Y0-CUY-378

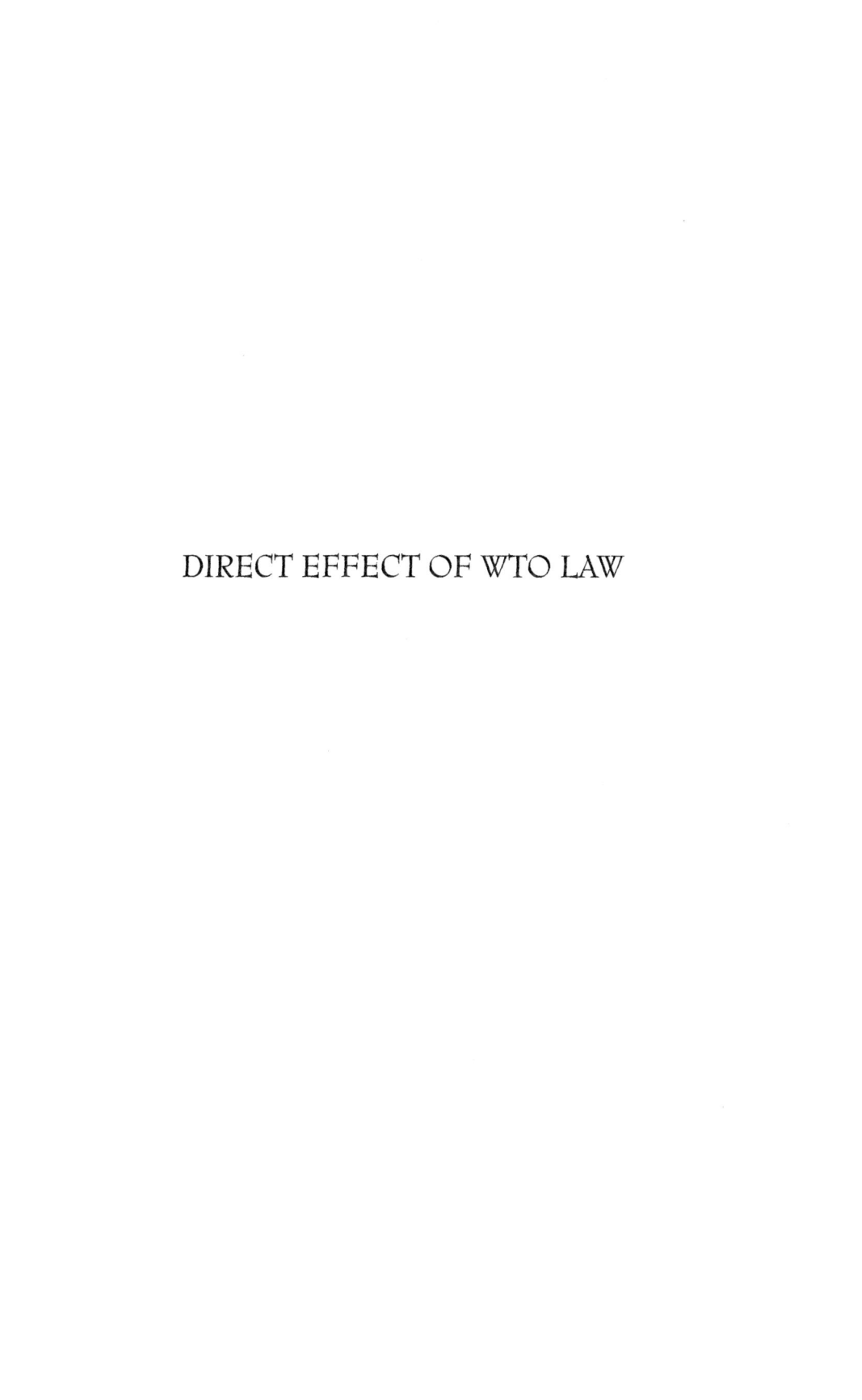

DIRECT EFFECT OF WTO LAW

DIRECT EFFECT OF WTO LAW

Geert A. Zonnekeyn

CAMERON MAY
INTERNATIONAL LAW & POLICY

Copyright © Cameron May

Published 2008 by Cameron May Ltd
7 Cornwall Crescent, Notting Hill, London W11 1PH
Tel: +44 (0)20 7792 0075 Fax: +44 (0)20 7792 1055
email: info@cameronmay.com
Website: http://www.cameronmay.com

All rights reserved. Except for the quotation of short passages for the purpose of criticism and review, no part of this publication may be reproduced, stored in a retrieval system or transmitted, in any form or by any means, electronic, mechanical, photocopying, recording or otherwise, without prior permission of the publisher.

This book is sold subject to the condition that it shall not by way of trade or otherwise, be lent, resold, hired out, or otherwise circulated without the publisher's prior consent in any form of binding or cover other than that in which it is published and without a similar condition including this condition being imposed on the subsequent purchaser.

ISBN 10: 1-905017- 60 X
ISBN 13: 978-1-905017-60 7

Printed in the United Kingdom by The Good News Press Ltd

TABLE OF CONTENTS

Introduction	11
PART I: DIRECT EFFECT	13

CHAPTER I 15
THE DIRECT EFFECT OF GATT IN COMMUNITY LAW: FROM
INTERNATIONAL FRUIT COMPANY TO THE BANANA CASES
  *Published in Internationational Trade Law & Regulation [1996]
  Pp. 63 To 71*

1.	Introduction	15
2.	The ECJ'S Case Law as Regards GATT 1947	16
3.	Conclusion	32

CHAPTER II 35
THE HÈRMES JUDGMENT – RECONCILING THE PRINCIPLES OF UNIFORM
AND CONSISTENT INTERPRETATION
  *Published in the Journal of World Intellectual Property [1999]
  pp. 495 to 508*

1.	Introduction	35
2.	Procedural Background	35
3.	Opinion of the Advocate General	38
4.	The Judgment of the ECJ	41
5.	Comment	43
6.	Conclusion	50

CHAPTER III 51
THE LEGAL STATUS OF WTO PANEL REPORTS IN THE EC LEGAL ORDER
– SOME REFLECTIONS ON THE OPINION OF ADVOCATE GENERAL
MISCHO IN THE ATLANTA CASE
  *Published in Journal of International Economic Law [1999] pp.
  713 to 722*

1.	Introduction	51
2.	The Opinion of the Advocate General	52
3.	The Interface Between Decisions of International Judicial Bodies and EC Law	53
4.	Conclusion	60

CHAPTER IV 61
THE STATUS OF ADOPTED PANEL AND APPELLATE BODY REPORTS IN THE EUROPEAN COURT OF JUSTICE AND THE EUROPEAN COURT OF FIRST INSTANCE – THE BANANA EXPERIENCE
Published in Journal of World Trade [2000] pp. 93 – 108

1. Introduction 61
2. An Analysis of the Judgments 62
3. The Interface Between Decisions of International Judicial Bodies and EC Law 65
4. Conclusion 78

CHAPTER V 79
THE STATUS OF WTO LAW IN THE EC LEGAL ORDER – THE FINAL CURTAIN?
Published in Journal of World Trade [2000] pp. 111 to 125

1. Introduction 79
2. Factual and Legal Background 80
3. The Opinion of the Advocate General 82
4. The Judgment of the ECJ 86
5. Observations 88
6. Conclusion: Implications of the Judgment 94

CHAPTER VI 97
THE BED LINEN CASE AND ITS AFTHERMATH – SOME COMMENTS ON THE EUROPEAN COMMUNITY'S WORLD TRADE ORGANISATION ENABLING REGULATION
Published in Journal of World Trade [2000] pp. 993 to 1003

1. Introduction 97
2. Factual Background 97
3. The WTO Enabling Regulation – Some Further Reflections 99
4. The Binding Nature of Reports Adopted by the DSB 100
5. The Reimbursement of Anti-dumping Duties 104
6. Conclusion 108

CHAPTER VII 111
THE LATEST ON INDIRECT EFFECT OF WTO LAW IN THE EC LEGAL ORDER – THE NAKAJIMA CASE LAW MISJUDGED?
Published in Journal of International Economic Law [2001] pp. 597 to 608

1. Introduction 111

2.	Factual Background	112
3.	The Judgments of the CFI	113
4.	Comments	114
5.	The Legal Status of Adopted Appellate Body Reports in the EC	118
6.	Conclusion	122

CHAPTER VIII   123
EC LIABLITY FOR NON-IMPLEMENTATION OF ADOPTED PANEL AND APPELLATE BODY REPORTS
Published in the European Union and the International Legal Order: Discord or Harmony [2001], TMC Asser Press, pp. 251-272

1.	Introduction	123
2.	The Cases – a Brief Overview	125
3.	Background	126
4.	The Implementation of Adopted WTO Panel and Appellate Body Reports – Is Implementation Compulsory?	129
5.	Non-Implementation by the EC of Adopted WTO Panel and Appellate Body Reports: Implications at EC Level	132
6.	Conclusion	143

CHAPTER IX   145
EC LIABILITY FOR THE NON-IMPLEMENTATION OF WTO DISPUTE SETTLEMENT DECISIONS – ADVOCATE GENERAL ALBER PROPOSES A 'COPERNICAN INNOVATION' IN THE CASE LAW OF THE ECJ
Published in Journal of International Economic Law [2003] pp. 761 to 769

1.	Introduction	145
2.	The Facts	145
3.	The Opinions – a Brief Analysis	147
4.	Conclusion	152

CHAPTER X   153
THE ECJ'S PETROTUB JUDGMENT: TOWARDS A REVIVAL OF THE NAKAJIMA DOCTRINE?
Published in Legal Issues of Economic Integration [2003] pp. 7249-266

1.	Introduction	153
2.	Factual Background	154

	3.	The Judgment	156
	4.	Analysis	158
	5.	Observations	164
	6.	Conclusion	167

CHAPTER XI
EC LIABILITY FOR THE NON-IMPLEMENTATION OF WTO DISPUTE   169
SETTLEMENT DECISIONS – ARE THE DICE CAST?
  Published in Journal of International Economic Law [2004] pp. 483 to 490

	1.	Introduction	169
	2.	Factual Background	170
	3.	The Judgments	172
	4.	Comment – a Sparkle in the Dark or a Pandora's Box?	174
	5.	Conclusion – What about the Future?	175

CHAPTER XII   177
ENFORCEABILITY OF WTO LAW FOR INDIVIDUALS: RIEN NE VA PLUS?

	1.	Introduction	177
	2.	Prelude	179
	3.	Recent Case Law – Nil Novi Sub Sole ?	181
	4.	Merck Genéricos - A Different Approach for the TRIPS Agreement?	186 / 190
	5.	Conclusion	

PART II: THE EU TRADE BARRIERS REGULATION   **191**

CHAPTER I
THE EC TRADE BARRIERS REGULATION: MORE OPPORTUNITTIES FOR   193
COMMUNIY INDUSTRIES?
  Published in International Trade Law & Regulation [1995] pp. 143 - 148

	1.	Introduction	193
	2.	Experiences to Date	194
	3.	The 'Full Exercise of the Rights of the Community': Complaints by Member States	194
	4.	'Illicit Commercial Practices': Complaints by Community Industries	195
	5.	Proposals to Amend the NCPI	197
	6.	The Trade Barriers Regulation: An Analysis	198
	7.	Procedural Aspects	203
	8.	Conclusion	205

CHAPTER II 207
THE EC TRADE BARRIERS REGULATION – THE EC'S MOVE TOWARDS A
MORE AGGRESSIVE MARKET ACCESS STRATEGY
Published in Journal of World Trade [1997] pp. 147 to 166

1.	Introduction	207
2.	Legislative Background	208
3.	Cases Brought under the NCPI	210
4.	The Trade Barriers Regulation	212
5.	The EC's New Market Access Strategy	220
6.	Cases Brought under the TBR	221
7.	Conclusion	228

CHAPTER III
THE PROTECTION OF INTELLECTUAL PROPERTY RIGHTS UNDER THE EC 231
TRADE BARRIERS REGULATION – AN ANALYSIS OF THE IMRO CASE
Published in the Journal of World Intellectual Property [1999] pp. 357 to 370

1.	Introduction	231
2.	Factual Background	232
3.	The Activity Under Investigation: Cross-Border Licensing of Music Works	233
4.	The Obstacle to Trade	234
5.	The Legality of Section 110(5)	238
6.	Recent Amendments to Section 110(5)of the US Copyright Act	245
7.	Conclusion	246

PART III: AMICUS BRIEFS AND THE WTO **249**

THE APPELLATE BODY COMMUNICATION ON AMICUS CURIAE BRIEFS 251
IN THE ASBESTOS CASE – AN ECHTERNACH PROCESSION?
Published in Journal of World Trade [2001] pp. 553 to 563

1.	Introduction	251
2.	The Communication – an Analysis	252
3.	Administration of the Communication	258
4.	Practice in other International Fora: the Example of The NAFTA Methanex Case	260
5.	Conclusion – Nil Novi Sub Sole?	261

About the author 263

Introduction

The effect of the WTO Agreements within the legal order of the EU has been the object of a fierce controversy in the case law of the Court of First Instance and of the European Court of Justice ever since the conception of the WTO. The case law of the Luxembourg Courts clearly indicates that practitioners seem to have explored practically all the boundaries of this extremely fascinating subject.

Direct Effect of WTO law is a collection of essays written over a period of more than ten years and chronicles the evolution in the case law of the European Courts in Luxembourg on the enforceability of GATT and WTO law in the EU legal order. Some of the essays concentrate on more controversial subjects such as the status in the EU legal order of decisions taken by the WTO dispute settlement bodies and the question whether the EU institutions should be held liable under EU law for not acting in conformity with WTO law. The book also contains some essays analyzing the opportunities given to EU companies to enforce WTO law through the application of the so-called Trade Barriers Regulation and gives an almost complete picture of how WTO law can be enforced in the EU legal order by individuals.

One essay has been co-authored with Michael Sanchez Rydelski, a former colleague of mine with whom I started my career in Brussels. I thank him for his inspired contribution, and for his willingness to appear in this book. I also thank Nick May for taking the initiative to assemble these essays, previously published in different sources, in one volume and Aster Tewelda for her meticulous production of the book. Last but not least I would like to thank my wife Petra and my children Helena and Benjamin for coping so well with my absence during the many hours that I spent on writing these essays. The text of the essays included here is practically identical to the original publications, except for a few editorial changes.

Geert A. Zonnekeyn,
Ronse, January 2008

PART I: DIRECT EFFECT

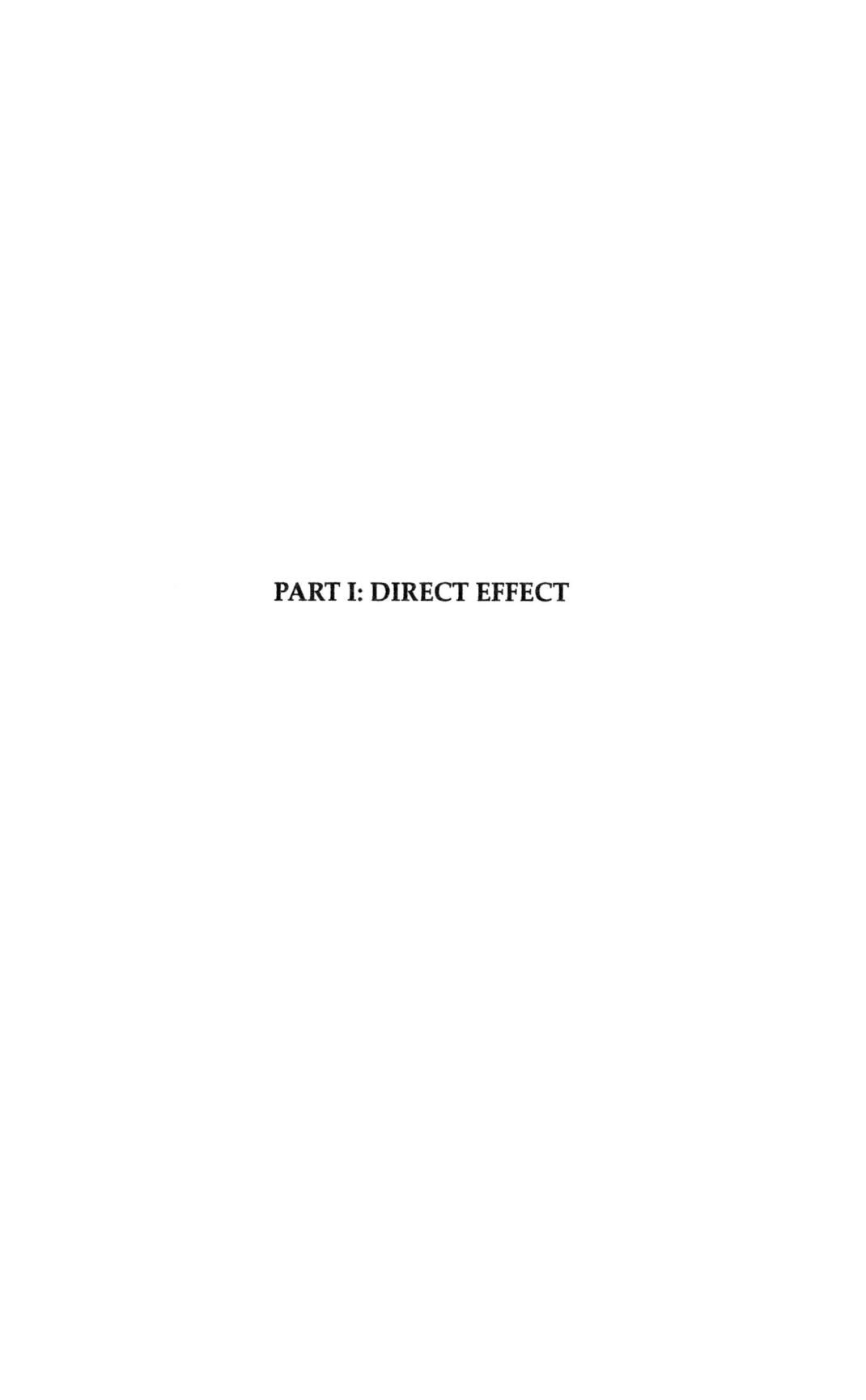

CHAPTER I

THE DIRECT EFFECT OF GATT IN COMMUNITY LAW: FROM
INTERNATIONAL FRUIT COMPANY TO THE BANANA CASES

1. Introduction

The reference for a preliminary ruling from the Finanzgericht (Finance Court) Hamburg to the European Court of Justice (ECJ)[1] represents a good opportunity to focus on the question of the legal status of the General Agreement on Tariffs and Trade (GATT) in European Community (EC) law.[2] The German court more specifically asked whether individuals are entitled to rely on GATT provisions in proceedings before the courts of Member States, ie whether those provisions produce direct effect.

As a matter of general principle, a legal provision cannot be directly effective unless two requirements are satisfied: the courts must recognise it as valid and binding law and, secondly, the provision must be appropriate to confer rights on individuals.[3]

The ECJ introduced the principle of direct effect as a general principle underlying the EC Treaty and secondary law in its landmark ruling *Van Gend & Loos*[4] and subsequently developed it in its well-known case law. The question, however, whether and to what extent agreements concluded by the EC with third states may give rise to equivalent or similar effects within its legal order does not seem to be entirely settled.[5] As far as the GATT is

---

[1] [1995] OJ C208/12. See Kuschel 'Die EG-Bananenmarktordung vor deutschen Gerichten' *EuZW* 689 (1995).
[2] On this question see Castillo de la Torre 'The Status of GATT in EC Law: Some New Developments' (1992) *JWT* 35; P-J Kuyper 'The New Dispute Settlement System: The Impact on the Community' in JHJ Bourgeois et al (eds) *The Uruguay Round Results: A European Lawyer's Perspective* (Brussels: European University Press, 1995) 87–114; P Mengozzi 'The Marrakesh DSU and its Implications on the International and European Level' in JHJ Bourgeois et al (eds) *The Uruguay Round Results: A European Lawyer's Perspective* (Brussels: European University Press, 1995) 115–33; CWA Timmermans 'The Implementation of the Uruguay Round by the EC in JHJ Bourgeois et al (eds) *The Uruguay Round Results: A European Lawyer's Perspective* (Brussels: European University Press, 1995) 501–9 and NAEM Neuwahl 'Individuals and the GATT: Direct Effect and Indirect Effects of the General Agreement on Tariffs and Trade in Community Law in N Emiliou and D O'Keeffe (eds) *The European Union and World Trade Law After the GATT Uruguay Round*, (Chichester: Wiley 1995) 313–28.
[3] TC Hartley *The Foundations of European Community Law* (Oxford: Clarendon Press, 1994) 195.
[4] Case 26/62 *Van Gend & Loos v Nederlandse Administratie der Belastingen* [1963] ECR 1.
[5] For example the question on the status of the EEA Agreement in EC law. See W van Gerven 'The Genesis of EEA Law and the Principles of Primacy and Direct Effect' (1993) *Fordham*
continued ...

concerned, the ECJ has in the past denied direct effect to GATT provisions as they were not considered 'capable of creating rights of which interested parties may avail themselves'.[6]

This article analyses the ECJ's case law in this field up to the *Banana* cases[7] with a view to identifying possible developments in the future. The analysis will be pursued alongside two main themes: what did the ECJ mean when it denied direct effect to the GATT and what were the reasons for the ECJ's doing so? On the basis of this study the question will be tackled whether the ECJ might alter its position in the future. The ECJ's possible views as regards the World Trade Organization Agreement (WTO Agreement) will be dealt with in a later article.[8] The WTO Agreement includes the 'General Agreement on Tariffs and Trade 1994' which is based upon the text of the original General Agreement on Tariffs and Trade referred to as 'GATT 1947'.[9] A distinction must therefore be made between the situation before (GATT 1947) and after (GATT 1994) the entry into force of the WTO Agreement on 1 January 1995.

2. The ECJ'S Case Law as Regards GATT 1947

The ECJ was faced with the question of the direct effect of international agreements for the first time in *International Fruit Company*[10] when it had to decide on the enforceability of certain GATT provisions. The outcome is well known and has been extensively reviewed.[11] It seems appropriate to take this case as a departure for developing the following analysis.

Int'l LJ 955. For a more general analysis of the effect of international agreements in the EC's legal order, see I Cheyne 'International Agreements and the European Community Legal System' [1994] *EL Rev* 581.

[6] Case 9/73 *Schlüter v Hauptzollamt Lörrach* [1973] ECR 1135. Similarly, Case 266/81 *Società Italiana per l'Oleodotto Transalpino (SIOT) v Ministero delle Finanze* [1983] ECR 731; Joined Cases 267–269/81, *Amministrazione dello Stato v Società Petrolifera Italiana (SPI)* [1983] ECR 801 and Joined Cases 290–291/81, *Compagnia Singer v Amministrazione delle Finanze dello Stato* [1983] ECR 847.

[7] Case C–280/93 *Germany v Council* [1994] ECR I–4973 and Case C–469/93 *Amministrazione delle Finanze dello Stato v Chiquita Italia SpA* judgment of 12 December 1995, ECR I – 4533. For an analysis of the first judgment, see eg GM Berrisch. (1994) EuR 461; M Dony 'L'Affaire des Bananes' (1994) *CDE* 461, F Castillo de la Torre 'The Status of GATT in EC Law Revisited' (1995) *JWT* 53 and P Foubert (1995) *The Columbia Journal of European Law* 312.

[8] On this question, see S Griller 'The Common Commercial Policy Instruments after the Uruguay Round - with some Implications for Austria in F Breuss (ed) *The World Economy after the Uruguay Round* (Wien: Service Fachverlag, 1995) 269–337 and Ph Lee and B Kennedy 'The Potential Direct Effect of GATT 1994 in European Community Law' (1996) *JWT* 67.

[9] For an analysis of the structure of the WTO Agreement and the content of its Annexes, see E-U Petersmann 'The Transformation of the World Trading System through the 1994 Agreement Establishing the World Trade Organization' (1995) *EJIL* 161 and, more generally, Th Flory (ed) *La Communauté européenne et le GATT* (Rennes: Editions Apogée, 1995).

[10] Joined Cases 21–24 *International Fruit Company v Produktschap voor Groenten en Fruit* [1972] ECR 1227.

[11] See, for example, C-D Ehlermann and J Formann (1973) *CML Rev* 336; PJG Kapteyn 'The Domestic Law Effect of Rules of International Law within the European Community System

continued ...

2.1　The Denial of Direct Effect: What Did the ECJ Mean?

Given the impressive case law and the enormous amount of doctrinal study concerning the concept of direct effect it may appear superfluous to pose this question. The initial case law of the ECJ, however, gave rise to some confusion.

In *International Fruit Company* the ECJ was asked to assess the validity of a regulation in the light of the GATT. After having held that the EC was bound by the GATT, the ECJ stated that '(B)efore invalidity can be relied upon before a national court, that provision of international law must also be capable of conferring rights on citizens of the Community which they can invoke before the courts'.[12] The ECJ established a link between the possibility of invoking an international agreement for the review of the validity of a Community act and the fact that certain provisions of this agreement may be relied upon by individuals before national courts. Consequently, the ECJ is not prepared to review the validity of such an act unless the agreement is capable of conferring rights on individuals. As Bebr rightly points out, the lacking direct effect of an agreement protects the validity of Community acts.[13]

This connection between the direct effect of EC law, which plays a role in the relationship between the EC and the national legal order and the possibility of invoking an international agreement, which refers to the relationship between the international and the EC legal orders, has been commented on by various scholars.[14] Nevertheless these two elements are still perceived as related to each other, as appears clearly from a statement made by the Council in *Nakajima* on the question whether the latter could rely on certain provisions of the GATT Anti-Dumping Code in an action for annulment. The Council argued that ' ... although the GATT and the GATT Anti-Dumping Code are binding on the Community under the

---

of Law and the Question of the Self-Executing Character of GATT Rules' (1974) *Int'l Lawyer* 784; A Riesenfeld 'The Doctrine of Self-Executing Treaties and Community Law' (1973) *AJIL* 504; HG Schermers 'Community Law and International Law' (1975) *CML Rev* 77; J and M Waelbroeck 'Effect of GATT within the Legal Order of the EEC' (1974) *JWTL* 614.
[12] Joined Cases 21–24/72 (n 10) at para 8 of the judgment.
[13] G Bebr 'Agreements Concluded by the Community and their Possible Direct Effect: from International Fruit Company to Kupferberg' (1983) *CML Rev* 35, at 46.
[14] See eg J Rideau 'Les accords internationaux dans la jurisprudence de la Cour de Justice des Communautés européennes: réflexions sur les relations entre les ordres juridiques international, communautaire et nationaux' (1990) *RDIP* 289; M Maresceau 'The GATT in the case-law of the European Court of Justice' in FG Jacobs et al (eds) *The European Community and GATT* (Deventer: Kluwer, 1986) 107–26; HN Tagaras 'L'effet direct des accords internationaux de la Communauté' (1984) *CDE* 20; JHJ Bourgeois 'Effects of International Agreements in European Community Law: Are the Dice Cast?' (1984) *Michigan Law Review* 1250 and E-U Petersmann 'Application of GATT by the Court of Justice of the European Communities' (1983) *CML Rev* 403.

rules of international law, they do not confer rights on individuals which can be relied on before the Court in proceedings under Article 173 EEC Treaty'.[15]

Generally speaking two ways of relying on GATT provisions can be distinguished: invoking the GATT either directly before national courts or as a ground of review before the ECJ. For the purpose of this chapter the former perspective represents the narrow view of the concept of direct effect whereas the latter will be described as the wider one.

Only if these two aspects are disassociated and separately dealt with will the scope of the ECJ's case law be clear enough to make a more reliable assessment of the most recent case law. The following chapters demonstrate that the consequences of the ECJ's repeated denial of direct effect to the GATT differ fundamentally according to the view taken in the above sense.

2.2 Direct Effect in the Wider Sense – the Binding Nature of the GATT

Article 228(2) EC Treaty, states that agreements concluded under the procedure provided therein 'shall be binding on the institutions of the Community and on Member States'. Such agreements are concluded by the Council. The EC Treaty does not determine the legal instrument to be used by the Council for such approval.

Whereas in the past the Council approved such agreements by way of a decision, it now does so in the form of a regulation. This practice may lead to confusion between direct effect in the wider and in the narrower sense as described above. The fact that regulations are directly applicable by virtue of Article 189 EC Treaty might induce courts to draw erroneous consequences as to the direct effect (in the narrow sense) of such agreements. This danger is not purely theoretical. In its reference for a preliminary ruling in *Polydor* the English Court of Appeal asked whether a provision of the EEC-Portugal free trade agreement could be invoked by individuals before a national court 'having full regard in particular to the said EEC Council Regulation'.[16] Similarly, a German court, when dealing with the association agreements concluded by the EC with Portugal and Spain, pointed out that 'both agreements have been transformed into Community law by means of regulations'.[17]

---

[15] Case C-69/89 *Nakajima All Precision Co Ltd v Council* [1991] ECR I-2069, Report for the Hearing, para 67(a).
[16] Case 270/80 *Polydor Ltd v Harlequin Record Shop Ltd* [1982] ECR 329, para 10 of the judgment.
[17] Bundesfinanzhof (Finance Court), judgment of 5 August 1980 (1980) RIW 786.

In both cases the respective national courts attached considerable importance to the legal nature of the instrument used by the Council. The ECJ on the other hand considers the form of the act of approval as being not of particular importance. Suffice it for this purpose to observe that the ECJ has recognised direct effect of provisions of agreements approved by the Council in the form of a decision.[18]

The GATT, however, was not an agreement signed and concluded by the EC within the meaning of Article 228 EC Treaty, but was signed by the later Member States before the setting up of the EC and neither was the EC a Contracting Party to the GATT. Although not quite clarified from a formal point of view, the other contracting parties were acting in practice as if they had formally accepted that the EC succeeded to the rights and duties of its Member States. The EC was therefore treated as a contracting party to GATT without there being a specific legal act.

The ECJ itself made it clear in *International Fruit Company* that the provisions of the GATT 'have the effect of binding the Community'.[19] In its reasoning the ECJ mentions several factors which determine the special relationship between the EC and the GATT.[20] In particular, the transfer of power from the Member States to the EC by virtue of Article 113 EC Treaty indicated that the former showed their willingness to bind the latter by the obligations entered into the framework of the GATT. This transfer had moreover been recognised by the other contracting parties. Finally, the ECJ pointed out that the EC – through its institutions – had participated in the operation of the GATT. By this reasoning the ECJ established its jurisdiction to construe even an agreement to which the EC became only subsequently a de facto party.

With regard to agreements concluded by the EC within the framework of Article 228 EC Treaty, the ECJ has been more explicit. In *Haegeman* the ECJ, after pointing out that the association agreement with Greece was concluded by the Council under Articles 228 and 238 EC Treaty, stated that '(T)his agreement is therefore ... an act of one of the institutions of the Community within the meaning of subparagraph (b) of the first paragraph of Article 177'. The provisions of the agreement ... form an integral part of Community law.[21]

Accordingly the ECJ considered itself competent to give a preliminary ruling on the interpretation of this agreement. As will be demonstrated later in this article the stance of the ECJ will be the same should this ground be raised in a direct action before it.

---

[18] Case 87/75 *Bresciani v Amministrazione delle Finanze dello Stato* [1976] ECR 129.
[19] Joined Cases 21–24/72 (n 10) at para 18 of the judgment.
[20] Joined Cases 21–24/72 (n 10) at paras 14 to 17 of the judgment.
[21] Case 181/73 *Haegeman v Belgium* [1974] ECR 449, at paras 3 to 6 of the judgment.

Bearing in mind the different and somehow more indirect approach adopted by the ECJ to establish that the EC is bound by the provisions of the GATT the question arises whether the GATT consequently forms part of the EC's legal order in the sense of the ECJ's ruling in *Haegeman*. One could use the ECJ's reasoning in *International Fruit Company* to reach this conclusion.[22] It seems, however, that the ECJ does not consider the GATT approach – the EC having replaced the Member States in respect of their obligations under the GATT – identical to the situation resulting from the use of Article 228 EC Treaty as in *Haegeman*.[23] If the replacement of the Member States by the EC is the logical consequence of the coming into effect of the EC's exclusive competence in the field of the common commercial policy (and therefore of the GATT) – as the ECJ indicated in its *SPI* ruling[24] – then the conclusion becomes inevitable that the GATT bound the Member States through EC law. It is in this sense that the ECJ's dictum in the *SIOT* case[25] may have to be understood when it confirmed the '... Community's obligation to ensure that the provisions of GATT are observed in its relations with non-Member States which are parties to GATT'.[26]

It has been argued that these observations do not necessarily lead to the GATT constituting an integral part of the EC legal system.[27] It is submitted that it is nevertheless reasonable to regard the provisions of the GATT – in any event in so far as the EC has replaced the Member States – as part of the EC legal order, simply because the GATT can be regarded as binding the EC just as if it were an agreement concluded pursuant to Article 228 EC Treaty, notwithstanding the different approach demonstrated above. In any case, the paragraph quoted from *SIOT* represents a clear assertion of the binding nature of GATT which can today be considered as undisputed.

2.3 Direct Effect in the Narrow Sense

The ECJ has, on numerous occasions, made clear what is meant by the notion of direct effect. If a provision of EC law is held to be directly effective it grants individuals rights which the national courts must protect. The test laid down by the ECJ, as developed in the case law following *Van Gend & Loos*, may be stated as follows.[28] The provision must be clear, unambiguous, unconditional and its operation must not be dependent on further action to be taken by EC or national authorities.

---

[22] G Bebr (n 13) at 43.
[23] ELM Völker 'The direct effect of international agreements in the Community's legal order' (1982/83) *LIEI* 131.
[24] Joined Cases 267–269/81 (n 6).
[25] Case 266/81 (n 6).
[26] ibid para 28 of the judgment.
[27] ELM Völker (n 23) at 142.
[28] See eg TC Hartley (n 3) at 188.

It is tempting to transfer the doctrine of direct effect thus developed to the relationship between international law and EC law. This is in fact more than a merely academic exercise. In view of the fact that practically all EC trade agreements contain clauses worded in terms similar or even identical to those of the EC Treaty such a transportation may have far-reaching consequences.[29] In order to avoid hasty conclusions in this context it seems appropriate to briefly recall the underlying reasoning of the ECJ's doctrine concerning direct effect.

This concept was developed within the framework of an autonomous, new legal order for the benefit of which the Member States have limited their sovereign rights and which not only refers to the latter but also to their nationals. Furthermore, the doctrine is closely linked to the establishment of institutions endowed with sovereign rights, especially the ECJ whose task it is to secure uniform interpretation of the EC Treaty which itself is more than an agreement merely creating mutual obligations between the parties but pursues the objective of establishing an internal market. Moreover, the direct effect doctrine has to be seen as a corollary to the concept of supremacy of EC law over inconsistent national legislation, as developed by the ECJ in *Costa v ENEL*.[30]

It remains, therefore, rather doubtful whether this fundamental principle which was developed within the genuine legal order of the EC for the purpose of its unprecedented objectives could be transported as such into a more flexible international legal system.[31] Advocate General Trabucci expressed similar doubts in his Opinion in *Bresciani* when he stated that '... it might seem contradictory and perhaps, in practice, also counter-productive ... simply to apply to the law of international agreements the Community concept of direct applicable law ...'.[32]

The ECJ itself set out some conditions under which its is prepared to consider a provision of an international agreement to be directly effective (in the narrower sense) as creating rights for individuals which they can rely upon before national courts. In *Pabst* the ECJ held that a provision of the association agreement with Greece was directly effective because it was 'a clear and precise obligation which is not subject, in its implementation or effects, to the adoption of any subsequent measure'.[33] The same wording has later been used by the ECJ in *Demirel*,[34] *Sevince*,[35] *Anastasiou*,[36] *Yousfi*[37]

---

[29] JHJ Bourgeois (n 14) at 1262.
[30] Case 6/64 *Costa v ENEL* [1964] ECR 585.
[31] G. Bebr (n 13) at 72.
[32] Opinion of 14 January 1976 in Case 87/75 (n 18) at 148.
[33] Case 17/81 *Pabst & Richarz KG v Hauptzollamt Oldenburg* [1982] ECR 1331, at para 27 of the judgment.
[34] Case 12/86 *Meryem Demirel v Stadt Schwäbisch Gmünd* [1987] ECR 3719, at para 14 of the judgment.

and, more recently, in *Krid*.[38] It is difficult to ignore the similarities between the conditions required by the ECJ for an EC and an international provision to be directly effective.

The ECJ has dealt with the question whether provisions of the GATT are capable of producing direct effect in the narrow sense on several occasions. The arguments that led the ECJ to its conclusion will be explored further below in detail. The systematic approach adopted by the ECJ will be analysed first.

The case law demonstrates that, in order to determine whether an agreement has direct effect, the ECJ considers the characteristics of the provision in question, as it does when applying EC rules sensu stricto. However, whereas under EC law it is automatically assumed that the Member States intended to confer rights on individuals and therefore the only requirement for direct effect is that the rules in question be precise and complete, the presumption of such intention may not as such be extended to international agreements.[39] On the contrary, the intention of the contracting parties to confer rights on individuals represents a preliminary condition for the possible effect of provisions of such an agreement. This condition must be established and verified in each individual case. In other words, if the direct effect of an international agreement is questioned, it is not sufficient to examine exclusively the 'classic' conditions of direct effect as related to the provision invoked (clear, precise and unconditional), but the preliminary condition has to be complied with in the first place.[40] Only after having established this precondition can the agreement be considered as being capable of producing such effect.

In order to ascertain the capability of an international agreement to produce direct effect, the ECJ undertakes a two-stage approach. First, it examines whether the agreement's nature and general scheme preclude direct reliance on one of its provisions. The second stage includes two steps. The provision in question must first be analysed '... in the light of both the object and purpose of the agreement and of its context' in order to answer then to the question 'whether such a stipulation is unconditional and sufficiently precise to have direct effect'.[41]

---

[35] Case C–18/90 *Office National de l'Emploi v Kziber* [1991] ECR I–199.
[36] Case C–432/92 *R v Minister of Agriculture, Fisheries and Food ex parte S.P. Anastasiou (Pissouri) Ltd* [1994] ECR I–3087.
[37] Case C–58/93 *Zoubir Yousfi v Belgium* [1994] ECR I–1353.
[38] Case C–103/94 *Zoulika Krid v CNAVTS* [1995] ECR I–719.
[39] HN Tagaras (n 14) at 29.
[40] HN Tagaras (n 14) at 30.
[41] Case 104/81 *Hauptzollamt Mainz v Kupferberg* [1982] ECR 3641 at paras 22 and 23of the judgment.

In other words, the ECJ is anxious to distinguish two aspects of direct effect in the narrow sense. On the one hand, there is the direct effect of the agreement as a whole, and, on the other hand, there is the direct effect of the individual provision in question.[42] Only if the agreement as such is capable of producing direct effect does the ECJ consider it appropriate to continue its analysis and to look at the provisions invoked.

It is also in this logical order that the ECJ proceeded when examining the direct effect in the narrow sense of the GATT in *International Fruit Company*. The ECJ considered for this purpose 'the purpose, the spirit, the general scheme and the terms' of the GATT[43] and denied direct effect on these grounds. Consequently the ECJ did not consider it necessary to go any further and to examine whether the provisions concerned would have complied with the standard requirements for direct effect of a Community rule and, more particularly, whether the general considerations concerning the nature, objectives and structure of the GATT 'are sufficient to show that ... Article XI is not capable of conferring on citizens of the Community rights which they can invoke before the courts'.[44]

2.3.1 The Development of the ECJ's Case Law

As it was pointed out above, the ECJ's ruling in *International Fruit Company* and in *Schlüter*[45] indicate that the ECJ considered the direct effect of an agreement in the narrower sense as a condition for such effect in the wider sense. In its later case law, however, the ECJ provided indications that it perceived the two meanings of direct effect in a more differentiated way. As will be shown later, the ECJ's most recent judgments on this subject made it clear that its denial of direct effect to the GATT does not to the same extent apply to the wider and the narrow concept. It seems that in its judgments following *International Fruit Company* and *Schlüter*, the ECJ abandoned the direct effect in the narrow sense as a precondition for the direct effect in the wider sense.[46]

In *Schroeder*,[47] the ECJ reviewed the validity of a Commission regulation allegedly infringing a provision of the association agreement with Greece without having first examined whether this provision conferred rights on individuals. The ECJ proceeded likewise in *Haegeman*. Of particular importance is the ECJ's judgment in *Nederlandse Spoorwegen*.[48] In this

---

[42] N March Hunnings 'Enforceability of the EEC-EFTA Free Trade Agreements' (1977) *EL Rev* 163.
[43] Joined Cases 21–24/72 (n 10) at para 20 of the judgment.
[44] ibid para 27 of the judgment.
[45] Case 9/73 *Schlüter v Hauptzollamt Lörrach* [1973] ECR 1135.
[46] G Bebr (n 13) at 46.
[47] Case 40/72 *Schroeder v Germany* [1973] ECR 125.
[48] Case 38/75 *Douaneagent der NV Nederlandse Spoorwegen v Inspecteur der Invoerrechten en Accijnzen* [1975] ECR 1439.

case the referring Dutch court asked the ECJ to assess the validity of a Community act in light of the GATT. The ECJ decided that '(I)n the light of the priority of Treaty obligations of the Community over acts of its organs and – independently of the question of whether a GATT provision is or is not suited to create rights in relation to citizens upon which he can rely before a court – is not ... a court bound ... to apply GATT provisions which are suitable for direct application ...?'[49]

Although Advocate General Reischl, referring to *International Fruit Company* and *Schlüter* still considered the direct effect of an international agreement in the narrow sense as a precondition for the wider notion of direct effect,[50] the ECJ reviewed the Community act in the light of Article II of the GATT without considering whether the GATT was directly effective in the narrow sense.

Advocate General Reischl upheld the approach laid down in *International Fruit Company* and *Schlüter* some years later in *Dürbeck*.[51] In this case the ECJ upheld a Commission regulation which introduced temporary import restrictions on apples. It merely observed that the plaintiff's submission based on the GATT 'is not capable in this case of putting the validity of those measures in question', thereby definitely rejecting the strict views still advocated by Reischl.[52]

Thus, the mere fact that the ECJ was prepared to interpret a provision of an agreement by no means implies that it also has direct effect in the narrow sense. But the contrary is also true. Even if an agreement is not directly effective in the narrow sense it still may be invoked as a ground of review.[53] Advocate General van Gerven pointed out in *Fediol* that the ECJ would interpret any provision of an agreement, 'regardless as to whether, to what extent and how easily individuals can derive rights from the provisions in question'.[54] There is in fact no need to introduce the controversy of the

---

[49] ibid at 1442.
[50] ibid at 1457.
[51] Case 112/80 *Dürbeck v Hauptzollamt Frankfurt* [1981] ECR 1095.
[52] Marescau, however, is of a different opinion and refuses to see this ruling as a modification of the ECJ's previous case law and says that it had more the character of an 'inadvertence', see M Marescau (n 14) at 121.
[53] As the ECJ put it in Case 70/87 *Fediol v Commission* [1989] ECR 1781, at para 20 of the judgment. The fact that the GATT does not produce any direct effect in the narrow sense 'does not, however, prevent the Court from interpreting and applying the rules of GATT with reference to a given case, in order to establish whether certain specific commercial practices should be considered incompatible with those rules. The GATT provisions have an independent meaning which, for the purposes of their application in specific cases, is to be determined by way of interpretation'. This judgment must, however, be seen in its specific context. The act to be assessed was a foreign one and its illegality was one of the conditions (not the only one) for the initiation of the procedure under the so-called 'New Commercial Policy Instrument'. Fediol did not derive any rights from the GATT, but only from the regulation making express reference to the GATT.
[54] ibid at 1806.

GATT's direct effect in the narrow sense in the situation of an individual relying on GATT in the wider sense, eg as a ground for annulment.[55]

Given its special circumstances the *Fediol* judgment is regarded by some legal writers[56] as not being a full-fledged authority for this purpose. The ECJ was more transparent in *Nakajima*. Nakajima was challenging a regulation imposing anti-dumping duties, relying first on the inapplicability of the basic regulation[57] and secondly on the illegality of the implementing regulation.

At this stage only Nakajima's effort to rely on the GATT Anti-Dumping Code as a ground of review of the regulation – thereby invoking the code's direct effect in the wider sense – is relevant. The Council objected to the possibility for Nakajima of invoking such effect with reference to the ECJ's ruling in *International Fruit Company*. It was of the opinion that since neither the code nor the GATT itself are directly effective in the narrow sense, there was no room for direct effect in the wider sense of these agreements.

Advocate General Lenz, after referring to the ECJ's GATT case law, dealt with the issue of the relationship between direct effect in the narrow and the wide sense as follows. He held that 'a mere review of validity does nor in any event presuppose that the question whether the relevant provision in the agreement governed by international law is directly applicable has already been determined'.[58]

In its judgment the ECJ also clearly distinguished the narrow from the wide meaning of direct effect by declaring that Nakajima did not evoke such effect in the narrow sense but merely wished to rely on the code's provisions as a ground of review.[59] This statement was generally interpreted at the time

---

[55] After pointing out the concept of direct effect in the narrow sense is foreign to the interpretation of the grounds for illegality, Maresceau considers it, correctly, as a somewhat artificial construction if the ECJ were to introduce in actions based on Article 173 EC Treaty the 'directly effective sword of Damocles'. See M Maresceau (n 14) at 116. Waelbroeck, however, does not consider it justified to maintain that, when raising the question of invalidity in an action for annulment, it would not be necessary to establish first that the agreement produces direct effect in the narrow sense. He argues that if an agreement was held not to have direct effect in the narrow sense, there is no reason to decide otherwise when looking at the agreement's possible direct effect in the wider sense. See M Waelbroeck (n 14) at 622.
[56] See eg F Castillo de la Torre (n 2) at 38.
[57] Council Regulation (EEC) No 2423/88 of 11 July 1988 on protection against dumped or subsidised imports from countries not members of the European Economic Community [1988] OJ L209/1.
[58] Opinion of 5 December 1990 in Case 69/89 (n 15) at para 56.
[59] Nakajima raised this issue under Article 184 EC Treaty. This seemed to have influenced the ECJ's reasoning as it stressed that '(...) the applicant is in fact questioning, in an incidental manner under Article 184 of the Treaty, the applicability of the new basic regulation...' However, the grounds for review under Article 184 EC Treaty are exactly the same as in the case of a direct challenge under Article 173 EC Treaty.

as an acceptance that direct effect is a requirement only if an action was brought before a national court.[60] For the purposes of establishing the code's direct effect in the wider sense the ECJ adopted its well-known reasoning.[61] The ECJ then entered into a detailed examination of various provisions of the GATT Anti-Dumping Code and concluded that the contested regulation was fully in accordance with the provisions of the code.

In the first *Banana* judgment, the ECJ concluded that '[T]hese features of GATT, from which the Court concluded that an individual within the Community cannot invoke it in a court to challenge the lawfulness of a Community act, also preclude the Court from taking provisions into consideration to assess the lawfulness of a regulation in an action brought ... under ... Article 173 of the Treaty'.[62] Surprisingly, no distinction is made between direct effect in national courts (the narrow view) and whether it is possible to invoke the GATT in a direct action before the ECJ (the broad view). However, the ECJ did not completely ignore its former case law and held that the GATT would remain enforceable in cases where 'the Community intended to implement a particular obligation entered into within the framework of GATT, or if the Community act expressly refers to specific provisions of GATT'.[63] The former possibility would be the application of the *Nakajima* case law, the latter of the *Fediol* case law.

After this analysis, the following observations can be made. On the one hand, the ECJ denied direct effect in the narrow sense to the GATT. The reasons for the ECJ's doing so will be explored here below. On the other hand, however, the ECJ recognised that the GATT may produce direct effect in the wider sense. It can be invoked by individuals before the ECJ as an interpretive criterion and – in particular circumstances – as a ground for of review of a Community act.[64] Direct effect in the narrow sense remains a requirement only if an action is brought before a national court. Consequently the general affirmation that individuals may not rely on the

---

[60] FC Castillo de la Torre (n 7) at 56. See also MJ Hahn and G Schuster 'Zum Verstoss von gemeinschaftlichen Sekundärrecht gegen das GATT' (1993) EuR 261. Kapteyn has even questioned whether the *International Fruit Company* case law was still valid. See PJG Kapteyn 'Quelques réflections sur les effets des accords internationaux liant la Communauté dans l'ordre juridique communautaire' in *Hacia un nuevo orden internacional y europeo. Estudios en hommaje al professor Don Manuel Diaz de Velasco* (Madrid: Tecnos, 1993) 1007–15.

[61] By referring to its ruling in *International Fruit Company*, the ECJ first recalled that the EC is bound by the GATT, what also applies to the Anti-Dumping Code adopted in application of article VI of GATT. The ECJ then concluded that the EC is obliged to ensure the observance of the GATT and the GATT Anti-Dumping Code when – as in this case – adopting a regulation.

[62] Case C–280/93 (n 7) at para 109 of the judgment.

[63] ibid para 111 of the judgment.

[64] In this context, Advocate General van Gerven referred to a 'certain direct effect' of the GATT and other agreements. See his Opinion in Case 70/87 (n 53) at 1806. It seems noteworthy, however, that the ECJ has not yet been prepared to declare a Community provision invalid on the ground of its incompatibility with the GATT.

GATT appears to be an over-simplification. It depends on the purpose for which the GATT is relied upon.

2.3.2 Is Judicial Control Desirable?

The fact that the ECJ considers itself competent to interpret and apply international agreements in cases pending before it calls for some observations.

Some legal writers will certainly welcome the willingness of the ECJ to let the GATT play a more prominent role in the judicial protection in the EC. Petersmann is of the opinion that the ECJ should 'exercise a stricter review of the observation of GATT obligations' by the Community and its Member States and protect individual freedoms and property rights against protectionist governmental interferences in contravention of legally binding clear and unconditional GATT obligations.[65]

Others have been less enthusiastic. They underline that the ECJ might move into an area which the Contracting Parties conferred to political negotiation.[66] Ehlermann warned in particular against the danger of interference with the GATT dispute settlement machinery. In his opinion, a judgment of the ECJ would tie the hands of the Community negotiators.[67]

It is not yet clear if the ECJ will listen to these voices. Advocate General van Gerven, however, perceived this issue and urged the ECJ to show some self-restraint when dealing with interpretation of the GATT: '... the Court cannot deliver interpretative judgments which are binding outside the Community, since it is not responsible vis-à-vis the other parties to the GATT for ensuring the uniform interpretation of GATT provisions. The court should therefore avoid broad interpretations of GATT provisions which go further than normal ... methods of interpretation if they cannot be based on explicit or implicit consensus between the parties to the GATT'.[68]

Thus, the ECJ should not substitute itself for any GATT institution. Neither should it assume a creative role in the interpretation of GATT provisions – in particular it ought to refrain from any kind of teleological interpretation.[69]

---

[65] Note 14 above at 404.
[66] JHJ Bourgeois 'Le GATT et le Traité CEE' (1980) Dir.comm.scamb.int. 30.
[67] Quoted in F Castillo de la Torre (n 2) at 42.
[68] Opinion of Advocate General van Gerven in Case 70/87 (n 53) at 1808.
[69] Ibid. Maresceau therefore suggests that only clear, open and well-substantiated conflicts between EC acts and GATT obligations should be considered by the ECJ. See M Maresceau (n 14) at 177. JHJ Bourgeois reveals that the ECJ, when dealing with multilateral rules, has to take due account of the international dimension: the ECJ – acting as a Community and not as an international institution – should be at pains not to introduce into EC law the Trojan horse of certain concepts of international law. See JHJ Bourgeois 'Les relations extérieurs de la
continued ...

The *Nakajima* judgment does not seem to reflect such self-restraint on the ECJ's side to the extent as it was suggested by van Gerven.

2.3.3 The Reasons for Denial – Are They Still Valid?

As already mentioned several times in the previous chapters, the ECJ, while admitting the direct effect of the GATT in the wider sense, has repeatedly denied such effect in the narrow sense. In the following chapters an attempt will be made to analyse the reasons given by the ECJ for such a denial. Some of them have been expressly spelled out by the ECJ, others can only be deduced from its reasoning whereas some further motives may merely be inferred.

The reasons put forward by the ECJ itself to start with are based not on the particular terms of the respective provision in question but on general grounds which relate to the spirit and general scheme of the GATT, consequently being relevant to all provisions of the GATT.

The ECJ pointed out that it was clear from its preamble that the GATT was founded on the principle of negotiations undertaken on a reciprocal basis and that it was important for its application that there should be a balance of advantages and disadvantages for the Contracting Parties. The GATT's provisions were flexible and allowed for derogations and for measures to be taken in cases of exceptional difficulty. Also of importance for the ECJ were the methods of dispute settlement, essentially based on consultations and negotiations. In the event of failure of a contracting party to carry out its obligations, the GATT allowed any other contracting party adversely affected thereby to suspend the application of their own obligations. Finally, there is the possibility of withdrawing from the GATT.[70]

2.3.4 Flexibility

In order to illustrate that the GATT was characterised by a considerable flexibility, in particular regarding the possibility of derogation and exceptional measures as well as the procedure of settling disputes, the ECJ referred to Articles XIX, XXII and XXIII of the GATT.[71]

Article XXII (Consultation) and Article XXIII (Nullification or Impairment) provide for a two-stage procedure. First, a bilateral agreement between the contracting parties concerned must be pursued whereby each party will give 'sympathetic consideration' to the other party's arguments. When this

---

Communautés européenne et la règle de droit: quelques reflections' in F Capotorti et al (eds) *Du droit international au droit de l'intégration. Liber Amicorum Pierre Pescatore* (Baden-Baden: Nomos Verlaggesellschaft, 1987) 65.

[70] Joined Cases 21–24/72 (n 10).
[71] Joined Cases 21–24/72 (n 10) at paras 22, 24 and 26 of the judgment.

initial attempt fails, the matter is referred to the other contracting parties who will initiate a conciliatory procedure, leaving retaliation as a last resort to the party adversely affected.[72] The wording of this provision indicates that its purpose is more to enable compromises to be found than to be applied under a strict legalistic interpretation.

As regards safeguard measures, the ECJ referred to Article XIX of the GATT which provides for the possibility for a party to suspend an obligation which effectively leads to increased imports, thereby actually or potentially causing serious injury to the party's domestic producers. The only condition which must be observed by the party concerned is the prior consultation with other interested parties, except in situations of urgency. This provision illustrates very well the flexible character of the GATT. This might well be the reason why the ECJ concentrated on this Article.[73]

It was in view of these characteristics that the ECJ denied direct effect to the GATT. More in particular, the pragmatic, non-legalistic dispute settlement system, aiming at consensus, and the possibilities for unilateral derogations. As Advocate General Reischl said, '(D)irect applicability – which is connected with rigidity – would obviously be out of place in a set of rules characterised by their flexibility'.

The judgment has been criticised. As Waelbroeck pointed out, there is no international treaty which imposes unconditional obligations.[74] Most international treaties provide for provisions such as those mentioned above, for the simple reason that the fluctuating character of international relations can always lead to unforeseen situations which may only be coped with if the agreement is sufficiently flexible.

Elements of flexibility are therefore by no means exclusive to the GATT. Does the approach adopted by the ECJ in *International Fruit Company* and *Schlüter* consequently lead to the denial of direct effect of all agreements containing comparable clauses?

This question is all the more important since, eg, Article XIX of the GATT is frequently taken as a model for similar safeguard clauses and consultation procedures in other trade agreements, including the free-trade agreements concluded by the EC. It was precisely in the case of such agreements that the ECJ had to decide on similar clauses.

In *Kupferberg* and in *Polydor* the ECJ was asked to a give preliminary ruling on the possible direct effect of certain provisions in an agreement with

---
[72] For a more detailed analysis of this procedure, see *Guide to GATT Law and Practice*, vol II (Geneva: World Trade Organization, 1995) 629–787.
[73] HN Tagaras (n 14) at 36.
[74] M Waelbroeck (n 14) at 617.

29

Portugal, which resembled provisions in the GATT.[75] Advocate General Rozes expressly referred to the agreement's flexibility as an argument against direct effect.[76] Moreover, the agreement with Portugal sets up its own dispute-settlement mechanism and provides for safeguard measures and derogations. Since the elements which led the ECJ to deny direct effect to the GATT are also present in the agreement with Portugal it was not surprising that the Advocate General suggested that the ECJ should come to a negative conclusion there as well.

The ECJ, however, decided otherwise. It held that neither the existence of an institutional framework for consultations and negotiations nor the existence of safeguard clauses (which only apply in specific situations) are sufficient to exclude direct effect.[77] It was submitted that the fundamental differences between these clauses and those included in the GATT were not that obvious. Furthermore, in both cases the parties may have recourse to emergency measures without consulting the other party (parties) in advance. Although there are indeed some differences it is nevertheless difficult to see how one can justify such a fundamental different approach as regards direct effect.

Can one infer from those rulings that the ECJ has reconsidered its previous case law, as Waelbroeck had advocated almost 10 years before the *Kupferberg* and *Polydor* judgments?[78] Such a conclusion would go too far. Although it can be said that these rulings amount to an evolution of the ECJ's approach in *International Fruit Company*,[79] the paragraphs dealing with dispute settlement and safeguard clause are worded very prudently,[80] leaving the ECJ a considerable scope for denying direct effect because of the flexibility of an agreement in the future[81] – as it has done in its *SIOT* and *SPI* judgments, cutting off any thoughts about a possible change in this respect.[82] It has furthermore been argued that in *Fediol* the ECJ, by holding that its previous case law concerning the flexibility of the GATT did not mean to '*exclure toute application juridictionelle de cet accord*', could

---

[75] Article 23 of the EC-Portugal free trade agreement, identically worded as Article 36 EC Treaty, is very similar to Article XX of the GATT.
[76] Opinion of Advocate General Rozes in Case 104/81 (n 41) at 3674.
[77] Case 104/81 (n 41) at paras 20 to 22 of the judgment.
[78] M Waelbroeck (n 14).
[79] HN Tagaras (n 14).
[80] 'The mere fact that ... have established a ... framework for consultation ... is not in itself sufficient ...; As regards safeguard clauses ... the existence of such clauses ... is not sufficient in itself ...' See Case 104/81 (n 41) at paras 20 and 21 of the judgment.
[81] *Kupferberg* therefore does not indicate a real change of approach, although it might seem surprising that the court neglected the structural differences between the EC-Portugal Agreement and the Treaty of Rome – all the more since it was precisely the GATT's structural weaknesses which led the ECJ to deny direct effect to the GATT. See JHJ Bourgeois (n 14) at 1267.
[82] For the purposes of denying direct effect to the GATT the ECJ referred to its position previously adopted in *International Fruit Company* and *Schlüter*.

have indicated a somewhat different approach.[83] However, this judgment dealt with direct effect of the GATT in the wider sense and is therefore of little relevance in the present context.

2.3.5 Reciprocity

As regards the direct effect of provisions of international agreements, reciprocity has been the most controversial one. The ECJ dealt with the question whether reciprocity – or the absence thereof – has any impact on the direct effect of such provisions in three cases. These are the *Bresciani, Polydor* and *Kupferberg* cases. It was in the latter where the ECJ stated, under the reservation that there must be bona fide performance of every international agreement that '... the fact that the courts of one of the parties consider that certain of the stipulations in the agreement are of direct application whereas the courts of the other parties do not recognise such direct application is not in itself such as to constitute a lack of reciprocity in the implementation of the agreement'.[84]

It follows from these judgments that neither the imbalance of obligations nor differences in the application are at odds with the principle of reciprocity. The question of direct effect of international agreements relates to their execution, the modalities of which international law leaves to the discretion of the parties (provided they act in good faith). The choice of a particular way of execution, as far as courts are concerned, should not be discussed under the heading of reciprocity.

Is this also so for the GATT? Petersmann argues that denial of direct effect on the ground of lack of reciprocity is unjustified since almost all international agreements are based on some kind of reciprocity.[85] The opposite point of view seems, however, more convincing. There is little doubt that the recognition of direct effect in the context of the GATT would impair reciprocity in the application of the GATT because most of the other contracting parties do not recognise direct effect of the GATT. Furthermore, it is difficult to see how such an imbalance might be remedied within the context of a multilateral agreement with more than hundred participants, whereas in the case of bilateral treaties (such as those at issue in *Bresciani, Polydor* and *Kupferberg*) the parties can more easily come to an understanding about problems arising from the performance of the agreement. Finally, the reservation made by the ECJ in *Kupferberg* relating to the issue of reciprocity should be kept in mind. The ECJ could therefore consider the divergent case law concerning the direct effect as running counter to the principle of reciprocity[86] and consequently deny such effect

---
[83] J Rideau (n 14) at 373.
[84] Case 104/81 (n 41) at para 18 of the judgment.
[85] E-U Petersmann (n 14) at 426.
[86] HN Tagaras (n 14) at 51.

on the ground of non-performance by a contracting party, ie absence of substantive reciprocity.[87]

2.3.6 The System and Objectives of the GATT

The ECJ based its rejection of the direct effect of the GATT on 'considerations concerning the general scheme of GATT'.[88] It may be regretted that the ECJ came to such far-reaching conclusions on an a priori approach without, as it usually does, examining the nature, purpose and terms of the specific provision in question which is then considered with regard to the general scheme of the agreement.

2.3.7 Uniformity

The issue of uniform interpretation and application may at first sight seem to be misplaced. Indeed, uniformity has not explicitly been mentioned by the ECJ as a reason for denying direct effect to the GATT. It was primarily for the purpose of establishing the ECJ's jurisdiction to interpret the GATT in cases pending before it, that uniformity was referred to. However, the issue of uniform application of the GATT within the EC legal order is linked to the denial of direct effect to the GATT. In *SPI* the ECJ held that it had jurisdiction because 'it is important that the provisions of GATT should ..., receive uniform application throughout the Community'.[89]

The ECJ tries to avoid any discrepancies in the interpretation and application of the GATT since such discrepancies might not only undermine the common commercial policy but also lead to distortions of trade between the Member States. It is true, of course, that this reference to uniformity was made within the context of a preliminary ruling, but there can be little doubt as to the overall importance attached to this principle by the ECJ.

3. Conclusion

By holding that the determination of the meaning and scope falls under the ECJ's jurisdiction and by denying direct effect to the GATT the ECJ secured control over the application of the GATT within the EC. The GATT cannot be relied upon before national courts to question the validity of a Community act or to avoid the application of national law.

This view has been criticised ever since the *International Fruit Company* judgment was rendered. The fact that the ECJ did not respond to this criticism in its GATT-rulings prompted most authors to consider the

---

[87] JHJ Bourgeois (n 14) at 1266.
[88] Joined Cases 267–269/81 (n 6) at para 23 of the judgment.
[89] Joined Cases 267–269/81 (n 6) at para 14 of the judgment.

ECJ's view as final.[90] This does not seem to correspond with the actual developments in the ECJ's case law.

The ECJ's denial of direct effect to the GATT is not surprising. The GATT could be subject to different application in various Member States. The common commercial policy would be seriously jeopardised, not to mention the economic implications of such disunity. These consequences are not confined to the divergent application of international treaty provisions within the EC's legal order. Similar problems may arise if national courts in the various Member States apply EC Treaty provisions differently.

However, the *Foto Frost* case[91] sheds another light on the problem referred to above. In this case, the ECJ decided that Member State courts '...do not have the power to declare acts of Community institutions invalid. ... Divergences between courts in Member States as to the validity of Community acts would be liable to place in jeopardy the very unity of the Community legal order .... where the validity of a Community act is challenged before a national court the power to declare the act invalid must ... be reserved to the Court of Justice'.[92] This judgment permits the ECJ to be less strict when it comes to the application of the GATT before the national courts.[93]

It is not impossible that the ECJ might alter its view in the future, especially as regards GATT 1994. Such a change would inevitably lead to an increased application of GATT provisions within the EC. However, the ECJ is perfectly aware of the economic and political consequences of such a development. The ECJ's decision to include a clause in the decision concluding the Uruguay Round Agreement which precludes the direct effect of the Agreement in EC law will make it very difficult for the ECJ to rule differently.[94]

---

[90] M Maresceau (n 14) at 124.
[91] Case 314/85 *Foto Frost v Hauptzollamt Lübeck-Ost* [1987] ECR 4225.
[92] ibid paras 14 to 17 of the judgment.
[93] JHJ Bourgeois 'International Jurisprudence and Domestic Law: Some Comments from a European Community Perspective' in KR Simmonds and BHW Hill (eds) *Law and Practice Under the GATT* (New York: Oceana Publications, 1993) 10.
[94] Council Decision of 22 December 1994 concerning the conclusion on behalf of the European Community, as regards matters within its competence, of the agreements reached in the Uruguay Round multilateral negotiations (1986–1994) [1994] OJ L336/1. The last recital of the preamble reads as follows: '(W)hereas, by its nature, the Agreement establishing the World Trade Organization, including the Annexes thereto, is not suspectible to being directly invoked in Community or Member State courts...'. The recital is justified by the Commission as follows: '... it is important for the WTO Agreement and its annexes not to have a direct effect, that is one whereby private individuals who are natural or legal persons could invoke it under national law. It is already known that the United States and many other of our trading partners will explicitly rule out any such direct effect. Without an express stipulation of such exclusion in the Community instrument of adoption, a major imbalance would arise in the actual management of the obligations of the Community and other countries' See COM(94) 414 final.

CHAPTER II

THE HERMÈS JUDGMENT: RECONCILING THE PRINCIPLES OF UNIFORM AND CONSISTENT INTERPRETATION

1. Introduction

The judgment of the European Court of Justice (ECJ) of 16 June 1998 in Hermès[1] represents a good opportunity to focus on the jurisdictional competence of the ECJ to interpret the Agreement on Trade-Related Aspects of Intellectual Property Rights (the TRIPs Agreement) and to answer the question of the direct effect of the TRIPs Agreement and WTO Agreement(s) in the European Community's (EC) legal order. This chapter first reviews the Opinion of Advocate General Tesauro and the judgment itself. It will then address the wider impact of the Hermès judgment and more particularly the ECJ's attempt to reconcile the principles of uniformity and consistent interpretation in relation to the TRIPs Agreement.

2. Procedural Background

In Hermès, the Arrondissementsrechtbank (District Court) of Amsterdam referred to the ECJ, for a preliminary ruling under Article 177 of the EC Treaty, a question on the interpretation of Article 50(6) of the TRIPs Agreement. The question was raised in proceedings between Hermès International BV (Hermès) and FHT Marketing Choice BV (FHT), concerning trade mark rights owned by Hermès.[2]

In 1995, Hermès, on the basis of its trade mark right to the name 'Hermès', asked a Dutch court to order the seizure of ties marketed by FHT. Moreover, Hermès applied for an interim order requiring FHT to cease the infringement of its copyright and trade mark and the adoption of all measures to bring the infringement definitively to an end. Hermès also

---

[1] Case C-53/96 Hermès International v FHT Marketing Choice BV [1998] ECR I-3603. For a comment, see GA Desmedt 'European Court Rules on TRIPS Agreement' (1998) Journal of International Economic Law 679; A Epiney 'Zur Stellung des Völkerrechts in der EU' (1999) *EuZW* 5 and GA Zonnekeyn 'Mixed Feelings About the Hermès Judgment' (1999) *Int TLR* 20.
[2] President Arrondissementsrechtbank Amsterdam, 1 February 1996. The full text of the judgment was published in (1996) Bijblad Industriële Eigendom 288. For a comment, see P van den Bossche 'Een vraag die vragen doet rijzen' (1996) *Nederlands Tijdschrift voor Europees Recht* 211.

requested the court to fix, under Article 50(6) of the TRIPs Agreement, a time limit of three months for FHT to request revocation of those provisional measures and a period of 14 days, counting from the date of the requested revocation, for Hermès to initiate proceedings on the merits of the case. However, the court considered that Article 50(6) of the TRIPs Agreement does not place any time limit on the defendant's right to request revocation of provisional measures and that therefore the request could not be granted.

Article 50(1) of the TRIPs Agreement provides that judicial authorities must have the authority to order provisional measures to prevent an infringement of any intellectual property right. Article 50(6) of the TRIPs Agreement more specifically provides that these provisional measures shall be revoked or cease to have effect, upon request by the defendant, if proceedings leading to a decision on the merits of the case are not initiated within a reasonable period, to be determined by the judicial authority or, in the absence of such determination, not to exceed 20 working days or 31 calendar days, whichever is the longer.

However, while it refused to fix a time limit for FHT to introduce a request for revocation of provisional measures, the Dutch court referred a question to the ECJ under Article 177 of the EC Treaty to determine whether an interim measure such as the one foreseen by the Dutch Code of Civil Procedure, whereby an immediate, enforceable measure may be sought, could be characterised as a 'provisional measure' within the meaning of Article 50(6) of the TRIPs Agreement. Given the fact that the Dutch court was of the opinion that this measure had direct effect, it considered that if the interim measure was a 'provisional measure' it could oblige Hermès, the plaintiff, to initiate a procedure on the merits of the case within the period established in Article 50(6) of the TRIPs Agreement.

The District Court rendered its decision on 23 July 1998 and decided, in conformity with the judgment of the ECJ, that the interim measure as foreseen under Dutch law qualified as a provisional measure within the meaning of Article 50 of the TRIPs Agreement.[3]

The direct effect of Article 50(6) of the TRIPs Agreement appears to be an object of great concern amongst the judiciary in the Netherlands.[4] Less than 10 days after the Hermès judgment was rendered, the District Court of The Hague referred a question to the ECJ under Article 177 EC

---

[3] President Arrondissementsrechtbank (District Court) Amsterdam, KG 96/100, stencilled version.

[4] See, for a general analysis of the situation in the Netherlands, T Cohen Jehoram and WJM Diekman 'De directe werking van TRIPs' (1996) *Informatierecht* 127.

Treaty asking whether 'Article 50(6) of the Agreement on trade-related aspects of intellectual property rights is to be interpreted as having direct effect in the sense that the legal consequences set out therein take effect even in the absence of any corresponding provision of national law?'[5] In addition, on 30 October 1998, the Hoge Raad der Nederlanden (Supreme Court of the Netherlands) also asked the ECJ to rule on the direct effect of Article 50(6) of the TRIPs Agreement.[6]

Also in the United Kingdom, the interpretation of the TRIPs Agreement has resulted in some controversial case law.[7] In Lenzing,[8] the English court held the TRIPs Agreement could not have direct effect for several reasons: (1) the ECJ had already held that GATT 1947 did not have direct effect and that there was nothing in the WTO Agreement which indicated that it was intended to be otherwise; (2) any distinctions between GATT 1947 and the WTO Agreement were 'inconsequential' and (3) the WTO Agreement, and the TRIPs Agreement in particular, were merely agreements between countries. In any event, the provision invoked (ie Article 32 of the TRIPs Agreement) was not sufficiently clear and precise to have direct effect. It is obvious that the court's judgment betrayed a cursory analysis of the issue before it and was too dismissive of the differences between GATT 1947 and the WTO Agreement.

In Azrak-Hamway International,[9] the court first looked at the area of intellectual property involved and then asked whether the EC had competence in that area (ie industrial designs). When it found that it had not, it concluded that Articles 25 and 26 of the TRIPs Agreement did not have direct effect.[10]

---

[5] Case C–300/98 *Parfums Christian Dior SA v Tuk Consultancy BV* [1998] OJ C299/25 of 26 September 1998. The full text of the judgment was published in (1998) Intellectuele Eigendom & Reclamerecht 204.
[6] Case C–392/98 *Assco Gerüste GmbH and R van Dijk, trading as Assco Holland Steigers Plettac Nederland v Wilhelm Layher GmbH & Co and Layher BV* [1999] OJC 1/6 of 4 January 1999.
[7] For an analysis, see P Ruttley 'The Effect Of WTO Agreements in EC Law: How private parties can use WTO Agreements in litigation before the EC courts and the national courts of Member States' in P Ruttley et al (eds) *The WTO and International Trade Regulation* (London: Cameron May, 1998) 130, at 149–54.
[8] R v the Controller of Patents, Designs and Trademarks, ex parte Lenzing AG judgment of 20 December 1996 [1997] RPC 245. For a comment. see W Cook 'Judicial Review of the EPO and the Direct Effect of TRIPs in the European Community' (1997) *EIPR* 367.
[9] Azrak-Hamway International Inc [1997] RPC 134.
[10] What is astonishing is that the court decided that the TRIPs provisions not coming within the EC's competence are not part of EC law. The court thus ignored Article 228(7) of the EC Treaty according to which agreements concluded by the Community are binding upon the institutions of the Community and its Member States. Such agreements are part of the EC's legal order. See Case 181/73 Haegeman v Belgium [1974] ECR 449.

3. Opinion of the Advocate General

3.1 Jurisdiction of the ECJ

In his Opinion of 13 November 1997,[11] Advocate General Tesauro relied on Opinion 1/94 of the ECJ as a starting point for his analysis.[12] In Opinion 1/94, the ECJ held that 'the Community and its Member States are jointly competent to conclude TRIPs'.[13] The ECJ came to that conclusion after finding that, despite the link with trade in goods, intellectual property does not fall within the scope of Article 113 of the EC Treaty. The ECJ considered the case of measures to prevent counterfeit goods entering the EC, which are already the subject of a regulation based on Article 113 of the EC Treaty and consequently come within the exclusive external competence of the EC. While recognising the connection between intellectual property and trade in goods, and the effects intellectual property rights may have on such trade, the ECJ held that this was not enough to bring them within the specific scope of Article 113 of the EC Treaty and, consequently, within the exclusive external competence of the EC.

The Advocate General stated that with regard to the essential core provisions on the protection of intellectual property rights, there was only a potential exclusive external competence for the EC when the Opinion was delivered and that this situation has not changed to date. The terms of the problem are therefore unaltered, in that the competence to conclude an agreement such as TRIPs is still held jointly by the Member States and the EC[14] and, more particularly, in cases where the

---

[11] The Opinion of the Advocate General has been further elaborated in G Tesauro, 'Rapporti tra la Communita Europea e l'OMC' (1997) Rivista di Diritto Europeo 369.

[12] Opinion 1/94 of the Court of Justice of 15 November 1994 on the competence of the Community to conclude international agreements concerning services and the protection of intellectual property – Article 228(6) of the EC Treaty [1994] ECR I–5267. For a comment, see JHJ Bourgeois 'The EC in the WTO and Advisory Opinion 1/94: An Echternach Procession' (1995) *CMLRev* 763 and M Hilf 'The ECJ's 1/94 Opinion on the WTO – No Surprise, but Wise?' (1995) *EJIL* 245.

[13] See para 105 of the Opinion.

[14] This state of affairs, as the Advocate General remarked, could change only if Article 113(5) EC Treaty, inserted under the Treaty of Amsterdam, were to be applied after it enters into force. That provision states that 'the Council, acting unanimously on a proposal from the Commission and after consulting the European Parliament, may extend the application of paragraphs 1 to 4 to international negotiations and agreements on services and intellectual property insofar as they are not covered by these paragraphs'. In other words, Article 113(5) EC Treaty allows provisions on intellectual property too to be included in the common commercial policy, from which they are at present excluded, and consequently to come within the exclusive competence of the EC. For an analysis of the common commercial policy after the Amsterdam Treaty, see O Belin 'L'Article 113 CE Après Amsterdam' (1998) *RMUE* 447; A Dashwood 'External Relations Provisions of the Amsterdam Treaty' (1998) *CMLRev* 1019 and E Neframi 'Quelques Réflections sur la

continued ...

EC's competence is (still and only) potential, the competence to conclude agreements remains vested in the Member States.

Nothwithstanding the mixed character of the TRIPs Agreement, the Advocate General concluded that the ECJ had jurisdiction to interpret the TRIPs Agreement. He essentially argued that the requirement of uniformity in the interpretation and application of the TRIPs Agreement, or provisions thereof, were fundamental reasons to give the ECJ jurisdiction.

3.2 Direct Effect of the WTO Agreement

Advocate General Tesauro pleaded in favour of direct effect of the WTO Agreement as far as its substance is concerned but denied direct effect on grounds of reciprocity.

He started his Opinion with an analysis of the Council's decision approving the WTO Agreement.[15] The last recital of the preamble to that decision provides that '(W)hereas, by its nature, the Agreement establishing the World Trade Organisation, including the Annexes thereto, is not susceptible to being directly invoked in Community or Member State courts...'. The recital is justified by the Commission as follows: '... it is important for the WTO Agreement and its annexes not to have a direct effect, that is one whereby private individuals who are natural or legal persons could invoke it under national law. It is already known that the United States and many others of our trading partners will explicitly rule out any such direct effect. Without an express stipulation of such exclusion in the Community instrument of adoption, a major imbalance would arise in the actual management of the obligations of the Community and other countries'.[16] The Advocate General argued that this statement, in the absence of a multilateral solution on this issue, is not binding on the ECJ and cannot prevent the ECJ from ruling differently.[17]

Réforme de la Politique Commerciale par le Traité d'Amsterdam: Le maintain du Status Quo et l'Unité de la réprésentation Internationale de Communauté' (1998) CDE 137.

[15] Council Decision of 22 December 1994 concerning the conclusion on behalf of the European Community, as regards matters within its competence, of the agreements reached in the Uruguay Round multilateral negotiations (1986–1994) [1994] OJ L336/1 of 23 December 1994.

[16] See the Explanatory Memorandum to COM(94) 143 final of 15 April 1994.

[17] A similar point of view based on the good faith principle has been expressed by Pescatore who argues that the attempt to alter ex post the effect of an international agreement is incompatible with good faith in international relations and with the principle of legal protection at home. See P Pescatore 'The New WTO Dispute Settlement Mechanism' in P Demaret et al (eds) *Regionalism and Multilateralism after the Uruguay Round* (Brussels:, European University Press, 1997) 703–14.

The Advocate General then reviewed the judgments of the ECJ in which it had held that the provisions of GATT 1947 had no direct effect and examined whether those reasons for denial were equally valid as regards the provisions of the WTO Agreement(s). In its judgment in International Fruit Company,[18] the ECJ held that GATT 1947 'which, according to its preamble, is based on the principle of negotiations undertaken on the basis of 'reciprocal and mutually advantageous arrangements' is characterised by the great flexibility of its provisions, in particular those conferring the possibility of derogation, the measures to be taken when confronted with exceptional difficulties and the settlement of conflicts between the contracting parties'. Those factors were held by the ECJ to be sufficient to indicate that the provision at issue in that case, more in particular Article XI of GATT 1947, was not capable of conferring on private parties rights which they can invoke before a national court. More generally, those factors led the ECJ to hold that the rules of GATT 1947 'are not unconditional and that an obligation to recognise them as rules of international law which are directly applicable in the domestic legal systems of the contracting parties cannot be based on the spirit, general scheme or terms of GATT'. These arguments, which have been strongly criticised in the legal literature,[19] are consistently upheld in all the subsequent case law on the subject.[20]

It is quite clear from this case law that the ECJ considers that direct effect depends upon two factors, namely the characteristics of the GATT system (objectives, structure, nature of the provisions, remedies in the event of infringement) and the content of the provision. However, as the case law demonstrates, the content of the provision has never been examined, in that the ECJ has not taken steps to ascertain whether the provision at issue was clear, precise and unconditional, in accordance with the traditional criteria the ECJ has used in deciding whether or not to attribute direct effect to EC measures or to provisions contained in other agreements concluded by the EC. This is because the ECJ has never gone beyond its initial investigation, which was concerned with the principal features of the GATT system, with the result that it has always ruled against direct effect.

---

[18] Joined Cases 21/72–24/72 *International Fruit Company v Produktschap voor Groenten en Fruit* [1972] ECR 1219.

[19] See eg MJ Hahn and G Schuster 'Le Droit des états membres de se prévaloir en justice d'un accord liant la Communauté. L'invocabilité du GATT dans l'affaire République fédérale d'Allemagne contre Conseil de l'Union européenne' (1995) *Revue Générale de droit international public* 367 and KJ Kuilwijk The European Court of Justice and the GATT Dilemma: Public Interest versus Individual Rights' *Critical European Studies Series – Volume 1*, (Meppel : Nexed Editions Academic Publishers, 1996) 372.

[20] See inter alia Case 9/73 Schlüter v Hauptzollamt Lörrach [1973] ECR 1135; Case 266/81 *SIOT v Ministero delle Finanze* [1983] ECR 731 and, most recently, Case C–469/93 *Amministrazione delle Finanze dello Stato v Chiquita Italia* [1995] ECR I–4533.

The Advocate General subsequently questioned whether the characteristics attributed to GATT 1947 and which have led to the conclusion that its provisions do not have direct effect, and in particular the flexibility of those provisions and the excessively loose, negotiated, mechanism for the settlement of disputes, can be considered obsolete in the context of the WTO. It is obvious, he concluded, that the WTO system is very different from GATT 1947 and that there have been profound changes in the factors on which the ECJ's case law has been based. The WTO has the structure of an international organisation, the relationship between rules and exceptions appears to be functional and the dispute settlement mechanism has improved in that the results have more binding force.[21] Based on these reasons, Advocate General Tesauro concluded that the change from GATT 1947 to the WTO should lead the ECJ to alter its position on the direct effect of the WTO Agreement. He therefore concluded that provisions of the WTO Agreement, including the TRIPs Agreement, were capable of having direct effect.

He then examined the relationship between direct effect and considerations of reciprocity. If the EC recognises direct effect of the WTO Agreement and other WTO members do not, EC individuals would consequently be disadvantaged with regard to their competitors from third countries. Under such circumstances, third country competitors could invoke the WTO rules before the national courts of the EC Member States whereas EC individuals would not be able to invoke those rules in third country courts. The Advocate General argued that the recognition of direct effect should be related to the principle of reciprocity in the application of the Agreement and suggested that the ECJ should follow the principle of reciprocity.

4. The Judgment of the ECJ

4.1 Jurisdiction of the ECJ

The three intervening Member States, France, the Netherlands and the United Kingdom, claimed that the ECJ had no jurisdiction to answer the question. They referred to paragraph 104 of Opinion 1/94 in which the ECJ held that the provisions of the TRIPs Agreement relating to

---

[21] See M Montañá i Mora 'A GATT with Teeth: Law Wins over Politics in the resolution of International Trade Disputes' (1993) *Columbia Journal of Transnational Law* 103; M Montañá i Mora *La OMC y el Reforzamiento del Systema GATT* (Madrid: McGraw-Hill, 1997) 214 and E-U Petersmann 'International Trade Law and the GATT/WTO Dispute Settlement System 1948-1996: An Introduction' in E-U Petersmann (ed) *International Trade Law and the GATT/ WTO Dispute Settlement System* (London: Kluwer Law International, 1997) 3. For a more general analysis of the strengthened 'WTO system' as such, see JH Jackson *The World Trade Organization. Constitution and Jurisprudence* (London: The Royal Institute of International Affairs, 1998) 193.

'measures ... to secure the effective protection of intellectual property rights', such as Article 50, essentially fall within the competence of the Member States and not that of the Community on the ground that, at the time when the Opinion was delivered, the EC had not yet exercised its internal competence in this area.[22]

The Commission on the other hand, claimed that the ECJ had jurisdiction for the following reasons: (i) there is no absolute parallelism between the EC's competence to conclude agreements and the ECJ's interpretative jurisdiction, as the former must be based on present and effective Community powers; (ii) a mixed agreement – such as the TRIPs Agreement – is a single agreement between the EC and the Member States, on the one hand and non-Member States, on the other, and the interpretation and application must therefore be uniform; (iii) the interpretation of EC provisions which have harmonised the sector, albeit to a limited extent, must be consistent with the interpretation of those provisions where no harmonisation has taken place and (iv) the WTO Agreements are to be considered as a single agreement that requires interpretation based on the same criteria, avoiding the risk of divergent interpretations by the ECJ and the national courts on questions of major importance, such as direct effect.[23]

In this regard, the ECJ considered that it had jurisdiction since the WTO Agreement was concluded by the EC and ratified by its members without any allocation between them of their respective obligations towards the other WTO members. In addition, at the time of the signature of the WTO Agreement, Regulation 40/94 on the Community trademark[24] had been in force for one month, thereby implying that the matter falls at least partly under the EC's competence. Moreover, the ECJ seemed to infer its competence for interpreting Article 50 of the TRIPs Agreement from the fact that this provision was relevant to the interpretation of national provisional measures which can be taken by virtue of Article 99 of Regulation 40/94. Article 99 allows for provisional measures to be imposed by courts entrusted with safeguarding EC trade mark rights under Regulation 40/94.

With regard to the argument that the dispute concerned a trademark for which the international registrations were only made in the Benelux, the ECJ held that 'where the question referred to it concerns a provision which it has jurisdiction to interpret, the Court of Justice is, in principle,

---

[22] See the Report for the Hearing of 27 May 1997, paras 17–27.
[23] See the Report for the Hearing of 27 May 1997, paras 28–38.
[24] Council Regulation (EC) No 40/94 of 20 December 1993 on the Community trade mark [1994] OJ L11/36 of 14 January 1994.

bound to give a ruling'.[25] Additionally, the ECJ stated that 'where a provision can apply both to situations falling within the scope of Community law, it is clearly in the Community interest that, in order to forestall future differences of interpretation, that provision should be interpreted uniformly, whatever the circumstances in which it is to apply'.[26]

4.2 Direct Effect of the TRIPs Agreement

The ECJ did not focus on the issue of direct effect but indicated how a national measure should be construed in order to qualify as a 'provisional measure' within the meaning of Article 50 of the TRIPs Agreement. It concluded that, according to a textual analysis of Article 50, a measure such as the order made by the Dutch court must be considered as a 'provisional measure' within the meaning of that provision.

5. Comment

5.1 The Principle of Uniform Interpretation

The ECJ has always considered the principle of uniform interpretation and application of GATT as essential. In SPI,[27] the ECJ held that 'it is important that the provisions of GATT should ... receive uniform application throughout the Community'. It illustrates that the ECJ is at pains to avoid any discrepancies in the interpretation and application of GATT since such discrepancies in the interpretation might not only undermine the unity of the common commercial policy but also lead to distortions of trade between Member States.

However, the ECJ has never clarified whether the principle of uniform interpretation applies to all the provisions of an agreement binding the EC or solely to those provisions coming within the exclusive competence of the EC. The essential question therefore is whether there exists a parallelism between the EC's competence to conclude agreements and the ECJ's interpretative jurisdiction. It would appear that the ECJ has no interpretative jurisdiction regarding provisions that come within the exclusive competence of the Member States. In Demirel,[28] concerning the interpretation of certain provisions of the EC's association agreement with Turkey, some governments had questioned the jurisdiction of the ECJ to interpret the provisions on freedom of movement of workers,

---
[25] See para 31 of the judgment.
[26] See para 32 of the judgment.
[27] Joined Cases 267–269/81 Amministrazione delle Finanze dello Stato v Società Petrolifera Italiana (SPI) [1983] ECR 847.
[28] Case 12/86 Meryem Demirel v Stadt Schwäbisch Gmünd [1987] ECR 3719.

stating that such provisions fell within the exclusive competence of the Member States. The ECJ replied that the problem of 'mixity' was not an issue in this particular case as the competence to conclude association agreements extends to all the areas covered by the EC Treaty.

On the contrary, one could infer from this judgment that the ECJ has to decline jurisdiction under Article 177 of the EC Treaty for those areas coming within the exclusive competence of the Member States. As Advocate General Tesauro argued, 'if it were to be accepted that there are sectors for which the Member States have sole competence (or which are reserved solely for them), it would certainly follow that it need not be necessary to have perfect harmony in the application, and consequently in the interpretation of the various provisions of a mixed agreement. There would be no need for a centralised interpretation by the Court of Justice for all the areas of the subject-matter in question, especially in view of the trouble it would cause if the ECJ were to be given the last word on the interpretation of all the provisions of mixed agreements. For example, it would naturally be asked why – in applying agreements to which, in effect, the State alone (not the Community) is a party – the national courts or authorities should be obliged to follow the interpretation handed down by the Court in preference, let us suppose, to their own interpretation of that of a WTO panel, under the mechanism for the settlement of disputes ...'.[29]

This reasoning would exclude the jurisdiction of the ECJ to interpret those provisions of the TRIPs Agreement that fall within the exclusive competence of the Member States. However, should one not take into consideration the existence of a so-called 'power of attraction' of EC law on mixed agreements in their entirety? The application of the power of attraction follows from two basic principles.

The first principle is the duty of cooperation between the EC institutions and the Member States as put forward in Opinion 1/94 where the ECJ held that 'where it is apparent that the subject-matter falls in part within the competence of the Community and in part within that of the Member States, it is essential to ensure close cooperation between Member States and the Community institutions, both in the process of negotiation and conclusion and in the fulfilment of the commitments entered into. That obligation to cooperate flows from the requirement of unity in the international representation of the Community'.[30] The duty of cooperation equally applies to the national courts of the Member States and the European courts and would lead to a centralised interpretation of the TRIPs Agreement.

---

[29] Paragraph 19 of the Opinion.
[30] Paragraph 108 of the Opinion.

Secondly, there is the international responsibility of the EC. In Demirel, the ECJ held that 'in ensuring respect for commitments arising from an agreement concluded by the Community institutions the Member States fulfil, within the Community system, an obligation in relation to the Community, which has assumed responsibility for the due performance of the agreement'. This obligation is incorporated in Article 5 of the EC Treaty which provides that 'Member States shall take all appropriate measures, whether general or particular, to ensure fulfilment of the obligations arising out of this Treaty or resulting from action taken by the institutions of the Community. They shall facilitate the achievement of the Community's tasks'.

Both principles imply that the TRIPs Agreement should be subject to a centralised interpretation by the ECJ.

5.2 Direct Effect of the WTO Agreement(s)

As far as GATT – in its pre-Uruguay Round version – is concerned, the ECJ has in the past denied direct effect to GATT provisions as they were not considered 'capable of creating rights of which interested parties may avail themselves'.[31] The ECJ has maintained this case law on the direct

---

[31] A vast amount of literature has been devoted to the question of the legal status of GATT/WTO in the EC's legal order. See eg RA Brand 'Direct Effect of International Economic Law in the United States and the European Union' (1996–97) *Northwestern Journal International Law & Business* 556; F Castillo de la Torre The Status of GATT in EC Law. Some New Developments' (1992) *JWT* 35; F Castillo de la Torre 'The Status of GATT in EC Law, Revisited' (1995) *JWT* 53; P Eeckhout 'The Domestic Legal Status of the WTO Agreement: Interconnecting Legal Systems' (1997) *CMLRev* 11; S Griller 'The Common Commercial Policy Instruments after the Uruguay Round - with some Implications for Austria' in F Breuss (ed) *The World Economy after the Uruguay Round* (Wien: Service Fachverlag, 1995) 269–337; P-J Kuyper 'The New Dispute Settlement System: The Impact on the Community' in JHJ Bourgeois et al (eds) *The Uruguay Round Results. A European Lawyers' Perspective* (Brussels: European University Press, 1995) 87–114; P Lee and B Kennedy 'The Potential Direct Effect of GATT 1994 in European Community Law' (1996) *JWT* 67; P Mengozzi 'The Marrakesh DSU and its Implications on the International and European Level' in JHJ Bourgeois et al (eds) *The Uruguay Round Results. A European Lawyers' Perspective* (Brussels:,European University Press, 1995) 115–33; P Mengozzi 'The World Trade Organization Law: An Analysis of its First Practice' (1998) *Rivista di Diritta Europeo* 3 at 29–30; M Montañà i Mora 'Equilibrium - A Rediscovered Basis for the Court of Justice of the European Communities to Refuse Direct effect to the Uruguay Round Agreements' (1996) *JWT* 43; J Osterhoudt Berkey 'The European Court of Justice and Direct Effect for the GATT: A Question Worth Revisiting' (1998) *EJIL*; CWA Timmermans 'The Implementation of the Uruguay Round by the EC' in JHJ Bourgeois et al (eds) *The Uruguay Round Results. A European Lawyers' Perspective* (Brussels: European University Press, 1995) 501–09 and G Zonnekeyn 'The Direct effect of GATT in Community Law: From International Fruit Company to the Banana Cases' (1996) *Int TLR* 63. For a more general and exhaustive analysis, see *A Ott GATT und WTO im Gemeinschaftsrecht. Die Integration des Völkervertrechts in die Europäische Gemeinschaftsordnung am Beispiel des GATT–Vertrags und der WTO-Übereinkünfte* (Cologne Carl Heymanns verlag, 1998) 317. For a specific analysis of the potential direct effect of the TRIPs Agreement, see T Einhorn 'The

continued ...

effect of GATT 1947, as promulgated in International Fruit Company,[32] in its Banana judgments.[33] According to the ECJ, GATT 1947 is based on the principle of reciprocal and mutually advantageous arrangements, as is written in its preamble and is characterised by three elements: (i) the great flexibility of its provisions, in particular those conferring the possibility of derogation; (ii) the measures to be taken when confronted with exceptional difficulties; and (iii) the settlement of disputes between contracting parties.

Those features show that GATT rules are not unconditional. The ECJ therefore concluded that the spirit, general scheme and terms of GATT preclude direct effect. Individuals are only allowed to invoke GATT provisions if EC legislation expressly referred to them,[34] or if the EC intended to implement an obligation entered into under GATT.[35]

The question now also arises whether the WTO Agreement(s) have direct effect. Apart from the Hermès case, this question has been recently dealt with in a number of other cases.

In Affish, the ECJ had the opportunity for the first time to decide upon the direct effect of the WTO Agreement.[36] In this particular case, the Commission prohibited Member States from importing fish from Japan. On the basis of the Commission's decision, the Dutch authorities refused to authorise the importation of Japanese products by an importer, Affish Co Ltd. The latter challenged the Commission decision in the Dutch Administrative Court for Trade and Industry and argued that this decision was inconsistent with the WTO Agreement on the application of sanitary and phytosanitary measures.[37]

Advocate General Cosmas denied direct effect to the provisions of the WTO Agreement on the same basis as that of the well established case law applied to GATT 1947.[38] He argued that the provisions of the WTO

Impact of the WTO Agreement on TRIPS (Trade-Related Aspects of Intellectual Property Rights) on EC Law' (1998) *CMLRev* 1069 at 1094–5 and M Miller 'The TRIPs Agreement and direct effect in European Community Law ' (1999) *Notre Dame Law Rev* 597.

[32] Joined Cases 21–24/72 *International Fruit Company v Produktschap voor Groenten en Fruit* [1972] ECR 1219.

[33] Case C–280/93 *Germany v Council* [1994] ECR I–4973 and Case C–469/93 *Amministrazione delle Finanze dello Stato v Chiquita Italia Spa* [1995] ECR I–4533.

[34] Case 70/87 *Fediol v Commission* [1989] ECR 1781.

[35] Case 69/89 *Nakajima All Precision Co Ltd v Council* [1991] ECR I–2069 and Case C–352/96 Italy v Council, not yet reported in the ECR.

[36] Case C–183/95 *Affish BV v Rijksdienst voor de Keuring van Vee en Vlees* [1997] ECR I–4315.

[37] For an analysis of the case before the Dutch court, see M Fierstra 'Rol CBb in communautair stelsel van rechtsbescherming' (1995) *Nederlands Tijdschrift voor Europees Recht* 135.

[38] Opinion of 17 July 1997 [1997] ECR I–4362, paras 112–28.

Agreement remain characterised by a great flexibility which does not allow recognition of their direct effect. The Advocate General further maintained that the 'spirit of negotiations' is not totally excluded from the WTO's new dispute settlement. The Advocate General also addressed the principle of reciprocity which had been used by the Commission as an argument against direct effect. Mr Cosmas considered this argument to be irrelevant and referred to the general rules of international law according to which there must be bona fide performance of every agreement. The ECJ has previously confirmed that although each contracting party is responsible for executing fully the commitments which it has undertaken, it is nevertheless free to determine the legal means appropriate for attaining that end in its legal system unless the agreement, interpreted in the light of its subject matter and purpose, itself specifies those means. Subject to that reservation, the fact that the courts of one of the parties consider that certain of the stipulations in the agreement are of direct application whereas the courts of the other party perhaps do not recognise such direct application is not in itself such as to constitute a lack of reciprocity in the implementation of the agreement.[39] By contrast, the ECJ did not refer to the question of direct effect since the national court had not explicitly asked the ECJ to rule on that particular issue.

In T Port, an importer of bananas challenged the legality of the EC's bananas Regulation under GATT/WTO rules.[40] Advocate General Elmer, in his Opinion of 24 June 1997, denied direct effect to the WTO Agreement by referring to the well-known case law of the ECJ and the preamble to the Council's decision concluding the WTO Agreements. The ECJ, again, avoided answering the question of direct effect.

5.3 The Reciprocity Principle

This chapter will only discuss the principle of reciprocity, as this was the sole argument relied on by the Advocate General to deny direct effect to the WTO Agreement. It will also adddress the issue of consistent interpretation as a substitute to the principle of direct effect.

As regards the direct effect of provisions of international agreements, reciprocity has been one of the most controversial reasons to deny direct effect to GATT 1947. The ECJ dealt with the question whether reciprocity – or the absence thereof – has any bearing on the direct effect of such

---

[39] See Case 104/81 *Hauptzollamt Mainz v Kupferberg* [1982] ECR 3641. The principle of good faith is a rule of customary international law and therefore binding on the EC. See in this respect Case T–115/94 *Opel Austria GmbH v Council* [1997] ECR II–39.
[40] Joined Cases C–364/95 and C–365/95 *T Port GmbH & Co v Hauptzollamt Hamburg-Jonas* [1997] ECR I–1023.

provisions in three cases: Bresciani,[41] Polydor[42] and Kupferberg.[43] It was in the latter case that the ECJ stated, under the reservation that there must be bona fide performance of every international agreement that 'the fact that the courts of one of the parties consider that certain of the stipulations in the agreement are of direct application whereas the courts of the other parties do not recognise such direct application is not in itself such as to constitute a lack of reciprocity in the implementation of the agreement'.

It follows from these judgments that neither the imbalance of obligations nor differences in the application are at odds with the principle of reciprocity. The question of direct effect of international agreements relates to their execution, the modalities of which international law leaves to the discretion of the parties (provided they act in good faith). The choice of a particular way of execution – especially as far as courts are concerned – should not be discussed under the heading of reciprocity. Is this also the case for the WTO Agreement? It has been argued that denial of direct effect on the basis of lack of reciprocity is unjustified since most international agreements are based on some kind of reciprocity.[44] The opposite point of view seems, however, more convincing: there is little doubt that the recognition of direct effect in the context of the WTO Agreement would impair reciprocity in the application of the Agreement because most of the other members do not recognise direct effect of the WTO Agreement. Moreover, it is difficult to see how such an imbalance might be remedied within the context of a multilateral agreement with more than 130 members, whereas in the case of bilateral treaties (such as those at issue in Bresciani, Polydor and Kupferberg) the parties can more easily come to an understanding about problems arising from the performance of the agreement. Finally, the reservation made by the ECJ in Kupferberg relating to the issue of reciprocity should be recalled: the ECJ could therefore consider the divergent case law concerning the direct effect as running counter to the principle of reciprocity and consequently deny such effect on the ground of non-performance by a contracting party, ie absence of substantive reciprocity. The same reasoning could apply to the WTO Agreement.

5.4 The Principle of Consistent Interpretation

However, as the Dutch court interpreted national law in accordance with the meaning given to Article 50(6) of the TRIPs Agreement by the

---

[41] Case 87/75 *Bresciani v Amministrazione delle Finanzedello Stato* [1976] ECR 129.
[42] Case 270/80 *Polydor Ltd v Harlequin Record Shop Ltd* [1982] ECR 329.
[43] Case 104/81 *Hauptzollamt Mainz v Kupferberg* [1982] ECR 3641.
[44] E-U Petersmann 'Application of GATT by the Court of Justice of the European Communities' (1983) *CMLRev* 397.

ECJ, the TRIPs Agreement certainly had an effect on the outcome of the case. One could therefore infer from this judgment that the WTO Agreement(s) certainly have an 'indirect effect'.[45] This has been referred to as 'the doctrine and principle of consistent interpretation'.[46] According to this principle, national law has to be interpreted in accordance with international obligations. Where national rules allow for different interpretation, the one in accordance with international obligations is to be adopted.

The ECJ has applied this principle in relation to the interpretation of EC law provisions in the Werner[47] and Leifer[48] judgments. In those cases the question arose whether Article 1 of Council Regulation No 2603/69 establishing common rules for exports, which prohibits quantitative restrictions on exports, extends to national licensing requirements for exports of so-called dual-use goods. The ECJ gave an affirmative reply and stated 'that finding is supported by Article XI of the General Agreement on Tariffs and Trade, which can be considered for the purposes of interpreting a Community instrument governing international trade'.[49] The ECJ has been more clear in Germany v Council[50] where it held that 'the primacy of international agreements concluded by the Community over provisions of secondary Community legislation means that such provisions must, so far as possible, be interpreted in a manner that is consistent with those agreements'.

---

[45] On the principle of indirect effect, see NAM Neuwahl 'Individuals and the GATT: Direct and Indirect Effects of the General Agreement on Tariffs and Trade in Community Law' in N Emiliou and D O'Keeffe (eds) *European Union and World Trade Law* (Chichester: John Wiley & Sons, 1996) 213. See also P Eeckhout 'The Domestic Legal Status of the WTO Agreement: Interconnecting Legal Systems' [1997] *CMLRev* 11 at 40–2.

[46] T Cottier 'The Impact of the TRIPs Agreement on Private Practice Litigation' in J Cameron and K Campbell (eds) *Dispute Resolution in the World Trade Organisation* (London: Cameron & May, 1998) 111 at 124–6 and P Manin 'A propos de l'accord instituant l'Organisation mondiale du commerce et de l'accord sur les marchés publics: la question de l'invocabilité des accords internationaux conclus par la Communauté européenne' [1997] *RTDE* 399 at 412–13. See also A Epiney, C Kaddous and C-A Ridore 'La Communauté européenne et l'OMC. A propos du statut des règles du GATT/OMC dans l'ordre juridique communautaire' (1998) *European Food Law Review* 291 at 315. The latter refer to the principle of consistent interpretation as a 'paliatif à l'absence d'effet direct'. The principle of consistent interpretation has also explicitly been recognised by Advocate General Tesauro in his Opinion in Hermès at para 38.

[47] Case C–70/94 *Fritz Werner Industrie-Ausrüstungen GmbH v Germany* [1995] ECR I–3189.

[48] Case 83/94 Peter Leifer and Others [1995] ECR I–3231.

[49] Paragraph 23 of the Werner judgment and para 24 of the Leifer judgment.

[50] Case C–61/94 *Commission v Germany* [1996] ECR II–3989, para 52. For an excellent comment on this case, see P Eeckhout (1998) *CMLRev* 557. This author argues that 'the Court appears to be stretching the requirement of consistent interpretation for reasons related to the lack of direct effect'.

6. Conclusion

The Hermès case has made it clear that in order to preserve uniformity in the interpretation of WTO law, the ECJ should have jurisdiction to interpret the WTO Agreement, even in those circumstances where the EC has to share its competences with the Member States such as under the TRIPs Agreement.

With regard to the direct effect of the WTO Agreement and the TRIPs Agreement in particular, it has become clear that the strongest candidate to substitute the structural weakness doctrine as a judicial doctrine to limit the effects of WTO law within the EC's legal order is the doctrine of non-reciprocity in respect of direct effect. One author has suggested that the reciprocity argument be replaced by the concept of 'equilibrium' which would entail that the ECJ should refuse to grant direct effect to the WTO Agreement in order not to create an imbalance of the rights and obligations of the WTO members under the WTO Agreement.[51] It is possible that the ECJ will alter its view regarding the direct effect of the WTO Agreement. Such a change would inevitably lead to an increased application of WTO law within the EC Member States. However, as the ECJ is perfectly aware of the economic and political consequences of such a development, it will be very difficult for the ECJ to rule differently. As the question of direct effect has not been dealt with by the ECJ in Hermès, as many had hoped or expected, it has left most of those – rightly – with 'mixed feelings'.

Notwithstanding those 'mixed feelings', the Hermès judgment has shed a light on the principle of consistent interpretation which is currently used as a surrogate for direct effect in correlation with the ECJ's jurisdiction to interpret the WTO Agreement(s), even in those areas where the EC and the Member States share competences. A 'reconciliation' between the principles of uniform and consistent interpretation could certainly help those national courts confronted with the interpretation of the WTO Agreement(s).

---

[51] See M Montañà i Mora (n 30) at 53.

CHAPTER III

THE LEGAL STATUS OF WTO PANEL REPORTS IN THE EC LEGAL ORDER – SOME REFLECTIONS ON THE OPINION OF ADVOCATE GENERAL MISCHO IN THE ATLANTA CASE

1. Introduction

In an Opinion delivered on 6 May 1999, Advocate General Mischo briefly focused on the question of the legal status of panel reports (in this particular case an Appellate Body report) adopted by the World Trade Organization's ('WTO') Dispute Settlement Body ('DSB') in the European Community ('EC') legal order.[1] This question has not yet inspired many legal scholars to date and therefore merits some closer attention.[2]

This comment will focus on the Opinion of the Advocate General and will refer to the factual background of the case where necessary. It will then concentrate on the question of whether WTO panel and Appellate Body reports can be invoked in legal actions brought before the European Court of First Instance (CFI) or the European Court of Justice (ECJ).

---

[1] Opinion of 6 May 1999 in Case C-104/97 P, *Atlanta AG v Commission and Council*, not yet reported in the ECR. At the time of writing only the French version of the Opinion was available.

[2] See on this particular question, J M Beneyto, 'The EU and the WTO. Direct Effect of the New Dispute Settlement System?', 1996, *EuZW*, 295; J H Jackson, 'The Legal Meaning of a GATT Dispute Settlement Report: Some Reflections', in *Towards More Effective Supervision by International Organisations. Essays in Honour of Henry G Schermers*, Vol 1, N. Blokker and S Muller, eds, (Dordrecht: Kluwer 1994, 149–64; N. Lavranos, 'Die Rechtswerkung von WTO panel reports im Europäischen Gemeinschaftsrecht sowie im deutschen Verfassungsrecht', Europarecht, May–June 1999, 289, and A Weber and F Moos, 'Rechtswirkungen von WTO-Streitbeilegungsentscheidungen im Gemeinschaftsrecht', *EuZW*, 1999, 229. Others have briefly touched upon the question, see, eg, J H J Bourgeois, 'International Jurisprudence and Domestic Law: Some Comments from a European Community Perspective', in *Law and Practice Under the GATT*, K R Simmonds and B H W Hill, eds (New York: Oceana Publications 1993), 10–13; P. Eeckhout, 'The Domestic Legal Status of the WTO Agreement: Interconnecting Legal Systems', *CML Rev* 11 (1994), 11, at 51–5; T Cottier, 'Dispute Settlement in the World Trade Organization: Characteristics and Structural Implications for the European Union', *CML Rev* (1998) 325, at 369–75; M. Montañà I Mora, 'A GATT with Teeth: Law Wins Over Politics in the Resolution of International Trade Disputes', *Colum J Transnat'l L* (1993) 103, at 175–6; J. Nyberg, 'Will the Fight against the European Community Common Banana Market Lead to Conflicts of a Constitutional Character?', ELSA Selected Papers on European Law (1997), 211, at 244–5; A Ott, *GATT und WTO im Gemeinschaftsrecht* (Cologne: Carl Heymanns Verlag 1997), 242–3 and C Schmid, 'Immer wieder Bananen: Der Status des GATT/WTO – Systems im Gemeinschaftsrecht', *NJW* (1998) 190, at 196.

2. The Opinion of the Advocate General

In the case at hand, Atlanta[3] sought the annulment of a CFI judgment rendered on 11 December 1996, rejecting Atlanta's request for damages based on Article 288 of the EC Treaty (ex Article 215).[4] Atlanta alleged that the WTO-incompatibility of Regulation 404/93,[5] in view of the Appellate Body report of 9 September 1997,[6] justified a claim for damages and emphasised that it was not invoking a breach of substantive WTO rules.

Advocate General Mischo disagreed with the applicant and argued that Atlanta was relying on substantive WTO law, since the Appellate Body report is a mere application (and interpretation) of WTO law. Consequently, the Advocate General considered that Atlanta should have tried to annul the CFI judgment on the ground that the latter did not give Atlanta the possibility of invoking GATT rules. As this argument was not included in Atlanta's submission, Advocate General Mischo concluded that the appeal was inadmissible.[7]

However, according to the Advocate General, even an explicit referral to an alleged infringement of substantive WTO law in Atlanta's submission would still not have constituted a valid ground on which to challenge the WTO-incompatibility of Regulation 404/93 as WTO rules cannot be invoked as a ground for annulment before the European courts.[8]

The Advocate General then examined whether the WTO Appellate Body report could constitute a ground for liability on the part of the EC. It follows from the case law of the ECJ that to impose liability upon the

---

[3] Atlanta is a German banana trader who has been involved in a number of legal proceedings before the CFI and the ECJ whereby it challenged the EC banana regime.

[4] Case T-521/93, *Atlanta AG and Others v EC*, [1996] ECR II-1707. See OJ 142/11 of 10 May 1997 for a summary of the pleas in law and the main arguments adduced in support. It is interesting to note that there are other cases pending before the CFI where reference has been made to the panel and Appellate Body reports issued in the banana case. See Case T-2/99, *T. Port GmbH & Co KG v Council*, OJ C 71/35 of 13 March 1999; Case T-3/99, *Bananatrading GmbH v Council*, OJ C 71/35 of 13 March 1999; Case T-18/99, *Cordis Obst- und Gemüsegrosshandel GmbH v Commission*, OJ C 86/28 of 27 March 1999; Case T-30/99, *Bocchi Food Trade International GmbH v Commission*, OJ C 86/33 of 27 March 1999 and T-52/99, *T. Port GmbH & Co KG v Commission*, OJ C 121/19 of 1 May 1999.

[5] Council Regulation (EC) No. 404/93 of 13 February 1993 on the common organisation of the market in bananas, OJ L 47/1 of 25 February 1993.

[6] WT/DS27/AB/R, *European Communities – Regime for the Importation, Sale and Distribution of Bananas*, report of the Appellate Body of 9 September 1997. The Advocate General refers to the Appellate Body report of 25 September 1997. This is the date on which the Appellate Body report was adopted by the Dispute Settlement Body ('DSB') as provided for by Article 17.14 of the Understanding on Rules and Procedures Governing the Settlement of Disputes ('DSU').

[7] Paras 3 to 23 of the Opinion.

[8] The Advocate General referred to Case C-208/93, *Germany v Council*, [1994] ECR I-4973.

EC, the law invoked must have 'direct effect', i.e. must be able to confer rights on individuals.[9]

The Advocate General finally argued that a ruling of the Appellate Body does not impose any obligation on the Member whose legislation has been found to be in breach of WTO law to amend its legislation immediately. According to Article 21(3) of the DSU, a Member has a 'reasonable period' of time to comply with the ruling of the Appellate Body and to bring its legislation in line with WTO law. Moreover, Article 22 of the DSU gives WTO Members the possibility of maintaining the legislation in force beyond the reasonable period of time if the parties to the dispute have agreed on suitable compensation. Therefore, the Advocate General considered that Atlanta would not be able to rely on the Appellate Body report to invoke a right to damages.[10]

3. The Interface Between Decisions of International Judicial Bodies and EC Law

According to the Opinion of the Advocate General, the status in EC law of decisions of (judicial) bodies established under the auspices of an international agreement, depends on the status and the effect of the particular international agreement in the EC legal system. This analysis is not entirely correct, as the legal status of decisions emanating from judicial entities established within the framework of an international agreement such as the WTO cannot – as such – be assimilated with the legal status of the agreement itself in so far as that agreement is binding for the EC and forms an integral part of the EC legal order.[11]

For the purposes of this comment, 'decisions of bodies established under the auspices of an international agreement' will refer either to decisions of international bodies administering international agreements or to decisions or judgments of judicial entities established within the framework of an international agreement.

---

[9] See Case 5/71, *Zuckerfabrik Schöppensted v Council*, [1971] ECR 975.
[10] Advocate General Lenz, however, did not exclude liability of the EC under such circumstances albeit under the 'old' GATT regime. He argued that one should '*not exclude the possibility that in exceptional cases an infringement of provisions of GATT might give rise to a liability in damages to the traders concerned. In particular, one might envisage a case where in such a situation the Community makes no use of the possibilities provided for in GATT of freeing itself from its obligations, but agrees that the dispute should be decided by a neutral tribunal, and then however refuses to comply with the decision.*' See paragraph 21 of his Opinion of 16 February 1995 in Case C-469/93, *Amministrazione delle Finanze dello Stato v Chiquita Italia SpA*, [1995] ECR I-4533. As Montañà I Mora phrased it, '*[O]ne may construe this intriguing statement as establishing that the Community's failure to comply with a World Trade Organization (WTO) panel report might give rise to liability in damages to the traders concerned.*' See M. Montañà I Mora, *AJIL* (1997), 152, at 155.
[11] *Contra*: J H J Bourgeois, above n 2, at 13.

3.1 Decisions of Bodies Administering International Agreements

Certain international agreements concluded by the EC establish institutions such as an Association Council, empowered to issue recommendations or to adopt decisions. One of the best known examples is the 'Council of Association' set up under the Association Agreement concluded between the EC and Turkey.[12] Under this Agreement, the Association Council has the power to take decisions and each of the parties to the agreement must take the measures necessary to implement the decisions taken.[13] It is important to distinguish between, on the one hand, the binding character of such decisions in the EC legal order and, on the other hand, the direct effect of such decisions.

3.1.1 The Binding Character in The EC Legal Order

The ECJ decided in *Greece v Council*[14] that decisions issued by the Association Council form an integral part of EC law from the moment of their entry into force. They do not necessarily require implementing measures by the EC for their application within the EC legal order. A specific act of the Council is only required if the substance of the particular decision does not allow it to be applied by the courts immediately.

3.1.2 Direct Effect

Individuals have successfully invoked decisions adopted by the Association Council before their domestic courts in order to invalidate national legislation inconsistent with such decisions. The majority of those cases were referred to the ECJ under Article 234 of the EC Treaty (ex Article 177).[15] The ECJ has held, on several occasions, that those decisions may have direct effect.

Lavranos[16] has argued that the legal effect of decisions taken by the Association Council set up under the EC-Turkey Association Agreement can be assimilated with the legal effects of WTO panel reports, because

---

[12] See the Agreement of 12 September 1963 establishing an Association between the European Economic Community and Turkey, OJ L 217/3687 of 29 December 1964.
[13] See Article 22(1) of the Association Agreement.
[14] Case 30/88, *Greece v Commission*, [1989] ECR 3711.
[15] See eg Case C-192/89, *S Z Sevince v Staatssecretaris van Justitie*, [1990] ECR I-3461; Case C-237/91, *Kazim Kus v Landeshauptstadt Wiesbaden*, [1992] ECR I-6781; Case C355/93, *Hayriye Eroglu v Land Baden-Württemberg*, [1994] ECR I-5113 and Case C-98/96, *Kasim Ertanir v Land Hessen*, [1997] ECR I-5179 and Case C-262/96, *Sema Sürül v Bundesanstalt für Arbeit*, Judgment of 4 May 1999, not yet reported in the ECR. For an analysis of the earlier case law, see eg P Gilsdorf, 'Les Organes institués par des Accords Communautaires: Effets Juridiques de leurs Décisions', *RMC* (1992) 328.
[16] See N Lavranos, above n 2.

both the EC and its Member States are signatories to the WTO Agreements as well as to the Association Agreement with Turkey, and because under both agreements a body was established entrusted with the power to take binding decisions. Although those decisions are different in form, they would have the same binding (legal) effect.

It is questionable, however, whether panel or Appellate Body reports can be assimilated with decisions taken by the Association Council. Certainly, there are similarities but they do not produce or intend to produce similar legal effects. The panels and the Appellate Body have a judicial function, whereas the Association Council rather acts as a kind of executive, administrative body.

It is also questionable whether decisions taken by the Association Council as a 'dispute settlement body' under the Association Agreement would have the same status and/or effect as panel or Appellate Body reports. Presumably not, since the dispute settlement system established in the framework of the Association Agreement with, for example Turkey, does not have the same judicial qualities and characteristics as the WTO dispute settlement mechanism. For example, the jurisdiction of the Association Council is not compulsory and there is no possibility for appeal.

3.2 Decisions of Judicial/Adjudicative-Type Entities

The ECJ has confirmed that the EC may enter into an international agreement whereby a judicial entity is established, provided that the structure and the jurisdiction of such entities are compatible with the EC Treaty. In 1991, the ECJ gave an opinion pursuant to Article 300 of the EC Treaty (ex Article 228) before the draft agreement on the European Economic Area ('EEA') was concluded with the Member States of the European Free Trade Association ('EFTA').[17] One of the crucial questions with which the ECJ dealt was whether the EEA Agreement's system of judicial supervision for the settlement of disputes was compatible with the EC Treaty. Under the EEA Agreement, an EEA Court was proposed with the jurisdiction to interpret and apply the provisions of the Agreement in disputes between the Contracting Parties.

The ECJ declared that the proposed jurisdiction given to the EEA Court was incompatible with the EC Treaty on the following grounds. Since the EEA Court had the competence to interpret the EEA Agreement of which the provisions were identical with the corresponding provisions of the EC Treaty, there was a risk that the EEA Court and the ECJ would make different interpretations, especially since the two agreements had

---
[17] Opinion 1/91, *Draft agreement relating to the creation of the European Economic Area*, [1991] ECR I-6079.

different purposes. Interpretations made by the EEA Court were therefore liable to affect EC law and, subsequently, the EEA court system would be in conflict with the role of the ECJ under Article 220 (ex Article 164) and Article 292 (ex Article 219) of the EC Treaty and therefore the very foundations of the EC.[18]

However, the ECJ declared that there are certain conditions under which it will be bound by the decisions of another court. After recalling its case law on the binding effect of international agreements concluded by the EC and on its own jurisdiction to interpret those agreements, the ECJ decided that

> [W]here, however, an international agreement provides for its own system of courts, including a court with jurisdiction to settle disputes between the Contracting Parties to the agreement, and, as a result, to interpret its provisions, the decisions of that court will be binding on the Community institutions, including the Court of Justice. Those decisions will also be binding in the event the Court of Justice is called upon to rule, by way of a preliminary ruling or in a direct action, on the interpretation of the international agreement, in so far as that agreement is an integral part of the Community legal order. An international agreement providing for such a system of courts is in principle compatible with Community law. The Community's competence in the field of international relations and its capacity to conclude international agreements necessarily entails the power to submit to the decisions of a court which is created or designated by such an agreement as regards the interpretation and application of its provisions.[19]

Here, the ECJ emphasised the binding character of judicial decisions on disputes between the contracting parties to an agreement for the ECJ where the ECJ is called upon to rule on the interpretation of the agreement.[20]

Moreover, a closer look at Opinion 1/91 reveals that the ECJ implicitly agreed with the concept that the binding character of judicial decisions on disputes between the contracting parties to an international agreement does not depend on the direct effect of such an agreement. In Opinion 1/91, the ECJ assumed that the EEA Agreement did not have direct effect.[21]

---

[18] In a subsequent opinion, the ECJ held that the new provisions of the EEA Agreement on the settlement of disputes were now compatible with the EC Treaty. See Opinion 1/92, *Opinion on the revised draft Agreement on the European Economic Area*, [1992] ECR I-2821.
[19] Paragraphs 39 and 40 of Opinion 1/91, *Draft agreement relating to the creation of the European Economic Area* [1991] ECR I-6079.
[20] P Eeckhout, above n 2, at 52.
[21] See in particular paragraph 21 of the Opinion. See W van Gerven, 'The Genesis of EEA Law and the Principles of Primacy and Direct Effect', *Fordham Int'l LJ* (1992/93), 955, at 968.

This did not prevent the ECJ from holding that the decisions of the EEA Court could be binding for the ECJ.

3.3 WTO Panel and Appellate Body Reports

3.3.1 The WTO Agreements are Part of the EC Legal Order

To date, there has been only one case where the ECJ explicitly referred to a GATT panel report. In *Dürbeck*,[22] which concerned imports of dessert apples from Chile, the ECJ was informed by the Commission at the hearing that a GATT panel[23] had not found an infringement of Articles I or II of GATT, as was alleged, and had only marginally criticised the protective measures adopted by the EC.[24] The ECJ therefore rejected the claim based on GATT and decided that

> (...) the argument advanced by the plaintiff in the main action that the protective measures in issue are contrary to the commitments entered into by the Community under GATT is not compatible in this case of putting the validity of these measures into question.[25]

It would appear that the ECJ was misinformed, as the GATT panel had found a number of infringements of Article XIII and Article XIX of GATT.[26]

As the *Dürbeck* judgment did not give any guidance as to how the ECJ would qualify the legal status of a (GATT) panel report, it is now essential to assess whether the line of reasoning maintained by the ECJ in Opinion 1/91 also applies to panel and Appellate Body reports adopted under the WTO dispute settlement mechanism.[27]

---

[22] Case 112/80, *Firma Anton Dürbeck v Hauptzollamt Frankfurt am Main-Flughafen* [1981] ECR 1095. For a comment see M C E J Bronckers, SEW (1982), 184.
[23] *EEC Restrictions on Imports of Apples from Chile*, report of the panel of 10 November 1980, BISD 27S/98.
[24] The ECJ decided that '[A]ccording to the uncontested information on this matter supplied by the Commission during the oral procedure the special GATT group charged with examining the conformity of the Community measures with the General Agreement found that in adopting the protective measures in issue the Commission did not infringe either Article I or Article II of that agreement.' See paragraph 46 of the judgment. 'Special GATT group' is a translation error. The ECJ obviously meant 'GATT panel' See also J H J Bourgeois, above n 2, at 13, fn 44.
[25] See paragraph 45 of the judgment.
[26] See also J H J Bourgeois, above n 2, at 13, fn 44; A. Ott, 'The Friction Between GATT/WTO Law and EC Law: Some Critical Remarks on the Case Law of the ECJ', in *International Law and the Hague's 750th Anniversary*, W. P. Heere, ed (The Hague: T M C Asser Press 1999), 323–32, at 327 and E.-U. Petersmann, 'Application of GATT by the European Communities', *CMLRev* 397 (1983), 409–10.
[27] The notion 'panel and Appellate Body reports' refers to reports adopted by the DSB pursuant to Article 17.14 of the DSU.

Under the GATT dispute settlement mechanism – in its pre-Uruguay Round version – it could have been argued that the reasoning of the ECJ in Opinion 1/91 would not have applied because the panels were not 'court-like' but rather conciliatory bodies.[28] Since the WTO dispute settlement mechanism is now far more judicial in nature,[29] it can be argued that if the ECJ were to maintain the reasoning of Opinion 1/91, it should be bound by the panel or Appellate Body reports adopted by the WTO Dispute Settlement Body.[30] This line of reasoning would be valid regardless of whether the ECJ grants direct effect to the WTO Agreement, since Opinion 1/91 of the ECJ provides that the decisions of a court set up under an international agreement to which the EC is a party would already bind the ECJ *'in so far as that agreement is an integral part of the Community legal order'*.[31] As the WTO Agreement is an integral part of the EC's legal order pursuant to Article 300 of the EC Treaty (ex Article 228),[32] the EC institutions, including the ECJ, are bound by panel and Appellate Body reports adopted under the WTO dispute settlement mechanism.[33]

---

[28] See M. Montañà i Mora, above n 2, at 175. The ECJ has established the following criteria in order to determine whether a national 'judicial' body qualifies as a court or tribunal for the purposes of establishing the ECJ's jurisdiction under Article 234 of the EC Treaty (ex Article 177): (i) the body concerned must be established by law; (ii) it must be a permanent body; (iii) its jurisdiction must be compulsory; (iv) the procedure before it must be inter partes; (v) it must apply the rule of law; and (vi) it must be an independent body. See, Case C-416/96, *Nour Eddline El-Yassini v Secretary of State for the Home Department*, Judgment of the ECJ of 2 March 1999, not yet reported in the ECR. Although in a different context, it is submitted that a panel and, undoubtedly, the Appellate Body would satisfy those criteria.

[29] The amount of literature devoted to the WTO dispute settlement mechanism is enormous. For a recent contribution, see D. Palmeter and Petros C Mavroidis, *Dispute Settlement in the World Trade Organization. Practice and Procedure*, (The Hague: Kluwer Law International 1999).

[30] Petersmann argues that the WTO dispute settlement system has contributed largely to a greater judicialisation of the international economic system and could inspire dispute settlement systems in other non-economic areas. See E-U Petersmann, 'Dispute Settlement in International Economic Law – Lessons for Strengthening International Dispute Settlement in Non-Economic Areas', *J Int'l Econ L* (1999), 189.

[31] Eeckhout argues that '[W]here a violation is established the binding character of the agreement and the principle of legality should in my view trump any lack of direct effect.' See P Eeckhout, above n 2, at 53. This line of reasoning implies that the direct effect of the WTO Agreement(s) is a *per se* condition which is then ignored.

[32] The EC is bound by the WTO Agreement(s) by virtue of Council Decision 94/800/EC of 22 December 1994 concerning the conclusion on behalf of the European Community, as regards matters falling within its competence, of the agreements reached in the Uruguay Round multilateral negotiations (1986–1994), OJ L 336/1 of 23 December 1994.

[33] Advocate General Saggio has recently argued that the WTO dispute settlement rules are not capable of limiting the competences of the ECJ for the following two reasons: (i) the WTO dispute settlement rules do not establish a judicial system but rather a conciliatory mechanism for the settlement of disputes (as the DSB is more political in nature and limits itself to the mere adoption of decisions or recommendations from the panels or the Appellate Body) and (ii) the establishment of a judicial body entrusted with the powers, not only to interpret and apply the WTO Agreements, but also to annul Community acts and decisions, would be incompatible with the EC's legal order and manifestly in breach of Article 220 of the EC Treaty (ex Article 164). See para 23 of the Opinion of 25 February 1999

continued...

However, a WTO panel or Appellate Body report can only be invoked in legal actions before the ECJ in those cases where the panel or Appellate Body has established that certain EC rules or practices are not in conformity with WTO law and has required the EC to bring them into conformity with WTO law.[34] This approach is correct in view of the limited precedential effect of WTO panel or Appellate Body reports which are only binding on the parties to the dispute.[35] This approach has been confirmed by the Appellate Body in *Japan – Taxes on Alcoholic Beverages*,[36] where it held that

> [A]dopted panel reports are an important part of the GATT acquis. They are often considered by subsequent panels. They create legitimate expectations among WTO members, and, therefore, should be taken into account where they are relevant to any dispute. However, they are not binding, except with respect to resolving the particular dispute between the parties to that dispute.

3.3.2 The binding nature of panel and Appellate Body reports

Finally, this comment will briefly focus on the argument brought forward by the Advocate General according to which a panel or Appellate Body report does not establish an (immediate) obligation for WTO Members to bring their legislation in conformity with WTO law. According to the Advocate General, individuals are not able to derive any rights from a panel or Appellate Body report. This is based on a misinterpretation of the relevant provisions of the DSU. Article 22.1 of the DSU provides that compensation is a purely provisional measure and that '(...) *neither compensation nor the suspension of concessions or other obligations is preferred to full implementation of a recommendation to bring a measure into conformity with the covered agreements* (...).' Compensation is not a method of settling disputes but simply a temporary instrument to ensure that any benefits accruing to the other members are not nullified or impaired as a result of the failure to comply within the reasonable period of time set in the particular case and that the defaulting party is not encouraged to persist indefinitely in its failure to comply.[37] As Eeckhout phrased it, '[T]*he DSU's*

---

in case C-149/96, *Portugal v Council*, not yet reported in the ECR. This line of reasoning is based on a misconception of the WTO dispute settlement mechanism as neither panels, nor the Appellate Body are able to invalidate Community acts. They can merely establish that a Community act infringes WTO law and recommend that the EC should bring its legislation in conformity with those rules. The 'invocability' of a panel or Appellate Body report in a legal proceeding before the CFI or the ECJ is a completely different matter.

[34] See P Eeckhout, above n 2, at 53–4.
[35] On this subject, see A Chua, 'The Precedential Effect of WTO Panel and Appellate Body Reports', *LJIL* (1998), 45.
[36] WT/DS8/AB/R, WT/DS10/AB/R, WT/DS11/AB/R, *Japan – Taxes on Alcoholic Beverages*, report of the Appellate Body of 4 October 1996.
[37] See also paragraph 29 of the Opinion of Advocate General Tesauro of 13 November 1997 in Case C-53/96, *Hermès International v FHT Marketing Choice*, [1998] ECR I-3603. Timmermans

continued...

rules on compensation should (...) not act as a barrier to acknowledging that WTO dispute settlement decisions are binding on the Community's judiciary.'[38]

Thus, adopted panel and Appellate Body reports are binding for the EC and the compensation mechanism cannot not prevent those reports from being invoked in a legal proceeding before the CFI or ECJ. By accepting compensation, the responding country in a dispute, *in se*, recognises the binding effect of a panel or Appellate Body report since it accepts that its legislation or other measures adopted by it are in breach with WTO law.

4. Conclusion

The question of the 'invocability' of panel and/or Appellate Body reports is a novelty in the case law of the ECJ. This explains why Advocate General Mischo has been very prudent in his Opinion and has taken a rather conservative approach. He was not prepared to accept any binding legal force emanating from panel or Appellate Body reports in cases brought before the ECJ. However, the case law of the ECJ in Opinion 1/91 makes it clear that the ECJ would be prepared to accept binding interpretations of WTO law by panels or the Appellate Body in cases brought before it. Taking into consideration the legalisation of the WTO dispute settlement mechanism, there is no doubt that this is the line of reasoning to be followed.

---

has suggested that it cannot in any way be excluded that the compensation may ultimately be a *'provisoire qui dure'*, see C W A Timmermans, 'The Implementation of the Uruguay Round by the EC', in *The Uruguay Round Results: A European Lawyers' Perspective* (Brussels: European Interuniversity Press 1995), 501–9, at 504. This might certainly be the case, but it would run counter to the spirit and objectives of the WTO dispute settlement mechanism as such. The fact of maintaining the 'illegal' measures in force would, in my view, give a right to damages to the European industries directly affected by the sanctions.
[38] P Eeckhout, above n 2, at 55.

CHAPTER IV

THE STATUS OF ADOPTED PANEL AND APPELLATE BODY REPORTS IN THE EUROPEAN COURT OF JUSTICE AND THE EUROPEAN COURT OF FIRST INSTANCE: THE BANANA EXPERIENCE[*]

1. Introduction

The judgments of the European Court of Justice (ECJ) in the *Atlanta* case[1] and of the European Court of First Instance (CFI) in the *Chemnitz* case[2] represent an excellent opportunity to focus on the question of the status of panel and Appellate Body reports, adopted by the World Trade Organization's Dispute Settlement Body, in the European Community legal order.[3] Both courts briefly looked into the issue but took a very careful position, as if they were at pains to open a Pandora's box filled with unanswered legal questions.

The question of the status of adopted WTO panel and Appellate Body reports in legal proceedings brought before the ECJ or CFI has not yet instigated a fierce legal debate to date and therefore merits some closer attention.[4] Thomas Cottier recently took a quite straightforward

---

[*] This article is a modified and extended version of a paper presented at the University of Cambridge under the auspices of the Centre for European Legal Studies on 10 November 1999.
[1] Case C–104/97 P Atlanta AG v Council and Commission, judgement of the European Court of Justice of 14 October 1999, not yet reported in the ECR
[2] Case T–254/97 Fruchthandelsgesellschaft mbH Chemnitz v Commission, judgement of the European Court of First Instance of 28 September 1999 [1999] 3 CMLR 508.
[3] The notion 'panel and Appellate Body reports' refers to reports adopted by the WTO Dispute Settlement Body (DSB) pursuant to Article 17.14 of the Understanding on Rules and Procedures Governing the Settlement of Disputes (DSU).
[4] See on this particular question, JM Beneyto 'The EU and the WTO. Direct Effect of the New Dispute Settlement System?' (1996) 7 *EuZW* 295–9; JHJ Bourgeois 'International Jurisprudence and Domestic Law: Some Comments from a European Community Perspective' in KR Simmonds and BHW Hill (eds) *Law and Practice Under the GATT* (New York: Oceana Publications, 1993) 10–13; T Cottier 'Dispute Settlement in the World Trade Organization: Characteristics and Structural Implications for the European Union' (1998) 35 *CMLRev* 325–78 at 369–75; P Eeckhout 'The Domestic Legal Status of the WTO Agreement: Interconnecting Legal Systems' (1997) 34 *CMLRev* 11–58 at 51–5; JH Jackson 'The Legal meaning of a GATT Dispute Settlement Report: Some Reflections' in Blokker and Muller (eds) *Towards More Effective Supervision by International Organisations. Essays in Honour of Henry G Schermers* (vol I, Dordrecht: Kluwer, 1994) 149–64; N Lavranos 'Die Rechtswirkung von WTO panel reports im Europäischen Gemeinschaftsrecht sowie im deutschen Verfassungsrecht' (1999) 34 *Europarecht* 289–308; M Montañà i Mora 'A GATT With Teeth: Law Wins Over Politics in the Resolution of International Trade Disputes' (1993) 31 *Colum*

continued ...

position and argued that in cases where adopted panel or Appellate Body reports are simply ignored, courts, both of the EC and the EC Member States, should no longer apply rules and measures inconsistent with the reports upon expiry of the reasonable time period given to the responding country for compliance.[5]

Whether this is indeed the road to be followed will be further explored in this article. The article first gives a brief description of the Atlanta and Chemnitz judgments and then concentrates on the crucial question of whether panel and Appellate Body reports adopted by the DSB can be invoked in legal actions brought before the ECJ or the CFI.

2. An Analysis of the Judgments

2.1 The Chemnitz Case

In 1996, Fruchthandelsgesellschaft mbH Chemnitz, a German fruit trading company, submitted an application to the Commission for a special grant of licenses for the importation of bananas pursuant to Article 30 of Regulation 404/93.[6] The Commission rejected this application and Chemnitz brought an action for annulment before the CFI against this decision under Article 230 of the EC Treaty (ex Article 173). Chemnitz based its action on the WTO Appellate Body report in the Bananas case where the Appellate Body had found that some features of Regulation 404/93 were inconsistent with WTO law.[7] Any decision based on an 'unlawful' Regulation would thus have to be declared null and void.

J Transnat'l L 103–80 at 175–6; J Nyberg 'Will the Fight against the European Community Common Banana Market lead to Conflicts of a Constitutional Character?' (1997) 8 *ELSA Selected Papers on European Law* 211–69 at 244–5; S Peers 'Banana Split: WTO Law and Preferential Agreements in the EC Legal Order' (1999) 4 *EFA Rev* 195–214 at 205–12; A Reinisch 'Entschädigung für die unbeteiligten 'Opfer des Hormon- und Bananensteites nach Art. 228 II EG?' (2000) 11 *EuZW* 42–51 at 48–9; C Schmid, 'Immer wieder Bananen: Der Status des GATT/WTO – Systems im Gemeinschaftrecht' (1998) *NJW* 190–7 at 196; A Weber and F Moos 'Rechtswirkungen von WTO-Streitbeilegungsentscheidungen im Gemeinschaftrecht' (1999) 10 *EuZW* 229–36 and GA Zonnekeyn 'The Legal Status of WTO Panel Reports in the EC legal Order. Some Reflections on the Opinion of Advocate General Mischo in the Atlanta Case' (1999) 2 *JIEL* 713–22.

[5] T Cottier 'Dispute Settlement in the World Trade Organization: Characteristics and Structural Implications for the European Union' (1998) 35 *CMLRev* 325–78 at 374.

[6] Council Regulation (EC) 404/93 of 13 February 1993 on the common organisation of the market in bananas [1993] OJ L47/1, as amended. Article 30 provides that '[I]f specific measures are required after July 1993 to assist the transition from arrangements existing before the entry into force of this Regulation to those laid down by this Regulation, and in particular to overcome difficulties of a sensitive nature, the Commission ... shall take any transitional measures it judges necessary'.

[7] WT/DS27/AB/R European Communities – Regime for the Importation, Sale and Distribution of Bananas, report of the Appellate Body of 9 September 1997.

At the hearing, the Spanish Government argued that the legal effect of an Appellate Body report was limited for the following two reasons. First, a report is a mere 'recommendation' addressed to a WTO member to bring its legislation into compliance with WTO law but does not oblige that member to amend its legislation. The Spanish Government referred to Article 22 of the Understanding on Rules and Procedures Governing the Settlement of Disputes (DSU) which gives WTO members the possibility to leave the illegal measures in place and offer compensation or agree with the suspension of concessions. Secondly, the Spanish Government argued that GATT, by its very nature, was not directly applicable and could not be invoked to call into question the validity of a Community rule and that such an effect would be tantamount to an exception to the jurisdictional monopoly conferred on the ECJ by Article 220 of the EC Treaty (ex Article 164).[8] Dashwood fully agrees with this and argues that it could not be admitted that the decisions of a judicial or quasi-judicial body operating outside the Community order could produce effects within it. This would, indeed, compromise the jurisdictional monopoly of the ECJ. The only argument that would be acceptable in his view, is that the GATT provisions applied by the WTO Appellate Body are directly effective and that the ECJ 'would do well to be guided by the specialist wisdom of that Body'.[9]

Two reasons were given by the ECJ for rejecting the arguments brought forward by the applicant. First, the ECJ ruled that the EC had amended Regulation 404/93 to bring it into compliance with the Appellate Body report by adopting Regulation 1637/98.[10] Chemnitz could therefore not rely on the report to claim that the arrangements establishing the common organisation of the market in bananas were not enforceable. In addition, the ECJ held that the applicant had not established a link in law between the Appellate Body report and the action for annulment. For a provision to have direct effect on a person other than the addressee, that provision

---

[8] The judgement of the CFI does probably not accurately reflect the arguments brought forward by the Spanish Government since it is not the direct applicability of GATT that would jeopardise the jurisdictional monopoly of the ECJ but rather the possibility to invoke a panel or Appellate Body report in a procedure before the ECJ and the obligation of the ECJ to comply with such a ruling.
[9] See A Dashwood 'Treatment of Public International Law by European Community Law' paper presented on 21 October 1999 at the Jean Monnet Symposium on the 'Fundamental principles as inspiration and as source of law in the systems of the European Union and the WTO'.
[10] Council Regulation (EC) 1637/98 of 20 July 1998 amending Regulation (EEC) 404/93 on the common organisation of the market in bananas [1998] OJ L210/98. A panel has ruled that also these amendments do not comply with WTO law. See WT/DS27/RW/EEC European Communities – Regime for the Importation, Sale and Distribution of Bananas – Recourse to Article 21.5 by the European Communities, report of the panel of 12 April 1999. For a comment on this report, see G Meier 'Bananas IV: der Bericht des WTO-Panels vom 12.4.99' (1999) 10 *EuZW* 428–31.

must impose on the addressee an unconditional and sufficiently clear and precise obligation vis-à-vis the person concerned.[11] Since the applicant did not put forward any arguments that these criteria were met, its arguments concerning the effects of the WTO Appellate Body report had to be rejected as unfounded, without there being any need for the ECJ to consider whether such reports could have direct effect.

2.2 The Atlanta Case

In this particular case, Atlanta sought the annulment of a CFI judgment of 11 December 1996, rejecting Atlanta's request for damages based on Article 288 of the EC Treaty (ex Article 215).[12] Atlanta alleged that the WTO-incompatibility of Regulation 404/93, in view of the Appellate Body report,[13] justified a claim for damages and emphasised that it was not invoking a breach of substantive WTO rules.

Advocate General Mischo disagreed with the applicant and argued that the latter was invoking substantive WTO law, since the Appellate Body report is a mere application (and interpretation) of WTO law.[14] Consequently, the Advocate General considered that Atlanta should have tried to annul the CFI judgment on the ground that the latter did not give Atlanta the possibility to invoke GATT rules. As this argument was not included in Atlanta's submission, Advocate General Mischo concluded that the appeal was inadmissible.

However, according to the Advocate General, even an explicit referral to an alleged infringement of substantive WTO law in Atlanta's submission would still not have constituted a valid ground to challenge the WTO-incompatibility of Regulation 404/93 as WTO rules cannot be invoked as a ground for annulment before the European courts.[15]

The Advocate General then examined whether the WTO Appellate Body report could constitute a ground for liability on the part of the EC. It follows from the case law of the ECJ that to impose liability upon the EC,

---

[11] Case 9/70 *Franz Grad v Finanzamt Traunstein* [1970] ECR 825; Case 104/81 *Hauptzollamt Mainz v CA Kupferberg KG* [1982] ECR 3641 and Case C–280/93 *Germany v Council* [1994] ECR I–4973.
[12] Case T–521/93 *Atlanta AG and Others v Commission* [1996] ECR II–1707.
[13] WT/DS27/AB/R European Communities – Regime for the Importation, Sale and Distribution of Bananas, report of the Appellate Body of 9 September 1997. The Advocate General referred to the Appellate Body report of 25 September 1997. This is the date on which the Appellate Body report was adopted by the Dispute Settlement Body as provided for by Article 17(14) of the DSU.
[14] Opinion of Advocate General Mischo of 6 May 1999.
[15] The Advocate General referred to Case C–208/93 Germany v Council [1994] ECR I–4973.

the measure invoked must aim to protect the interests of individuals.[16] It is therefore crucial to determine whether the Appellate Body (report) intends to protect the interests of the applicant in this particular case. In order to answer this question, the Advocate General considered the characteristics of the WTO dispute settlement mechanism. In line with the argument brought forward by the Spanish Government in the Chemnitz case, he argued that a ruling of the Appellate Body does not impose any obligation on the member, whose legislation has been found to be in breach of WTO law, to amend its legislation immediately. According to Article 21(3) of the DSU, a member has a 'reasonable period' of time to comply with the ruling of the Appellate Body and to bring its legislation into line with WTO law. Moreover, Article 22 of the DSU gives WTO members the possibility of maintaining the unlawful measures in place beyond the reasonable period of time if the parties to the dispute have agreed on a suitable compensation. The Advocate General therefore concluded that Atlanta was not able to rely on the Appellate Body report to substantiate its right to damages.[17]

The ECJ did not focus on the issue at all and decided that the arguments brought forward by Atlanta with regard to the effects of the WTO Appellate Body report were simply inadmissible.

3. The Interface Between Decisions of International Judicial Bodies and EC Law

According to the Opinion of Advocate General Mischo, the status in EC law of decisions of (judicial) bodies established under the auspices of an international agreement, would depend on the status and the effect of the particular international agreement in the EC legal system. This analysis is not entirely correct, as the legal status of decisions from judicial entities established within the framework of an international agreement, such as the WTO, cannot – as such – be assimilated with the

---

[16] Case 5/71 *Zuckerfabrik Schöppensted v Council* [1971] ECR 975.
[17] Advocate General Lenz, however, did not exclude liability of the EC institutions for breach under such circumstances albeit under the 'old' GATT regime. He argued that one should 'not exclude the possibility that in exceptional cases an infringement of provisions of GATT might give rise to a liability in damages to the traders concerned. In particular, one might envisage a case where in such a situation the Community makes no use of the possibilities provided for in GATT of freeing itself from its obligations, but agrees that the dispute should be decided by a neutral tribunal, and then however refuses to comply with the decision'. See para 21 of his Opinion of 16 February 1995 in Case C-469/93 *Amministrazione della Finanze dello Stato v Chiquita Italia SpA* [1995] ECR I-4533. As Montañà i Mora phrased it, '[O]ne may construe this intriguing statement as establishing that the Community's failure to comply with a World Trade Organization (WTO) panel report might give rise to liability in damages to the traders concerned'. See M Montañà i Mora 'Equilibrium – A Rediscovered Basis for the Court of Justice of the European Communities to refuse Direct effect to the Uruguay Round Agreements?' (1996) 30 *JWT* 43–59 at 50–1.

legal status of the agreement itself insofar as that agreement is binding for the EC and forms an integral part of the EC legal order.[18]

For the purposes of this article 'decisions of bodies established under the auspices of an international agreement' will refer either to decisions of international bodies administering international agreements or to decisions or judgments of judicial entities established within the framework of an international agreement.

3.1 Decisions of Bodies Administering International Agreements

Certain international agreements concluded by the EC established institutions such as an Association Council, empowered to issue recommendations or to adopt decisions. One of the best-known examples is the 'Council of Association' set up under the Association Agreement concluded between the EC and Turkey.[19] Under this Agreement, the Association Council has the power to take decisions and each of the parties to the Agreement must take the measures necessary to implement the decisions taken.[20] It is important to distinguish between, on the one hand, the binding character of such decisions in the EC legal order and, on the other hand, the direct effect of such decisions.

3.1.1 The Binding Character in the EC Legal Order

The ECJ decided in Greece v Council[21] that decisions issued by the Association Council form an integral part of EC law from the moment of their entry into force. They do not necessarily require implementing measures by the EC for their application within the EC legal order. A specific act of the Council is only required if the substance of the particular decision does not allow it to be applied by the courts immediately.

3.1.2 Direct Effect

Individuals have successfully invoked decisions adopted by the Association Council in the domestic courts of the EC Member States to invalidate national legislation inconsistent with such decisions. The majority of those cases were referred to the ECJ under Article 234 of the EC Treaty (ex Article 177). The ECJ has held, on several occasions, that such decisions may have direct effect.[22]

---

[18] Contra: JHJ Bourgeois (n 4) 13.
[19] See the Agreement of 12 September 1963 establishing an Association between the European Economic Community and Turkey [1964] OJ L217/3687.
[20] See Article 22 (1) of the Association Agreement.
[21] Case 30/88 *Greece v Commission* [1989] ECR 3711.
[22] See eg Case C–192/89 *SZ Sevince v Staatssecretaris van Justitie* [1990] ECR I–3461; Case
continued ...

Lavranos[23] has argued that the legal effect of decisions taken by the Association Council set up under the EC–Turkey Association Agreement can be assimilated with the legal effect of WTO panel reports for the following two basic reasons. First, both the EC and its Member States are signatories to the WTO Agreements as well as to the Association Agreement with Turkey. Secondly, under both agreements a body was established entrusted with the power to take binding decisions. Although those decisions are different in form, they would have the same binding (legal) effect.

It is questionable, however, whether panel or Appellate Body reports can be assimilated with decisions taken by the Association Council. Certainly, there are formal similarities but they do not have or intend to have identical legal effects. The panels and the Appellate Body are judicial entities, whereas the Association Council rather acts as a kind of executive, administrative body. Even the decisions taken by the Association Council as a 'dispute settlement body' under the Association Agreement would, in my view, not have the same status and/or effect as panel or Appellate Body reports since the dispute settlement system established in the framework of the Association Agreement with, for example Turkey, does not have the same judicial characteristics as the WTO dispute settlement mechanism. For example, the jurisdiction of the Association Council is not compulsory and there is no possibility for appeal.

3.2. Decisions of Judicial/Adjudicative-Type Entities

The ECJ has confirmed that the EC may enter into an international agreement whereby a judicial entity is established, provided that the structure and the jurisdiction of such entities are compatible with the EC Treaty. In 1991, the ECJ gave an opinion pursuant to Article 300 of the EC Treaty (ex Article 228) before the draft agreement on the European Economic Area (EEA) was concluded with the Member States of the European Free Trade Association (EFTA).[24] One of the crucial questions with which the ECJ dealt was whether the EEA Agreement's system of judicial supervision for the settlement of disputes was compatible with the EC Treaty. Under the EEA Agreement, an EEA Court was proposed with the jurisdiction to interpret and apply the provisions of the Agreement in disputes between the Contracting Parties.

C–237/91 *Kazim Kus v Landeshauptstadt Wiesbaden* [1992] ECR I–6781; Case C355/93 *Hayriye Eroglu v Land Baden-Württemberg* [1994] ECR I–5113; Case C–98/96 *Kasim Ertanir v Land Hessen* [1997] ECR I–5179 and Case C–262/96 *Sema Sürül v Bundesantalt für Arbeit* judgement of 4 May 1999, not yet reported in the ECR.

[23] N Lavranos (n 4). See also A Reinish (n 4) 48.

[24] Opinion 1/91, Draft agreement relating to the creation of the European Economic Area [1991] ECR I–6079.

The ECJ declared that the proposed jurisdiction given to the EEA Court was incompatible with the EC Treaty on the following grounds. Since the EEA Court had the competence to interpret the EEA Agreement of which the provisions were identical with the corresponding provisions of the EC Treaty, there was a risk that the EEA Court and the ECJ would make different interpretations, especially since the two agreements had different purposes. Interpretations make by the EEA Court were therefore liable to affect EC law and, subsequently, the EEA court system would be in conflict with the role of the ECJ under Article 220 (ex Article 164) and Article 292 (ex Article 219) of the EC Treaty and therefore the very foundations of the EC.[25]

However, the ECJ declared that there were certain conditions under which it would be bound by the decisions of another court. After recalling its case law on the binding effect of international agreements concluded by the EC and on its own jurisdiction to interpret those agreements, the ECJ decided that '[W]here, however, an international agreement provides for its own system of courts, including a court with jurisdiction to settle disputes between the Contracting Parties to the agreement, and, as a result, to interpret its provisions, the decisions of that court will be binding on the Community institutions, including the Court of Justice. Those decisions will also be binding in the event the Court of Justice is called upon to rule, by way of a preliminary ruling or in a direct action, on the interpretations of the international agreement, in so far as that agreement is an integral part of the Community legal order. An international agreement providing for such a system of courts is in principle compatible with Community law. The Community's competence in the field of international relations and its capacity to conclude international agreements necessarily entails the power to submit to the decisions of a court which is created or designated by the such an agreement as regards the interpretations and application of its provisions'.[26]

Here, the ECJ emphasised the binding character of judicial decisions on disputes between the contracting parties to an agreement for the ECJ, where the ECJ is called upon to rule on the interpretation of the agreement.[27] Moreover, a closer look at Opinion 1/91 reveals that the ECJ implicitly agreed with the concept that the binding character of judicial decisions on disputes between the contracting parties to an

---

[25] In a subsequent opinion, the ECJ held that the new provisions of the EEA Agreement on the settlement of disputes were now compatible with the EC Treaty. See Opinion 1/92, Opinion on the revised draft Agreement on the European Economic Area [1992] ECR I–2821.

[26] Paragraphs 39 and 40 of Opinion 1/91, Draft agreement relating to the creation of the European Economic Area [1991] ECR I–6079.

[27] P Eeckhout (n 4) at 52.

international agreement does not depend on the direct effect of such an agreement. In Opinion 1/91, the ECJ assumed that the EEA Agreement did not have direct effect.[28] This did not prevent the ECJ from holding that the decisions of the EEA Court could be binding for the ECJ.

3.2.1 The WTO Agreements are Part of the EC Legal Order

To date, there has been only one case where the ECJ explicitly referred to a GATT panel report. In Dürbeck,[29] which concerned imports of dessert apples form Chile, the ECJ was informed by the Commission at the hearing that a GATT panel[30] had not found an infringement of Articles I or II of GATT, as was alleged, and had only marginally criticised the protective measures adopted by the EC.[31] The ECJ therefore rejected the claim based on GATT and decided that '… the argument advanced by the plaintiff in the main action that the protective measures in issue are contrary to the commitments entered into by the Community under GATT is not compatible in this case of putting the validity of these measures not question'.[32] It appeared that the ECJ had been misinformed, as the GATT panel had found a number of infringements of Article XIII and Article XIX of GATT.[33]

As the Dürbeck judgment did not give any guidance as to how the ECJ would qualify the legal status of a (GATT) panel report, it is now essential to assess whether the line of reasoning maintained by the

---

[28] See in particular paras 21 and 27 of the Opinion. See W van Gerven 'The Genesis of EEA Law and the Principles of Primacy and Direct Effect' (1992–92) 16 *Fordham International Law Journal* 955–89 at 968. It should be emphasised that the EEA Agreement as it now stands, has direct effect if the criteria for direct effect are fulfilled. See S Norberg et al The *European Economic Area. EEA Law. A Commentary on the EEA Agreement* (Stockholm: Fritzes, 1993) 203.

[29] Case 112/80 Firma Anton Dürbeck v Hauptzollamt Frankfurt am Main-Flughafen [1981] ECR 1095.

[30] EEC Restrictions on Imports of Apples from Chile, report of the panel of 10 November 1980, BISD 27S/98.

[31] The ECJ decided that '[A]ccording to the uncontested information on this matter supplied by the Commission during the oral procedure the special GATT group charged with examining the conformity of the Community measures with the General Agreement found that in adopting the protective measures in issue the Commission did not infringe either Article I or Article II of that agreement'. See para 46 of the judgement. 'Special GATT group' is a translation error. The ECJ obviously meant 'GATT panel'. See also JHJ Bourgeois (n 4) at 13, fn 44.

[32] See para 45 of the judgement.

[33] See also JHJ Bourgeois (n 4) at 13, fn 44; A Ott 'The Friction Between GATT/WTO Law and EC Law: Some Critical Remarks on the Case Law of the ECJ' in Heere (ed) *International Law and the Hague's 750th Anniversary* (The Hague: TMC Asser Press, 1999) 323–32 at 327; E-U Petersmann 'Constitutional Principles Governing the EEC's Commercial Policy' in Marescau (ed) *The European Community's Commercial Policy after 1992: The Legal Dimension* (Martinus Nijhoff Publishers, 1993) 21–62 at 47 and E-U Petersmann 'Application of GATT by the European Communities' (1983) 20 *CMLRev* 397–437 at 409–10.

ECJ in Opinion 1/91 also applies to panel and Appellate Body reports adopted under the WTO Dispute settlement mechanism.

Under the GATT dispute settlement mechanism – in its pre-Uruguay Round version – it could have been argued that the reasoning of the ECJ in Opinion 1/91 would not have applied because the panels were not 'court-like' but rather conciliatory bodies.[34] Since the WTO dispute settlement mechanism is now far more judicial in nature,[35] it can be argued that if the ECJ were to maintain the reasoning of Opinion 1/91, it should be bound by the panel or Appellate Body reports adopted by the WTO Dispute Settlement Body. This line of reasoning would be valid regardless of whether the ECJ grants direct effect to the WTO Agreement, since Opinion 1/91 of the ECJ provides that the decisions of a court set up under an international agreement to which the EC is party would already bind the ECJ 'in so far as that agreement is an integral part of the Community legal order'.[36] As the WTO Agreement is an integral part of the EC's legal order pursuant to Article 300 of the EC Treaty (ex Article 228),[37] the EC institutions, including the ECJ, are bound by panel and Appellate Body reports adopted under the WTO dispute settlement mechanism.[38]

---

[34] See M Montañà i Mora (n 4) at 175. The ECJ has established the following criteria in order to determine whether a national 'judicial' body qualifies as a court for tribunal for the purposes of establishing the ECJ's jurisdiction under Article 234 of the EC Treaty (ex Article 177): (i) the body concerned must be established by law; (ii) it must be a permanent body; (iii) its jurisdiction must be compulsory; (iv) the procedure before it must be inter partes; (v) it must apply the rule of law; and (vi) it must be an independent body. See Case C–416/96 Nour Eddline El-Yassinin v Secretary of State for the Home Department [1999] ECR I–1209. Although in a different context, it is submitted that a panel and, undoubtedly, the Appellate Body, would satisfy these criteria.

[35] Petersmann argues that the WTO dispute settlement system has contributed largely to a greater judicialisation of the international economic system and could inspire dispute settlement systems in other non-economic areas. See E-U Petersmann 'Dispute Settlement in International Economic Law – Lessons for Strengthening International Dispute Settlement in Non-Economic Areas' (1999) 2 JIEL 189–248.

[36] Eeckhout argues that '[W]here a violation is established the binding character of the agreement and the principle of legality should in my view trump any lack of direct effect'. See P Eeckhout (n 4) at 53. This line of reasoning implies that the direct effect of the WTO Agreement(s) is a per se condition which is then ignored.

[37] The EC is bound by the WTO Agreement(s) by virtue of Council Decision 94/800/EC of 22 December 1994 concerning the conclusion on behalf of the European Community, as regards matters falling within is competence, of the agreements reached in the Uruguay Round multilateral negotiations (1986–1994) [1994] OJ L336/1.

[38] Advocate General Saggio has argued that the WTO dispute settlement rules are not capable of limiting the jurisdiction of the ECJ for the following two reasons: (i) the WTO dispute settlement rules do not establish a judicial system but rather a conciliatory mechanism for the settlement of disputes (as the DSB is more political in nature and limits itself to the mere adoption of decisions or recommendations from the panels or the Appellate Body) and (ii) the establishment of a judicial body entrusted with the powers, not only to interpret and apply the WTO Agreements, but also to annul Community acts
continued ...

However, a WTO panel or Appellate Body report can only be invoked in legal actions before the ECJ in those cases where the panel or Appellate Body has established that certain EC rules or practices are not in conformity with WTO law and has required the EC to bring them into conformity with the WTO law.[39] This approach is correct in view of the limited precedential effect of WTO panel or Appellate Body reports which are only binding on the parties to the dispute.[40] This approach has been confirmed by the Appellate Body in Japan – Taxes on Alcoholic Beverages,[41] where it held that '[A]dopted panel reports are an important part of the GATT acquis. They are often considered by subsequent panels. They create legitimate expectations among the WTO members, and, therefore, should be taken into account where they are relevant to any dispute. However, they are not binding, except with respect to resolving the particular dispute between the parties to that dispute'.

3.2.2 The Binding Nature of Adopted Panel and Appellate Body Reports

This chapter will focus on the argument brought forward by the Advocate General Mischo in the Atlanta case and the Spanish government in the Chemnitz case, according to which a panel or Appellate Body report would not establish an (immediate) obligation for WTO members to bring their legislation in conformity with WTO law. In bringing up this issue, the Advocate General entered into the sensitive debate on the interpretation of the nature of the legal obligations of WTO members under the WTO dispute settlement mechanism. Some have argued that WTO obligations need not be implemented given that compensation or even the acceptance of retaliation, are separate options.[42] They consider

---

and decisions, would be incompatible with the EC's legal order and manifestly in breach of Article 220 of the EC Treaty (ex Article 164). See paragraph 23 of the Opinion of 25 February 1999 in Case C–149/96 Portugal v Council judgement of the European Court of Justice of 24 November 1999, not yet reported in the ECR (author's translation). This line of reasoning is based on a misconception of the WTO dispute settlement mechanism as neither panels, nor the Appellate Body are able to invalidate Community acts. They can merely establish that a Community act infringes WTO law and recommend that the EC should bring its legislation in conformity with those rules. The 'invocability' of a panel or Appellate Body report in a legal proceeding before the CFI or the ECJ is a complete different matter.

[39] See P Eeckhout (n 4) at 53–4.
[40] On this subject, see A Chua 'The Precedential Effect of WTO Panel and Appellate Body Reports' (1998) 11 LJIL 45–61.
[41] WT/DS8/AB/R, WT/DS10/AB/R, WT/DS11/AB/R Japan – Taxes on Alcoholic Beverages, report of the Appellate Body of 4 October 1996.
[42] JH Bello 'The WTO Dispute Settlement Understanding: Less is More' (1996) 90 *Am J Int'l L* 416 and TM Reiff and M Forestal 'Revenge of the Push-me, Pull-You: The Implementation Process Under the WTO Dispute Settlement Understanding' (1998) 32 *Int'l L* 755–93 at 763.

compensation as one possible option, which is independent of the obligation to comply with WTO law.

Jackson has – rightly – argued that the obligation to comply with WTO rules can be inferred from the language of the DSU itself and that compliance is the preferred option.[43] Indeed, Article 22.1 of the DSU provides that compensation is a purely provisional measure and that '… neither compensation nor the suspension of concessions or other obligations is preferred to full implementation of a recommendation to bring a measure into conformity with the covered agreements …'. Compensation is not a method of settling disputes but simply a temporary instrument to ensure that any benefits accruing to the other members are not nullified or impaired as a result of the failure to comply within the reasonable period of time set in the particular case and that the defaulting party is not encouraged to persist indefinitely in its failure to comply.[44] As Eeckhout phrased it, '[T]he DSU's rules on compensation should … not act as a barrier to acknowledging that WTO dispute settlement decisions are binding on the Community's judiciary'.[45]

Consequently, adopted panel and Appellate Body reports are binding for the EC and the compensation mechanism cannot prevent those reports from being invoked in legal proceedings before the CFI or the ECJ. By accepting compensation, the responding member in a dispute, in se, recognises the binding effect of a panel or Appellate Body report since it acknowledges that its legislation or other measures are in breach with WTO law. The compensation mechanism was not meant to give WTO members a complete freedom to leave WTO-inconsistent measures in place and does not, as a matter of principle, accord a 'right' to violate a legal obligation entered into under an international agreement. It merely

---

[43] H Horn and P Mavroidis 'Remedies in the WTO Dispute Settlement System and developing Country Interests' paper dated 11 April 1999, at 14; JH Jackson 'The WTO Dispute Settlement Understanding – Misunderstandings on the Nature of Legal Obligation' in Cameron & Campbell (eds) *Dispute Resolution in the WTO* (London: Cameron May, 1998) 69–74 at 73 and JH Jackson 'Dispute Resolution and the WTO' paper presented at the Center for International Development, Harvard University, 5–6 November 1999 at 7.

[44] See also paragraph 29 of the Opinion of Advocate General Tesauro of 13 November 1997 in Case C–53/96 Hermès International v FHT Marketing Choice [1998] ECR I–3603. Timmermans has suggested that it cannot in any way be excluded that compensation may ultimately be a 'provisoire qui dure', see C Timmermans 'The Implementation of the Uruguay Round by the EC' in *The Uruguay Round Results: A European Lawyers' Perspective* (Brussels: European Interuniversity Press, 1995) 501–09 at 504. This situation cannot – a priori – be excluded but it would run counter to the spirit and objectives of the WTO dispute settlement mechanism. The fact of maintaining the 'illegal' measures in force would, in my view, give a right to damages to the European industries directly affected by the illegal measures or the sanctions.

[45] P Eeckhout (n 4) 55.

constitutes a practical option to temporarily defuse a dispute between WTO members, parties to a dispute.

3.2.3 The Alternative: EC Treaty Conform Interpretation

To date, the ECJ and the CFI have manifestly refused to take the rulings of WTO panels and the Appellate Body into consideration in their judgments. However, it would appear that the ECJ is prepared to apply principles of WTO law, but without explicitly referring to them. In T Port III,[46] the ECJ annulled part of the EC banana regime based on an identical reasoning as maintained by the Appellate Body in the Bananas case. However, the ECJ never mentioned the Appellate Body report but confined itself to referring to provisions of the EC Treaty.[47]

In T Port III, the ECJ was asked to assess the validity of the system for the allocation of tariff quotas under Regulation 478/95[48] in the light of the general principle of non-discrimination, as stated in Article 34(2) of the EC Treaty (ex Article 40(3)). T Port alleged that the allocation of country quotas to certain third countries, under Article 1(1) of Regulation 478/95, limited the import opportunities of economic operators who traditionally imported bananas from other third countries. It also argued that, in the case of imports from the third countries to which country quotas had been allocated, Regulation 478/95 discriminated against Category A and C operators, as compared with Category B operators, in that, by virtue of Article 3(2), only the former were required to obtain export licences from the competent authorities in the third countries concerned in order to import bananas from those countries.

The ECJ held that the exemption of Category B operators from the export-licence system and the difference in treatment followed from the fact that, among the EC operators who had entered into commercial relations with third countries imports from which were subject to the export-licence system, some were under an obligation to obtain export licences whilst others were exempt from that requirement. It constituted, moreover, a clear difference in the treatment of Category A and C operators as compared with Category B operators since application of the export-licence system to Category A and C operators meant that they

---

[46] Joined Cases C–364/95 and C–365/95 T Port GmbH v Hauptzollampt Hamburg-Jonas [1998] ECR I–1023.
[47] For an analysis of this case, see S Peers 'Constitutional Principles and International Trade' (1999) 24 ELRev 185–95.
[48] Commission Regulation (EC) 478/95 of 1 March 1995 on additional rules for the application of Council (EEC) Regulation 404/93 as regards the tariff quota arrangements for imports of bananas into the Community and amending Regulation (EEC) 1442/93 [1995] OJ L49/13.

had to pay a price for bananas from the third countries concerned which was some 33 per cent higher than that paid by Category B operators.

The ECJ therefore said that it was necessary to consider whether that difference of treatment was incompatible with the prohibition laid down in the second subparagraph of Article 34(2) of the EC Treaty (ex Article 40(3)) which is merely a specific enunciation of the general principle of equality, one of the fundamental principles of EC law, or whether, on the contrary, it could be objectively justified by the need to restore the competitive balance between those categories of operators. In that regard, the ECJ emphasised that, as it had recognised in *Germany v Council*,[49] the common organisation of the market in bananas, as established by Regulation 404/93, and in particular the system of tariff-quota allocation, involved certain restrictions or differences of treatment detrimental to Category A and C operators, whose opportunities for importing bananas from third countries had thereby been restricted, whereas Category B operators, who had previously been obliged to market essentially Community and ACP bananas, had gained an opportunity to import specific quantities of third country bananas.

The ECJ further held that such a difference in treatment was not contrary to the general principle of non-discrimination in so far as it was inherent in the objective of integrating previously compartmentalised markets, bearing in mind the different situations of the various categories of economic operators before the establishment of the common organisation of the market, and that pursuit of the objective of the common organisation, which is to guarantee disposal of EC production and traditional ACP production, entailed the striking of a balance between the various categories of economic operators in question. Accordingly, where the balance thus achieved by Regulation 404/93 was disturbed because one or more of the parameters on which it was based – such as, for example, the level of the tariff quota or that of the customs duties on imports – had been changed, albeit for reasons unconnected with the common organisation of the market in the bananas sector, it might have been proven necessary to restore that balance. The question remained, however, whether in this case it was proper to do so, to the detriment of Category A and C operators, by means of a measure such as the exemption of Category B operators from the export-licence system, as provided for in Article 3(2) of Regulation 478/95.

The system for the allocation of the tariff quota, as established by Regulation 404/93, which reserved 30 per cent of it to Category B operators, also applied to the increase of that quota agreed upon in

---

[49] Case C–208/93 *Germany v Council* [1994] ECR I–4973.

the Framework Agreement on Bananas (FAB).[50] Category B operators therefore benefited, in the same way as Category A and C operators, from the quota increase and the concomitant lowering of customs duties which were the cause of the disturbance of the balance between the various categories of operator concerned. In addition, the restrictions and differences in treatment to which Category A and C operators were subject as a result of the banana import regime set up by Regulation 404/93 also applied to the part of the quota corresponding to that increase.

Therefore, recourse to a measure such as the one contained in Article 3(2) of Regulation 478/95 could only be justified if it was shown that the balance disturbed by the increase in the tariff quota and the concomitant lowering of customs duties, which also benefited Category B operators, could be restored only by granting a substantial advantage to that same category of operators and, thus, at the cost of introducing a new difference in treatment detrimental to the other categories of operators who had already, when the tariff quota and the machinery for dividing it up were introduced, been subjected to similar restrictions and differences in treatment. As was clear from the judgment delivered by the ECJ in *Germany v Council*,[51] that was not the case.

The ECJ therefore decided that that Regulation 478/95 was invalid to the extent to which Article 3(2) of that Regulation imposed only on Category A and C operators the obligation to obtain export licences for bananas from Colombia, Costa Rica or Nicaragua.

The WTO panel and the Appellate Body had – earlier – come to the same conclusion as the ECJ.[52] Both had concluded that the requirement that import licenses only be granted to Category A and C operators having an export license in the case of imports from Colombia, Costa Rica and Nicaragua was inconsistent with Article I:1 of GATT which essentially contains a non-discrimination principle. They reasoned that this requirement provided an 'advantage' to bananas from these FAB countries within the scope of Article I of GATT, since it created the potential for quota-rents associated with banana regime tariff quotas to benefit producers of bananas from those countries, and thereby created more favourable competitive opportunities vis-à-vis non FAB third countries.

---

[50] Framework Agreement on Bananas, Annex to Part I, Section I–B (tariff quotas) in Schedule LXXX – European Communities.
[51] Case C–122/95 Germany v Council [1998] ECR I–973.
[52] WT/DS27/R European Communities – Regime for the Importation, Sale and Distribution of Bananas, report of the panel of 22 May 1997. WT/DS27/AB/R European Communities – Regime for the Importation, Sale and Distribution of Bananas, report of the Appellate Body of 9 September 1997.

One could thus argue that the ECJ has been prepared to apply the findings of the Appellate Body but without explicitly referring to them. This reflects, in my view, a 'reception' of WTO law principles in EC law.[53] Pescatore seemed to have detected in these cases 'a glimmer of hope' but also noted that the ECJ judgments were not based on GATT itself but on the EC Treaty.[54]

3.2.4 Epilogue – Liability for Non-Implementation?

Finally, the question will be tackled whether the EC institutions can be held liable for (persistent and conscious) non-implementation of WTO panel and Appellate Body reports. This is the fourth and final scenario outlined by Cottier. He suggested that when the EC consciously chooses not to give effect to a panel or Appellate Body report, knowing that other WTO members will then be allowed to retaliate under the rules of the DSU pending specific performance, such report should be directly effective depending on the 'motives and reasons stated in support of non-compliance'. There would be no direct effect if there were 'compelling reasons' not to implement the report, but direct effect if the report is flouted due to 'arbitrary non-compliance and mere political expediency'.[55]

Peers has argued that the bananas case does not fall within this category since the EC has purported to implement the ruling. However, since it was obvious that the legislation adopted by the EC in 1998 to implement the findings of the Appellate Body report, would still not satisfy the rules imposed by WTO law, the scenario referred to by Cottier applies and the Appellate Body report would have 'direct effect'.

Cottier did not address the problem of liability but only the direct effect of WTO panel and Appellate Body reports. The question of the liability of the EC for non-compliance with a ruling of a panel or of the Appellate Body is, indeed, a different problem. The thesis defended in this article, is that the EC's non-compliance with a WTO panel or Appellate Body should, in principle, lead to liability of the EC under Article 228 of the EC Treaty (ex Article 215).

---

[53] Peers argues that the T Port III judgement reflects the willingness of the ECJ to extend (modestly) the general principles of EC law to international trade. See S Peers (n 47) at 195. The author suggests reversing the order and argues that the ECJ was willing to apply international trade law (read WTO law) principles in the context of the EC legal order.

[54] P Pescatore 'Free World Trade and the European Union – The Reconciliation of Interests and the Revision of Dispute Resolution Procedures in the Framework of the WTO' lecture presented in June 1998 in Brussels at a conference organised by the Academy of European Law Trier. The 'glimmer of hope' detected by Pescatore refers to issue of direct effect of WTO law rather than the effect of Appellate Body reports in the EC legal order.

[55] T Cottier (n 4) at 374–5.

Private parties could envisage instituting an action for damages based on Article 228 of the EC Treaty (ex Article 215) when the EC refuses to implement a panel or Appellate Body report. In the bananas dispute, for example, this procedure could be initiated by two different groups of companies. The first are these banana operators whom are still denied the volume of licenses and tariff quota to which they are entitled on the basis of the Appellate Body ruling. The second are the European companies affected by the sanctions imposed by the United States following the EC's failure to implement the rulings of the panels and the Appellate Body in the *Bananas* dispute.[56]

According to settled case law, in order for the EC to incur non-contractual liability, a number of conditions must be met: (i) the conduct of the EC institutions in question must be unlawful; (ii) there must be a real and certain damage and (iii) a direct causal link must exist between the conduct of the institution concerned and the alleged damage.[57] Since the EC banana regime entails the adoption of legislative measures involving a choice of economic policy, an action under Article 228 of the EC Treaty (ex Article 215) would only be successful if it can be demonstrated that the EC institutions have acted in breach of a 'manifest and grave or sufficiently serious violation of a superior rule of law for the protection of individuals'.[58] In order to establish such an infringement, account will be taken of the level of importance of the infringed rule, the degree of blame to be attributed to the author of the measure and the extent of the loss suffered.

In *Odigitria*,[59] the Court of First Instance accepted this condition as also being relevant to determining EC liability in the field of external relations. In the light of this judgment Gasparon recently posed the question 'whether this condition tying Community liability to a violation of 'a superior rule for the protection of individuals' requires that that rule has direct effect'.[60] In view of the fact that ECJ would be prepared to consider itself bound by a panel or Appellate Body report irrespective of the direct applicability of the WTO Agreements, it seems plausible to

---

[56] Reinish has argued that the European companies affected by the sanctions imposed by the Untied States following the EC's non-compliance with the Appellate Body reports in the bananas and hormones cases would be entitled to claim damages. See A Reinish (n 4). Bronckers has taken a similar view. See MCE.J Bronckers 'Aansprakelijkheid EU voor WTO-schending wel mogelijk' (1999) VNO-NCW Forum.

[57] See eg Case T–231/97 *New Europe Consulting Ltd and Michael P Brown v Commission* [1999] CMLR 1452, judgement of 9 July 1999.

[58] Case T–521/93 *Atlanta AG and others v Council and Commission* [1996] ECR II–1707.

[59] Case T–572/93 *Odigitria AAE v Council and Commission* [1995] ECR II–2025.

[60] P Gasparon 'The Transposition of the Principle of Member State Liability into the Context of External Relations' (1999) 10 *EJIL* 605–24 at 620. See also more generally, S Schmall 'Ungereimtheiten und Rchtsschutzlücken bei der ausservertraglichen Haftung der Europäischen Gemeinschaft' (1999) 2 *ZeuS* 415–29.

argue that this question is superfluous. Direct effect may only be used as a precondition when the liability of the EC would follow from a breach of an international agreement to which it is a signatory.[61]

Whether the conditions referred to above would be complied with by the companies who suffered damages as a result of the EC's non-implementation or 'implementation avoidance' of the panel and Appellate Body reports, must be dealt with on a case by case basis. The author takes the view that these companies have a fundamental economic right to be compensated and must be able to invoke the non-implementation of these reports as a basis for liability of the EC.

4. Conclusion

The question of the 'invocability' of WTO panel and Appellate Body reports is a novelty in the case law of the ECJ and the CFI. This explains why both the ECJ and CFI, as well as Advocate General Mischo, have been very prudent and why they have taken a rather conservative approach. They were not prepared to accept any binding legal force emanating from panel or Appellate Body reports in cases brought before the ECJ or CFI. However, the case law of the ECJ in Opinion 1/91 makes it clear that the ECJ should be prepared to accept binding interpretations of WTO law by panels or the Appellate Body in cases brought before it. Taking into consideration the judicialisation of the WTO dispute settlement mechanism, there is no doubt that this is the line of reasoning to be followed. The margin of discretion left to WTO members whether or not to implement a panel or Appellate Body ruling can certainly not be an obstacle for parties to invoke such rulings in legal proceedings before the ECJ or the CFI.

---

[61] See P Gasparon (n 60) at 620–3 and the references to relevant case law and literature.

CHAPTER V

THE STATUS OF WTO LAW IN THE EC LEGAL ORDER – THE FINAL CURTAIN?

1. Introduction

The judgment of the European Court of Justice (ECJ) in the *Portuguese Textiles* case[1] represents an excellent opportunity to readdress the question of the status of the GATT/WTO Agreements in the EC legal order.[2] In the case at hand, the ECJ ruled on an action for annulment introduced by Portugal against a Council decision approving two Memoranda of Understanding on market access arrangements for textile products originating in Pakistan and India. With regard to the argument invoked by the Portuguese Government that the WTO Agreements could serve as a legal ground to invalidate the contested Decision, the ECJ replied that these agreements could not, in principle, be used as a standard for reviewing the legality of Community acts. However, the ECJ did not completely ignore its former case law and ruled that the WTO Agreements could serve as a ground for review in cases where the Community intends to implement a particular obligation entered into within the framework of the WTO (the *Nakajima* doctrine),[3] or if the Community act expressly refers to specific provisions of the WTO Agreements (the *Fediol* doctrine).[4]

The *Portuguese Textiles* case therefore indicates that the fundamental changes in the GATT system have not induced the ECJ to depart from its former case law as regards the status of GATT in the EC legal order. It will be recalled that in *International Fruit Company* and a string of subsequent cases, the ECJ had previously held that the GATT Agreements preceding the WTO

---

[1] Case C–149/96 *Portugal v Council* judgement of 23 November 1999, not yet reported in the ECR. For a brief comment, see A Desmedt 'ECJ Restricts Effect of WTO Agreements in the EC Legal Order' (2000) *JIEL* 191.
[2] See M Waelbroeck 'Effect of GATT Within the Legal Order of the EEC' (1974) *JWT* 6; J Steenbergen 'The Status of GATT in Community Law' (1981) *JWT* 337; F Castillo de la Torre 'The Status of GATT in EEC Law. Some New Developments' (1992) *JWT* 35; F Castillo de la Torre 'The Status of GATT in EC Law, Revisited – The Consequences of the Judgement on the Banana Import Regime for the Enforcement of the Uruguay Round Agreements' (1995) *JWT* 53; P Lee and B Kennedy 'The Potential Direct Effect of GATT 1994 in European Community Law' (1996) *JWT* 67 and M Montañà i Mora 'Equilibrium – A Rediscovered Basis for the Court of Justice of the European Communities to Refuse Direct effect to the Uruguay Round Agreements' (1996) *JWT* 43.
[3] See Case C–69/89 *Nakajima All Precision Co Ltd v Council* [1991] ECR I–2069.
[4] See Case C–70/87 *Fediol v Commission* [1989] ECR 1781.

were devoid of direct effect, enabling individuals to invoke them before the national courts of the EC Member States.[5] In *Germany v Council*,[6] the ECJ also denied a Member State the right to invoke the provisions of GATT to challenge the legality of acts taken by the EC institutions.

The ECJ now, essentially, upheld this 'old' case law, but partly based on new arguments. The ECJ underlined the nature of the WTO Agreements as a forum of intergovernmental negotiation between the WTO members and also ruled that the WTO Agreements themselves did not determine how they should be implemented nationally but left this to the WTO members.[7] The judgment will undoubtedly settle much of the uncertainty surrounding the status of the WTO Agreements in EC law.[8] However, it can be argued that the judgment is doing injustice to the WTO system as it undermines the relevance of the WTO Agreements as restraints on the conduct of the EC institutions and ground for individuals and Member States to challenge that conduct.

2. Factual and Legal Background

In May 1996, Portugal introduced an action for annulment under Article 230 of the EC Treaty (ex Article 173) against Council Decision 96/386/EC of 26 February 1996 'concerning the conclusion of Memoranda of Understanding between the European Community and the Islamic Republic of Pakistan and between the European Community and the

---

[5] See Joined Cases 21–24/72 *International Fruit Company NV v Produktschap voor Groenten en Fruit* [1972] ECR 1219 and Case 9/73 *Schlüter v Hauptzollamt Lörrach* [1973] ECR 1135; Case 266/81 *Società Italiana per l'Oleodotto Transalpino (SIOT) v Ministero delle Finanze* [1983] ECR 731; Joined Cases 267–269/81 *Amministrazione dello Stato v Società Petrolifera Italiana (SPI)* [1983] ECR 801; Joined Cases 290–291/81 *Compagnia Singer v Amministrazione delle Finanze dello Stato* [1983] ECR 847 and Case C–469/93, *Amministrazione delle Finanze dello Stato v Chiquita Italia SpA* [1995] ECR I–4533.

[6] Case C–280/93 *Germany v Council* [1994] ECR I–4973.

[7] Shortly after the ECJ had rendered its judgement, a WTO panel contained a passage to the same effect but from the point of view from the WTO legal system. See *United States – Sections 301-310 of the Trade Act of 1974*, report of the panel released on 22 December, WT/DS152/R, at para 7.72. The panel held that '[U]nder the doctrine of direct effect, which has been found to exist most notably in the legal order of the EC but also in certain free trade agreements, obligations addressed to States are construed as creating legally enforceable rights and obligations for individuals. Neither the GATT nor the WTO has so far been interpreted by GATT/WTO institutions as a legal order producing direct effect. Following this approach, the GATT/WTO did not create a new legal order the subjects of which comprise both contracting parties or Members and their nationals'.

[8] There have been several cases where the ECJ has been confronted with this question but declined to give an answer. See Case 183/95 *Affish BV v Rijksdienst voor de Keuring van vee en vlees* [1997] ECR I–4315; Joined Cases C–364/95 and C–365/95 *T Port GmbH v Hauptzollampt Hamburg-Jonas* [1998] ECR I–1023; Case C–53/96 *Hermès International v FHT Marketing Choice BV* [1998] ECR I–3603; Case C–100/96 *Queen v Ministry of Agriculture, Fisheries and Food* [1999] ECR I–1499 and Case C–104/97 P *Atlanta AG v Council and Commission* judgement of 14 October 1999, not yet reported in the ECR.

Republic of India on arrangements in the area of market access for textile products' (Council Decision 96/386).[9] The Memoranda of Understanding implemented by Council Decision 96/386 envisaged reciprocal market access concessions between Pakistan, India and the EC.

Under the Memorandum signed by Pakistan and the EC on 27 March 1996, Pakistan agreed to eliminate all quantitative restrictions applicable to a series of textile products listed in Annex II to the Memorandum. The Commission undertook to give favourable consideration to requests from Pakistan with regard to the management of existing tariff restrictions for exceptional flexibility and to initiate immediately the necessary internal procedures in order to ensure that all the restrictions which affected the importation of products of the handloom and cottage industries of Pakistan were removed before the entry into force of the WTO. Pursuant to the Memorandum signed by India and the EC on 8 March 1996, India agreed to bind the tariffs which it applied to the textiles and clothing items listed in the Attachment to the Memorandum and to notify these tariffs to the WTO Secretariat. In return, the EC agreed to remove all the restrictions applicable to India's exports of handloom products and cottage industry products as referred to in the EC–India Agreement on trade in textile products. The EC also undertook to give favourable consideration to requests for exceptional flexibilities in the administration of quantitative restrictions and tariff restrictions on textile products.

Portugal alleged that the implementation of the Memoranda adversely affected its textile industry and decided to introduce an action for annulment against Council Decision 96/386. It argued that the Memoranda infringed certain provisions and principles included in the WTO Agreements.[10] Portugal invoked provisions of GATT 1994, the WTO Agreement on Textile and Clothing Products and the WTO Agreement on Licensing Procedures. It argued that these Agreements were a valid ground to challenge the legality of Council Decision 96/386 since this decision constituted a mere implementation of the Memoranda of Understanding negotiated with India and Pakistan for the specific purpose of applying the rules in GATT 1994 and the WTO Agreement on Textile and Clothing Products.

The Council, supported by the Commission and France, took the position that WTO Agreements did not have direct effect and could not be used as a ground to review the legality of Community acts. It argued that the

---

[9] [1996] OJ L153/47 of 27 June 1996.
[10] Portugal also invoked certain rules and fundamental principles of EC law. Portugal alleged the violation of principles or rules concerning the publication of Community acts, transparency, and loyal co-operation between Member States and Community institutions, legitimate expectations, non-retroactivity, economic and social cohesion and equality between economic operators. However, that part of the claim falls outside the scope of this article which will focus solely on the WTO-related arguments.

case law of the ECJ regarding GATT – in its pre-Uruguay Round version – also applied to the WTO Agreements. In addition, the Council argued that the Memoranda did not envisage any implementation of the WTO Agreements referred to by Portugal. The *Fediol* and *Nakajima* doctrines did therefore not apply and excluded any possibility for judicial review of the contested decision based on WTO law.

3. The Opinion of the Advocate General

Advocate General Saggio delivered his Opinion on 25 February 1999. He followed an approach that was quite different from the reasoning maintained by the ECJ and entered into a discussion on the legal status and nature of the WTO Agreements like Advocate General Tesauro had done in the *Hermès* case.[11] His point of departure was Article 300(7) of the EC Treaty (ex Article 288(7)) according to which international agreements concluded by the EC with other states 'shall be binding on the institutions of the Community and on Member States' and the case law of the ECJ starting with *Haegeman*[12] according to which these agreements form an integral part of Community law.[13]

Recalling thereafter the ECJ's case law on direct effect, he provided a summary of the ECJ's reasoning in its *International Fruit Company* line of case law as well as in *Germany v Council*, including the *Fediol* and *Nakajima* 'exceptions'.[14] The Advocate General expressed his disagreement with the stance taken by the ECJ that the right, particularly of a Member State, to challenge the legality of a Community act ought to be subordinated to the question of whether the GATT Agreements had direct effect. Accordingly, he argued that international agreements, such as the WTO Agreements, could serve as a ground for the control of the legality of Community acts, even in the absence of direct effect. The limitation of the 'invocability' of the WTO Agreements as a ground to review the legality of Community acts to the situations covered by the '*Fediol* and *Nakajima*' doctrines would, according to the Advocate General, restrict the breadth of Article 300(7) EC Treaty.[15]

The Advocate General then reviewed the legal nature of the WTO Agreements and the changes brought about by the Uruguay Round. He

---

[11] See Opinion of 16 June 1998 in Case C–53/96 *Hermès International v FHT Marketing Choice BV* [1998] ECR I–3603.

[12] Case 181/73 *Haegeman v Belgium* [1974] ECR 449, para 5. See the reformulation of the *Haegeman* principle in Case 12/86 *Meryem Demirel v Stadt Schäbisch Gmünd* [1987] ECR 3719, para 7. The *Demirel* formulation was recently reiterated in Case C–321/97 *Ulla-Brith Anderson and Susanne Wåkerås-Andersson v Sweden* judgement of 15 June 1999, not yet reported in the ECR.

[13] Paragraphs 14 to 16 of the Opinion.

[14] Paragraphs 14 to 18 of the Opinion.

[15] Paragraph 18 of the Opinion.

referred to the new institutional framework and the numerous provisions of the WTO Agreements, which contain unconditional and precise commitments. He also mentioned the new dispute settlement system that, in his view, left a much more limited margin of manoeuvre for a WTO member which considered itself a victim of the illegal behaviour on the part of another WTO member.[16] He also commented upon the arguments brought forward by the Council that the WTO dispute settlement mechanism is an autonomous system that would prevent the ECJ from interpreting WTO law.[17] Saggio replied that the WTO dispute settlement rules are not capable of limiting the competences of the ECJ because the WTO dispute settlement rules do not establish a judicial body but rather a conciliatory mechanism for the settlement of disputes (as the DSB is more political in nature, limits itself to the mere adoption of decision or recommendations and is not accessible for private parties) and because the establishment of a judicial body entrusted with the powers, not only to interpret and apply the WTO Agreements, but also to annul Community acts and decisions, would be incompatible with the EC legal order and a manifest breach of Article 220 EC Treaty (ex Article 164).[18] He continued that nothing prevented the EC from going further than the WTO dispute settlement system and thus from annulling Community acts as being considered contrary to the WTO.

The Advocate General also focused on the legal status of the preamble to Council Decision 94/800 implementing the Uruguay Round Agreements.[19] The last recital of the Preamble provides that:

> [W)]hereas, by its nature, the Agreement establishing the World Trade Organisation, including the Annexes thereto, is not susceptible to being directly invoked in Community or Member State courts ...

The recital was justified by the Commission as follows:

---

[16] Paragraph 19 of the Opinion. The Advocate General – incorrectly – argued that WTO panel reports are adopted by majority voting. Article 16(4) of the Understanding on Rules and Procedures Governing the Settlement of Disputes (DSU) provides that a panel report is adopted by the Dispute Settlement Body (DSB) 'unless ... the DSB decides by consensus not to adopt the report'.

[17] Paragraph 23 of the Opinion.

[18] This line of reasoning is based on a misconception of the WTO dispute settlement mechanism as neither panels, nor the Appellate Body are able to invalidate Community acts. They can merely establish that a Community act infringes WTO rules and recommend that the EC should bring its legislation in conformity with these rules. See GA Zonnekeyn 'The Legal Status of WTO Panel Reports in the EC Legal order. Some Reflections on the Opinion of Advocate General Mischo in the Atlanta Case' (1999) *JIEL* 713 at 720, fn 33.

[19] Council Decision of 22 December 1994 concerning the conclusion on behalf of the European Community, as regards matters within its competence, of the agreements reached in the Uruguay Round of multilateral negotiations (1986–1994) [1994] OJ L336/1 of 23 December 1994.

... it is important for the WTO Agreement and its annexes not to have a direct effect, that is one whereby private individuals who are natural or legal persons could invoke it under national law. It is already known that the United States and many other of our trading partners will explicitly rule out any such direct effect. Without an express stipulation of such exclusion in the Community instrument of adoption, a major imbalance would arise in the actual management of the obligations of the Community and other countries.[20]

Contrary to some of the earlier Opinions on this subject,[21] Advocate General Saggio did not accord much weight to that statement. The Advocate General argued that such a unilateral declaration could not, at the level of international law, limit the effects of an international agreement and that the text of the agreement is the primary source of interpretation.[22] He also argued that, at the level of EC law, the Council could not by secondary legislation, limit the competence of the ECJ or national courts to apply Community agreements.[23] Therefore, the Advocate General concluded that the Council's statement on the effect of the WTO Agreements was a mere political statement that could not affect the jurisdiction of a national or EC court to interpret WTO law.[24]

---

[20] See the Explanatory Memorandum to COM(94) 143 final of 15 April 1994.
[21] Opinion of Advocate General Cosmas of 17 July 1997 in Case C–183/95 *Affish BV v Rijksdienst voor de Keuring van Vee en Vlees* [1997] ECR I–4315, at para 127 and Opinion of Advocate General Elmer of 24 June 1997 in Joined Cases C–364/95 and C–365/95 *T Port GmbH & Co v Hauptzollamt Hamburg-Jonas* [1997] ECR I–1023, paras 28–9.
[22] The Advocate General referred to Articles 31 and 32 of the Vienna Convention on the Law of Treaties as well as to the judgement of the International Court of Justice of 3 February 1994 in 'The Case concerning the Territorial Dispute (Libyan Arab Jamahiriya v Chad)' (1994) ICJ Reports 6. See para 20 of the Opinion. Pescatore has followed a similar approach and argued that the attempt to alter ex-post the effect of an international agreement is incompatible with the principle of good faith in international (trade) relations. See P Pescatore 'The New WTO Dispute Settlement Mechanism' in P Demaret et al (eds) *Regionalism and Multilateralism after the Uruguay Round* (Brussels: European University Press, 1997) 703-14.
[23] See para 20 of the Opinion. Advocate General Saggio referred in this context to the Opinion of Advocate General Tesauro in the *Hermès* case, who argued that the Council's statement, in the absence of a multilateral solution on this issue, was not binding for the ECJ and could not prevent the ECJ from ruling differently. See para 24 of the Opinion. Similar views have been expressed by Dashwood who argued that in the absence of a clear indication as to the parties' intentions, it is for the ECJ alone to determine the internal effects that the WTO Agreements may produce within the Community order and that the recital merely provides an indication as to how the matter was understood by the members of the Council at the time Decision 94/800 was adopted. See A Dashwood 'Treatment of Public International Law by European Community Law' paper presented on 21 October 1999 at the Jean Monnet Symposium on the 'Fundamental principles as inspiration and as source of law in the systems of the European Union and the WTO'.
[24] The reference to 'interpretation' is not entirely correct. The recital in the preamble was clearly addressing the question of direct effect. Interpretation is a different issue, which is relevant, for example, when applying the principle of consistent interpretation as reflected in *Hermès*. See GA Zonnekeyn 'The Hermès Judgement – Reconciling the Principles of Uniform and Consistent Interpretation' (1999) *JWIP* 495.

The Advocate General finally considered the reciprocity principle which was also mentioned by Advocate General Tesauro in *Hermès*.[25] This principle essentially implies that the denial of direct effect to the WTO Agreements by the EC's other trading partners would be a sufficient reason to refuse direct effect of these Agreements in the EC legal order. Advocate General Saggio, however, took the view that the absence of direct effect of the WTO Agreements in other WTO members' legal system should not affect the legal effect of these Agreements in the EC legal order. Only non-compliance by a WTO member of the rules of the WTO Agreements (ie substantive non-compliance rather than the absence of direct effect), could justify the suspension of the operation of these Agreements by other members. This decision to suspend the application of an international agreement could even be taken by the national or Community courts. This argument reflected the reasoning of Advocate General Tesauro in *Hermès* and was most likely used to counter the argument that the absence of direct effect of the WTO Agreements in the legal order of the EC's major trading partners constituted an imbalance in the fulfilment of the obligations undertaken. Since the absence of direct effect was not a sufficient proof of such an imbalance, Saggio argued that effective non-compliance would be a sufficient reason for the non-application of the WTO Agreements by the EC courts and would leave no possibility for Member States and individuals to invoke their provisions directly.[26]

Saggio consequently concluded that '[C]ompte tenu des considérations dévéloppées jusqu'ici, nous estimons que dans le cas d'espèce, s'agissant d'un recours direct foné sur l'article 173 du traité, introduit par un Etat membre à l'encontre d'un acte du Conseil, l'invocation des accords de l'OMC par le requérant ne soulève aucun problème de recevabilité'.[27]

As far as the substance of the case was concerned, Saggio's answer was negative. Part of the reasoning was based on the Commission's argument that any possible departure from WTO rules had to be considered, under EC law, as legally valid, since under customary international law, as codified by Article 41 of the Vienna Convention on the Law of Treaties, parties to a multilateral agreement are authorised, within certain limits, to derogate by a bilateral agreement from the application inter se of the provisions of the multilateral agreement. As he did not find any violation of EC law principles either, the Advocate General concluded that the application had to be dismissed.

---

[25] See para 21 of the Opinion. See also paras 31–5 of the Opinion of Advocate General Tesauro in *Hermès*.
[26] Mengozzi also argued that the principle of 'substantial reciprocity', ie the correct implementation of the WTO Agreements, would be a precondition for their enforcement in the EC and national courts. See P Mengozzi 'The World Trade Organization Law: An Analysis of its First Practice' (1998) *Rivista di Diritta Europeo* 3 at 32–5.
[27] Paragraph 24 of the Opinion.

4. The Judgment of the ECJ

The ECJ recalled at the outset that the contracting parties to an international agreement are free to agree what effect the provisions of the agreement are to have in the internal legal order of the contracting parties. Only if that question has not been settled by the agreement, does it have to be decided by the courts having jurisdiction in the matter, and in particular, as far as the EC is concerned, by the ECJ within the framework of its jurisdiction under the EC Treaty, in the same manner as any question of interpretation relating to the application of the agreement in the EC.[28] It further recalled that, while parties are bound by the principle of good faith in the implementation of international agreements, they are, in principle, free to determine the legal means appropriate to implement the commitments they have undertaken, unless the agreement itself provides for those means.[29] The ECJ thus started by examining whether the WTO Agreements contained specific means to ensure the implementation of the obligations contained in these Agreements in the internal legal order of the WTO members.

The ECJ admitted that, when compared with the 'old' GATT, the WTO had undergone significant changes. It referred to the new dispute settlement mechanism and the safeguards regime, which were, under the 'old' GATT, the main obstacles for the ECJ to grant direct effect to GATT and the reasons to limit the judicial review of Community acts on the basis of GATT.[30] Notwithstanding these changes, the ECJ argued that the WTO Agreements still leave significant room for negotiation between its members. The ECJ emphasised that although the DSU, in Articles 3(7), 22(1) and 22(2), expresses a clear preference for the withdrawal of the measure found to be inconsistent with WTO law, mutually acceptable compensation is considered as a valuable – albeit temporary – alternative. The ECJ further emphasised that Article 22(2) of the DSU provides for negotiations between the parties to a dispute if the party whose measure has been found to be incompatible with WTO law has failed to implement the recommendations and decisions of the Dispute Settlement Body within a reasonable period of time.

Consequently, the ECJ ruled that imposing upon courts the obligation to refrain from applying these rules which are inconsistent with WTO law, would deprive the legislative and executive bodies of WTO members of the right to negotiate an – albeit temporary – mutually acceptable

---

[28] The ECJ here referred to its judgement in Case 104/81 *Hauptzollamt Mainz v Kupferberg*, [1982] ECR 3641, para 17.
[29] The ECJ here again referred to *Kupferberg*, para 18.
[30] For an overview, see G Zonnekeyn 'The Direct Effect of GATT in Community Law: From International Fruit Company to the Banana Cases' [1996] *Int TLR* 63.

solution.³¹ In view of these characteristics, the ECJ concluded that the WTO Agreements, interpreted in the light of their object and purpose, do not determine how the obligations entered into under these Agreements have to be implemented in good faith in the legal order of the WTO members.

The ECJ then gave its views on the status of the WTO Agreements in the EC legal order. It argued that the WTO Agreements were still based on the principle of negotiations and 'reciprocal and mutually advantageous arrangements', as mentioned in the preamble to the Marrakesh Agreement Establishing the World Trade Organization.³² This feature of the WTO legal system distinguished it from certain agreements to which the ECJ had previously accorded direct effect, more in particular these agreements 'which introduce a certain asymmetry of obligations, or create special relations of integration with the Community, such as the agreement which the Court was required to interpret in *Kupferberg*'.³³

Notwithstanding the ECJ's adherence to the *Kupferberg* ruling, ie that the absence of direct effect on the part of another contracting party does not, for the EC, necessarily constitute an absence of reciprocity in the implementation of an agreement, the ECJ remarked that most of the EC's major trading partners did not accord direct effect to the WTO Agreements. The lack of reciprocity in that regard on the part of the EC's most important commercial partners in relation to the WTO Agreements, which are based on 'reciprocal and mutually advantageous arrangements' and which differ in this respect with from the agreements to which direct effect had previously been granted, would, according to the ECJ, lead to an imbalance in the application of WTO rules. To accept that the role of ensuring that these rules comply with EC law be given to the 'Community judicature', would deprive the legislative or executive organs of the Community of the scope of manoeuvre enjoyed by similar organs of the EC's major trading partners.

The ECJ therefore concluded that '[I]t follows from these considerations that having regard to their nature and structure, the WTO agreements are not in principle among the rules in the light of which the Court is to review the legality of measures adopted by the Community institutions'.³⁴ It added that '[T]hat interpretation corresponds, moreover, to what is

---

[31] Similar arguments (against direct effect or invocability of the WTO Agreements) were brought forward by others. See especially J Osterhoudt Berkey 'The European Court of Justice and Direct Effect for the GATT: A Question Worth Revisiting' (1998) *EJIL* 626, at 641–7.
[32] Paragraph 3 of the preamble.
[33] Paragraph 42 of the judgement.
[34] Paragraph 47 of the judgement.

stated in the final recital in the preamble to Decision 94/800 ...'.[35] The ECJ thus ruled that this statement was, indeed, relevant, although it was only used after it had reached its conclusions on the nature of the WTO Agreements as such.

The ECJ finally ruled that, in the case at hand, the *Fediol* and *Nakajima* case law did not apply as Council Decision 96/386 only approved the Memoranda with India and Pakistan and did not imply the implementation of a specific WTO obligation nor did it expressly refer to a WTO rule. The conclusion of the ECJ therefore was that 'the claim of the Portuguese Republic that the contested decision was in breach of certain rules and fundamental principles of the WTO is unfounded'.[36] Also, the ECJ found that there was no violation of any EC law principle and dismissed the application.

5. Observations

5.1 Nil Novi Sub Sole?

The final outcome of the ECJ's judgment in the *Portuguese Textiles* case does not differ substantially from the approach taken by the ECJ in relation to its 'GATT case law'. However, in the case at hand, the ECJ seems to attach more importance to the nature of the WTO as a forum of negotiations aiming at a system of reciprocal and mutually advantageous arrangements. The ECJ had already ruled in *International Fruit Company*, that GATT – in its pre-Uruguay Round version – was based on the principle of negotiations undertaken on the basis of reciprocal and mutually advantageous arrangements.[37] Indeed, paragraph 3 of the preamble to GATT 1947 is identical to paragraph three of the Marrakesh Agreement Establishing the World Trade Organization. The argument invoked by the ECJ in the *Portuguese Textiles* case is therefore not entirely new. The ECJ did recognise this in its judgment.[38]

The real novelty of the *Portuguese Textiles* case therefore is the ECJ's emphasis on the compliance mechanism of the WTO dispute settlement system as an obstacle to invoke the WTO Agreements as a ground for legality control of Community acts, and the implicit recognition that international trade relations within the WTO are essentially governed by politics, rather than by the rule of law.

---

[35] Paragraph 48 of the judgement.
[36] Paragraph 52 of the judgement.
[37] Paragraph 21 of the judgement.
[38] Paragraph 42 of the judgement.

5.2 Direct Effect and Invocability: Two Distinct Concepts

The ECJ refused to depart from its now well established case law, that the direct effect of GATT (read WTO Agreements) serves as a pre-condition for using these Agreements as a ground for judicial review in a direct action brought before the ECJ or the European Court of First Instance (CFI). Already in 1972, in *International Fruit Company*, the ECJ was asked to assess the validity of a Community regulation in the light of GATT. After having held that the EC was bound by GATT, the ECJ ruled that:

> Before invalidity can be relied upon before a [national] court, that provision of international law must also be capable of conferring rights on citizens of the Community which they can invoke before the courts.[39]

The ECJ thus established a link between the possibility of invoking an international agreement for reviewing of the validity of a Community act and the fact that certain provisions of this agreement may be relied upon by individuals before national courts. As a consequence of this link, the ECJ was not prepared to review the validity of such an act unless the agreement was capable of conferring rights on individuals. As Bebr – rightly – pointed out, the absence of direct effect of an international agreement protected the validity of Community acts.[40]

This connection between the direct effect of EC law, which plays a role in the relationship between the EC and the national legal order of the EC Member States, and the possibility of invoking an international agreement, which refers to the relationship between the international and the EC legal order, was subject to fierce criticism,[41] also by Advocate General Saggio in the case at hand. As Maresceau – almost poetically – phrased it: '[A]s far as GATT is concerned it would now seem a somewhat artificial construction if the court were to introduce in actions based on Art. 173 the directly effective sword of Damocles'.[42]

---

[39] Paragraph 8 of the judgement.
[40] G Bebr 'Agreements Concluded by the Community and their Possible Direct Effect: From International Fruit Company to Kupferberg' (1983) *CMLRev* 35 at 46.
[41] See eg J Rideau 'Les accords internationaux dans la jurisprudence de la Cour de Justice des Communautés européennes: réflections sur les relations entre les ordres juridiques international, communautaire et nationaux' (1990) *RDIP* 289; M Maresceau 'The GATT in the case-law of the European Court of Justice' in FG Jacobs et al (eds) *The European Community and GATT* (Deventer: Kluwer, 1986) 107–26; HN Tagaras 'L'effet direct des accords internationaux de la Communauté' (1984) CDE 20; JHJ Bourgeois 'Effects of International Agreements in European Community Law: Are the Dice Cast?' (1984) *Michigan Law Review* 1250 and E-U Petersmann 'Application of GATT by the Court of Justice of the European Communities' (1983) *CMLRev* 403.
[42] M Maresceau (n 41) 116.

5.3 Judicial Self-Restraint – The Trias Politica in Danger?

The ECJ essentially rejected Portugal's request because a legal assessment by the ECJ of the WTO Agreements would bind the EC's legislative and executive bodies so that they would no longer be able to enjoy identical discretionary powers as similar bodies of the EC's major trading partners. This implies that legality control of acts adopted by the Community institutions on the basis of WTO law is impossible because the ECJ must leave the necessary 'freedom' to the EC legislator in order not to endanger the EC's future negotiating position towards its trading partners in the WTO. This is clearly not a legal argument and an obvious assault to the 'trias politica' principle, which ought to be the cornerstone of every legal system.

It raises the fundamental question of the ECJ's willingness to let WTO law play a more prominent role as a standard for reviewing the legality of acts adopted by the Community institutions. Some would certainly have welcomed such an approach. Petersmann, for example, argued that the ECJ should '… exercise a stricter review of the observation of GATT obligations by the Community …'.[43] Others have been less enthusiastic and underlined that the ECJ might move to an area which the WTO members conferred to political negotiation.[44] Ehlermann warned against the danger of interference with the GATT dispute settlement mechanism. In his view, a judgment of the ECJ would tie the hands of the Community negotiators.[45]

5.4 Reciprocity

Even though the WTO Agreements were concluded in order to enter into 'reciprocal and mutually advantageous arrangements', it is very clear that some of the provisions of the WTO Agreements do contain reciprocal trade concessions. The 'national treatment' principle, for example, is a rule that is susceptible of being invoked by both EC nationals and non-EC nationals. That principle constitutes a general rule of law under the WTO and is not a trade concession that the EC exchanged in order to obtain a reciprocal concession from its trading partners. Other general principles from the WTO Agreements could be referred to, to illustrate that the WTO has matured from a multilateral trade forum based on reciprocal concessions, to an international rule-based system where obligations are enforced through

---
[43] E-U Petersmann (n 41) 404.
[44] JHJ Bourgeois 'Le GATT et le Traité CEE' (1980) *Dir Comm Scamb Int* 30 at 54.
[45] As quoted by Castillo de la Torre. See F Castillo de la Torre (n 2) 42, fn 40. The arguments of both Petersmann, Bourgeois and Ehlermann were made in the context of the 'old' GATT See also P-J Kuyper 'The New WTO Settlement System: The Impact on the Community' in JHJ Bourgeois et al (eds) *The Uruguay Round Results. A European Lawyers' Perspective* (Brussels: European Interuniversity Press, 1995) 87–114 at 105.

a binding dispute settlement system. For the application of these rules, the question of reciprocity is simply not relevant. In view of the evolution of the WTO system, the ECJ's reliance on the reciprocal character of the WTO Agreements is anachronistic.

5.5 Implementation – Obligatory, or Not?

The judgment is also of significant importance because the ECJ focused – for the first time – on the legal nature of the WTO dispute settlement mechanism. This issue had already been raised in two earlier cases brought before the European Court of First Instance (CFI) and the ECJ, but both courts avoided ruling on it.[46]

However, in the *Atlanta* case,[47] Advocate General Mischo did focus on the issue and argued that, in line with the arguments brought forward by the Spanish government in the *Chemnitz* case,[48] that a ruling of the Appellate Body does not impose any obligation on the WTO member, whose legislation has been found to be in breach of WTO law, to amend its legislation immediately. He referred to Article 21(3) of the DSU, according to which a member has a 'reasonable period' of time to comply with the ruling of the Appellate Body and to bring its legislation into line with WTO law. Moreover, Article 22 of the DSU gives WTO members the possibility of maintaining the unlawful measures in place beyond the reasonable period of time if the parties to the dispute have agreed on a suitable compensation.

In bringing up the issue, the ECJ entered into the sensitive debate on the interpretation of the nature of the legal obligations of WTO members under the WTO dispute settlement mechanism. Some have argued that WTO obligations need not be implemented given that compensation or even the acceptance of retaliation, are separate options.[49] The Commission also seems to have taken the approach that full implementation is not an absolute obligation.[50] Indeed, one could argue that the DSU, even as

---

[46] See Case T–254/97 *Fruchthandelsgesellschaft mbH Chemnitz v Commission* judgement of the European Court of First Instance of 28 September 1999, not yet reported in the ECR and Case C–104/97 P *Atlanta AG v Council and Commission* judgement of the European Court of Justice of 14 October 1999, not yet reported in the ECR.

[47] Case C–104/97 P *Atlanta AG v Council and Commission*, judgement of the European Court of Justice of 14 October 1999, not yet reported in the ECR. For a comment on the Opinion of Advocate General Mischo, see GA Zonnekeyn (n 18).

[48] Case T–254/97 *Fruchthandelsgesellschaft mbH Chemnitz v Commission* judgement of the European Court of First Instance of 28 September 1999, not yet reported in the ECR.

[49] JH Bello 'The WTO Dispute Settlement Understanding: Less is More' (1996) *Am J Int'l L* 416 and TM Reiff and M Forestal 'Revenge of the Push-me, Pull-You: The Implementation Process Under the WTO Dispute Settlement Understanding' (1998) *Int'l Law* 755 at 763.

[50] See in this respect the remarks made by Gusetti from EC Commission Legal Service. L Gusetti 'WTO: Implementation of DSU Findings by Compensation' lecture given on 7

continued ...

a preference to the withdrawal of WTO-incompatible measures, seems to favour solutions 'mutually acceptable' to the parties. Article 22(8) of the DSU provides that the suspension of concessions shall cease not only if the incompatible measure is withdrawn or the member concerned has provided a solution to the nullification and impairment of benefits, but also if a 'mutually satisfactory solution is reached'. Article 3(7) of the DSU further provides that what is 'clearly to be preferred' is a mutually acceptable solution 'consistent with the covered agreements'. Another option is the possibility for the member whose legislation has been found to be in breach with WTO law to tolerate the suspensions of concessions instigated by the other party to the dispute. Such suspension of concessions must be 'equivalent' to the level of the nullification and impairment caused by the measure to be WTO-inconsistent and is not of a punitive nature but has as its main objective to restore the imbalance in concessions caused by the measure found to be incompatible.[51] It should be recalled that the EC has chosen to accept retaliation by the United States in the bananas and hormones cases. The suspension of concessions is regulated by Article 22 of the DSU, including the possibility to request binding arbitration to ensure that the suspension sought is, indeed, 'equivalent' In addition, Article 26(1) of the DSU provides that in case of so-called non-violation cases under Article XXIII of GATT 1994, there is no obligation to withdraw the measure.

Jackson who has – rightly – argued that the 'unconditional' obligation to comply with WTO rules can be inferred from the language of the DSU itself and that compliance is the preferred option.[52] Indeed, Article 22.1 of the DSU provides that compensation is a purely provisional measure and that '… neither compensation nor the suspension of concessions or other obligations is preferred to full implementation of a recommendation to bring a measure into conformity with the covered agreements …'.

March 2000 at a luncheon organised by the European Trade law association. The author will refrain from quoting any statement made by Mr Gusetti and will approach the subject in a neutral way.

[51] See *European Communities – Regime for the Importation, Sale and Distribution of Bananas – Recourse to Arbitration by the European Communities under Article 22.6 of the DSU*, decision by the arbitrators of 9 April 1999, WT/DS27/ARB. The arbitrators decided that '[W]e agree with the United States that this temporary nature indicates that it is the purpose of countermeasures to induce compliance. But this purpose does not mean that the DSB should grant authorization to suspend concessions beyond what is equivalent to the level of nullification or impairment. In our view, there is nothing in Article 22.1 of the DSU, let alone in paragraphs 4 and 7 of Article 22, that could be read as a justification for countermeasures of a punitive nature'. See para 6.3 of the decision.

[52] H Horn and P Mavroidis 'Remedies in the WTO Dispute Settlement System and developing Country Interests' paper dated 11 April 1999, 14; JH Jackson 'The WTO Dispute Settlement Understanding – Misunderstandings on the Nature of a Legal Obligation' in Cameron & Campbell (eds) *Dispute Resolution in the WTO* (London: Cameron May, 1998) 69–74 at 73 and JH Jackson 'Dispute Resolution and the WTO' paper presented at the Center for International Development, Harvard University, 5–6 November 1999, 7.

Compensation is not a method of settling disputes but simply a temporary instrument to ensure that any benefits accruing to the other members are not nullified or impaired as a result of the failure to comply within the reasonable period of time set in the particular case and that the defaulting party is not encouraged to persist indefinitely in its failure to comply.[53]

Consequently, adopted panel and Appellate Body reports are binding for the EC and the compensation mechanism cannot prevent the WTO Agreements from being invoked in a direct legal proceeding before the CFI or the ECJ. By accepting compensation, the responding member in a dispute, in se, recognises the binding effect of WTO law since it acknowledges that its legislation or other measures are in breach with WTO law. The compensation mechanism was not meant to give WTO members a complete freedom to leave WTO-inconsistent measures in place and does not, as a matter of principle, accord a 'right' to violate a legal obligation entered into under an international agreement. It merely constitutes a practical option to temporarily defuse a dispute between WTO members, parties to a dispute.

Moreover, the reasoning maintained by the ECJ would imply that the EC's trading partners are entitled to compensation when the EC does not respect its obligations under WTO law, whereas a legal action introduced by an individual or an EC Member State in the CFI or ECJ to annul a Community act based on an identical breach of WTO law, would have to be rejected. The report of the panel in *United States – Section 301–310 of the Trade Act of 1974*[54] contains an interesting obiter dictum in this respect. The panel held that 'whether there are circumstances where obligations in any of the WTO agreements addressed to members would create rights for individuals which national courts must protect, remains an open question, in particular in respect of obligations following the exhaustion of DSU procedures in a specific dispute'. The panel further argued that '[T]he fact that WTO institutions have not to date construed any obligations as producing direct effect does not necessarily preclude that in the legal system of any given Member, following internal constitutional principles, some obligations will be found to give right to individuals'.

---

[53] See also para. 29 of the Opinion of Advocate General Tesauro in *Hermès*. Timmermans has suggested that it cannot in any way be excluded that compensation may ultimately be a 'provisoire qui dure', see C Timmermans, 'The Implementation of the Uruguay Round by the EC' in JHJ Bourgeois et al (eds) *The Uruguay Round Results: A European European Lawyers' Perspective*, (Brussels: European Interuniversity Press, 1995) 501–09 at 504. This situation cannot – a priori – be excluded but it would run counter to the spirit and objectives of the WTO dispute settlement mechanism.

[54] *United States – Sections 301–310 of the Trade Act of 1974*, report of the panel released on 22 December, WT/DS152/R, para 7.72, fn 661.

5.6 Alternatives for Legality Control or Direct Effect

The judgment of the ECJ in the *Portuguese Textiles* case does not deprive the WTO Agreements of their relevance under EC law. In the *International Dairy Agreement* case[55] and the *Hermès* case, the ECJ recognised the principle or duty of consistent interpretation, which implies that WTO law should be interpreted in the light of WTO law. As Dashwood phrased it, '[I] am beginning to wonder whether it worth spilling so much learned ink over the WTO's direct effect. The lesson might be drawn from the International Dairy Agreement case and from Hermès that the duty of consistent interpretation can do pretty much the same job, while sparing the Court intellectual acrobatics'.[56] The question whether this principle will develop as a valuable alternative, will have to be developed on a case by case basis. Moreover, the ECJ may apply its *Fediol* and *Nakajima* case law to review the legality of Community legislation on the basis of WTO law under the conditions referred to above.

6. Conclusion: Implications of the Judgment

The impact of the ECJ's judgment cannot be underestimated. It is the first time that the ECJ itself has given a clear signal that the WTO Agreements have no direct effect and that it is not prepared to depart from its case law first established in *International Fruit Company*. In essence, The ECJ maintained its existing case law according to which the GATT Agreements preceding the WTO were devoid of direct effect, but partly based on new arguments. The ECJ now emphasised the nature of the WTO Agreements as a forum of intergovernmental negotiation between the WTO members and that the WTO Agreements themselves did not determine how they should be implemented nationally but left this to the WTO members.

The judgment will undoubtedly settle much of the uncertainty surrounding the status of the WTO Agreements in EC law. However, it can be argued that the judgment is doing injustice to the WTO system as it undermines the relevance of the WTO Agreements as restraints on the conduct of the EC institutions and ground for individuals and Member States to challenge that conduct. The non-recognition of direct effect linked to the impossibility of legality control of Community acts on the basis of WTO law must be regretted. However, one should not be desperate since the ECJ has developed an alternative. The *Hermès* case has shown that the principle of consistent interpretation could well develop into a valuable substitute for direct effect.

---

[55] Case C–61/94 *Commission v Germany* [ECR] I–4021.
[56] See n 23.

I would nevertheless like to conclude this article with the comment that ECJ's ruling is clearly inspired by political motives. This must be regretted, but it was probably unavoidable. The ECJ has chosen for a 'real-politik' and has sacrificed the 'trias politica' doctrine, a well-known principle on the continent, to give leeway to the political institutions of the EC.

CHAPTER VI

THE BED LINEN CASE AND ITS AFTERMATH –
SOME COMMENTS ON THE EC's 'WTO ENABLING REGULATION'

1. Introduction

It is not the objective of the present article to discuss the substantive and more technical issues of the *Bed Linen* case but rather to focus on the legislative measures adopted by the European Community (EC) to comply with the panel and Appellate Body reports in *Bed Linen*, with special attention for the so-called 'WTO enabling regulation' adopted by the EC.[1] The WTO enabling regulation and the proposal leading to its adoption contain some statements made by the European Commission and the Council of the European Union which are disputable and which give food for thought. These thoughts will be further developed in the present article.

2. Factual Background

On 12 March 2001 the WTO Dispute Settlement Body (DSB) adopted the Appellate Body report[2] and the panel report,[3] as modified by the Appellate Body in *European Communities – Anti-Dumping Duties on Imports of Cotton-Type Bed Linen from India*. These reports concluded that the imposition by the EC of definitive anti-dumping duties on imports of cotton-type bed linen from India was inconsistent with the Agreement on Implementation of Article VI of the General Agreement on Tariffs and Trade 1994 (the Anti-Dumping Agreement). Pursuant to the recommendations of these reports, the DSB requested the EC to bring its measure into conformity with its obligations under the Anti-Dumping Agreement. In accordance with Article 21.3(b) of the Understanding on Rules and Procedures Governing the Settlement of Disputes (DSU) the EC and India mutually agreed on a reasonable period of five months and two days to implement the recommendations and rulings adopted by the DSB.[4]

---

[1] For a more in-depth analysis of the *Bed Linen* case, see JB Kim 'Fair Price Comparison in the WTO Anti-dumping Agreement. Recent WTO Panel Decisions against the "Zeroing" Method' (2002) *JWT* 39.
[2] WT/DS141/AB/R of 1 March 2001.
[3] WT/DS141/R of 30 October 2000.
[4] WT/DS141/10 of 1 May 2001.

In order to provide the EC with the necessary legal framework to implement these recommendations and rulings, the Council adopted a regulation 'on the measures that may be taken by the Community following a report adopted by the WTO Dispute Settlement Body concerning anti-dumping and anti-subsidy matters' (ie the so-called WTO enabling regulation).[5] On 7 August 2001, in application of Regulation 1515/2001, the EC adopted Regulation 1644/2001 amending the original definitive anti-dumping duties on bed linen from India, purporting to comply with the DSB's recommendations and rulings, whilst simultaneously suspending its application.[6]

India disagreed that this re-determination complied with the panel and Appellate Body rulings.[7] The re-determination was amended by Council Regulation 160/2002 terminating the proceeding against Pakistan.[8] On 13 February 2002, the EC initiated a so-called 'partial interim review' against India[9] and on 14 March 2002 the EC terminated the anti-dumping proceeding with respect to Egypt.[10] On 22 April 2002, the Council adopted Regulation 696/2002 confirming the definitive anti-dumping duty imposed on imports of cotton-type bed linen originating in India by Regulation 2398/97, as amended and suspended by Regulation 1644/2001.[11] In May 2002, the EC announced that it would review, on request, all the anti-dumping measures based on methodologies found to be incompatible with WTO rules in the *Bed Linen* case.[12] The Commission argued that the EC had fully implemented the rulings and recommendations of the panel and Appellate Body and that these reviews were an additional

---

[5] Council Regulation (EC) 1515/2001 of 23 July 2001 [2001] OJ L201/10 of 26 July 2001. For a comment, see J Branton 'The EC Washes its Dirty Bed Linen – Is the Saga Over Yet?' (2002) *Int TLR* 64; D Horovitz 'A Regulated Scope for EU Compliance with WTO Rulings' (2001) *Int TLR* 153 and GA Zonnekeyn 'Enkele kanttekeningen bij Verordening 1515/2001 inzake de tenuitvoerlegging van besluiten van het Orgaan voor Geschillenbeslechting van de WTO' (2002) *SEW* 97.

[6] Council Regulation (EC) 1644/2001 of 7 August 2001 amending Regulation (EC) 2398/97, imposing a definitive anti-dumping duty on imports of cotton-type bed linen originating in Egypt, India and Pakistan and suspending its application with regard to imports originating in India [2001] OJ L219/1 of 14 August 2001.

[7] WT/DS141/11, para 4.

[8] Council Regulation (EC) 160/2002 of 28 January 2002 amending Regulation (EC) 2398/97 imposing a definitive anti-dumping duty on imports of cotton-type bed linen originating in Egypt, India and Pakistan and terminating the proceeding with regard to imports originating in Pakistan [2002] OJ L26/1 of 30 January 2002.

[9] Notice of initiation of a partial interim review of the anti-dumping measures applicable to imports of cotton-type bed linen originating in India [2002] OJ C39/17 of 13 February 2002.

[10] Notice of the expiry of certain anti-dumping measures [2002] OJ C65/12 of 14 March 2002.

[11] Council Regulation (EC) 696/2002 of 22 April 2002 confirming the definitive anti-dumping duty imposed on imports of cotton-type bed linen originating in India by Regulation (EC) 2398/97, as amended and suspended by Council Regulation (EC) 1644/2001 [2002] OJ L109/3 of 25 April 2002.

[12] Notice regarding the anti-dumping measures in force following a ruling of the Dispute Settlement Body of the World Trade Organization adopted on 12 March 2001 [2002] OJ C111/4 of 8 May 2002.

implementation step, to conform WTO compliance of all other existing anti-dumping measures.[13]

India argues that the re-determination, as amended, as well as the further actions, failed to bring the EC into compliance with the recommendations and rulings adopted by the DSB and is inconsistent with WTO law. It is of the opinion that the redetermination is inconsistent with Articles 2, 3, and 15 of the ADA, as was the original measure, and that the re-determination and the further actions have also introduced further inconsistencies with the Anti-Dumping Agreement.

On 8 March 2002, India initiated procedures under Article 21.5 of the DSU by requesting the EC to enter into consultations.[14] Consultations were held in Geneva on 25 and 26 March 2002. These consultations have allowed a better understanding of the respective positions but have failed to settle the dispute. Accordingly, 'there is disagreement as to the existence or consistency with a covered agreement of measures taken to comply with the recommendations and rulings' of the DSB between India and EC within the terms of Article 21.5 of the DSU. Pursuant to Articles 6 and 21.5 of the DSU, Article 17 of the Anti-Dumping Agreement and Article XXIII of GATT 1994, and as envisaged in the Agreement of 13 September 2001 on the 'Agreed Procedures between India and the European Communities under Articles 21 and 22 of the Understanding on Rules and Procedures Governing the Settlement of Disputes (DSU) in the follow-up to the dispute *European Communities – Anti-Dumping Duties on Imports of Cotton-Type Bed Linen from India*, India requested the establishment of a panel. A panel was established on 2 July 2002.[15]

3. The WTO Enabling Regulation – Some Further Reflections

Regulation 1515/2001 was adopted to enable the EC, whenever a need was created by an unfavourable WTO ruling, to digress from the rigid framework of the anti-dumping and anti-subsidy regulations, in order to remedy the adverse WTO ruling. The WTO enabling regulation empowers the EC to take whatever steps it sees fit to amend existing anti-dumping or anti-subsidy measures on account of future unspecified WTO rulings. The reason for adopting the WTO enabling regulation was that the basic regulations, as they stood,[16] did not allow for special types of reviews of existing measures such as in *Bed Linen*.[17]

---

[13] See Press Release IP/02/685 of 8 May 2002, 'European Commission to review anti-dumping measures to confirm compliance with WTO recommendations'.
[14] WT/DS141/12 of 14 March 2002.
[15] WT/DS141/14 of 2 July 2002.
[16] Only the traditional newcomer, interim and sunset review options were available, all of which require new investigation periods and new calculations, rather than revisiting old investigation periods and recalculating via different methods.
[17] See J Branton (n 5) at 65.

The Commission proposal[18] and the final regulation as adopted by the Council, contain two particular statements which are quite controversial. The Commission argues that 'although WTO rules do not oblige the Community to implement a report adopted by the DSB, in certain circumstances the Community might find it appropriate to amend anti-dumping or anti-subsidy regulations to bring them in line with such reports'.[19] In addition, both the proposal and the WTO enabling regulation provide that 'recommendations in reports adopted by the DSB only have prospective effect'.[20] Both statements will be further examined below.

4. The Binding Nature of Reports Adopted by the DSB

In its proposal, the Commission entered into the sensitive debate on the interpretation of the nature of the legal obligations of WTO members under the WTO dispute settlement mechanism. The Commission seems to have taken the approach that full implementation is not an absolute obligation. The question whether panel and Appellate Body reports, as adopted by the DSB, are binding upon WTO members has been the object of a fierce debate in legal doctrine.[21]

---

[18] COM(2001) 379 final of 5 July 2001 and [2001] OJ C270 E/242 of 25 September 2001.

[19] Paragraph 2 of the explanatory memorandum to the Commission proposal.

[20] Paragraph 6 of the explanatory memorandum to the Commission proposal and para 6 of the preamble to the WTO enabling regulation.

[21] I refer in particular to the stimulating discussion between JH Bello 'The WTO Dispute Settlement Understanding: Less is More' (1996) *AJIL* 416 and JH Jackson 'The WTO Dispute Settlement Understanding- Misunderstandings on the Nature of a Legal Obligation' (1997) *AJIL* 60 reprinted in J Cameron and K Campbell (eds) *Dispute Resolution in the World Trade Organisation* (London: Cameron May, 1998) 69–74. Corroborating the view of Bello, see AO Sykes 'The Remedy for Breach of Obligations under the WTO Dispute Settlement Understanding: Damages or Specific Performance?' in M Bronckers and R Quick (eds) *New Directions in International Economic Law* (The Hague: Kluwer Law International, 2000) 349; TM Reif and M Florestal 'Revenge of the Push-Me, Pull-You: The Implementation Process Under the WTO Dispute Settlement Understanding' (1998) The International Lawyer 755 and P Ruttley and M Weisberger 'The WTO Agreement in European Community Law: Status, Effect and Enforcement' to be published in P McRoy, A Appleton and M Plummer (eds) *The Kluwer Companion to the WTO Agreement* (Kluwer Law International). Corroborating the view of Jackson, see eg S Griller 'Judicial Enforceability of WTO law in the European Union. Annotation to Case C–149/96 *Portugal v Council*' (2000) *JIEL* 441; RE Hudec 'Broadening the Scope of Remedies in WTO Dispute Settlement' in F Weiss (ed) *Improving WTO Dispute Settlement Procedures: Issues and Lessons From the Practice of Other International Courts and Tribunals* (London: Cameron May, 2000) 377; PC Mavroidis 'Remedies in the WTO Legal System: Between a Rock and a Hard Place' (2000) *EJIL* 763; J Pauwelyn 'Enforcement and Countermeasures in the WTO: Rules and Rules – Towards a More Collective Approach' (2000) *AJIL* 335; PX Pierros and M Maciejewski 'Specific Performance or Compensation and Countermeasures – Are These Alternative Means of Compliance Under the WTO Dispute Settlement System?' (2001) *Int TLR* 167 and F Roessler, A Ellard and R Elliot 'Performance of the System IV: Implementation' (1998) The International Lawyer 789. For an overview of these different views, see J Waincymer *WTO Litigation. Procedural aspects of Formal Dispute Settlement* (London: Cameron May, 2002) 659–64.

In an attempt to respond to 'some claims that faceless, unelected, unaccountable bureaucrats in Geneva have usurped U.S. sovereignty by writing rules for Americans that should be determined only by Americans', Bello emphasised that:

> Like the GATT rules that preceded them, the WTO rules are simply not binding in the traditional sense. ... Rather, the WTO – essentially a confederation of sovereign national governments – relies upon voluntary compliance. The genius of the GATT/WTO system is the flexibility with which it accommodates the national exercise of sovereignty, yet promote compliance with its trade rules through incentives.

She subsequently argued that if its law or measure is successfully challenged a WTO member has three options: first, it may (and preferably would) come into compliance with the ruling; secondly, it may maintain the offending measure but provide compensatory benefits instead; or thirdly, it may choose to make no change in its law and decline to provide compensation, and, instead, suffer from retaliation against its exports. Bello thus argues that a WTO member is not required to comply with an adverse WTO dispute settlement ruling, but instead may choose to comply, to compensate or to stonewall and suffer retaliation against its exports. In addition, the opinion of Bello is based on an assumption that 'the only truly binding WTO obligation is to maintain the balance of concessions negotiated among Members'.

Jackson has – rightly – argued that this conception constitutes 'a misunderstanding of the nature of legal obligation'. He argues that the 'adopted dispute settlement report establishes an international law obligation upon the member in question to change its practice to make it consistent with the rules of the WTO Agreement and its annexes'. In his view compensation or subsequent suspension of concessions are only 'a fallback in the event of non-compliance'. To support his views, he emphasised that, already under GATT 1947, contracting parties were treating the results of an adopted panel report as legally binding. He then relied on textual arguments, describing 11 clauses of the DSU which, read together, 'strongly suggest' that the legal effect of an adopted panel report is the international law obligation to perform the recommendation of the panel report.

The view taken by Jackson seems to be correct for a number of reasons. First, also under traditional international law the objective of countermeasures is to induce compliance of the state that has committed an internationally wrongful act. It is clear from the text of the ILC's Final Draft Rules on State Responsibility that, as under WTO law, countermeasures do not constitute an alternative means of reparation for the injured party.[22] Article19.1 of the DSU seems to confirm this understanding since it provides that '[W]here a panel or the Appellate Body concludes that a measure is inconsistent with a covered agreement, it shall recommend that the Member concerned bring the measure into conformity with that agreement'. The DSU thus seems to indicate that withdrawal or modification of the measure concerned includes both 'cessation' and 'reparation'.[23] There is no possibility of *restitutio in integrum* in WTO law and no financial compensation is available.[24] It is fundamental therefore to understand that there is only one real remedy available that panels and the Appellate Body can provide and this is the recommendation to bring the measure into conformity, ie withdrawal or modification of the contested measure(s) and the possible suggestion of how this can be done. Consequently, there is no 'choice' available to the parties. Compensation and suspension of concessions are merely potential default remedies that could be requested only if recommendations are not being implemented.

Secondly, the text of the DSU supports the view taken by Jackson. There are at least 11 separate passages in the DSU which seem to indicate that there is an obligation to comply with panel or Appellate Body rulings, as adopted by the DSB.[25] It is not necessary to analyse all of these provisions in detail. A closer look at article 3.7 DSU leaves little doubt as to the hierarchy and the character of measures that should be taken following the adoption of a panel or Appellate Body report.[26] Article 3.7 DSU provides that:

---

[22] See Article 49 of the ILC's Final Draft Rules on State Responsibility. The Final draft articles were adopted in August 2001. See ILC Report on the work of its fifty-third session (23 April–1 June and 2 July–10 August 2001), General Assembly, Official Records, Fifty-fifth Session, Supplement No 10 (A/56/10). The draft Articles are on pp 43–59 (posted at http://www.un.org/law/ilc/reports/2001/2001report.htm). Article 49(1) provides that '[A]n injured State may only take countermeasures against a State which is responsible for an international wrongful act in order to induce that State to comply with its obligations ...'.

[23] Pauwelyn, however, argues that the 'WTO enforcement regime lacks the remedy of reparation - at least in the traditional sense of compensation for damages in the past'. He concludes that '[I]n this sense, the WTO offers less than the ICJ'. See J Pauwelyn (n 21) 359. One could also argue that, under WTO law, cessation and reparation are 'compressed' in the withdrawal or the modification of the measure in question.

[24] However, in December 2001 the US agreed to pay the EC $3 million in compensation in the context of settling *U.S. – Section 110(5) of the U.S. Copyright Act* (WT/DS160). The statute at issue in the case allows the broadcasting of music in certain US restaurants and bars without paying EC rights holders. This has been estimated to cost the EC roughly $1 million per year in lost royalties. The settlement reached envisages an anticipated US payment of more than $3 million over three years into a fund for European musicians while the legislation remains in effect. See European Commission Press Release IP/01/1860 of 19 December 2001, 'EU and US agree on temporary compensation in copyright dispute'.

[25] See JH Jackson (n 21) 63.

[26] See PX Pierros and M Maciejewski (n 21) 168 and GA Zonnekeyn (n 21) 99.

In the absence of a mutually agreed solution, the first objective of the dispute settlement mechanism is usually to secure the withdrawal of the measures concerned if these are found to be inconsistent with the provisions of any of the covered agreements. The provision of compensation should be resorted to only if the immediate withdrawal of the measure is impracticable and as a temporary measure pending the withdrawal of the measure which is inconsistent with a covered agreement. The last resort which this Understanding provides to the Member invoking the dispute settlement procedures is the possibility of suspending the application of concessions or other obligations under the covered agreements on a discriminatory basis vis-à-vis the other Member, subject to authorization by the DSB of such measures.

This article reveals that the withdrawal of a WTO inconsistent measure is the primary objective of the WTO dispute settlement mechanism. Some scholars have questioned the importance of this provision. Sykes, for example, argued that if the objective of the system is 'usually' to secure the withdrawal of the measure, it is impliedly not always the objective.[27] This interpretation is only correct to the extent that it confirms that the word 'usually' refers to the discretion of panels and the Appellate Body in drafting their recommendations and suggestions and in applying the most efficient solutions to resolve a dispute (without obliging them to withdrawal where a mere modification would be sufficient). It does not imply that compensation is seen as an equal alternative for withdrawal.[28] On the contrary, the use of compensation is subject to two basic conditions: (a) compensation may be used only if immediate withdrawal is impracticable and (b) compensation is temporary. The first condition excludes compensation as an alternative to performance whereas the second condition emphasises the strictly temporarily character of compensation.[29]

Thirdly, it is important to understand that the remedy provided by Article 19.1 DSU, ie the recommendation that the member concerned – the party to the dispute to whom the panel or Appellate Body recommendations are addressed – bring the measure into conformity with the relevant agreement(s), is by itself very flexible. It has been clearly established that even though Article 19.1 DSU provides that a panel or the Appellate Body may suggest ways in which it believes the member could appropriately

---

[27] AO Sykes (n 21) 349.
[28] See PX Pierros and M Maciejewski (n 21) 168 and GA Zonnekeyn (n 21) 99.
[29] Timmermans admits that compensation is seen as only a temporarily solution but that it cannot in any way be excluded that compensation may ultimately be a 'provisoire qui dure', see CWA Timmermans 'The Implementation of the Uruguay Round by the EC' in JHJ Bourgeois et al (eds) *The Uruguay Round Results: A European European Lawyers' Perspective* (Brussels: European Interuniversity Press, 1995) 501–9 at 504.

implement that recommendation,[30] the modalities of implementation of a panel or Appellate Body recommendation are up to the member concerned to determine. This means that there is a clear distinction between the recommendations of a panel and of the Appellate Body and the means by which that recommendation is to be implemented. 'The former is governed by Art.19.1 and is limited to a particular form. The latter may be suggested by a panel, but the choice of means is decided, in the first instance, by the Member concerned'.[31] A recommendation under article 19.1 DSU to bring the measure into conformity with the relevant agreement(s) should thus be interpreted 'as referring to whatever actions the Member in question should undertake to ensure that it does fulfil its obligations.'[32] Obviously, it is possible that the prevailing member is not satisfied with the implementation. Then, the DSU provides for recourse to the dispute settlement procedure – and not to any other means – to resolve any such a disagreement.[33] In the meantime, if the responding party decides to follow the suggestion(s) of the panel or the Appellate Body, it would be logical to assume that the implementing measure confirms these suggestions.

5. The Reimbursement of Anti-dumping Duties

Regulation 1644/2001 does not provide for a reimbursement of anti-dumping duties. This is not surprising since the duties have merely been suspended and not repealed. In addition, article 3 of the WTO enabling Regulation explicitly provides that '[A]ny measures adopted pursuant to this Regulation shall take effect from the date of their entry into force and shall not serve as basis for the reimbursement of the duties collected prior to that date, *unless otherwise provided for*'.(own emphasis).

Horovitz has questioned the WTO-compatibility of this provision.[34] He argues that the DSU does not provide for any general principle to limit the effect in time, whether prospective or retrospective, of adopted panel of Appellate Body reports. Article 19.1 DSU only provides that where a measure is found to be incompatible with a covered agreement, the DSB recommendation to the member concerned would be 'to bring the measure into conformity with that agreement'. Accordingly, the DSU

---

[30] For a good example, see *India – Patent Protection for Pharmaceutical and Agricultural Chemical Products*, report of the panel of 5 September 1997, WT/DS50/R at para 8.2. For a comprehensive study of the non-binding character of the 'suggestion' of the adjudicating bodies, see PC Mavroidis (n 21) 777–8.

[31] *Guatemala – Antidumping Investigation Regarding Portland Cement from Mexico*, report of the panel of 16 June 1998, WT/DS60/R at para 8.3.

[32] *Guatemala – Antidumping Investigation Regarding Portland Cement from Mexico*, report of the panel of 16 June 1998, WT/DS60/R at para 7.26.

[33] See Article 21.5 DSU. For a recent analysis of the practice under Article 21.5 DSU, see JE Kearns and S Charnovitz 'Adjudicating Compliance in the WTO: A Review of DSU Article 21.5' (2002) *JIEL* 331.

[34] D Horovitz (n 5) 155.

would not allow a restriction as provided for by Article 3 of the WTO enabling regulation. Horovitz therefore concludes that the EC would be obliged to reimburse the anti-dumping duties paid.[35]

However, article 3 does leave some scope for manoeuvre since it provides that the measures will enter into force *ex nunc*, 'unless otherwise provided for'. It has not been explained what this specifically means.

The thesis defended by Horovitz with regard to the retrospective effect of recommendations and findings adopted by the DSB does not seem to correspond with prior rulings of panels and the Appellate Body and with the principle that recommendations and findings of the DSB are prospective in nature.[36] As far as the case-law of panels is concerned, a distinction must be made between GATT practice and WTO practice.[37]

5.1 GATT Practice

Under the GATT-regime, some panels had recommended, as Kuyper phrased it, a 'specific performance' by ruling that the anti-dumping duties imposed should be revoked and that the anti-dumping duties collected should be reimbursed.[38] In *New Zealand – Imports of Electrical Transformers from Finland*, the panel proposed to the Council 'that it addresses to New-Zealand a recommendation to revoke the anti-dumping determination and to reimburse the antidumping duty paid'.[39] Especially the United States opposed to a reimbursement of the anti-dumping duties and therefore decided not to adopt the report in *United States – Imposition of Anti-Dumping Duties on Imports of Seamless Stainless Steel Hollow Products from Sweden*. This panel had recommended 'to revoke the antidumping duties imposed' en 'reimburse the anti-dumping duties paid'.[40] In *United States – Anti-Dumping Duties On Gray Portland Cement and Cement Clinker from Mexico*, the panel even went further and recommended that 'the

---

[35] D Horovitz (n 5) 156.
[36] See eg PJ Kuyper 'The Law of GATT as a Special Field of International Law' in *Netherlands Yearbook of International Law* (vol XXV, Dordrecht, Martinus Nijhoff Publishers, 1994) 227 at 252–3; A Rosas 'Implementation and Enforcement of WTO Dispute Settlement Findings: An EU Perspective' (2001) *JIEL* 131 at 140–1 and P Ruttley 'WTO Dispute Settlement and Private Sector Interests: A Slow but Gradual Improvement?' in P Ruttley, I MacVay and M Weisberger (eds) *Due Process in WTO Dispute Settlement* (London: Cameron May, 2001) 177–9.
[37] This article will only focus on the case-law with regard to anti-dumping duties. The case law with regard to anti-subsidy measures will not be dealt with. For an overview also encompassing GATT and WTO practice with regard to anti-subsidy measures, see P Grane 'Remedies under WTO Law' (2001) *JIEL* 755 at 763–9.
[38] PJ Kuyper 'Het GATT en het Volkenrecht' in *Mededelingen van de Nederlandse Vereniging voor Internationaal Recht* (The Hague: Kluwer, 1993) 52.
[39] *New Zealand – Imports of Electrical Transformers from Finland*, report of the panel of 18 July 1985, BISD, 32S/55 at para 4.11.
[40] *United States – Imposition of Anti-Dumping Duties on Imports of Seamless Stainless Steel Hollow Products from Sweden*, report of the panel of 20 August 1990, ADP/47 at para 5.24.

Committee request the United States to revoke the anti-dumping duty order on gray portland cement and cement clinker from Mexico and to reimburse any anti-dumping duties paid or deposited under this order'.[41] Also the EC opposed, under the GATT-regime, to the reimbursement of anti-dumping duties. In *Brazil – Imposition of Provisional and Definitive Anti-Dumping Duties on Milk Powder and Certain Types of Milk from the European Economic Community*, the EC had eventually asked for the reimbursement of the anti-dumping duties but later withdrew its request.[42]

5.2 WTO Practice

Where a panel or the Appellate Body concludes that a measure is incompatible with a covered agreement, it shall recommend that the member concerned bring the measure into conformity with that agreement.[43] Article 19.1 DSU appears to follow GATT practice.[44] Panels and the Appellate Body may suggest ways in which the member concerned could bring its measure into conformity.[45] It is not yet clear how far these 'suggestions' may reach.

In *Guatemala – Anti-Dumping Investigation regarding Portland Cement from Mexico*,[46] Mexico requested the panel to recommend that Guatemala revoke the measure and also 'refund those anti-dumping duties already collected'.[47] The panel declined, noting that Article 19.1 DSU confines panels to recommending that the member concerned bring the measure into conformity. However, the panel added that Article 19.1 DSU did permit a panel to 'suggest' ways in which the member concerned could bring its measure into conformity. In this particular case, the panel ruled that the revocation of the duties collected was the only appropriate means to implement its recommendation since the entire anti-dumping investigation rested on an insufficient basis and therefore never should have been initiated. The ruling of the panel was appealed. The Appellate Body overturned the panel report

---

[41] *United States – Anti-Dumping Duties On Gray portland Cement and Cement Clinker from Mexico*, report of the panel of 7 September 1992, ADP/82 at para 6.2.

[42] *Brazil – Imposition of Provisional and Definitive Anti-Dumping Duties on Milk Powder and Certain Types of Milk from the European Economic Community*, report of the panel of 27 December 1993, SCM/179, para 200.

[43] Article 19.1 DSU.

[44] *Contra*: C Charmody 'Remedies and Conformity under the WTO Agreement' (2002) *JIEL* 307.

[45] D Palmeter and PC Mavroidis *Dispute Settlement in the World Trade Organization* (The Hague: Kluwer Law International, 1999) 164.

[46] *Guatemala – Antidumping Investigation Regarding Portland Cement from Mexico*, report of the panel of 16 June 1998, WT/DS60R. For an analysis of this report and other related reports, see DA Yocis 'Hardened Positions: Guatemala Cement and WTO Review of National Antidumping Determinations' (2001) *New York University Law Review* 1259.

[47] *Guatemala – Antidumping Investigation Regarding Portland Cement from Mexico*, report of the panel of 16 June 1998, WT/DS60R, at para 8.1.

on other grounds.[48] In a follow-up case, the panel refused to make a specific recommendation of reimbursement of anti-dumping duties.[49] It is important to note that the panel did not rule that a reimbursement of anti-dumping duties is per se excluded.

5.3   EC Law

If one accepts that the EC was obliged to revoke the anti-dumping duties after the ruling of the Appellate Body in *Bed Linen*, rather than to suspend these duties, the question arises whether these duties ought to be reimbursed on the basis of EC law as such. The WTO enabling Regulation precludes, in principle, a reimbursement of anti-dumping duties. However, if it is established that the legal basis of the anti-dumping duties imposed by the EC is in breach with WTO law, than the regulation imposing these duties should be null and void *ab initio*.[50] Consequently, a reimbursement of the anti-dumping duties collected ought to be considered by the EC.[51] The notice concerning the reimbursement of anti-dumping duties, which was recently adopted by the Commission, could provide a legal basis for such a reimbursement.[52] The aim of the notice is to 'allow for the reimbursement of anti-dumping duties which have already been paid where it is shown that the dumping margin on the basis of which duties were paid has been eliminated ...'.

The possibility provided by article 3 of the WTO enabling regulation, more in particular the provision that 'measures adopted pursuant to this Regulation shall take effect from the date of their entry into force and shall not serve as basis for the reimbursement of the duties collected prior to that date, unless otherwise provided for', does not appear to exclude such reimbursement.

An obvious question is whether there are any legal remedies available for exporters if the EC would decide not to reimburse the collected anti-dumping duties. One option is the initiation of an action for damages under article 288(2) EC Treaty. Article 288(2) EC Treaty imposes an obligation upon the EC to 'make good any damage caused by its institutions' and this 'in accordance with the general principles common to the laws of the Member States'. According to established case law,

---

[48] *Guatemala – Antidumping Investigation Regarding Portland Cement from Mexico*, report of the Appellate Body of 2 November 1998, WT/DS60/AB/R.
[49] *Guatemala – Antidumping Investigation Regarding Portland Cement from Mexico (II)*, report of the Panel of 24 October 2000, WT/DS156/R, at paras 9.5–9.7.
[50] See also J Branton (n 5) 65.
[51] Mavroidis reaches a similar conclusion in his comments on *Guatemala – Anti-Dumping Investigation regarding Portland Cement from Mexico*. See PC Mavroidis (n 21) 388.
[52] [2002] OJ C127/10 of 29 May 2002.

in order for the EC to incur non-contractual liability the applicant must prove the unlawfulness of the alleged conduct of the institution concerned, actual damage and the existence of a causal link between that conduct and the alleged damage.[53] Moreover, in the case of legislative measures involving choices of economic policy, an action under Article 288(2) EC Treaty will only be successful if the rule of law infringed is intended to confer rights on individuals.[54]

The illegality (ie WTO-incompatibility) of Regulation 2398/97, imposing anti-dumping duties, was clearly established in *Bed Linen* by a WTO panel and also by the Appellate Body. It would not be difficult to demonstrate that damages occurred a result of anti-dumping duties that were unlawfully imposed. In addition, the *nexus* between the regulation imposing the duties and the damages seems obvious. However, the *Bergaderm* test will be more difficult to comply with. It will be very difficult to demonstrate that the WTO rules infringed are intended to confer rights on individuals especially since the Court of First Instance has recently decided that '[T]he purpose of the WTO agreements is to govern relations between States or regional organisations for economic integration and not to protect individuals'.[55]

6. Conclusion

The analysis of the WTO enabling regulation has demonstrated that rulings of the WTO dispute settlement organs have a direct impact on intra European Community law. The statement that decisions of the DSB are not binding is not correct. One has to take into consideration that such decisions can even be invoked in legal actions before the Court of First Instance or the European Court of Justice.[56] A reimbursement of the unlawfully collected anti-dumping duties cannot a priori be excluded. The case-law of GATT and WTO panels is not always very clear on this subject, but there is nothing that seems to prevent a reimbursement on the basis of EC law as such. A refusal of the EC to do so, could result in the initiation of legal actions before the European courts in Luxembourg as indicated above. The statements made by the Commission and the

---

[53] See eg Case 26/81 *Oleifici Mediterranei v EEC* [1982] ECR 3057, para 16; Case T–175/94 *International Procurement Services v Commission* [1996] ECR II–729, para 44; Case T–113/96 *Edouard Dubois et Fils v Council and Commission* [1998] ECR II–125, para 54 and Case T–178/98 *Fresh Marine Company SA v Commission* [2000] ECR II–3331, para 54.
[54] Case C–352/98P *Laboratoires pharmaceutiques Bergaderm SA and J-J Goupil v Commission* [2000] ECR I–5291, paras 41–2.
[55] Case T–174/00 *Biret International SA v Council and Commission* not yet published in the ECR at para 62.
[56] See GA Zonnekeyn 'The Status of Adopted Panel and Appellate Body Reports in the European Court of Justice and the European Court of First Instance – The Banana Experience' (2000) *JWT* 93.

Council in the text of the WTO enabling regulation are disputable and should give rise to further thought and discussion.

CHAPTER VII

THE LATEST ON INDIRECT EFFECT OF WTO LAW IN THE EC
LEGAL ORDER – THE NAKAJIMA CASE LAW MISJUDGED?

CASE NOTE ON THREE JUDGMENTS OF THE COURT OF FIRST INSTANCE
IN THE INTERNAL EC BANANA BATTLE

The judgments of the Court of First Instance (CFI) in the banana cases of 20 March 2001 have shed some light on how the CF or the Court of Justice interpret the Nakajima line of case law, pursuant to which WTO law can serve as grounds for review in cases where the EC intends to implement a particular WTO obligation. The narrow interpretation given by the CFI to the '*Nakajima* doctrine' will make it very difficult to review the legality of EC law in the light of the obligations of the EC under WTO law.

1.   Introduction

The three *Bananas* judgments of the Court of First Instance in *Cordis*, *Bocchi* and *T Port*[1] represent an excellent opportunity to focus on two particular questions of enforceability of WTO law within the European Community legal order. First is the question of whether or not the CFI correctly applied the *Nakajima* line of case law, pursuant to which WTO law can serve as grounds for review in cases where the EC intends to implement a particular WTO obligation.[2] Second is the question of the status of adopted WTO panel and Appellate Body reports in the EC legal order.[3]

---

[1] Case T–18/99 *Cordis Obsst und Gemüse Grosshandel GmbH v Commission*; Case T–30/99 *Bocchi Food Trade International GmbH v Commission* and Case T–52/99 *T Port GmbH & Co KG v Commission*, judgements of 20 March 2001, not yet published in the ECR

[2] Case C–69/89 *Nakajima All Precision Co Ltd v Council* [1991] ECR I–2069. This case law has been explicitly confirmed by the ECJ in the *Portuguese Textiles* case. See Case C–149/96 *Portugal v Council* [1999] ECR I–8395. For a comment, see eg GM Berrisch and HG Kamann 'WTO-Recht im Gemeinschaftsrecht – (k)eine Kehrwende des EuGH' (2000) *EWS* 89; F Berrod 'La Cour de justice refuse l'invocabilité des accords OMC: essai de regulation de la mondialisation' (2000) *RTDE* 419; S Griller 'Judicial Enforceability of WTO law in the European Union. Annotation to Case C–149/96 *Portugal v Council*' (2000) *JIEL* 441; P Mengozzi 'La Cour de justice et l'applicabilité des règles de l'OMC en droit communautaire à la lumière de l'affaire Portugal c Conseil' (2000) *RDUE* 509; A Rosas, annotation on Case C–149/96 *Portugal v Council* (2000) CMLRev 797; N van den Broek 'Portugal v Council and the distinctive nature of the WTO Agreements' (2001) *JIEL* forthcoming copy on file with the author) and GA Zonnekeyn 'The Status of WTO Law in the EC Legal Order – The Final Curtain?' (2000) *JWT* 111.

[3] See on this subject, GA Zonnekeyn 'The Legal Status of WTO Panel Reports in the EC Legal Order. Some Reflections on the Opinion of Advocate General Mischo in the Atlanta Case' (1999) *JIEL* 723 and ibid 'The Status of Adopted Panel and Appellate Body Reports

continued ...

2. Factual Background

The factual background of the three cases is similar. The applicants were not satisfied with the annual quantity of bananas allocated to them following the adoption of Regulation 2362/98.[4] They asked for compensation for the loss suffered as a result of the adoption of Regulation 2362/98 by the Commission. Regulation 2362/98 laid down detailed rules for the implementation of Regulation 404/93 regarding imports of bananas into the EC. These rules allegedly conflicted with WTO law and certain general principles of EC law.[5]

The applicants submitted that the Commission's unlawful conduct included an infringement of GATT, GATS and the Agreement on Import Licensing Procedures (contained in Annex 1 to the WTO Agreement) as well as the arbitrary establishment of reference periods and infringement of the obligation to state reasons. They contended that the provisions of GATT constitute superior rules of law in which the prohibitions on discrimination and the most-favoured-nation clause were to be regarded as rules for the protection of individuals.

The applicants further considered that the WTO Agreement and the annexes thereto constitute a genuine world trade order with its own legal system and jurisdiction. WTO law is not negotiable and contains strict prohibitions, which can be restricted or temporarily set aside only by measures of the WTO, and not by unilateral measures on the part of a member. Some of the provisions of that new law are therefore directly applicable in EC law.

In regards to the possible inferences to be drawn from *Portugal v Council*, the applicants acknowledged that the ECJ had held that the WTO provisions did not have general direct effect within the EC legal system. They added, however, that this judgment did not conflict with the arguments submitted in support of their action to the effect that the EC institutions were guilty of misuse of power. The fact that the EC banana regime had been declared incompatible with WTO law by a panel and the Appellate Body, decisions having the force of *res judicata* and the efforts the EC had undertaken to rectify the infringements concerned, precluded the EC institutions from adopting further provisions in breach of those rules. The applicants further argued that since the EC had given an undertaking to the Dispute Settlement Body to repeal the provisions of its regulations

---

in the European Court of Justice and the European Court of First Instance – The Banana Experience' (2000) *JWT* 93.

[4] Commission Regulation (EC) 2362/98 of 28 October 1998 laying down detailed rules for the implementation of Council Regulation (EEC) 404/93 regarding imports of bananas into the Community [1998] OJ L293/32 of 31 October 1998.

[5] This article will only address the WTO-related arguments.

which conflicted with WTO rules, it had acted in breach of the principle *nemini licet venire contra factum proprium* when putting that undertaking into practice by adopting a regulation containing infringements of those rules. They explained that the principle expressed in that maxim (derived from the principle of good faith), constitutes a principle of EC law by which the legality of EC measures can be assessed by the EC judicature. The applicants are therefore entitled to plead infringement of the WTO rules on those grounds also.

In addition, the applicants stated that they did not seek to establish that the defendant was pursuing unlawful aims. Their contention was that the Commission, with full knowledge of the facts, infringed upon WTO rules in order to achieve its ends, namely, control of the market in bananas. Such conduct constitutes a new category of misuse of powers and means that the Commission is under an obligation to provide compensation irrespective of whether the WTO rules in question are designed to protect individuals. Individuals enjoy absolute protection against misuse of power by the EC institutions.

3. The Judgments of the CFI

The CFI ruled that in order for the EC to incur non-contractual liability, the applicant must prove the unlawfulness of the alleged conduct of the EC institution concerned, actual damage and the existence of a causal link between that conduct and the alleged damage.[6] In addition, the right to reparation also requires that the rule of law infringed upon be one that confers rights on individuals and that the breach of such a rule be sufficiently serious.[7]

With reference to *Portugal v Council*, the CFI ruled that since the WTO Agreement and its annexes are not, in principle, intended to confer rights on individuals, the EC cannot incur non-contractual liability as a result of infringement of them. As far as the misuse of powers is concerned, the CFI concluded that it is established case law that an act of an EC institution is vitiated by misuse of power only if it was adopted with the exclusive purpose of achieving an end other than that stated[8] and that a finding of misuse of powers may be made only on the basis of objective, relevant and consistent evidence.[9] Pursuant to the CFI, the applicants did

---

[6] See eg Case 26/81 *Oleifici Mediterranei v EEC* [1982] ECR 3057, para 16; Case T–113/96 *Dubois et Fils v Council and Commission* [1998] ECR II–125, para 54 and Case T–178/98 *Fresh Marine Company SA v Commission*, judgement of 24 October 2000, not yet reported in the ECR para 54.
[7] See Case C–352/98 P *Bergaderm and Others v Commission* [2000] ECR I–5291, paras 41 and 42.
[8] Case C–285/94 *Italy v Commission* [1997] ECR I–3519, para 52.
[9] Joined Cases T–551/93, T–231/94, T–232/94, T–233/94 and T–234/94 *Industrias Pesqueras Campos and Others v Commission* [1996] ECR II–247, para 168.

not establish, or even allege, that the Commission adopted Regulation 2362/98 or some of its provisions with the purpose of achieving an end other than that stated, which was to adopt all the provisions needed in order to bring into effect the arrangements for importing bananas into the EC introduced by Regulation 404/93. The applicants' argument that this was a new category of misuse of powers was, therefore, rejected.

In addition, the CFI ruled that the applicants' argument that the EC was guilty of misuse of powers in adopting a regulation containing infringements of WTO rules, or by continuing infringements already established when it had undertaken to comply with those rules, also had to be rejected. The CFI referred in this respect to the *Nakajima* and *Fediol* case law, according to which it is only where the EC intends to implement a particular obligation assumed in the context of the WTO, or where the EC measure refers expressly to the precise provisions of the agreements contained in the annexes to the WTO Agreement, that it is for the ECJ and the CFI to review the legality of the EC measure in question in light of the WTO rules. Pursuant to the CFI, neither the panel report of 22 May 1997[10] nor the Appellate Body report of 9 September 1997,[11] included any special obligations which the Commission intended to implement, within the meaning of the *Nakajima* case law, in Regulation 2362/98.[12] The regulation does not make express reference either to any specific obligations arising out of the reports of the WTO dispute settlement organs, or to specific provisions of the agreements contained in the annexes to the WTO Agreement.

4. Comments

4.1 Nakajima Misjudged?

In *Nakajima*, the applicant challenged a regulation imposing definitive anti-dumping duties on dot-matrix printers in Japan. Nakajima raised an exception of inapplicability of the basic anti-dumping regulation. On the other hand, it submitted grounds for the annulment of the definitive regulation. The plea of inapplicability was essentially based on the incompatibility of the basic anti-dumping regulation with the GATT

---

[10] WT/DS27/R *European Communities – Regime for the Importation, Sale and Distribution of Bananas*, report of the panel of 22 May 1997.

[11] WT/DS27/AB/R *European Communities – Regime for the Importation, Sale and Distribution of Bananas*, report of the Appellate Body of 9 September 1997.

[12] The English language version of the judgement refers in para 64 to a 'judgement' that does not make express reference to any specific obligations arising out of the panel or Appellate Body reports, or to specific provisions of the agreements contained in the annexes to the WTO Agreement. Obviously, the word judgement must be replaced by a reference to Regulation 2362/98. This follows clearly from the original German version of the judgement where it is said that 'Ebenso wenig verweist die "Verordnung Nr. 2362/98" ausdrücklich ...'.

Anti-Dumping Code, in connection with the calculation of the normal value. The ECJ rejected the pleading on the lack of direct effect of the GATT Anti-Dumping Code, because the applicant was not invoking the direct effect, but the compatibility of an EC measure with an international agreement that it was intended to implement. The ECJ concluded that such an incompatibility did not exist.

The most important part of the judgment referred to the possibility of invoking provisions of GATT in a direct action before the ECJ. The ECJ made a clear distinction between the direct effect of GATT as such, which plays a role in the relationship between national and EC law, and the possibility of invoking international agreements when challenging EC acts, which belongs to the relationship between international law and EC law. The ECJ emphasized that it was a direct action and that the regulation was adopted in order to implement the GATT Anti-Dumping Code. The relevant provisions of the GATT Anti-Dumping Code could therefore be invoked.

The distinction between the direct effect of GATT and the invocability of GATT, referred to in *Nakajima*, was also made by Advocate General Saggio in *Portugal v Council* with regard to the WTO Agreements.[13] The Advocate General argued that 'a provision of an agreement may be held not to have direct effect but that does not justify failing to recognize it as binding on the Community institutions and hence excluding it as a criterion for legality'.[14] The ECJ, however, disagreed and refused to depart from its now well-established case law, that the direct effect of the WTO Agreements serves as a pre-condition for using these as a ground for judicial review in a direct action before the ECJ or CFI. Already in 1972, in *International Fruit Company*,[15] the ECJ was asked to assess the validity of an EC regulation on the light of GATT. After having held that the EC was bound by GATT, the ECJ ruled that: '[B]efore invalidity can be relied upon before a [national] court, that provision of international law must also be capable of conferring rights on citizens of the Community which they can invoke before the courts'. The ECJ thus established a link between the possibility of invoking an international agreement for reviewing the legality of a Community act and the fact that certain provisions of that

---

[13] For a good analysis of the different concepts used to describe the 'effect' of international agreements, see JHJ Jackson 'Status of Treaties in Domestic Legal Systems: A Policy Analysis' (1992) *AJIL* 310.

[14] Paragraph 18 of the Opinion of Advocate General Saggio of 25 February 1999 in Case C–149/96 *Portugal v Council* [1999] ECR I–8395. See also A Desmedt 'Rechtstreekse werking van WTO-akkoorden via de achterdeur? De bevoegdheid van de nationale rechter tot de interpretatie van het TRIPS-akkoord na de Dior-zaak' (2001) *Nederlands Tijdschrift voor Europees Recht* 79 at 80; N van den Broek (n 2) and G Zonnekeyn (n 2) 120.

[15] Joined Cases 21–24/72 *International Fruit Company NV v Produktschap voor Groenten en Fruit* [1972] ECR 1219.

agreement may be relied upon by individuals before national courts. As a consequence of this link, the ECJ was not prepared to review the validity of such an act unless the agreement was capable of conferring rights on individuals. As Bebr – rightly – pointed out, the absence of direct effect of an international agreement protects the validity of Community acts.[16] The nexus between the direct effect and the invocability of an international agreement, was subject to criticism by some,[17] including Advocate General Saggio in *Portugal v Council*. As Maresceau phrased it: '[A]s far as GATT is concerned it would now seem a somewhat artificial construction if the court were to introduce in actions based on Article 173 the directly effective sword of Damocles'.[18]

As far as the application of the *Nakajima* case law is concerned, it might not always be easy to know when the EC intends to implement a particular obligation undertaken in the framework of the WTO.[19] In *Nakajima*, the anti-dumping regulation clearly implemented the GATT Anti-Dumping Code and references to this effect could be found in the recitals. The situation may not be so clear when an explicit reference is omitted. It is questionable, however, whether the absence of an explicit reference to the WTO Agreement(s) in a regulation would suffice to deprive applicants of the possibility to have the legality of the provisions of such a regulation assessed by the ECJ or CFI.[20] A rational reading of the *Nakajima* judgment reveals that the ECJ used a contextual and teleological approach.[21] It is therefore impossible for the EC to avoid review of the compatibility of a regulation with WTO law, simply by not referring to the relevant provisions of the WTO Agreement(s) which it intends to implement.[22]

Following the judgment of the ECJ in *Portugal v Council*, it was argued that there was still room for clarification as to the limits of the *Nakajima*

---

[16] G Bebr 'Agreements concluded by the Community and their Possible Direct Effect: from International Fruit Company to Kupferberg' (1983) *CMLRev* 35 at 46.

[17] See eg J Rideau 'Les accords internationaux dans la jurisprudence de la Cour de Justice des Communautés européennes: réflextions sur les relations entre les ordres juridiques international, communautaire et nationaux' (1990) *RGDIP* 289; M Maresceau 'The GATT in the case-law of the European Court of Justice' in FG Jacobs et al (eds) *The European Community and GATT* (Deventer: Kluwer, 1986) 107–26; HN Tagaras 'L'effet direct des accords internationaux de la Communauté' (1984) *CDE* 20; JHJ Bourgeois 'Effects of International Agreements in European Community Law: Are the Dice Cast?' (1984) *Michigan Law Review* 1250 and E-U Petersmann 'Application of GATT by the Court of Justice of the European Communities' (1983) *CMLRev* 403.

[18] M Maresceau (n 17) 116.

[19] As argued by F Castillo de la Torre 'The Status of GATT in EC Law, Revisited – The Consequences of the Judgement on the Banana Import Regime for the Enforcement of the Uruguay Round Agreements' (1995) *JWT* 53 at 59–60.

[20] F Castillo de la Torre 'The Status of GATT in EC Law Revisited – The Consequences of the Judgement on the Banana Import Regime for the Enforcement of the Uruguay Round Agreements' (1995) *JWT* 53 at 60 and F Berrod (n 2) 442.

[21] Similarly, see GM Berrisch and HG Kamann (n 2) 95.

[22] *Contra*: S Griller (n 2) 464.

ruling.[23] Griller even questioned whether the ECJ had not departed from the *Nakajima* case law and alleged that the legality of the regulations amending the EC's 1993 banana regime could not be reviewed in the light of WTO law.[24] He argues that the principle of reciprocity, used by the ECJ in *Portugal v Council* as one of the arguments to refute the possibility of invoking WTO law as a standard for review in a direct action before the ECJ, also applies once internal legislation has been enacted in the application of a particular obligation under WTO law.[25] He concluded that the intention to observe WTO obligations is not sufficient to activate the ECJ's competence to review secondary EC legislation in the light of WTO law, and that the future would have to determine which direction the ECJ would take.

It was finally not the ECJ, but the CFI that gave an indication about what the future case law would look like. The CFI is walking on very thin ice when it argues that Regulation 2362/98 was not adopted by the EC with the intention to implement any WTO obligation. A WTO panel, for example, explicitly referred to a statement of the EC that 'in order to live up to its WTO obligations as contained in its Schedules of GATS commitments, it had adopted an entirely new banana import regime, as set out in Regulations 1637 and 2362'.[26] It is obvious that Regulations 1637/98 and 2362/98 were adopted with a view to establishing a WTO-compatible banana regime. It can be argued therefore that the CFI 'misjudged' the principles of the *Nakajima* case law. In addition, paragraph 2 of the preamble to Regulation 1637/98,[27] which gives the Commission a 'mandate' to establish a WTO-compatible banana regime, explicitly provides as follows: '[W]hereas the Community's international commitments under the World Trade Organisation (WTO) and to the other signatories of the Fourth ACP-EC Convention should be met, whilst achieving at the same time the purposes of the common organisation of the market in bananas'. This would indicate that Regulation 2362/98 was, indeed, adopted with a view to implement the WTO obligations of the EC.[28]

[23] See A Rosas (n 2) 815.
[24] S Griller (n 2) 463–7.
[25] A similar point was raised by Berrisch and Kamman, see GM Berrisch and HG Kamman (n 2) 95. They argued that '[U]nerklärt bleibt allerdings, wie diese Lösung der mittelbaren Wirkung mit dem Kriterium der Gegenseitigkeit vereinbar ist'.
[26] WT/DS27/RW/ECU *European Communities – Regime for the Importation, Sale and Distribution of Bananas – Recourse to Article 21.5 by Ecuador*, report of 12 April 1999, para 4.56. This also follows from the judgement itself. In para 8, the CFI explicitly says that in order to comply with the panel and Appellate Body reports, the Council adopted Regulation 1637/98 and subsequently Regulation 2362/98. It would seem that CFI has contradicted itself.
[27] Council Regulation (EC) 1637/98 of 20 July 1998 amending Regulation (EEC) 404/93 on the common organisation of the market in bananas [1998] OJ L210/28 of 28 July 1998.
[28] The action for damages by Chiquita is noteworthy in this respect. Chiquita argues that '[F]ollowing a dispute settlement procedure in the WTO finding aspects of this regime to be WTO-incompatible, the EC agreed to make its banana regime compatible ... This was

continued ...

It is interesting to note in this context, that the EC's new banana regime, which entered into force on 1 July 2001, does not refer to any obligation of the EC under WTO law.[29] It does mention, however, that using the three-year period 1994 to 1996 'can also resolve a dispute which has been going on for a number of years with certain of the Community's trading partners'.[30] This statement, in combination with the numerous press statements made by the EC clearly indicate that Regulation 896/2001 intends to bring the EC banana regime into compliance with WTO law. A narrow, textual interpretation of the *Nakajima* case law would possibly exclude the possibility to review this new regulation in the light of WTO law. However, when looking at the objective of Regulation 896/2001, that is the establishment of a WTO-compatible banana regime in view of the earlier panel and Appellate Body reports, there cannot be any doubt that it purports to implement the WTO obligations of the EC.

5. The Legal Status of Adopted Appellate Body Reports in the EC

The applicants argued that the EC arrangements for banana imports had been declared incompatible with WTO law by 'a decision' having the force of *res judicata* and that the EC had undertaken to rectify the infringements concerned. This precluded the EC institutions from adopting further provisions in breach of those rules. The idea that panel reports have the legal authority of *res judicata* had already been advocated in the past,[31] and also, more recently, with regard to WTO panel and Appellate Body reports.[32]

---

purportedly done by Council Regulation No 1634/98 and Commission Regulation No 2362/98'. See Case T–19/01, *Chiquita Brands International Inc Chiquita Banana Company BV and Chiquita Italia SpA v Commission* [2001] OJ C108/23 of 7 April 2001.

[29] Commission Regulation (EC) 896/2001 of 7 May 2001 laying down detailed rules for applying Council Regulation (EEC) 404/93 as regards the arrangements for importing bananas into the Community [2001] OJ L126/6 of 8 May 2001. Corrigendum [2001] OJ L133/19 of 16 May 2001.

[30] See the 5th recital of the preamble to Regulation 896/2001.

[31] P Pescatore 'The GATT Dispute Settlement Mechanism. Its Present Situation and its Prospects' (1993) *JWT* 5 at 16.

[32] See eg JM Beneyto 'The EU and the WTO. Direct Effect of the New Dispute Settlement System?' (1996) *EuZW* 295; JHJ Bourgeois 'International Jurisprudence and Domestic Law: Some Comments from a European Community Perspective' in KR Simmonds and BHW Hill (eds) *Law and Practice Under the GATT* (New York: Oceana Publications, 1993) 10–13; T Cottier 'Dispute Settlement in the World Trade Organization: Characteristics and Structural Implications for the European Union' (1998) *CMLRev* 325 at 369–75; P Eeckhout 'The Domestic Legal Status of the WTO Agreement: Interconnecting Legal Systems' (1997) *CMLRev* 11 at 51–5; JH Jackson 'The Legal Meaning of a GATT Dispute Settlement Report: Some Reflections' in Blokker and Muller (eds) *Towards More Effective Supervision by International Organisations. Essays in Honour of Henry G Schermers* (vol I, Dordrecht: Kluwer, 1994) 149–64; N Lavranos 'Die Rechtswirkung von WTO panel reports im Europäischen Gemeinschaftrecht sowie im deutschen Verfassungsrecht' (1999) Europarecht 289; M Montañà i Mora 'A GATT With Teeth: Law Wins Over Politics in the Resolution of International Trade Disputes' (1993) *Colum J Transnat'l L* 103 at 175–6; J Nyberg 'Will the Fight against

continued ...

The ECJ has confirmed that the EC may enter into an international agreement whereby a judicial entity is established, provided that the structure and the jurisdiction of such entities are compatible with the EC Treaty. In 1991, the ECJ gave an opinion pursuant to Article 300 of the EC Treaty (ex Article 228) before the draft agreement on the European Economic Area (EEA) was concluded between the Member States of the European Free Trade Association (EFTA).[33] One of the crucial questions with which the ECJ dealt was whether the EEA Agreement's system of judicial supervision for the settlement of disputes was compatible with the EC Treaty. Under the EEA Agreement, an EEA Court was proffered the jurisdiction to interpret and apply the provisions of the Agreement in disputes between the Contracting Parties.

The ECJ declared that the proposed jurisdiction given to the EEA Court was incompatible with the EC Treaty on the following grounds. Since the EEA Court had the competence to interpret the EEA Agreement of which the provisions were identical with the corresponding provisions of the EC Treaty, there was a risk that the EEA Court and the ECJ would make different interpretations, especially since the two agreements had different purposes. Interpretations made by the EEA Court were therefore liable to affect EC law and, subsequently, the EEA court system would be in conflict with the role of the ECJ under Article 220 (ex Article 164) and Article 292 (ex Article 219) of the EC Treaty, and therefore, in conflict with the very foundations of the EC.[34]

However, the ECJ declared that there were certain conditions under which it would be bound by the decisions of another court. After recalling its case law on the binding effect of international agreements concluded by the EC and on its own jurisdiction to interpret those agreements, the ECJ decided that:

> [W]here, however, an international agreement provides for its own system of courts, including a court with jurisdiction to settle disputes between the Contracting Parties to the agreement, and, as

the European Community Common Banana Market lead to Conflicts of a Constitutional Character?' (1997) *ELSA Selected Papers on European Law* 211 at 244–5; S Peers 'Banana Split: WTO Law and Preferential Agreements in the EC Legal Order' (1999) *EFA Rev* 195 at 205–12; A Reinisch 'Entschädigung für die unbeteiligten "Opfer" des Hormon- und Bananensteites nach Art. 228 II EG?' (2000) *EuZW* 42 at 48–9; C Schmid 'Immer wieder Bananen: Der Status des GATT/WTO – Systems im Gemeinschaftrecht' (1998) *NJW* 190 at 196; A Weber and F Moos 'Rechtswirkungen von WTO-Streitbeilegungsentscheidungen im Gemeinschaftrecht' (1999) *EuZW* 229 and the contributions by GA Zonnekeyn (n 3).

[33] Opinion 1/91 *Draft agreement relating to the creation of the European Economic Area* [1991] ECR I–6079.

[34] In a subsequent opinion, the ECJ held that the new provisions of the EEA Agreement on the settlement of disputes were now compatible with the EC Treaty. See Opinion 1/92 *Opinion on the revised draft Agreement on the European Economic Area* [1992] ECR I–2821.

a result, to interpret its provisions, the decisions of that court will be binding on the Community institutions, including the Court of Justice. Those decisions will also be binding in the event the Court of Justice is called upon to rule, by way of a preliminary ruling or in a direct action, on the interpretations of the international agreement, in so far as that agreement is an integral part of the Community legal order. An international agreement providing for such a system of courts is in principle compatible with Community law. The Community's competence in the field of international relations and its capacity to conclude international agreements necessarily entails the power to submit to the decisions of a court which is created or designated by the such an agreement as regards the interpretations and application of its provisions.[35]

Here, the ECJ emphasised the binding character of judicial decisions on disputes between the contracting parties to an agreement for the ECJ, where the ECJ is called upon to rule on the interpretation of the agreement.[36] Moreover, a closer look at Opinion 1/91 reveals that the ECJ implicitly agreed with the concept that the binding character of judicial decisions on disputes between the contracting parties to an international agreement does not depend on the direct effect of such an agreement. In Opinion 1/91, the ECJ assumed that the EEA Agreement did not have direct effect.[37] This did not prevent the ECJ from holding that the decisions of the EEA Court could be binding for the ECJ.

Under the GATT dispute settlement mechanism – in its pre-Uruguay Round version – it could have been argued that the reasoning of the ECJ in Opinion 1/91 would not have applied because the panels were not 'court-like' but rather conciliatory bodies.[38] Since the WTO dispute settlement mechanism is now far more judicial in nature,[39] it can be argued

---

[35] Paragraphs 39 and 40 of Opinion 1/91 *Draft agreement relating to the creation of the European Economic Area* [1991] ECR I–6079.

[36] P Eeckhout (n 4) 52.

[37] See in particular paras 21 and 27 of the Opinion. See W van Gerven 'The Genesis of EEA Law and the Principles of Primacy and Direct Effect' (1992) *Fordham International Law Journal* 955 at 968. It should be emphasised that the EEA Agreement as it now stands, has direct effect if the criteria for direct effect are fulfilled See S Norberg et al *The European Economic Area. EEA Law. A Commentary on the EEA Agreement* (Stockholm: Fritzes, 1993) 203.

[38] See M Montañà i Mora (n 23) 175. The ECJ has established the following criteria in order to determine whether a national 'judicial' body qualifies as a court for tribunal for the purposes of establishing the ECJ's jurisdiction under Article 234 of the EC Treaty (ex Article 177): (i) the body concerned must be established by law; (ii) it must be a permanent body; (iii) its jurisdiction must be compulsory; (iv) the procedure before it must be inter partes; (v) it must apply the rule of law; and (vi) it must be an independent body. See Case C–416/96 *Nour Eddline El-Yassinin v Secretary of State for the Home Department* [1999] ECR I–1209. Although in a different context, it is submitted that a panel and, undoubtedly, the Appellate Body would satisfy these criteria.

[39] Petersmann argues that the WTO dispute settlement system has contributed largely to a greater judicialisation of the international economic system and could inspire dispute settlement systems in other non-economic areas. See E-U Petersmann, 'Dispute Settlement
continued ...

that if the ECJ were to maintain the reasoning of Opinion 1/91, it should be bound by the panel or Appellate Body reports adopted by the WTO Dispute Settlement Body. This line of reasoning would be valid regardless of whether the ECJ grants direct effect to the WTO Agreement, since Opinion 1/91 of the ECJ provides that the decisions of a court set up under an international agreement to which the EC is party would already bind the ECJ 'in so far as that agreement is an integral part of the Community legal order'.[40] As the WTO Agreement is an integral part of the EC's legal order pursuant to Article 300 of the EC Treaty (ex Article 228),[41] the EC institutions, including the ECJ, are bound by panel and Appellate Body reports adopted under the WTO dispute settlement mechanism.[42]

However, a WTO panel or Appellate Body report can only be invoked in legal actions before the ECJ or CFI, in those cases in which the panel or Appellate Body has established that certain EC rules or practices are not in conformity with WTO law and has required the EC to bring them into conformity with the WTO law.[43] This approach is correct in view of the limited precedential effect of WTO panel or Appellate Body reports which are only binding on the parties to the dispute.[44] It is unthinkable that the EC would be bound by a ruling of the Appellate Body in a dispute in which it has not at all been involved. This approach has been confirmed

in International Economic Law – Lessons for Strengthening International Dispute Settlement in Non-Economic Areas' (1999) *JIEL* 189.

[40] Eeckhout has argued that '[W]here a violation is established the binding character of the agreement and the principle of legality should in my view trump any lack of direct effect'. See P Eeckhout (n 23) 53. This line of reasoning implies that the direct effect of the WTO Agreement(s) is a per se condition which is then ignored.

[41] The EC is bound by the WTO Agreement(s) by virtue of Council Decision 94/800/EC of 22 December 1994 concerning the conclusion on behalf of the European Community, as regards matters falling within is competence, of the agreements reached in the Uruguay Round multilateral negotiations (1986–1994) [1994] OJ L336/1.

[42] Advocate General Saggio has argued that the WTO dispute settlement rules are not capable of limiting the jurisdiction of the ECJ for the following two reasons: (i) the WTO dispute settlement rules do not provide for the establishment of a judicial body but for a system for the settlement of disputes between persons subject to international law (the body which adopts the decisions or recommendations is a political body to which individuals within a particular domestic legal order have no access) and (ii) the establishment of a judicial body whose jurisdiction was not limited to interpreting and applying the agreement but also included the power to annul measures of the EC institutions would be incompatible with the EC legal order inasmuch as it would clearly conflict with Article 220 of the EC Treaty (ex Article 164). See para 23 of the Opinion of 25 February 1999 in Case C–149/96 *Portugal v Council* [1999] ECR I–8395. This line of reasoning is based on a misconception of the WTO dispute settlement mechanism as neither panels, nor the Appellate Body are able to invalidate Community acts. They can merely establish that a Community act infringes WTO law and recommend that the EC should bring its legislation in conformity with those rules. The 'invocability' of a panel or Appellate Body report in a legal proceeding before the CFI or the ECJ is a completely different matter.

[43] See P Eeckhout (n 23) 53–4.

[44] On this subject, see A Chua 'The Precedential Effect of WTO Panel and Appellate Body Reports' (1998) *LJIL* 45.

by the *Appellate Body in Japan – Taxes on Alcoholic Beverages*,[45] where it held that '[A]dopted panel reports are an important part of the GATT acquis. They are often considered by subsequent panels. They create legitimate expectations among the WTO members, and, therefore, should be taken into account where they are relevant to any dispute. However, they are not binding, except with respect to resolving the particular dispute between the parties to that dispute'.

6. Conclusion

The most important aspect of the judgments analysed above is the minimalist application of the *Nakajima* doctrine by the CFI. The CFI argued that Regulation 2362/98, adopted by the EC with a view to establishing a WTO-compatible banana regime, did not intend to implement any WTO obligations stemming from the panel and Appellate Body reports in the banana case. The approach followed by the CFI is not correct since Regulation 2362/98 was clearly adopted to establish a WTO-compatible regime in line with the panel and Appellate Body reports. An overly narrow interpretation of the *Nakajima* case law will further limit the possibilities of applicants to invoke WTO law as a standard for reviewing EC law in actions before the ECJ and CFI. Taking into consideration the increasing relevance of WTO law for private companies, it can only be hoped that either the CFI or the ECJ will choose for a teleological and broad interpretation of the *Nakajima* line of case-law, which will extend the possibilities for reviewing the legality of Community acts in the light of WTO law. In order for the '*Nakajima* doctrine' to apply, an implicit reference to WTO law should suffice.

In addition, the CFI did not accord any legal value to the panel and Appellate Body reports referred to by the applicants. Nevertheless, adopted panel and Appellate Body reports are binding for the EC and the compensation mechanism cannot prevent those reports from being invoked in legal proceedings before the CFI or the ECJ. By accepting compensation, the responding member in a dispute, *in se*, recognises the binding effect of a panel or Appellate Body report, since it acknowledges that its legislation or other measures are in breach of WTO law. The compensation mechanism was not meant to give WTO members complete freedom to leave WTO-inconsistent measures in place and does not, as a matter of principle, accord a 'right' to violate a legal obligation entered into under an international agreement. It merely constitutes a practical option temporarily to defuse a dispute between WTO members who are parties to a dispute.

---

[45] WT/DS8/AB/R, WT/DS10/AB/R, WT/DS11/AB/R *Japan – Taxes on Alcoholic Beverages*, report of the Appellate Body of 4 October 1996.

CHAPTER VIII

EC LIABILITY FOR NON-IMPLEMENTATION OF ADOPTED WTO PANEL AND APPELLATE BODY REPORTS – THE EXAMPLE OF THE 'INNOCENT EXPORTERS' IN THE BANANA CASE

'Darf die EG die völkerrechtlichen WTO-Streitbeilegungsverfahren ignorieren, wenn sie die Völkerrechtswidrigkeit des EG-Rechts festgestellt haben?'[1]

Summary

The question whether the European Community can be held liable, at the Community level, for the non-implementation of adopted WTO panel and Appellate Body reports has yet not been answered by the European Court of Justice or the European Court of First Instance. The actions for damages introduced by five European companies adversely affected by the sanctions imposed by the United States following non-compliance by the European Community with the WTO panel and Appellate Body reports in the transatlantic banana dispute, represent an excellent opportunity to address the aforementioned question. It will be argued that the legal proceedings initiated by these companies, also referred to as the 'innocent exporters', may be successful and that the EC can be held liable for the non-implementation of the WTO panel and Appellate Body reports in the transatlantic banana dispute.

1. Introduction

The relationship between the European Community (EC) and the World Trade Organization (WTO) is one of discord *and* harmony, rather than discord *or* harmony. Discord, because WTO panels and the Appellate Body have ruled against the EC in a number of cases.[2] Harmony, because

---

[1] E-U Petersmann 'Darf die EG das Völkerrecht ignorieren?' (1997) *EuZW* 325–31.
[2] See eg WT/DS26/48/R *European Communities – Measures Affecting Meat and Meat Products (Hormones)*, report of the panel of 18 August 1997; WT/DS26/48/AB/R *European Communities – Measures Affecting Meat and Meat Products (Hormones)*, report of the Appellate Body of 16 January 1998; WT/DS27/R *European Communities – Regime for the Importation, Sale and Distribution of Bananas*, report of the panel of 22 May 1997; WT/DS27/AB/R *European Communities – Regime for the Importation, Sale and Distribution of Bananas*, report of the Appellate Body of 9 September 1997; WT/DS62/67/68/R *European Communities – Customs Classification of Certain Computer Equipment*, report of the panel of 5 February 1998; WT/DS62/67/68/AB/R *European Communities – Customs Classification of Certain Computer*

continued ...

the EC is generally considered as a vigorous proponent of international trade liberalisation.

This article will focus on the subject of discord rather than harmony and will address the question whether the EC institutions can be held liable, under EC law, for the continuous and conscious non-implementation of panel and Appellate Body reports adopted by the WTO Dispute Settlement Body (DSB). The panel and Appellate Body reports adopted in the *Bananas* case and the sanctions imposed by the United States following the non-implementation of these reports are a well-known example.[3] The article will shed some light on the question whether European companies can claim compensation from the EC for the damages they suffered following the imposition of punitive import duties by the United States.[4] The subject is certainly not at all hypothetical. This is evidenced by the five actions for damages that have been introduced before the Court of First Instance of the European Communities (CFI) by the companies adversely affected by the sanctions imposed by the United States.[5]

Equipment, report of the Appellate Body of 5 June 1998; WT/DS69/R *European Communities – Measures affecting the Importation of Certain Poultry Products*, report of the panel of 12 March 1998; WT/DS69/AB/R *European Communities – Measures affecting the Importation of Certain Poultry Products*, report of the Appellate Body of 13 July 1998 and WT/DS141/R *European Communities – Anti-Dumping Duties on Imports of Cotton-Type Bed Linen From India*, report of the panel of 30 October 2000.

[3] For an excellent overview of the 'banana saga', both on the EC and WTO level, see N Komuro 'The EC Banana Regime and Judicial Control', *JWT* 5 (2000), pp. 1-87 and M Salas and JH Jackson 'Procedural Overview of the WTO EC – Banana Dispute' (2000) *JIEL* 145–66. For a very recent overview of the banana dispute, see E Patterson 'The US-EU Banana Dispute' (February 2001) ASIL Insight.

[4] See on the same subject, A Reinisch 'Entschädigung für die unbeteiligten "Opfer" des Hormonen- und Bananenstreites nach Art. 288 II EG?' (2000) *EuZW* 2 42–51.

[5] The Understanding on Rules and Procedures governing the Settlement of Disputes (DSU) does not use the term 'sanction'. The DSU provides that if a government fails to bring a measure found to be inconsistent with a WTO rule into compliance, it must enter into negotiations with the government invoking dispute settlement and that if no mutually acceptable compensation is agreed upon, the complaining Member may seek authorisation from the WTO Dispute Settlement Body (DSB) to suspend the application to the member concerned of concessions or other obligations under the covered agreements. This wording was based on the provisions of GATT 1947 which provided that the Contracting Parties may give a ruling in a complaint regarding the failure of a party to carry out its obligations, and if the Contracting Parties 'consider that the circumstances are serious enough to justify such action, they may authorize a contracting party or parties to suspend the application to any other contracting party or parties of such concessions or other obligations as they determine to be appropriate in the circumstances' (Article XXX:2 of GATT). See S Charnovitz 'Should the Teeth Be Pulled? A Preliminary Assessment of WTO Sanctions' paper prepared for a conference on *The Political Economy of International Trade Law* (University of Minnesota Law School, 15 September 2000) (available at www.gets.org.).

2. The Cases – a Brief Overview

In *Fiamm*,[6] the applicant is an Italian battery manufacturer exporting to the United States. In support of its claims, Fiamm argues that the retaliatory measures imposed by the United States are the direct consequence of the EC maintaining in force a system of rules which the WTO has already ruled unlawful and that there has been a serious breach of a number of higher legal rules protecting individuals, such as the principle of '*pacta sunt servanda*', the protection of legitimate expectations, legal certainty, the right to property, and the right to pursue an economic activity, and also of the principle of sound administration.

In *Le Laboratoire du Bain*,[7] the applicant is a French company specialising in the development and manufacture of effervescent cosmetic bath products, exporting a significant proportion of its production to the United States. It maintains that the damages which it has suffered are a direct consequence of the adoption and retention by the EC of a system for the importation of bananas in breach of WTO rules and of the fact that the EC omitted to take into account the situation of companies subject to sanctions, which was bound to result from the approach followed by the EC. It claims a violation of the principles of equality and non-discrimination, the protection of legitimate expectations, freedom to pursue a professional activity and proportionality.

In *Claude-Anne de Solène*[8] and *Groupe Fremaux and Palais Royal Inc*,[9] the applicants are manufacturers of cotton bed linen, a significant proportion of which is marketed in the United States, who seek compensation for the losses caused by the sanctions applied by the United States. In support of their action, the applicants claim first, that by adopting and maintaining in force an 'unlawful' banana regime, the EC is acting in breach of the rules laid down by the WTO. Second, the applicants rely on an infringement of the principles of equality, non-discrimination and protection of legitimate expectations, to the extent that the EC unlawfully failed to have regard to the situation of companies affected by the sanctions. Finally, the applicants base their action, in the alternative, on the objective responsibility of the EC for the unequal discharge of public burdens.

In *Cartondruck*,[10] the applicant is a German manufacturer of printed and processed collapsible cardboard cartons for proprietary products,

---

[6] Case T–69/00 *Fiamm SpA and Fiamm Technologies Inc v Commission and Council* [2000] OJ C135/30.
[7] Case T–151/00 *Le Laboratoire du Bain v Council and Commission* [2000] OJ C247/30.
[8] Case T–297/00 *Claude-Anne de Solène v Council and Commission* [2000] OJ C355/30.
[9] Case T–301/00 *Groupe Fremaux SA and Palais Royal Inc v Council and Commission* [2000] OJ C355/32.
[10] Case T–320/00 *CD Cartondruck GmbH & Co KG v Commission and Council* [2000] OJ C355/39.

largely intended for the United States market. Cartondruck alleges that the adoption of Regulations 1637/98 and 2362/98,[11] which were found to be inconsistent with WTO law, and the subsequent failure by the EC to adopt a WTO-compatible banana regime, infringe WTO law. This would follow in particular from the fact that the reformed organisation of the market for bananas is intended to transpose WTO law and from the very nature of WTO law and the compulsory WTO dispute settlement mechanism. The applicant further maintains that the conduct of the EC infringes the principle of the protection of legitimate expectations, the right to engage freely in economic activity, the right to property and the prohibition of discrimination. In respect of all these infringements, the applicant alleges that the EC has acted negligently. In addition, the applicant has instigated a claim for compensation in respect of lawful conduct on behalf of the EC.

In *Beamglow*,[12] the applicant is an English company active in the business of high quality printing on folding carton packaging for products such as cosmetics and fragrances. The applicant argues that, as a result of the retaliatory measures taken by the United States, the United States market has been entirely closed off, so that heavy investments in capital adapted specifically to the needs of this market have been rendered worthless. The company therefore decided to claim damages from the EC. In support of this claim the applicant submits that the damages it has suffered are the direct result of the EC's unlawful failure to comply with its international obligations.

3. Background

Following the EC's non-compliance with the findings of the Appellate Body in the banana case, the United States Trade Representative (USTR) announced in December 1998 that the United States would impose increased import duties of 100 per cent on selected products from the EC as from 3 March 1999.[13] Consequently, the United States customs authorities started to withhold liquidation on imports from the EC concerning a list of products, together valued at US$520 million on an annual basis and to impose a contingent liability for 100 per cent duties on each individual importation of affected products as from 3 March

---

[11] Council Regulation (EC) 1637/98 of 20 July 1998 amending Regulation (EEC) 404/93 on the common organisation of the market in bananas [1998] OJ L210/28 of 28 July 1998 and Commission Regulation (EC) 2362/98 of 28 October 1998 laying down detailed rules for the implementation of Council Regulation (EC) 404/93 regarding imports of bananas into the Community [1998] OJ L293/32.

[12] Case T–383/00 *Beamglow Ltd v Council, European Parliament and Commission* [2001] OJ C61/21.

[13] See Office of the United States Trade Representative 'USTR Announces List of European Products Subject to Increased Tariffs' Press Release 98–113 of 21 December 1998.

1999.[14] Later, in response to the decision by the arbitrators that the EC's amended banana regime was incompatible with WTO law and that the United States was entitled to suspend tariff concessions covering trade to an amount of US$191.4 million per year,[15] the USTR announced the final list of products on which the United States imposed a 100 per cent ad valorem duty as from 3 March 1999.[16] After having obtained the approval of the WTO Dispute Settlement Body on 19 April 1999, the United States effectively imposed the punitive import duties.[17] The imposition of the punitive import duties by the USTR was taken under the authority granted under Section 301 of the Trade Act.

The EC rejected the retroactive application of the punitive import duties as a blatant violation of the explicit obligations that the United States had accepted under WTO law and contended that the measure made effective by the United States as of 3 March 1999 deprived EC imports into the United States (of the products in question) of the right to a duty not in excess of the rate bound in the United States schedule of commitments. The EC further contended that, by requiring the deposit of a bond to cover the contingent liability for 100 per cent duties, the United States customs had effectively imposed 100 per cent duties on each individual importation. The EC alleged violations of Articles 3, 21, 22 and 23 of the Understanding on Rules and Procedures governing the Settlement of Disputes (DSU) and Articles I, II, VIII and XI of GATT 1994. The EC also alleged nullification and impairment of benefits under GATT 1994, as well as the impediment of the objectives of the DSU and GATT 1994. The EC had requested urgent consultations pursuant to Article 4.8 of the DSU.

The panel issued its report on 17 July 2000.[18] In its view, by putting that measure into place prior to the time authorised by the DSB, the United States had made a unilateral determination that the revised EC banana regime in respect of its banana imports, sales and distribution regime violated WTO rules, contrary to Articles 23.2(a) and 21.5, first sentence, of the DSU. In doing so, the United States did not abide by the DSU

---

[14] See Office of the United States Trade Representative 'United States Takes Customs Action on European Imports' Press Release 99–17 of 3 March 1999.
[15] WT/DS27/ARB *European Communities – Regime for the Importation, Sale and Distribution of Bananas – Recourse to Arbitration by the European Communities Under Article 22.6 of the DSU*, decision by the arbitrators of 9 April 1999.
[16] See Office of the United States Trade Representative 'USTR Announces Final Product List in Bananas Dispute' Press Release 99–35 of 9 April 1999.
[17] See the Notice published in the Federal Register of 19 April 1999 on the 'Implementation of WTO Recommendations Concerning the European Communities' Regime for the Importation, Sale and Distribution of Bananas'.
[18] WT/DS165/R United States – *Import Measures on Certain Products from the European Communities*, report of the panel of 17 July 2000.

and thus also violated Article 23.1 together with Articles 23.2(a) and 21.5 of the DSU. The panel further found that the increased bonding requirements of the measure of 3 March 1999 as such led to violations of Articles II:1(a) and II:1(b), first sentence. The increased interest charges, costs and fees resulting from the 3 March measure violated Article II:1(b), last sentence. The measure in question also violated Article I of the GATT 1994. In light of these conclusions, the measure of 3 March 1999 constituted a suspension of concessions or other obligations within the meaning of Articles 3.7, 22.6 and 23.2(c) of the DSU imposed without DSB authorisation and during the ongoing Article 22.6 arbitration process. In suspending concessions in those circumstances, the United States did not abide by the DSU and thus violated Article 23.1 together with Articles 3.7, 22.6 and 23.2(c) of the DSU.

On 12 September 2000, the EC notified its intention to appeal certain issues of law and legal interpretations developed by the panel. The Appellate Body issued its report on 11 December 2000 and concluded that the panel had erred by stating that the WTO consistency of a measure taken by a member to comply with recommendations and rulings of the DSB can be determined by arbitrators appointed under Article 22.6 of the DSU, and, thus, concluded that the panel's statements on this issue had no legal effect.[19] It also concluded that the panel had erred by stating that '[o]nce a Member imposes DSB authorised suspensions of concessions or obligations, that Member's measure is WTO compatible (it was explicitly authorised by the DSB)', and, thus, concluded that this statement has no legal effect. The Appellate Body also reversed the panel's findings that the increased bonding requirements were inconsistent with Articles II:1(a) and II:2(b), first sentence, of the GATT 1994, and reversed the panel's finding that, by adopting the 3 March measure, the United States acted inconsistently with Article 23.2(a) of the DSU. As it upheld the panel's finding that the 3 March 1999 measure, the measure at issue in this dispute, was no longer in existence, the Appellate Body did not make any recommendation to the DSB pursuant to Article 19.1 of the DSU.

The findings of the Appellate Body, that the retroactive application of the punitive import duties to 3 March 1999 did not constitute an infringement of WTO law, could have repercussions for the actions for damages introduced by the companies referred to above. If the duties imposed as from 3 March 1999 had been unlawful under WTO law, as the panel had ruled, the European exporters would not have been able to request compensation from the EC since the United States was not entitled to impose the punitive import duties. Under these conditions,

---

[19] WT/DS165/AB/R *Import Measures on Certain Products from the European Communities*, report of the Appellate Body of 11 December 2000.

they should have initiated legal actions in the national courts of the United States.

On 19 December 2000, the EU Agriculture Council adopted the Commission's proposal for a new import system for bananas.[20] It was decided to implement a transitional tariff quota regime on the basis of a first come, first served (FCFS) system. The regulation should come into force on 1 April 2001. The Council agreed that the tariff quotas are a transitional measure leading to a flat tariff in 2006 at the latest. Before a flat tariff can be applied, the Commission will have to conduct negotiations with the main banana suppliers under Article XXVIII of GATT. The Commission strongly believes that its proposal will put an end to the banana dispute. The United States, however, seems to take a more careful approach and is still casting doubts on the WTO compatibility of the Commission proposal.[21]

4. The Implementation of Adopted WTO Panel and Appellate Body Reports – is Implementation Compulsory?

The question whether there is an obligation for WTO members to implement adopted panel or Appellate Body reports has been the object of a fierce debate in legal doctrine.[22] The author takes the view that WTO rules, as well as DSB recommendations, should be considered to be binding legal obligations.

In the *Portuguese Textiles* case,[23] the ECJ focused – for the first time – on the legal nature of the WTO dispute settlement mechanism. The issue

---

[20] See Commission Press Release IP/00/1502 of 20 December 2000 'Fischler Welcomes Council Decision Designed to End the Banana Dispute'. For the text of the Commission proposal, see COM(2000) of 4 October 2000 'Communication from the Commission to the Council on the "First Come, First Served" method for the banana regime and the implications of "a tariff only" system'.
[21] See 'EU banana decision leaves wiggle room' (2000) *Inside US Trade* 22–3.
[22] See JH Bello 'The WTO Dispute Settlement Understanding: Less is More' (1996) *Am J Int'l L* 416–18. A – in my view – correct response to this article was provided by JH Jackson 'The WTO Dispute Settlement Understanding – Misunderstandings on the Nature of Legal Obligation' (1996) *Am J Int'l L* 60–4 reprinted in Cameron & Campbell (eds) *Dispute Resolution in the WTO* (London: Cameron May, 1998) 69–74; J Pauwelyn 'Enforcement and Countermeasures in the WTO: Rules Are Rules – Toward a More Collective Approach' (2000) *Am J Int'l L* 335–47 and TM Reiff and M Forestal 'Revenge of the Push-me, Pull-You: The Implementation Process Under the WTO Dispute Settlement Understanding' (1998) 3 *Int'l Law* 755–88.
[23] Case C–149/96 *Portugal v Council* [1999] ECR I–8395. For a comment, see eg G Berrisch and H-G Kamann 'WTO-Recht im Gemeinschaftsrecht – (k)eine Kehrwende des EuGH' (2000) 3 *EWS* 89–97; F Berrod 'La Cour de justice refuse l'invocabilité des accords OMC: essai de regulation de la mondialisation' (2000) 3 *RTDE* 419–50; A Desmedt 'European Court of Justice on the Effect of WTO Agreements in the EC Legal Order' (2000) 1 *LIEI* 93–101; N Forwood 'The Status of WTO Law in the Community Legal Order' paper presented on 10 November 2000 in London at the 4th Annual Conference of the World
continued ...

had already been raised in two earlier cases brought before the ECJ and the CFI, but both courts avoided ruling on it.[24] However, in the *Atlanta* case,[25] Advocate General Mischo did focus on the issue and argued that, in line with the arguments brought forward by the Spanish Government in the *Chemnitz* case,[26] that a ruling of the Appellate Body does not impose any obligation on the WTO member, whose legislation has been found to be in breach of WTO law, to amend its legislation promptly. He referred to Article 21(3) of the DSU, according to which a WTO member has a 'reasonable period' of time to comply with the ruling of the Appellate Body and to bring its legislation into line with WTO law. The Advocate General also argued that Article 22 of the DSU gives WTO members the possibility of keeping the unlawful measures in place beyond the reasonable period of time, if the parties to the dispute have agreed on suitable compensation.

Some have argued that WTO obligations need not be implemented given that compensation or even the acceptance of retaliation are separate options.[27] Indeed, one could argue that the DSU, even as a preference to the withdrawal of WTO-incompatible measures, seems to favour solutions which are 'mutually acceptable' to the parties. Article 22(8) of the DSU provides that the suspension of concessions shall cease not only if the incompatible measure is withdrawn or the member concerned has provided a solution to the nullification and impairment of benefits, but also if a 'mutually satisfactory solution is reached'. Article 3(7) of the DSU further provides that what is 'clearly to be preferred' is a mutually acceptable solution 'consistent with the covered agreements'.

Trade Law Association; M Hilf and F Schorkopf 'WTO und EG: Rechtskonflikte vor der EuGH?' (2000) 1 *EuR* 74–91; A Rosas 'Annotation on Case C-149/96 *Portugal v Council*' (2000) 3 *CMLRev* 797–816; and GA Zonnekeyn 'The Status of WTO Law in the EC Legal Order – The Final Curtain?' (2000) 3 *JWT* 111–25.

[24] See Case T-254/97 *Fruchthandelsgesellschaft mbH Chemnitz v Commission* [1999] ECR II-2743 and Case C-104/97 P *Atlanta AG v Council and Commission* [1999] ECR I-6983.

[25] Case C-104/97 P *Atlanta AG v Council and Commission* [1999] ECR I-6983. For a comment on the Opinion of Advocate General Mischo, see GA Zonnekeyn 'The Legal Status of WTO Panel Reports in the EC Legal Order. Some Reflections on the Opinion of Advocate General Mischo in the Atlanta Case' (1999) *JIEL* 713–22.

[26] Case T-254/97 *Fruchthandelsgesellschaft mbH Chemnitz v Commission* [1999] ECR II-2743. At the hearing, the Spanish Government had argued that the legal effect of an Appellate Body report was limited for the following two reasons. First, a report is a mere 'recommendation' addressed to a WTO member to bring its legislation into compliance with WTO law but does not oblige that member to amend its legislation. The Spanish Government referred to Article 22 of the Understanding on Rules and Procedures Governing the Settlement of Disputes (DSU), which gives WTO members the possibility to leave the illegal measures in place and offer compensation or agree with the suspension of concessions. Secondly, the Spanish Government argued that GATT, by its very nature, was not directly applicable and could not be invoked to call into question the validity of a Community rule and that such an effect would be tantamount to an exception to the jurisdictional monopoly conferred on the ECJ by Article 220 EC Treaty (ex Article 164).

[27] JH Bello (n 21) 418 and TM Reiff and M Forestal (n 21) 763.

Another option is the possibility for the member whose legislation has been found to be in breach with WTO law to tolerate the suspensions of concessions instigated by the other party to the dispute. Such suspension of concessions must be 'equivalent' to the level of the nullification and impairment caused by the measure to be WTO inconsistent and is not of a punitive nature but has as its main objective to restore the imbalance in concessions caused by the measure found to be incompatible.[28] It should be recalled that the EC has chosen to accept retaliation by the United States in the banana case. The suspension of concessions is regulated by Article 22 of the DSU, including the possibility to request binding arbitration to ensure that the suspension sought is, indeed, 'equivalent'. In addition, Article 26(1) of the DSU provides that in case of so-called non-violation cases under Article XXIII of GATT 1994, there is no obligation to withdraw the measure.

Jackson has – rightly – argued that the 'unconditional' obligation to comply with WTO rules can be inferred from the language of the DSU itself and that compliance is the preferred option.[29] Indeed, Article 22.1 of the DSU provides that compensation is a purely provisional measure and that '... neither compensation nor the suspension of concessions or other obligations is preferred to full implementation of a recommendation to bring a measure into conformity with the covered agreements ...'. Indeed, compensation is not a method of settling disputes but simply a temporary instrument to ensure that any benefits accruing to the other members are not nullified or impaired as a result of the failure to comply within the reasonable period of time set in the particular case and that the defaulting party is not encouraged to persist indefinitely in its failure to comply.[30]

---

[28] See *European Communities – Regime for the Importation, Sale and Distribution of Bananas – Recourse to Arbitration by the European Communities under Article 22.6 of the DSU*, decision by the arbitrators of 9 April 1999, WT/DS27/ARB. The arbitrators decided that '[W]e agree with the United States that this temporary nature indicates that it is the purpose of countermeasures to induce compliance. But this purpose does not mean that the DSB should grant authorization to suspend concessions beyond what is equivalent to the level of nullification or impairment. In our view, there is nothing in Article 22.1 of the DSU, let alone in paragraphs 4 and 7 of Article 22, that could be read as a justification for countermeasures of a punitive nature'. See para 6.3 of the decision.

[29] Jackson (n 21) 73. See also H Horn and P Mavroidis 'Remedies in the WTO Dispute Settlement System and Developing Country Interests' World Bank paper dated 11 April 1999, 14 (available at www.worldbank.org).

[30] See also para 29 of the Opinion of Advocate General Tesauro of 16 June 1998 in Case C–53/96 *Hermès International v FHT Marketing Choice BV* [1998] ECR I–3603. Timmermans has suggested that it cannot in any way be excluded that compensation may ultimately be a 'provisoire qui dure', see C Timmermans 'The Implementation of the Uruguay Round by the EC' in JHJ Bourgeois et al (eds) *The Uruguay Round Results: A European Lawyers' Perspective* (Brussels: European Interuniversity Press, 1995) 504. This situation cannot – a priori – be excluded but it would run counter to the spirit and objectives of the WTO dispute settlement mechanism.

The thesis here defended is that adopted panel and Appellate Body reports are binding on the EC. By accepting compensation, the responding member in a dispute, in se, recognises the binding effect of WTO law since it acknowledges that its legislation or other measures are in breach of WTO law. The compensation mechanism was not meant to give WTO members a complete freedom to leave WTO-inconsistent measures in place and does not, as a matter of principle, accord a 'right' to violate a legal obligation entered into under an international agreement. It merely constitutes a practical option temporarily to defuse a dispute between WTO members.

5. Non-Implementation by the EC of Adopted WTO Panel and Appellate Body Reports: Implications at EC Level

5.1 EC Liability for Non-Implementation

This section will focus on the question whether the EC can be held liable for the damages suffered by European exporters as a result of the import duties imposed by the United States following the EC's non-compliance with the panel and Appellate Body reports in the *Bananas* case. Article 288(2) EC Treaty imposes an obligation upon the EC to 'make good any damage caused by its institutions' and this 'in accordance with the general principles common to the laws of the Member States'. The principle of non-contractual liability, embedded in this Article, has given rise to a considerable amount of case law of the ECJ and the CFI.[31]

According to established case law, in order for the EC to incur non-contractual liability the applicant must prove the unlawfulness of the alleged conduct of the institution concerned, actual damage and the existence of a causal link between that conduct and the alleged damage.[32]

---

[31] For an analysis of this case law, see eg M Brealey and M Hoskins *Remedies in EC Law* (2nd edn, London: Sweet & Maxwell, 1998) 350–72; P Craig and G de Búrca *EU Law: Texts, Cases, and Materials* (2nd edn, Oxford: Oxford University Press, 1998) 516–47; P Gilsdorf and P Oliver 'Artikel 215 – Haftung der Gemeinschaft und ihrer Bediensteten' in H von der Groeben, J Thiesing and C-D Ehlermann (eds) *Kommentar zum EWG-Vertrag* (Band 4, Baden-Baden: Nomos Verlagsgesellschaft, 1991); T Heukels and A McDonnell (eds) *The Action for Damages in Community Law* (The Hague: Kluwer Law International, 1997); I Pernice 'Le recours en indemnité' (1995) CDE 641–60; S Schmahl 'Ungereimtheiten und Rechtschhutzlücken bei der ausservertralichen Haftung der Europaïschen Gemeinschaft' (1999) *ZeuS* 415–29; F Schockweiler, G Wivenes and JM Godart 'Le regime de la responsabilité extra-contractuelle du fait d'actes juridiques dans la Communauté européenne' (1990) 1 RTDE 27–74; A von Bogdandy 'Kommentar zum Artikel 215 EWG-Vertrag' in E Grabitz and M Hilf (eds) *Das Recht der Europäischen Union* (Altband II, München: CH Beck, 1999); HG Schermers T Heukels and P Mead *Non-Contractual Liability of the European Communities* (Dordrecht: Martinus Nijhoff Publishers, 1981) and A Ward *Judicial Review and the Rights of Private Parties in EC Law* (Oxford: Oxford University Press, 2000) 288–322.

[32] See eg Case 26/81 *Oleifici Mediterranei v EEC* [1982] ECR 3057, para 16; Case T–175/94 *International Procurement Services v Commission* [1996] ECR II–729, para 44; Case T–113/96

continued ...

Moreover, in the case of legislative measures involving choices of economic policy, an action under Article 288(2) EC Treaty will only be successful if a sufficiently serious breach of a superior rule of law for the protection of individuals has occurred (the so-called *Schöppenstedt* formula).[33] Much EC legislation of a type liable to give rise to a claim for damages is concerned with economic policy and involves the exercise by the political institutions of discretionary powers, especially in the agricultural field as is evidenced by the contested banana legislation.

The restrictive application of these criteria tends to frustrate, rather than foster, the chances of success of those seeking relief under the EC provisions on non-contractual liability.[34] It is therefore very difficult to assess whether the 'innocent exporters' will be able to comply with the criteria referred to above. However, the present article will demonstrate that these companies have a reasonable chance to succeed when bringing an action for damages before the CFI. It will therefore analyse in detail each of these criteria in the light of the factual background of the banana case.

5.2   A Legislative Act

The question whether the contested banana regulation(s) are legislative measures does not create any substantial problems. The basic Regulation 404/93[35] and the implementing regulations, as amended, are legislative acts within the meaning of Article 288(2) EC Treaty. In determining whether a measure is to be treated as legislative for the purposes of a claim under Article 288(2) EC Treaty, it is the substance, not the form, of the measure that is important.[36] The test is therefore the same as under Article 230 EC Treaty. The ECJ's case law under the latter Article shows that a legislative act is one which is of general application in the sense that it applies to 'categories of persons viewed abstractly and in their entirety'.[37] Both regulations and directives will normally satisfy that test.[38] Where that is so, as in the cases at hand, claims for compensation arising from such measures will have to satisfy the *Schöppenstedt* test.

Edouard Dubois et Fils v Council and Commission [1998] ECR II–125, para 54 and Case T–178/98 *Fresh Marine Company SA v Commission* judgement of 24 October 2000, not yet reported para 54.

[33] As first established in Case 5/71 *Zuckerfabrik Schöppenstedt v Council* [1971] ECR 975, at para 11. More recently confirmed in Case T–521/93 *Atlanta AG and Others v Council and Commission* [1996] ECR II–1707, at para 83. For an analysis of the case law of the ECJ and CFI on the EC's liability for legislative acts, see A Arnull 'Liability for Legislative Acts under Article 215(2) EC' in T Heukels and A McDonnell (eds) *The Action for Damages in Community Law* (The Hague: Kluwer Law International, 1997) 129–51.

[34] Ward (n 30) 288.

[35] Council Regulation (EEC) 404/93 of 13 February 1993 on the common organisation of the market in bananas [1993] OJ L47/1.

[36] Arnull (n 32) 135.

[37] Joined Cases 16 and 17/62 *Producteurs de Fruits v Council* [1962] ECR 471 at 478.

[38] Arnull (n 32) 135.

5.3 Choices of Economic Policy

A legislative measure, which involves choices of economic policy, presupposes discretionary power.[39] However, the case law of the ECJ indicates that the EC legislator does not enjoy an unlimited discretion. In *Sofrimport*, for example, compensation was sought for loss suffered as a result of three Commission regulations suspending the issue of import licences for dessert apples originating in third countries.[40] The applicant was an importer and wholesaler of fresh fruit. Before the contested regulations were adopted, it shipped a cargo of Chilean dessert apples to the EC. It subsequently submitted applications for import licences to the intervention agency in the Member State where the cargo was due to arrive. Those applications were rejected on the basis of two of the contested regulations. In a parallel action for annulment, all three contested regulations were declared void in so far as they concerned products in transit towards the EC. As for the claim under Article 288(2) EC Treaty, the ECJ concluded that the Commission had committed a sufficiently serious breach of one of the contested regulations without invoking any overriding public interest and that the damages alleged by Sofrimport went beyond the limits of the economic risks inherent in the business concerned.

5.4 Unlawfulness

The requirement of a breach of a superior rule of law appears to be the expression that liability for damages presupposes the existence of an unlawful act. The WTO dispute settlement organs repeatedly confirmed the unlawfulness of the EC's banana regime. It is questionable, however, whether this suffices to trigger the liability of the EC in the light of the *Schöppenstedt* formula referred to above.

5.4.1 The '*Schutznormtheorie*'

In order to establish the liability of the EC under the *Schöppenstedt* test, the applicant must be able to invoke a breach of a superior rule of law 'for the protection of the individual.' Grabitz argued that this requirement resembles the German '*Schutznormtheorie*', which concerns the liability of the government. According to this theory, the government is liable only when, in addition to causing injury, it breaches a '*Schutznorm*', which is a legal norm protecting a subjective public right of the injured party and which is intended not only to protect individuals in general, but

---

[39] G van der Wal and WBJ Van Overbeek 'Commentary on Article 215 EC Treaty' in H Smit and PE Herzog (eds) *The Law of the European Community. A Commentary on the EEC Treaty* (vol 5, New York: Matthew Bender, 1994) paras 6–138.2 and 6–138.3.
[40] Case 152/88 *Sofrimport SARL v Commission* [1990] ECR I–2477.

also to protect a specific circle of individuals to which the injured party belongs.[41]

This requirement is applied more liberally by the CFI and ECJ. In proceedings under Article 288(2) EC Treaty, it is enough if the applicant can show that the superior rule of law alleged to have been breached is for the protection of individuals generally. In *Kampffmeyer*,[42] the ECJ rejected the argument that the legal norm, which had been infringed was not intended to protect the interests of the applicants and decided that one of the purposes of the provision embodying the rule in question was to protect certain interests. The ECJ held that:

> [T]he fact that these interests are of a general nature does not prevent their including the interests of individual undertakings such as the applicants (…). Although the application of the rules of law in question is not in general capable of being of direct and individual concern to the said undertakings, that does not prevent the possibility that the protection of their interests may be (…) intended by those rules of law.[43]

An essential question is whether the WTO Agreements contain legal provisions aimed at the protection of the individual. Although the WTO is essentially an intergovernmental organisation in which private business operators do not have any direct role, they are the main beneficiaries of the multilateral trading system. They are the ones who are expected to take advantage of the rules negotiated by governments and to convert them into export opportunities.[44] The wording of the panel in the *Section 301* case[45] is very instructive in this respect:

> … it would be entirely wrong to consider that the position of individuals is of no relevance to the GATT/WTO legal matrix. Many of the benefits to Members which are meant to flow as a result of the acceptance of various disciplines under the GATT/WTO depend on the activity of individual economic operators in the national and global market places. The purpose of many of these disciplines, indeed one of the primary objects of the GATT/WTO as a whole, is to produce certain market conditions which would allow this individual activity to flourish.[46]…

---

[41] E Grabitz 'Liability for Legislative Acts' in *Non-Contractual Liability of the European Communities* (Dordrecht: Martinus Nijhoff Publishers, 1981) 6–7. See also P Gilsdorf and P Oliver (n 30) paras 38–42.
[42] Joined Cases 5, 7 and 13–24/66 *Kampffmeyer v Commission* [1967] ECR 245.
[43] ibid.
[44] E Kessie 'Enhancing Security and Predictability for Private Business Operators under the Dispute Settlement System of the WTO' (2000) *JWT* 1–17.
[45] WT/DS152/R *United States – Sections 301-310 of the Trade Act of 1974*, report of the panel of 22 December 1999.
[46] WT/DS152/R *United States – Sections 301–310 of the Trade Act of 1974*, report of the panel of 22 December 1999, at para 7.73.

The security and predictability in question are of 'the multilateral trading system'. The multilateral trading system is, per force, composed not only of States but also, indeed mostly, of individual economic operators. The lack of security and predictability affects mostly these individual operators.[47]

Trade is conducted most often and increasingly by private operators. It is through improved conditions for these private operators that Members benefit from WTO disciplines. The denial of benefits to a Member which flows from a breach is often indirect and results from the impact of the breach on the market place and the activities of individuals within it.[48]

These obiter dicta seem to indicate that the WTO rules do envisage the protection of the interests of individuals. As Petersmann has phrased it:

[T]he formulation of international trade rules in terms of rights and obligations of states is ... no convincing reason for preventing individuals from invoking precise and unconditional guarantees of freedom and non-discrimination, such as the customs union rules of the EC Treaty and their underlying worldwide GATT rules.[49]

5.4.2 A Superior Rule of Law

The ECJ has followed two different approaches to define the concept of a 'superior rule of law'. First, there is the approach where superior is equated with 'important'.[50] Secondly, there is the formalistic approach, which appears to be the one most often used by the ECJ and the CFI.[51] In the latter context, the hierarchy between rules is considered. In the majority of cases, however, general principles of EC law have been invoked as superior rules of law. These include the principle of protection of legitimate expectations, the principle of proportionality, the principle of equal treatment, the principle of care, the principle of proper administration and the prohibition of misuse of powers. Fundamental rights, such as the right to property, the right to be heard and the freedom to pursue an economic activity, are also recognised as being superior rules of law.[52]

---

[47] WT/DS152/R *United States – Sections 301–310 of the Trade Act of 1974*, report of the panel of 22 December 1999, at para 7.76.
[48] WT/DS152/R *United States – Sections 301–310 of the Trade Act of 1974*, report of the panel of 22 December 1999, at para 7.77.
[49] E-U Petersmann *The GATT/WTO Dispute Settlement System: International Law, International Organizations and Dispute Settlement* (Deventer: Kluwer Law International, 1996) 238.
[50] P Craig and G de Búrca (n 30) 519.
[51] TC Hartley *The Foundations of European Community Law* (4th edn, Oxford: Oxford University Press, 1998) 467.
[52] See K Lenaerts and D Arts in R Gray (ed) *Procedural Law of the European Union* (London: Sweet & Maxwell, 1999) 264–5.

Of great significance to the present case, is the principle of proportionality. It can certainly be argued that the 'innocent' EC exporters have suffered disproportionately compared to other EC exporters whose products could also have appeared on the United States' retaliation list. In a sense, they have suffered on behalf of the entire EC and should therefore be compensated.[53]

An issue of crucial importance is whether a violation of an international agreement such as the WTO Agreement(s) can give rise to the liability of the EC.[54] International agreements, which form an integral part of EC law, have priority over secondary EC law by virtue of Article 300(7) EC Treaty. It is therefore generally accepted that provisions of international agreements qualify as superior rules of law and are able to trigger the liability of the EC. It is unclear, however, whether an international agreement should have direct effect in order to be invoked in a procedure under Article 288(2) EC Treaty. This question has not yet inspired many legal scholars to date, but the few who have considered the question generally argue that direct effect is a prerequisite.[55]

This would imply that the WTO Agreements could not be invoked as a standard for reviewing the conduct of the EC institutions in an action under Article 288(2) EC Treaty since the ECJ has held that these Agreements are deprived of direct effect.[56] As far as GATT or the WTO Agreements are concerned, neither the ECJ nor the CFI explicitly ruled that these agreements should have direct effect in order to be invoked in an action under Article 288(2) EC Treaty. In *Stimming v Commission*,[57] an importer of prepared meat claimed compensation for damages, which he had allegedly suffered as a result of the adoption of a regulation raising the levies on such imports without requiring transitional measures. The applicant argued that the regulation infringed GATT. However, because the applicant did not specify which GATT rules he was referring to, the ECJ decided to dismiss the application in its entirety. The Opinion of Advocate General Mayras was more

---

[53] A member of the European Parliament proposed to establish a compensation fund for these companies. See *Agence Europe* of 4 and 5 May 1999, at p 10. It is questionable, however, whether such compensation would not amount to an unlawful subsidy under WTO law.

[54] For an analysis, see P Gasparon 'The Transposition of the Principle of Member State Liability into the Context of External Relations' (1999) *EJIL* 605–24.

[55] See eg M Maresceau 'The GATT in the Case Law of the European Court of Justice' in M Hilf, F Jacobs and E-U Petersmann (eds) *The European Community and GATT* (Deventer: Kluwer, 1986) 118–19 and Gilsdorf and Oliver (n 30) at para 36.

[56] See Case C–149/96 *Portugal v Council* [1999] ECR I–8395. See also Joined Cases C–300/98 and C–392/98 *Parfums Christian Dior SA and Others* judgement of 14 December 2000, not yet reported at paras 43 and 44.

[57] Case 90/77 *Helmut Stimming KG v Commission* [1978] ECR 995.

convincing. He raised substantial doubts whether an individual could found an action for damages on an infringement of GATT.[58]

Other cases that could provide some guidance are the *Atlanta* cases.[59] The CFI rejected Atlanta's request for damages, which was, *inter alia*, based on an infringement of GATT rules. Atlanta argued that the import restrictions of Regulation 404/93 were contrary to GATT law. The CFI rejected this argument and simply referred to the judgment of the ECJ in *Germany v Council*[60] where the ECJ had discarded a similar argument put forward by the German Government.[61] Atlanta sought the annulment of the CFI's judgment and alleged that the WTO incompatibility of Regulation 404/93, in view of the Appellate Body report of 9 September 1997, justified a claim for damages. It emphasised that it was not invoking a breach of substantive WTO rules but that it was relying on the ruling of the Appellate Body. Atlanta did not seek the annulment of Regulation 404/93 but contended that the Regulation had been 'unlawfully' applied to it in view of the ruling of the Appellate Body. The applicant therefore alleged that the EC was liable, not for unlawful legislative conduct but for unlawful administrative conduct. The ECJ did not focus on the question and held that the arguments brought forward by Atlanta were inadmissible on procedural grounds.

Advocate General Lenz, however, took a straightforward position in the Italian bananas case.[62] He argued that one should:

> [n]ot exclude the possibility that in exceptional cases an infringement of provisions of GATT might give rise to a liability in damages to the traders concerned.... [I]n particular, one might envisage a case where in such a situation the Community makes no use of the possibilities provided for in GATT of freeing itself from its obligations, but agrees that the dispute should be decided by a neutral tribunal, and then however refuses to comply with the decision.[63]

---

[58] Opinion of 14 March 1978 in Case 90/77 *Helmut Stimming KG v Commission* [1978] ECR 995 at 1016.

[59] Case T–521/93 *Atlanta AG and Others v Council and Commission* [1996] ECR II–1707 and Case C–104/97 P *Atlanta AG and Others v Council and Commission* [1999] ECR I–6983. For an analysis of these cases, see GA Zonnekeyn 'The Legal Status of WTO Panel Reports in the EC Legal Order. Some Reflections on the Opinion of Advocate General Mischo in the Atlanta Case' (1999) *JIEL* 713–22 and GA Zonnekeyn, 'The Status of Adopted Panel and Appellate Body Reports in the European Court of Justice and the European Court of First Instance – The Banana Experience' (2000) 2 *JWT* 93–108.

[60] Case C–404/93 *Germany v Council* [1994] ECR I–4973.

[61] Case T–521/93 *Atlanta AG and Others v Council and Commission* [1996] ECR II–1707 at para 77.

[62] Case C–469/93 *Amministrazione della Finanze dello Stato v Chiquita Italia SpA* [1995] ECR I–4533.

[63] See para 21 of the Opinion of Advocate General Lenz of 16 February 1995 in Case C–469/93 *Amministrazione della Finanze dello Stato v Chiquita Italia SpA* [1995] ECR I–4533.

continued ...

One scholar alleged that '[O]ne may construe this intriguing statement as establishing that the Community's failure to comply with a World Trade Organization (WTO) panel report might give rise to liability in damages to the traders concerned'.[64]

Reinisch suggested that the so-called *Fediol* and *Nakajima* line of case law could offer a solution in this particular case.[65] According to this case law, which was developed by the ECJ in relation to the legal effects of GATT within the EC legal order, the WTO Agreements may serve as a ground for review in cases where the EC intends to implement a particular obligation entered into within the framework of the WTO (the *Nakajima* doctrine).[66] or if the EC act expressly refers to specific provisions of the WTO Agreements (the *Fediol* doctrine).[67] In *Cartondruck*, the applicant argues that 'the reformed organisation of the market for bananas is intended to transpose WTO law'.[68] This could amount to an application of the Nakajima doctrine since Regulations 1637/98[69] and 2362/98[70] were presented by the EC as an implementation of its obligations under WTO law. When invoking the liability of the EC on the basis that these regulations are contrary to WTO law, the direct effect of WTO law would be a non-issue and would imply that the EC could be held liable on the basis of a breach of WTO law.

5.4.3 A sufficiently serious breach of law

Where the EC institutions have caused damage to individuals through a legislative act, it must be demonstrated that the superior rule of law has been infringed in a sufficiently flagrant manner.[71] In *HNL*, the applicants claimed damages for losses allegedly resulting from a Council Regulation on the

---

André Nollkaemper, writing on behalf of the Board of Editors of *Legal Issues of Economic Intergation*, argued that this Opinion could imply that liability for breach of international (WTO) law may ensue, even where direct effect is excluded See A Nollkaemper 'Reconsidering the Direct Effect of International Law in the EU Legal Order' (2000) 3 *LIEI* 213–15.

[64] See M Montañà i Mora 'Equilibrium – A Rediscovered Basis for the Court of Justice of the European Communities to Refuse Direct effect to the Uruguay Round Agreements?' (1996) *JWT* 50–1.

[65] Reinisch (n 4) 47–8.

[66] Case C–69/89 *Nakajima All Precision Co Ltd v Council* [1991] ECR I–2069.

[67] Case C–70/87 *Fediol v Commission* [1989] ECR 1781.

[68] Case T–320/00 *CD Cartondruck GmbH & Co KG v Commission and Council* [2000] OJ C355/39.

[69] Council Regulation (EC) 1637/98 of 20 July 1998 amending Regulation (EEC) 404/93 on the common organisation of the market in bananas [1998] OJ L210/28. Recital 2 of the regulation, for example, specifies that the EC's international commitments under the WTO should be met.

[70] Commission Regulation (EC) 2362/98 of 28 October 1998 laying down detailed rules for the implementation of Council Regulation (EC) 404/93 regarding imports of bananas into the Community [1998] OJ L293/32.

[71] Arnull (n 32) 139.

compulsory purchase of skimmed-milk powder for use in feeding stuffs.[72] The ECJ emphasised that the EC institutions can only exceptionally and in special circumstances incur liability for legislative measures, which are the result of choices of economic policy. Individuals therefore have to accept within reasonable limits certain harmful effects on their economic interests as a result of a legislative measure without being able to obtain compensation from public funds. In a legislative field such as agriculture, in which the EC enjoys a wide discretion which is necessary for the implementation of the common agricultural policy, the EC does not therefore incur liability unless the institution concerned has 'manifestly and gravely disregarded the limits on the exercise of its powers'.[73] In *Amylum*, where the ECJ applied an even stricter test, the applicants sought to recover compensation for the damages they had suffered following the imposition of a production levy on isoglucose by the Council.[74] In earlier proceedings, under Article 234 EC Treaty (ex Article 177), the ECJ had found that the Council regulation imposing the production levy was invalid.[75] The ECJ concluded that the errors it had found in the contested regulation were not of such gravity as to trigger the non-contractual liability of the EC.[76] However, in *Ireks-Arkady*, the ECJ concluded that a violation of the principle of equality, as embodied in Article 34(2) EC Treaty (ex Article 40 (3)), did constitute a ground for EC liability because the disregard of that principle affected a limited and clearly defined group of commercial operators and went beyond the bounds of the economic risks inherent in the activities in the sector concerned.[77]

The ECJ seems to have taken a less restrictive approach in *Brasserie du Pêcheur*, which concerned the liability of Member States.[78] It has been argued that the criteria used by the ECJ in that case to establish 'a serious breach of law' would also apply in the context of Article 288(2) EC Treaty,

---

[72] Joined Cases 83 and 94/76, 4, 15 and 40/77 *HNL and Others v Council and Commission* [1978] ECR 1209.
[73] Joined Cases 83 and 94/76, 4, 15 and 40/77 *HNL and Others v Council and Commission* [1978] ECR 1209, para 6.
[74] Joined Cases 116 and 124/77 *GR Amylum NV and Tunnel Refineries Limited v Council and Commission* [1979] ECR 3497.
[75] Joined Cases 103 and 145/77 *Koninklijke Scholten Honig NV v Intervention Board for Agricultural Produce* [1978] ECR 3583.
[76] Joined Cases 116 and 124/77 *GR Amylum NV and Tunnel Refineries Limited v Council and Commission* [1979] ECR 3497, para 19.
[77] Case 238/78 *Ireks-Arkady GmbH v Council* [1979] ECR 2955, para 11. The ECJ held that the principle of equality occupied a particularly important place among the rules of Community law intended to protect the interests of the individual.
[78] Joined Cases C–46/93 and C–48/93 *Brasserie du Pêcheur v Germany* and *The Queen v Secretary of State for Transport, ex parte Factortame* [1996] ECR I–1029. For an analysis, see DF Waelbroeck 'Treaty Violations and Liability of Member States: The Effect of the Francovich Case Law' in T Heukels and A McDonnell (eds) *The Action for Damages in Community Law* (The Hague: Kluwer Law International, 1997) 311–37. Waelbroeck also argues that the *Brasserie du Pêcheur* judgement 'gives hope for a widening of the conditions of liability' with explicit reference to the strict approach taken by the ECJ in the *Isoglucose* case.

taking into consideration the parallelism between Member State and EC liability.[79] In *Brasserie du Pêcheur*, the ECJ referred to factors such as the clarity and precision of the rule breached, the measure of discretion left by that rule, whether the infringement and the damage caused was intentional or involuntary, whether any error of law was excusable or not, the fact that the position taken by an EC institution may have contributed towards the omission and the adoption or retention of national measures or practices contrary to EC law.

When applying these criteria to the legal position of the innocent exporters, it could, in the author's view, certainly be argued that a 'sufficiently serious breach of law' did occur. The punitive import duties applied to a particular group of products clearly affect a limited and clearly defined group of companies. In addition, the legislation regulating the banana market in the EC has been found to violate WTO law on several occasions. Also the amendments adopted by the EC to bring its legislation into compliance with WTO law were found to be WTO inconsistent.[80] It was so obvious that these amendments were contrary to WTO law that one could argue that the EC consciously tried to avoid the implementation of the WTO rulings. Such conduct undoubtedly qualifies as a 'sufficiently serious breach of law', certainly in view of the more relaxed criteria established by the ECJ in *Brasserie du Pêcheur*.

5.5 Damages

The damages for which compensation is sought must be actual and certain. The fact that the amount of damages cannot be precisely quantified in the application will not render the claim inadmissible.[81] A claim will be admissible where it sets out 'imminent damage foreseeable with sufficient certainty even if the damage cannot yet be precisely assessed.'[82] In *Kampffmeyer II*, German meal producers claimed that a system of aid to durum wheat growers wrongfully put them at a disadvantage vis-à-vis their French competitors, the production of durum wheat being localised in France (durum wheat is ground into meal, which is then used to make pasta). They claimed damages for loss of profit, which they would suffer in the future. The ECJ held that such a claim was admissible, stating that such a loss was imminent and that the applicants could reserve the right to quantify the amount at a later stage, restricting themselves in the application to asking for a finding of the Community's liability.[83]

---

[79] Craig and de Búrca (n 31) 527 and von Bogdandy (n 31) para 5.
[80] See T Jürgensen 'WTO-Konformität der reformirten Gemeinsamen Marktorganisation für Bananen' (1999) 4 RIW 241–9 and H-D Kuschel 'Auch die rividierte Bananenmarktordung is nicht WTO-Konform' (1999) *EuZW* 74–7.
[81] Case 5/71 *Zuckerfabrik Schöppenstedt v Council* [1971] ECR 975, para 14.
[82] Joined Cases 5, 7 and 13–24/66 *Kampffmeyer v Commission* [1967] ECR 245, at para 8 (*Kampffmeyer II*).
[83] Joined Cases 5, 7 and 13–24/66 *Kampffmeyer v Commission* [1967] ECR 245, at para 8.

However, the ECJ has not always been so 'generous'. For example, in the *CNTA* case, the ECJ held that lost profits were not recoverable where the claim for damages was based on the concept of legitimate expectations, the argument being that this concept only served to ensure that losses were not suffered owing to an unexpected change in the legal position. It did not serve that profits would be made.[84] A similar argument could be developed in the present case. It could be argued that the EC exporters did not have a legitimate right to expect that the import duties imposed by the United States would never be altered, especially since Article XXVIII of GATT (Modification of Schedules) entitles WTO members, albeit under strict conditions, to modify their schedule of concessions either by agreement with the affected members or in the last resort unilaterally.[85] However, whether this line of thought would also apply to the situation where the EC refuses to implement a WTO panel or Appellate report and accepts retaliation as an alternative, is questionable. In the case of the innocent exporters, for example, it was impossible for an exporter to anticipate that the EC would continue to disregard its obligations under WTO law and, more importantly, that the exporters' own products would be subjected to a punitive import duty.

The economic loss suffered by the exporters is, in the author's view, not difficult to prove. These companies must be able to demonstrate that their profits in the United States were reduced drastically since the United States imposed the sanctions. It must be recalled, however, that companies who abandon their intended transactions to the United States, will encounter major difficulties when claiming compensation since the ECJ has refused to grant compensation for abandoned intended transactions that would have produced profits.[86]

5.6 Causality

The causation between the unlawful conduct of the EC institutions and damages is explicitly required by Article 288(2) EC Treaty. It follows from the case law of the ECJ and CFI that causality is assessed from a hypothetical perspective according to which a causal link is excluded when the damages would also have occurred in the absence of the (unlawful) act.[87] The CFI decided that there is a causal link where there is a direct causal nexus between the fault committed by the EC institution concerned and the injury pleaded, the burden of proof of which rests

---

[84] Joined Cases 89 and 91/86 *L'Étoile commerciale and comptoir national technique agricole (CNTA) v Commission* [1987] ECR 3005, at paras 45–7.
[85] For an analysis of Article XXVIII of GATT, see eg E McGovern *International Trade Regulation* (Exeter: Globefield Press, 2000) 5.13–1.
[86] Joined Cases 5, 7 and 13–24/66 *Kampffmeyer v Commission* [1967] ECR 245 (*Kampffmeyer I*).
[87] Case T–572/93 *Odigitria AAE v Council and Commission* [1995] ECR II–2025, at para 65.

on the applicant.[88] In addition, the EC cannot be held liable for any damage other than that which is a sufficiently direct consequence of the misconduct of the institution concerned.[89] It could be argued that the ECJ and CFI follow, to a certain extent, the German '*Adäquanztheorie*' pursuant to which the 'wrongful' act and the damages occurred have to be linked in a normal, ordinary and more or less predictable way.

The 'innocent exporters' would, in the author's view, be able to demonstrate that without the enactment of the EC's WTO-incompatible banana legislation no punitive import duties would have been imposed by the United States and that the exporters would not have suffered any damages. It could be argued, for example, that the 'direct causal nexus' is not found in the unlawful conduct of the EC but rather in the imposition of the sanctions by the United States. However, these sanctions could be considered as a direct and foreseeable consequence of the EC's unlawful conduct, which would re-establish the direct causal nexus.[90] It follows from the case law of the ECJ that the conduct of national authorities of a third country does not necessarily disrupt the causal link.[91] The disruption would only occur if the national measure would be unlawful as such and would thus be the cause of the damage which occurred.[92] The punitive import duties imposed by the United States were approved by the WTO DSB and therefore conform to the WTO. These measures are therefore not unlawful and have no impact on the existing causal link.[93]

6. Conclusion

The thesis defended in this chapter is that the EC can be held liable for the non-implementation of the WTO panel and Appellate Body reports in the transatlantic banana case and that the EC exporters, adversely affected by the sanctions imposed by the United States following this non-implementation, can be compensated for their losses. However, the hurdles imposed by the case law of the ECJ and CFI will be difficult to overcome. The granting of compensation to the 'innocent' businesses of the banana war would be a clear signal to the institutions of the EC that

---

[88] Case T–178/98 *Fresh Marine Company SA v Commission* judgement of 24 October 2000, not yet reported para 118.
[89] Case T–178/98 *Fresh Marine Company SA v Commission* judgement of 24 October 2000, not yet reported, para 118. See also Joined Cases 64/76 and 113/76, 167/78 and 239/78, 27/79, 28/79 and 45/79 *Dumortier and Others v Council* [1979] ECR 3091, para 21; Case T–168/94, *Blackspur and Others v Council and Commission* [1995] ECR II–2627, para 52.
[90] Reinisch (n 4) 51.
[91] von Bogdandy (n 31) para 106.
[92] Joined Cases 89 and 91/86 *L'Étoile commerciale and comptoir national technique agricole (CNTA) v Commission* [1987] ECR 3005.
[93] One could argue, however, that it is the persistence of the United States in 'retaliating' against the EC under Article 22(6) of the DSU (suspension of concessions), rather than accepting compensation, that is at the origin of the damage. Obviously, this rationale would only apply to the extent that the EC had actually offered compensation.

they should take up their responsibility. It can only be hoped that the CFI will see to it that justice is done by granting the European exporters the compensation they are entitled to.

CHAPTER IX

EC LIABILITY FOR THE NON-IMPLEMENTATION OF WTO
DISPUTE SETTLEMENT DECISIONS – ADVOCATE GENERAL ALBER
PROPOSES A 'COPERNICAN INNOVATION' IN THE CASE LAW OF
THE ECJ

1. Introduction

In two identical Opinions delivered on 15 May 2003 in the *Biret* cases, Advocate General Alber of the European Court of Justice (ECJ), proposes that the European Community (EC) may be held liable under EC law for the non-implementation of WTO dispute settlement decisions within the prescribed reasonable period of time and the damages resulting therefrom for economic operators.[1] The Advocate General opines that, in such circumstances, WTO law has direct effect and can thus be invoked by private parties in proceedings before the European courts in Luxembourg in order to trigger the liability of the EC. It remains to be seen whether the ECJ will be prepared to follow the 'Copernican innovation' proposed by the Advocate General.

This note does not purport to give an exhaustive analysis of the Opinions of the Advocate General. It will focus on some of the more controversial issues dealt with in both Opinions.

2. The Facts

The origins of the *Biret* case can be traced back to the *hormones* dispute between the EC and the United States (US).[2] On 29 April 1996, the Council adopted Directive 96/22/EC concerning the prohibition on the use in stock farming of certain substances having a hormonal or thyrostatic action and of ß-agonists.[3] In January 1996, the US, considering that the EC legislation was restricting its exports to the EC of beef and veal treated with certain hormones, in breach of the obligations the EC had entered into within the framework of the WTO,

---

[1] Case C–93/02 P *Biret International v Council* and Case C–94/03 P *Établissements Biret and Cie SA v Council*.
[2] For a recent analysis of this dispute and the implementation problems, see D Wüger 'The never ending story: the implementation phase in the disputes between the EC and the United States on hormone-treated beef' (2002) *Law & Policy in International Business* 777.
[3] [1996] OJ L125/3.

brought dispute settlement proceedings before the competent WTO organs.[4]

On 18 August 1997, the panel set up in respect of this procedure concluded that the EC was in breach of various provisions of the WTO Agreement on Sanitary and Phytosanitary Measures (SPS).[5] In response to an appeal lodged by the EC, the Appellate Body delivered a report on 16 January 1998 amending certain aspects of the report of the panel, but finding none the less that the EC was in breach of Article 3(3) and Article 5(1) of the SPS Agreement, essentially on the ground that there had not been a sufficiently specific scientific analysis of the cancer risks associated with the use of certain hormones as growth hormones.[6] The Appellate Body recommended that 'the Dispute Settlement Body request the European Communities to bring the SPS measures found ... to be inconsistent with the SPS Agreement into conformity with the obligations of the European Communities under that Agreement'. On 13 February 1998 the WTO Dispute Settlement Body (DSB) adopted the report of the Appellate Body and the reports of the panels, as amended by the Appellate Body.

As the EC had stated that it intended to comply with its WTO obligations but that it needed a reasonable time to do so,[7] under Article 21(3) of the Understanding on Rules and Procedures Governing the Settlement of Disputes (DSU), it was granted a period of 15 months for that purpose, which expired on 13 May 1999.[8]

On the basis of the results of further analysis of the risks associated with the use of the substances in question the European Commission adopted on 24 May 2000, and submitted to the Parliament and the Council on 3 July 2000, a proposal for a Directive of the European Parliament and the Council amending Directive 96/22 and seeking in particular to maintain the prohibition.[9] In January 2003, the Council adopted a common position 'with a view to the adoption of a Directive of the European Parliament and of the Council amending Council Directive 96/22/EC concerning the prohibition on the use in stock farming of certain substances having a

---

[4] WT/DS26/1 *EC – Measures Concerning Meat and Meat Products (Hormones)*, Request for Consultations by the United States of 31 January 1996 and WT/DS26/13 *EC – Measures Concerning Meat and Meat Products (Hormones)*, Request for the Establishment of a Panel by the United States of 25 April 1996.
[5] WT/DS26/R/USA *EC – Measures Concerning Meat and Meat Products (Hormones)*, report of the panel of 18 August 1997.
[6] WT/DS26/AB/R *EC – Measures Concerning Meat and Meat Products (Hormones)*, report of the Appellate Body of 16 January 1998.
[7] WT/DS/M/43 Minutes of the Meeting of the DSB held in Geneva on 13 March 1998.
[8] WT/DS26/15 *EC – Measures Concerning Meat and Meat Products (Hormones)*, Arbitration under Article 21.3(c) of the Understanding on Rules and Procedures Governing the Settlement of Disputes, Award of the Arbitrator of 29 May 1998.
[9] [2000] OJ C337 E/163 of 28 November 2000.

hormonal thyrostatic action and of beta-agonists'. The proposal is still going through the legislative process and no definitive text has yet been adopted, more than four after the reasonable period of time granted to the EC to comply with the adverse panel and Appellate Body rulings has lapsed.

In June 2000, *Biret* brought an action against the Council before the CFI seeking compensation for damages suffered as a result of the ban on the import into the EC of hormone treated beef. The CFI dismissed the application for damages and referred to the now firmly established case law according to which: (i) the WTO Agreements do not in principle form part of the rules by which the ECJ and the CFI review the legality of acts adopted by the EC institutions under Article 230 EC Treaty, (ii) that individuals cannot rely on them before the courts and (iii) that any infringement of them will not give rise to liability on the part of the EC.[10] In addition, the CFI emphasised that 'the purpose of the WTO Agreements is to govern relations between States or regional organisations for economic integration and not to protect individuals'.[11]

On 16 March 2002, *Biret* introduced an appeal against the judgment of the CFI, requesting, inter alia, that the ECJ should 'acknowledge that all or part of the WTO Agreements have direct effect'. Advocate General Alber appears to be willing to honour this request.

3. The Opinions – a Brief Analysis

The Advocate General starts his Opinions with an analysis of the conditions required to trigger the liability of the EC under Article 288(2) EC Treaty. This Article imposes an obligation upon the EC to 'make good any damage caused by its institutions' and this 'in accordance with the general principles common to the laws of the Member States'. According to established case law, in order for the EC to incur non-contractual liability the applicant must prove the unlawfulness of the alleged conduct of the institution concerned, actual damage and the existence of a causal link between that conduct and the alleged damage. Moreover, in the case of legislative measures involving choices of economic policy, an action under Article 288(2) EC Treaty will only be successful if a sufficiently serious breach of a superior rule of law for the protection of individuals has occurred (the so-called *Schöppenstedt* formula).[12] The test was reformulated somewhat in *Bergaderm* so that the first requirement for

---

[10] Case T–174/00 *Biret International SA v Council* [2002] ECR II–17, para 61 and Case T–210/00 *Établissements Biret et Cie SA v Council* [2002] ECR II–47, para 71.
[11] Case T–174/00 *Biret International SA v Council* [2002] ECR II–17, para 62 and Case T–210/00 *Établissements Biret et Cie SA v Council* [2002] ECR II–47, para 72.
[12] As first established in Case 5/71 *Zuckerfabrik Schöppenstedt v Council* [1971] ECR 975, para 11.

liability is a sufficiently serious breach of law intended to confer rights on individuals.[13]

In this particular case the unlawful conduct would consist in the adoption, by the EC, of the contested directives imposing a ban on hormone treated beef and the subsequent failure to withdraw or amend these WTO incompatible directives within the specified reasonable period of time. The EC was legally obliged to bring these directives into conformity with WTO law in accordance with the rulings and recommendations of the Dispute Settlement Body (DSB) and was given a reasonable time of 15 months to do so. No WTO compatible legislation has been enacted so far.

In an important but somewhat hidden statement, the Advocate General argues that the relevant WTO rules which the applicant wishes to submit should have direct effect and should have as their objective the protection of the individual in order for the liability claim to be successful.

This is an argument with which I tend to disagree. Although the CFI has previously ruled that that since the WTO Agreements are not, in principle, intended to confer rights on individuals, the EC cannot incur liability as a result of infringement of them[14], it can be argued that direct effect is not a precondition for the invocability of WTO law in an action for damages under Article 288(2) EC Treaty. First, the CFI did not explicitly say that direct effect of WTO law is as pre-condition. The reference to 'the rights of individuals' cannot be assimilated with direct effect. It is the first condition that must be fulfilled in an action for damages. Secondly, if one looks at the case law of the ECJ with regard to the liability of the EC Member States for infringement of EC law, there seems to be no requirement that the measure invoked must have direct effect. In *Francovich*,[15] for example, Italy was held liable for all damages caused by its failure to transpose an EC directive in its national legislation notwithstanding the fact that the directive did not have direct effect. There seems to be no compelling reason why this should not apply to the liability of the EC.[16] Alber, however, takes the position that such directives are suddenly 'blessed' with direct effect in the framework of a damages claim and that the same reasoning should

---

[13] Case C-352/98 P *Laboratoires Pharmaceutiques Bergaderm SA and J-J Goupil v Commission* ECR [2000] I-5291.

[14] See in particular Case T-254/97 *Fruchthandelsgesellschaft mbH Chemnitz v Commission* [1999] ECR II-2743; Case C-104/97 P *Atlanta AG v Council and Commission* [1999] ECR I-6983; Case T-18/99 *Cordis Obst und Gemüse Grosshandel GmbH v Commission* [2001] ECR II-4619; Case T-30/99, *Bocchi Food Trade International GmbH v Commission* [2001] ECR II-4619 and Case T-52/99 *T Port GmbH & Co KG v Commission* [2001] ECR II-981.

[15] Case C-6/90 *Francovich* [1991] ECR I-5354, paras 10ff.

[16] See, for a similar approach, B Schoißwohl 'The ECJ's Atlanta Judgement: Establishing a Principle of Non-Liability?' in F Breus, S Griller and E. Vranes (eds) *The Banana Dispute. An Economic and Legal Analysis* (Vienna – New York: Springer, 2003) 315–24.

apply to WTO law. I find this reasoning quite unconvincing and it would be better to argue that direct effect is irrelevant in a damages claim.

Advocate General Alber starts his analysis of the DSU with a reference to *Atlanta*[17] where the ECJ ruled that 'the applicant could have ... adduced in particular the dispute settlement mechanism set up within the WTO in 1995 in support of its argument that the provisions of GATT were of direct effect'.[18] This obiter dictum reflects the possibility, according to the Advocate General, that the 'new' WTO dispute settlement mechanism could alter the effects of WTO law in the EC legal order. In order to support this thesis, Advocate General Alber continues with a quite detailed analysis of the WTO dispute settlement system. He essentially argues, with reference to several articles of the DSU, that parties to a dispute must comply with rulings and recommendations of the DSB and that there are no permanent alternatives available.

Alber AG then continues with a rebuttal of some of the arguments tabled by the Council. At the hearing before the ECJ, the Council explicitly referred to the possibility for WTO members to negotiate a 'waiver'. Alber AG argues, however, that the possibility provided for in Article XXIII:2 of GATT 1947 to authorise the suspension of concessions or other obligations has substantially been modified by the WTO dispute settlement mechanism. He emphasises again that WTO members, parties to a dispute, have no other choice but to implement the rulings and recommendations of the DSB and relies therefore on a reading of Article 22 of the DSU. He therefore concludes that the alleged scope of manoeuvre for the legislative and executive bodies of WTO members cannot be curtailed by granting direct effect to WTO law since there is no room for further negotiations once a panel or the Appellate Body have ruled that a particular measure is contrary to WTO law.

The Council also referred to Article XXV:5 of GATT 1947 which provides that the members may waive an obligation imposed upon a member under WTO law. Alber argues that such a waiver requires a 'joint action' by the members and that a two-thirds majority of the votes cast is necessary to approve a waiver. An agreement between two members involved in a dispute does not satisfy these conditions.

Alber AG further argues that the implementation of DSB rulings and recommendations requires the adoption of a legislative act by the EC. He

---

[17] Case C–104/97 P *Atlanta AG v Council and Commission* [1999] ECR I–6983. For a comment, see GA Zonnekeyn 'The Status of Adopted Panel and Appellate Body Reports in the European Court of Justice and the European Court First Instance – The Banana Experience' (2000) *JWT* 93–108.

[18] Case C–104/97 P *Atlanta AG v Council and Commission* [1999] ECR I–6983, para 21.

relies, first, on the language used by the Appellate Body in the *Hormones* case pursuant to which the DSB should request the EC to bring the SPS measures found to be inconsistent with the SPS Agreement into conformity with the obligations of the EC under that Agreement and, secondly, on the text of Article 3(7) of the DSU. But even if an intervention of the legislative bodies of the EC is mandatory, the question should be raised, according to the Advocate General, whether the applicant can rely on the DSB decision in a procedure under Article 288(2) EC Treaty. Since the EC has not yet implemented the DSB decision in the *Hormones* case, even four years after the reasonable period of time has lapsed, there seems to be a strong argument in favour of such an approach.

In addition, such an approach will not limit the scope of manoeuvre of the legislative and executive bodies of the EC to implement the DSB decision since an individual will never be able to oblige the EC to implement the decision in a particular way.

I would tend to agree with the overall approach defended by Alber AG . There are two issues on which I would like to comment. First, there is the binding nature of DSB decisions. The question whether panel and Appellate Body reports, as adopted by the DSB, are binding upon WTO members has been the object of a fierce debate in legal doctrine.[19] Without starting a debate over this issue, I would like to remark that adopted panel and Appellate Body reports, certainly after the reasonable period has lapsed, are indeed binding. Parties to a dispute have no other choice but to implement such rulings. Secondly, there is the issue of the 'invocability' of panel and Appellate Body reports before the CFI or ECJ. Alber essentially argued that these may serve as a legal ground for a damages action. Here again, I would tend to agree with the Advocate General. I have already defended the thesis earlier that such reports have 'direct effect' and may be invoked as a ground for review in proceedings before the European courts in Luxembourg.[20]

I would like to conclude with another important conclusion of the Advocate General. He argues that it does not suffice that WTO law has direct effect in order to be invoked before the ECJ or CFI in damages procedure before

---

[19] I refer in particular to the stimulating discussion between JH Bello 'The WTO Dispute Settlement Understanding: Less is More' (1996) *AJIL* 416 and JH Jackson 'The WTO Dispute Settlement Understanding – Misunderstandings on the Nature of a Legal Obligation' (1997) *AJIL* and to GA Zonnekeyn 'The *Bed Linen* Case and its aftermath. Some Comments on the European Community's "World Trade Organization Enabling Regulation"' (2002) *JWT* 993. For an overview of these different views, see J Waincymer *WTO Litigation. Procedural aspects of Formal Dispute Settlement* (London: Cameron May, 2002) 659–64.

[20] GA Zonnekeyn 'The Legal Status of WTO Panel Reports in the EC Legal Order. Some Reflections on the Opinion of Advocate General Mischo in the Atlanta Case' (1999) *JIEL* 723 and ibid 'The Status of Adopted Panel and Appellate Body Reports in the European Court of Justice and the European Court of First Instance – The Banana Experience' (2000) *JWT* 93.

the ECJ, it must also be aimed protecting the rights of individuals. The CFI had ruled, in first instance, that the purpose of the WTO Agreements is to govern relations between states or regional organisations for economic integration and not to protect the individual.[21] Alber disagrees with this part of the CFI's reasoning. He submits that the WTO Agreements primarily govern customs law issues and international trade law in general. Provisions on customs law, such as Article 25 EC Treaty, which is similar to certain provisions of WTO law, are directly applicable within the EC legal order. Alber emphasises that companies are the real actors in international trade law and the main beneficiaries of free trade. In this respect, Alber argues that the provisions of the SPS Agreement are particularly relevant since they aim to abolish discriminatory measures. These are of major importance for guaranteeing free trade for economic operators. Again, I agree with this statement. Although the WTO is essentially an intergovernmental organisation in which private business operators do not have any direct role, they are the main beneficiaries of the multilateral trading system. They are the ones who are expected to take advantage of the rules negotiated by governments and to convert them into export opportunities.[22] The wording of the panel in the *Section 301* case[23] is very instructive in this respect:

> ... it would be entirely wrong to consider that the position of individuals is of no relevance to the GATT/WTO legal matrix. Many of the benefits to Members which are meant to flow as a result of the acceptance of various disciplines under the GATT/WTO depend on the activity of individual economic operators in the national and global market places. The purpose of many of these disciplines, indeed one of the primary objects of the GATT/WTO as a whole, is to produce certain market conditions which would allow this individual activity to flourish.[24]
>
> ...
>
> The security and predictability in question are of 'the multilateral trading system'. The multilateral trading system is, per force, composed not only of States but also, indeed mostly, of individual economic operators. The lack of security and predictability affects mostly these individual operators.[25]

---

[21] Case T–174/00 *Biret International SA v Council* [2002] ECR II–17, at para 61 and Case T–210/00 *Établissements Biret et Cie SA v Council* [2002] ECR II–47, at para 71.

[22] E Kessie 'Enhancing Security and Predictability for Private Business Operators under the Dispute Settlement System of the WTO' (2000) *JWT* 1–17.

[23] WT/DS152/R *United States – Sections 301–310 of the Trade Act of 1974*, report of the panel of 22 December 1999.

[24] WT/DS152/R *United States – Sections 301–310 of the Trade Act of 1974*, report of the panel of 22 December 1999, at para 7.73.

[25] WT/DS152/R *United States – Sections 301–310 of the Trade Act of 1974*, report of the panel of 22 December 1999, at para 7.76.

> Trade is conducted most often and increasingly by private operators. It is through improved conditions for these private operators that Members benefit from WTO disciplines. The denial of benefits to a Member which flows from a breach is often indirect and results from the impact of the breach on the market place and the activities of individuals within it.[26]

These obiter dicta seem to indicate that the WTO rules do envisage the protection of the interests of individuals. As Petersmann has phrased it: '[T]he formulation of international trade rules in terms of rights and obligations of states is ... no convincing reason for preventing individuals from invoking precise and unconditional guarantees of freedom and non-discrimination, such as the customs union rules of the EC Treaty and their underlying worldwide GATT rules'.[27]

4. Conclusion

The Opinions of Advocate General Alber in the *Biret* cases are quite revolutionary. It is the first time that direct effect of WTO law and of DSB decisions has been contemplated. The analysis made by Alber AG of the WTO dispute settlement mechanism is instructive and he comes to the correct conclusion, ie that DSB decisions are binding for WTO members. I also tend to agree with most of his other conclusions such as the effect that must be given to adopted panel and Appellate Body reports and the resulting liability of the EC for the damages incurred by private companies as a result of non-implementation by the EC. His reasoning, however, is not always convincing and he should, in my, view, have analysed in more depth the applicable conditions under Article 288(2) EC Treaty leading to the liability of the EC.

It is my personal feeling that it is very unlikely that the ECJ will adhere to the 'Copernican innovation(s)' proposed by its Advocate General.

---

[26] WT/DS152/R *United States – Sections 301–310 of the Trade Act of 1974*, report of the panel of 22 December 1999, at para 7.77.

[27] E-U Petersmann *The GATT/WTO Dispute Settlement System: International Law, International Organizations and Dispute Settlement* (Deventer: Kluwer Law International, 1996) 238.

CHAPTER X

THE ECJ'S PETROTUB JUDGMENT: TOWARDS A REVIVAL OF THE 'NAKAJIMA DOCTRINE'?

1. Introduction

The judgment of the European Court of Justice (ECJ) in *Petrotub*[1] represents a good opportunity to readdress some of the questions surrounding the enforceability of WTO law in the European Community (EC) legal order.[2] In *Petrotub*, the ECJ confirmed a key opening in its case law through which private parties can invoke WTO law to test the legality of Community acts. Pursuant to this line of case law, better known as the *Nakajima* doctrine, WTO law can serve as a ground for review in cases where the EC intends to implement a particular obligation entered into within the framework of the WTO.[3] The ECJ, first in *Portugal v Council*[4] and later in *OGT Fruchthandelsgesellschaft*,[5] and the Court of First Instance (CFI), in some of the banana judgments,[6] had advocated a narrow interpretation of the *Nakajima* doctrine. The judgment of the ECJ in *Petrotub* confirms that the *Nakajima* line of case law has not been abandoned.

---

[1] Case C–76/00 P *Petrotub SA and Republica SA v Council and Commission*, judgement of 9 January 2003.
[2] For recent surveys of the case law of the European Court of Justice and of the Court of First Instance on this issue, see eg A Davies 'Bananas, Private Challenges, the Courts and the Legislature' in P Eeckhout and T Tridimas (eds) *Yearbook of European Law 2002* (Oxford: Oxford University Press, 2003) 299–326; P Eeckhout 'Judicial enforcement of WTO Law in the European Union – Some Further Reflections' (2002) *JIEL* 91–110; S Griller 'Enforcement and Implementation of WTO Law in the European Union' in F Breus S Griller and E Vranes (eds) *The Banana Dispute. An Economic and Legal Analysis* (Vienna – New York: Springer, 2003) 247–307 and F Snyder 'The Gatekeepers: The European Courts and WTO Law' (2003) *CMLRev* 313–67. For an interesting overview of the case law of the ECJ and CFI with regard to the enforceability of WTO law in the context of breaches of WTO law by the EC, see the Opinions of Advocate General Alber of 16 May 2003 in Case C–93/02 P *Biret International SA v Council* and Case C–94/02 P *Établissements Biret et Cie SA v Council*. In two fascinating Opinions – of which an analysis goes beyond the scope of this note – the Advocate General concludes that the EC can be held liable for the non-implementation of WTO panel and Appellate Body reports.
[3] Case C–69/89 *Nakajima All Precision Co Ltd v Council* [1991] ECR I–2069.
[4] Case C–149/96 *Portugal v Council* [1999] ECR I–8395.
[5] Case C–307/99 *OGT Fruchthandelsgesellschaft* [2001] ECR I–3159.
[6] Case T–18/99 *Cordis Obst und Gemüse Grosshandel GmbH v Commission* [2001] ECR II–4619; Case T–30/99 *Bocchi Food Trade International GmbH v Commission* [2001] ECR II–4619 and Case T–52/99 *T Port GmbH & Co KG v Commission* [2001] ECR II–981.

2. Factual Background

In 1997, the Council imposed definitive anti-dumping duties on imports of certain seamless pipes and tubes of iron or non-alloy steel originating in Romania and other countries.[7] Petrotub, one of the companies whose products were subject to the anti-dumping duties, submitted an action for annulment under Article 230 EC Treaty before the CFI seeking the annulment of the contested regulation. In one of its pleas it alleged that the Council had infringed Article 2(11) of the EC Anti-dumping Regulation[8] by, inter alia, failing to provide justification for its choice of the asymmetrical method in order to determine the anti-dumping margin. The CFI dismissed the action brought by Petrotub.[9] In March 2000, Petrotub brought an appeal before the ECJ against the judgment of the CFI. The ECJ's judgment of 9 January 2003 and its further implications are the subject of the present case note.

It may be helpful to set out first the underlying issue, that of the calculation of dumping margins by the 'asymmetrical method'. Article 2.4 of the WTO Anti-dumping Agreement[10] requires that a fair comparison be made between the export price and the normal value (which is in principle the price normally charged in domestic trade but may also be, where no such price is available, constructed on the basis of specified rules). Article 2.4.2 of the WTO Anti-dumping Agreement provides that 'the existence of margins of dumping during the investigation phase shall normally be established on the basis of a comparison of a weighted average normal value with a weighted average of prices of all comparable export transactions ["first symmetrical method"] or by a comparison of normal value and export prices on a transaction-to-transaction basis ["second symmetrical method"]. A normal value established on a weighted average basis may be compared to prices of individual export transactions ['asymmetrical method'] if the authorities find a pattern of export prices which differ significantly among different purchasers, regions or time periods, and *if an explanation is provided as to why such differences cannot be taken into account appropriately by the use of a*

---

[7] Council Regulation (EC) 2320/97 of 17 November 1997 imposing definitive anti-dumping duties on imports of certain seamless pipes and tubes of iron or non-alloy steel originating in Hungary, Poland, Russia, the Czech Republic, Romania and the Slovak Republic, repealing Regulation (EEC) 1189/93 and terminating the proceeding in respect of such imports originating in the Republic of Croatia [1997] OJ L322/1 of 25 November 1997.

[8] Council Regulation (EC) 384/96 of 22 December 1995 on protection against dumped imports from countries not members of the European Community [1996] OJ L56/1 of 6 March 1996 (as amended).

[9] Joined Cases T-33/98 and T-34/98 *Petrotub SA and Republica SA v Council* [1999] ECR II-3837.

[10] Agreement on Implementation of Article VI of the General Agreement on Tariffs and Trade 1994 [1994] OJ L336/103 of 23 December 1994.

weighted average-to-weighted average or transaction-to-transaction comparison. (own emphasis)

Article 2(10) of the EC Anti-dumping Regulation embodies the same requirement of a fair comparison and provides, in Article 2(11) that 'the existence of margins of dumping during the investigation period shall normally be established on the basis of a comparison of a weighted average normal value with a weighted average of prices of all export transactions to the Community ["first symmetrical method"], or by a comparison of individual normal values and individual export prices to the Community on a transaction-to-transaction basis ["second symmetrical method"]. However, a normal value established on a weighted average basis may be compared to prices of all individual export transactions to the Community ['asymmetrical method'], if there is a pattern of export prices which differs significantly among different purchasers, regions or time periods, and *if the methods specified in the first sentence of this paragraph would not reflect the full degree of dumping being practised'.* (own emphasis).

These provisions are thus substantially the same, each providing for the same three possible methods of calculation, although the definition of the circumstances in which the third method (the so-called asymmetrical method) may be used differs – 'if an explanation is provided as to why such differences cannot be taken into account appropriately by the use of [the first two methods]' as opposed to 'if the [first two methods] would not reflect the full degree of dumping being practised'.

One of Petrotub's main arguments is that the CFI erred in law by ruling that the Council's decision to use the asymmetrical method was adequately reasoned. Paragraph 108 of the judgment refers to the statement that the asymmetrical method was necessary to reflect the full degree of dumping. Without further explanation, that is merely self-justifying and thus an inadequate statement of reasons. Petrotub argues that a mere reference to the existence of a pattern of export prices which differs significantly by region or time period is not itself an adequate statement of reasons. Before using the asymmetrical method, the Council must also satisfy itself that the symmetrical methods would not reflect the full degree of dumping and adequate reasons must be given to establish the logical link between Article 2(11) of the EC Anti-dumping Regulation and the Council's decision to use the asymmetrical method.

Petrotub points out that, unlike Article 2(11) of the EC Anti-dumping Regulation, Article 2.4.2 of the WTO Anti-dumping Agreement provides that, in order to have recourse to the asymmetrical method, the authority is required to provide an explanation as to why significant differences in export prices among different purchasers, regions or time periods cannot be taken appropriately into account. Petrotub refers in this regard to the reply given on 15 February 1996 by the European Commission to questions raised by certain WTO members concerning those textual differences, according to which '[t]he term "full degree of dumping" simply refers to targeted dumping which is the heading under which this problem was addressed in the Uruguay Round negotiations. This is understood as meaning that there may be occasions where an average to average or transaction to transaction methods may not be appropriate where targeted dumping is taking place. Any departure from the above-mentioned methods will be explained both to the parties concerned and in Regulations imposing anti-dumping measures'.[11] According to Petrotub, it can be seen from that statement that the EC considers that the 'explanation ... as to why ...' referred to in Article 2.4.2. of the WTO Anti-dumping Agreement must be provided as part of the statement of reasons required by Article 253 EC Treaty, that is to say, the adequacy of the reasons for recourse to the asymmetrical method must be assessed in the light of in the light of Article 2.4.2 of the WTO Anti-dumping Agreement. Petrotub therefore concludes that the CFI erred in law insofar as it did not take into account of Article 2.4.2 of the WTO Anti-dumping Agreement in determining whether the Council had given an adequate statement of reasons as required by Article 253 EC Treaty.

3. The Judgment

The ECJ ruled, contrary to what the CFI had held, that it is necessary to take account of Article 2.4.2 of the WTO Anti-dumping Agreement in so far as that provision states that an explanation must be provided as to why significant differences in the pattern of export prices as among different purchasers, regions or time periods cannot be taken into account appropriately by the use of the symmetrical methods.

The ECJ recalled that it is settled case law that the WTO Agreement(s) are not in principle among the rules in the light of which the ECJ is to review the legality of measures adopted by the EC.[12] It then referred to its well-known 'Fediol' and 'Nakajima' doctrines and ruled that where the EC intends to implement a particular obligation assumed in the context of the WTO (the *Fediol* doctrine), or where a EC measure refers expressly to precise provisions of the WTO Agreement(s) (the *Nakajima* doctrine),

---

[11] G/APD/W/301 and G/SCM/W/309 of 4 March 1996, Communication from the European Commission of 15 February 1996.

[12] Paragraph 53 of the judgement with reference to Case C–149/96 *Portugal v Council* [1999] ECR I–8395 and Case C–307/99 *OGT Fruchthandelsgesellschaft* [2001] ECR I–3159.

it is for the ECJ to review the legality of the EC measure in question in the light of the WTO rules.[13]

The ECJ pointed out that the preamble to the EC Anti-dumping Regulation, and more specifically the fifth recital therein, clearly shows that the purpose of that regulation is, inter alia, to transpose into EC law as far as possible the new and detailed rules contained in the WTO Anti-dumping Agreement, which include, in particular, those relating to the calculation of dumping, so as to ensure a proper and transparent application of those rules.[14] It is therefore established, according to the ECJ, that the EC adopted the Anti-dumping Regulation in order to satisfy its obligations arising from the WTO Anti-dumping Agreement and that, by means of Article 2(11) of the Anti-dumping Regulation, it intended to implement the particular obligations laid down by Article 2.4.2 of that Agreement. The ECJ therefore concluded that it was able to review the legality of the contested regulation in the light of the WTO Anti-dumping Agreement.[15]

The ECJ also recalled that EC law must, so far as possible, be interpreted in a manner that is consistent with international law, in particular where its provisions are intended specifically to give effect to an international agreement concluded by the EC. The fact that Article 2(11) of the EC Anti-dumping Regulation did not explicitly provide that the explanation required by Article 2.4.2 of the WTO Anti-dumping Agreement had to be given by the Council in the event of recourse to the asymmetrical method could be explained by Article 253 EC Treaty, the ECJ ruled. Once Article 2.4.2 is transposed by the EC, the specific requirement to state reasons laid down by that provision can be considered to be subsumed under the general requirement imposed by the Treaty for acts adopted by the institutions to state the reasons on which they are based. Such an interpretation coincides, according to the ECJ, with the international assurances given in the communication of 15 February 1996 from the Commission to the Secretariat of the WTO Committee on Anti-Dumping Practices, according to which the explanation referred to in Article 2.4.2 of the WTO Anti-dumping Agreement will be given directly to the parties and in regulations imposing anti-dumping duties.

The ECJ concluded that a Council regulation imposing definitive anti-dumping duties, using the asymmetrical method is used for the purposes of calculating the dumping margin, must in particular contain, as part of the statement of reasons required by Article 253 EC Treaty, the specific

---

[13] Paragraph 54 of the judgement with reference to Case C–149/96 *Portugal v Council* [1999] ECR I–8395.
[14] Paragraph 55 of the judgement.
[15] Paragraph 56 of the judgement.

explanation provided for in Article 2.4.2 of the WTO Anti-dumping Agreement. The ECJ ruled that is evident in this case that the contested regulation does not contain even the merest reference to the second symmetrical method or, a fortiori, the slightest explanation as to why that method would not enable significant differences in the pattern of export prices among different purchasers, regions or time periods to be taken appropriately into account. In those circumstances, it must be held that the CFI erred in law by holding that there was no need to take into consideration Article 2.4.2 of the WTO Anti-dumping Agreement for the purposes of determining whether the Council had fulfilled the obligation to state reasons for the contested regulation and by therefore finding that the statement of reasons given for that regulation was adequate for the purposes of Article 253 EC Treaty.

The ECJ therefore decided that the contested judgment had to be annulled on the ground referred to above without there being any need to rule on the other parts of the plea put forward by Petrotub in support of its appeal.

4. Analysis

The *Petrotub* judgment is not a landmark ruling. It does, however, clearly confirm that the *Nakajima* line of case law, which gives private parties an important tool for testing the legality of Community acts in view of the EC's commitments under WTO law, has not been abandoned. After the ECJ refused to apply the *Nakajima* doctrine in *Portugal v Council*,[16] Griller pointed out that the future would determine which direction the ECJ would take with regard to the application of *Nakajima*.[17] It was finally not the ECJ, but the CFI that gave an indication about what the future case law would look like. The minimalist application of the *Nakajima* doctrine, by the CFI in some banana cases, and later by the ECJ in *OGT Fruchthandelsgesellschaft*, seemed to indicate that both the ECJ and the CFI wanted to limit as much as possible the possibilities for individuals to rely on WTO law in proceedings before the European courts in Luxembourg.[18] The *Petrotub* judgment appears to indicate the opposite.

This case note will give an overview of the application of the *Nakajima* doctrine by the ECJ and the CFI with some further reflections on the ramifications of the *Petrotub* judgment if the ECJ were to follow this line of case law in the future.

---

[16] Case C–149/96 *Portugal v Council* [1999] ECR I–8395.
[17] S Griller 'Judicial Enforceability of WTO Law in the European Union. Annotation to Case C–149/96 *Portugal v Council*' (2000) *JIEL* 466.
[18] GA Zonnekeyn 'The Latest on Indirect Effect of WTO Law in the EC Legal Order. The Nakajima Case law Misjudged?' (2001) *JIEL* 608.

4.1 The *Nakajima* Doctrine – the Origins

In *Nakajima*,[19] the applicant (ie Nakajima) challenged a regulation imposing definitive anti-dumping duties on dot-matrix printers originating in Japan. Nakajima raised an exception of inapplicability of the EC Anti-dumping Regulation.[20] On the other hand, it submitted grounds for the annulment of the regulation imposing anti-dumping duties. The plea of inapplicability was essentially based on the incompatibility of the EC Anti-dumping Regulation with the GATT Anti-dumping Code, in connection with the calculation of the normal value. The ECJ rejected the pleading on the lack of direct effect of the GATT Anti-dumping Code, because the applicant was not invoking the direct effect of the GATT Anti-dumping Code, but the compatibility of an EC measure with an international agreement that it was intended to implement. The ECJ concluded that such an incompatibility did not exist.

The most important part of the judgment referred to the possibility of invoking provisions of GATT in a direct action before the ECJ. The ECJ made a clear distinction between the direct effect of GATT as such, which plays a role in the relationship between national and EC law, and the possibility of invoking international agreements when challenging EC acts, which belongs to the relationship between international law and EC law. The ECJ emphasised that it was a direct action and that the regulation was adopted in order to implement the GATT Anti-dumping Code. The relevant provisions of the GATT Anti-dumping Code could therefore be invoked.

4.2 The *Nakajima* Doctrine – Evolution

4.2.1 Nakajima Consistent Application

The ECJ has applied its *Nakajima* case law in a number of cases following the judgment in *Nakajima*.

Portugal v Commission[21] concerned the Uruguay Round Blair House Agreement (BHA), setting a maximum guaranteed area for the production of oilseeds. The EC implemented the BHA by Council Regulation 232/94 amending Council Regulation 1765/95 on oilseeds in part by adopting the area figures in the BHA annex. Portugal asked for the annulment of the

---

[19] Case C–69/89 *Nakajima All Precision Co Ltd v Council* [1991] ECR I–2069.
[20] Then, Council Regulation (EEC) 2423/88 of 11 July 1988 on protection against dumped or subsidised imports from countries not members of the European Economic Community[1988] OJ L209/1 of 2 August 1988.
[21] Case C–150/95 *Portugal v Council* ECR [1997] I–5863.

Commission implementing regulation, which had the effect of reducing the final regional reference amounts for oilseeds. The ECJ used the BHA to assess and confirm the legality of the Commission regulation.

In *BEUC v Commission*,[22] a consumer association invoked the WTO Anti-dumping Agreement to annul a Commission decision refusing to recognise it as an interested party in an anti-dumping procedure. Article 6.11 of the WTO Anti-dumping Agreement sets out a non-exhaustive list of interested parties for the purposes of the agreement. In adopting Articles 5(10), 6(7) and 21 of the EC Anti-dumping Regulation, the EC used the possibility given by the WTO Anti-dumping Agreement to recognise consumer organisations as interested parties. The CFI ruled that 'these articles correctly implement WTO rules, which allow consumer organisations access to non-confidential information in relation to all elements of the proceeding, including dumping, injury and causality' and annulled the Commission decision.

In *Euroalliages*,[23] the applicant sought the annulment of a Commission decision terminating anti-dumping duties following an expiry review. It argued that the EC Anti-dumping Regulation required the retention of duties, on expiry of the original period, where it was shown that injurious dumping was likely to recur. Whereas the applicant did not invoke WTO law, the CFI used the WTO anti-dumping Agreement as a criterion to assess the legality of ...[].

4.2.2 The Nakajima Doctrine Curtailed?

In *Portugal v Council*,[24] the ECJ ruled on an action for annulment introduced by Portugal against a Council decision approving two Memoranda of Understanding on market access arrangements for textile products originating in Pakistan and India. The Portuguese government argued that these Memoranda of Understanding and – by approving them, also the respective Council decision – were incompatible with certain provisions of GATT 1994 and the WTO Agreement on Textile and Clothing Products which they purported to implement. The ECJ was rather restrictive in its application of the Nakajima doctrine and ruled that 'the contested decision is not designed to ensure the implementation in the Community legal order of a particular obligation assumed in the context of the WTO agreements, nor does it make express reference to any specific provisions of the WTO agreements. Its purpose is merely to approve the Memoranda of Understanding negotiated by the Community with Pakistan and

---
[22] Case T–256/97 *Bureau Européen des Unions de Consommateurs (BEUC) v Commission* [1999] ECR I–169.
[23] Case T–188/89 *Euroalliages v Commission* [2001] ECR II–1757.
[24] Case C–149/96 *Portugal v Council* [1999] ECR I–8395.

India'.[25] Consequently, the ECJ was not prepared to review the legality of the Council decision approving the Memoranda.

It is correct that the two Memoranda, by mutually enhancing market access in the field of textiles and clothing, are not implementing a precise obligation stemming from GATT 1994 or the WTO Agreement on Textile and Clothing Products. It is clear, however, that the parties intended to act in accordance with the aim of the WTO Agreement on Textile and Clothing Products to gradually integrate the products covered by the agreement into the GATT 1994, thereby reducing quota restrictions as well as customs duties.[26] It should suffice to refer to one particular example to demonstrate that the ECJ could have used the *Nakajima* doctrine in this particular case. The preamble to the Council decision approving the Memoranda clearly reflects the objective of integrating the textiles and clothing sector into GATT 1994. It provides that 'in the framework of the GATT market access negotiations, the Commission conducted negotiations with the Republic of India and the Islamic Republic of Pakistan in the area of market access for textile products'.[27] This context and motivation is also reflected in the frequent references to GATT and the WTO in the Memoranda themselves, which are attached to the Council decision.

Following the judgment of the ECJ in *Portugal v Council*, it was argued that there was still room for clarification as to the limits of the *Nakajima* ruling.[28] Griller even questioned whether the ECJ had not departed from the *Nakajima* case law.[29] He argues that the principle of reciprocity, used by the ECJ in *Portugal v Council* as one of the arguments to refute the possibility of invoking WTO law as a standard for review in a direct action before the ECJ, also applies once internal legislation has been enacted in the application of a particular obligation under WTO law and he concluded that the intention to observe WTO obligations is not sufficient to activate the ECJ's competence to review secondary EC legislation in the light of WTO law.[30]

---

[25] Case C–149/96 *Portugal v Council* [1999] ECR I–8395, para 51.
[26] Similarly, S Griller 'Enforcement and Implementation of WTO Law in the European Union' in F Breus, S Griller and E Vranes (eds) *The Banana Dispute. An Economic and Legal Analysis* (Vienna – New York: Springer, 2003) 264.
[27] Second recital of the preamble to Council Decision 96/386/EC of 26 February 1996 concerning the conclusion of Memoranda of Understanding between the European Community and the Islamic Republic of Pakistan and between the European Community and the Republic of India on arrangements in the area of market access for textile products [1996] OJ L153/47 of 27 June 1996.
[28] A Rosas 'Annotation on Case C–149/96 *Portugal v Council*' (2000) *CMLRev* 815.
[29] S Griller 'Judicial Enforceability of WTO law in the European Union. Annotation to Case C–149/96 *Portugal v Council*' *JIEL* (2000) 463–7.
[30] A similar point was raised by Berrisch and Kamman. See GM Berrisch and HG Kamann 'WTO-Recht im Gemeinschaftsrecht – (k)eine Kehrwende des EuGH' (2000) *EWS* 95. They
continued ...

In *Cordis Obst, Bocchi* and *T Port*,[31] the CFI favoured, what has been referred to as a *'minimalist application of the Nakajima doctrine'*.[32] In these cases, the applicants were not satisfied with the annual quantity of bananas allocated to them following the adoption of Regulation 2362/98.[33] They asked for compensation for the loss suffered as a result of the adoption of Regulation 2362/98 by the Commission. Regulation 2362/98 laid down detailed rules for the implementation of Regulation 404/93 regarding imports of bananas into the EC. These rules were said to conflict with WTO law.

In regards to the possible inferences to be drawn from *Portugal v Council*, the applicants acknowledged that the ECJ had held that the WTO provisions did not have general direct effect within the EC legal system. They added, however, that this judgment did not conflict with the arguments submitted in support of their action to the effect that the EC institutions were guilty of misuse of power. The fact that the EC banana regime had been declared incompatible with WTO law by a panel and by the Appellate Body – decisions having the force of *res judicata* – and the efforts the EC had undertaken to rectify the infringements concerned, precluded the EC institutions from adopting further provisions in breach of those rules. The applicants further argued that since the EC had given an undertaking to the WTO Dispute Settlement Body to repeal the provisions of its regulations which conflicted with WTO rules, it had acted in breach of the principle *nemini licet venire contra factum proprium* when putting that undertaking into practice by adopting a regulation containing infringements of those rules.

As far as the application of the *Nakajima* doctrine is concerned, the CFI ruled that neither the panel report of 22 May 1997,[34] nor the Appellate Body report of 9 September 1997[35] included any special obligations which the Commission intended to implement, within the meaning of the *Nakajima* case law, in Regulation 2362/98.[36] The regulation does not make

---

argued that '[U]nerklärt bleibt allerdings, wie diese Lösung der mittelbaren Wirkung mit dem Kriterium der Gegenseitigkeit vereinbar ist'.

[31] Case T–18/99 *Cordis Obst und Gemüse Grosshandel GmbH v Commission* [2001] ECR II–4619; Case T–30/99 *Bocchi Food Trade International GmbH v Commission* [2001] ECR II–4619 and Case T–52/99 *T Port GmbH & Co KG v Commission* [2001] ECR II–981.

[32] GA Zonnekeyn 'The Latest on Indirect Effect of WTO Law in the EC Legal Order. The Nakajima Case law Misjudged?' (2001) *JIEL* 608.

[33] Commission Regulation (EC) 2362/98 of 28 October 1998 laying down detailed rules for the implementation of Council Regulation (EEC) 404/93 regarding imports of bananas into the Community [1998] OJ L293/32 of 31 October 1998.

[34] WT/DS27/R *European Communities – Regime for the Importation, Sale and Distribution of Bananas*, report of the panel of 22 May 1997.

[35] WT/DS27/AB/R *European Communities – Regime for the Importation, Sale and Distribution of Bananas*, report of the Appellate Body of 9 September 1997.

[36] The English language version of the judgement refers in para 64 to a 'judgement' that does not make express reference to any specific obligations arising out of the panel or Appellate

continued ...

express reference either to any specific obligations arising out of the reports of the WTO dispute settlement organs, or to specific provisions of the agreements contained in the annexes to the WTO Agreement.

These judgments of the CFI have been subject to fierce criticism because the CFI completely ignored the *Nakajima* line of case law.[37] Indeed, the CFI is walking on very thin ice when it argues that Regulation 2362/98 was not adopted by the EC with the intention to implement any WTO obligation. A WTO panel, for example, explicitly referred to a statement of the EC that 'in order to live up to its WTO obligations as contained in its Schedules of GATS commitments, it had adopted an entirely new banana import regime, as set out in Regulations 1637 and 2362'.[38] It is obvious that Regulations 1637/98 and 2362/98 were adopted with a view to establishing a WTO-compatible banana regime. It can be argued therefore that the CFI 'misjudged' the principles of the *Nakajima* case law. In addition, paragraph 2 of the preamble to Regulation 1637/98,[39] which gives the Commission a 'mandate' to establish a WTO-compatible banana regime, explicitly provides as follows: '[W]hereas the Community's international commitments under the World Trade Organisation (WTO) and to the other signatories of the Fourth ACP-EC Convention should be met, whilst achieving at the same time the purposes of the common organisation of the market in bananas'. This would indicate that Regulation 2362/98 was, indeed, adopted with a view to implement the WTO obligations of the EC.[40]

It is interesting to note in this context, that the EC's new banana regime, which entered into force on 1 July 2001, does not refer to any obligation of the EC under WTO law.[41] It does mention, however, that using the

Body reports, or to specific provisions of the agreements contained in the annexes to the WTO Agreement. Obviously, the word judgement must be replaced by a reference to Regulation 2362/98. This follows clearly from the original German version of the judgement where it is said that 'Ebenso wenig verweist die "Verordnung Nr. 2362/98" ausdrücklich ...'.

[37] See in particular J Gerkrath (2002) RAE 619–25; S Peers 'WTO dispute settlement and Community law' (2001) *ELRev* 605–15 and G A Zonnekeyn 'The Latest on Indirect Effect of WTO Law in the EC Legal Order. The *Nakajima* Case law Misjudged?' (2001) *JIEL* 597–608.

[38] WT/DS27/RW/ECU *European Communities – Regime for the Importation, Sale and Distribution of Bananas – Recourse to Article 21.5 by Ecuador*, report of 12 April 1999, para 4.56. This also follows from the judgements itself. In para 8, the CFI explicitly says that in order to comply with the panel and Appellate Body reports, the Council adopted Regulation 1637/98 and subsequently Regulation 2362/98. It would seem that CFI has contradicted itself.

[39] Council Regulation (EC) 1637/98 of 20 July 1998 amending Regulation (EEC) No. 404/93 on the common organisation of the market in bananas [1998] OJ L210/28 of 28 July 1998.

[40] The action for damages by Chiquita is noteworthy in this respect. Chiquita argues that '[F]ollowing a dispute settlement procedure in the WTO finding aspects of this regime to be WTO-incompatible, the EC agreed to make its banana regime compatible ... This was purportedly done by Council Regulation No. 1634/98 and Commission Regulation No. 2362/98'. See Case T–19/01 *Chiquita Brands International Inc Chiquita Banana Company BV and Chiquita Italia SpA v Commission* [2001] OJ C108/23 of 7 April 2001.

[41] Commission Regulation (EC) 896/2001 of 7 May 2001 laying down detailed rules for applying Council Regulation (EEC) 404/93 as regards the arrangements for importing

continued ...

three-year period 1994 to 1996 'can also resolve a dispute which has been going on for a number of years with certain of the Community's trading partners'.[42] This statement, in combination with the numerous press statements made by the EC clearly indicate that Regulation 896/2001 intends to bring the EC banana regime into compliance with WTO law. A narrow, textual interpretation of the *Nakajima* case law would possibly exclude the possibility to review this new regulation in the light of WTO law. However, when looking at the objective of Regulation 896/2001, that is the establishment of a WTO-compatible banana regime in view of the earlier WTO panel and Appellate Body reports, there cannot exist any doubt that it purports to implement the WTO obligations of the EC.

The ECJ adhered to an identical interpretation of the *Nakajima* doctrine in *OGT Fruchthandelsgesellschaft* and ruled – by reasoned order and thus not prepared to spill too much learned ink over the legal issue at hand – that the banana regime 'as introduced by Regulation 404/93 and subsequently amended, is not designed to ensure implementation in the Community legal order of a particular obligation assumed in the context of GATT'.[43]

5. Observations

5.1 What's in a Name?

The ECJ has recognised that WTO law can serve as a ground to review the legality of EC law in cases where the EC intends to implement a particular obligation entered into within the framework of the WTO (the *Nakajima* doctrine),[44] or if an EC act expressly refers to specific provisions of the WTO law (the *Fediol* doctrine).[45] Both doctrines have been referred to as embodying the so-called 'principle of implementation' since they both involve the implementation of WTO law in the EC legal order.[46]

It is better, however, as Snyder has suggested to explicitly distinguish between these two exceptions and refer to them as the 'clear reference exception' (*Fediol*) and the 'implementation exception' (*Nakajima*).[47]

---

bananas into the Community [2001] OJ L126/6 of 8 May 2001. Corrigendum, see [2001] OJ L133/19 of 16 May 2001.
[42] See the 5th recital of the preamble to Regulation 896/2001.
[43] Case C–307/99 *OGT Fruchthandelsgesellschaft* [2001] ECR I–3159.
[44] Case C–69/89 *Nakajima All Precision Co Ltd v Council* [1991] ECR I–2069.
[45] Case C–70/87 *Fediol v Commission* [1989] ECR 1781.
[46] P Eeckhout 'The Domestic Legal Status of the WTO Agreements: Interconnecting legal Systems' (1997) *CMLRev* 56 and ibid 'Judicial enforcement of WTO Law in the European Union – Some Further Reflections' (2002) *JIEL* 104. Eeckhout distinguishes the two doctrines but refers to them as a single category.
[47] F Snyder 'The Gatekeepers: The European Courts and WTO Law' (2003) *CMLRev* 342.

Without purporting to put too much emphasis on pure semantics, this distinction does have the disadvantage that it refers to both doctrines as exceptions to the non-recognition of direct effect of GATT law and WTO law in the EC legal order. The *Nakajima* doctrine for example cannot be considered as an exception *per se* to the absence of direct effect of WTO law since the question of direct effect is a non-issue where the EC intends to implement a particular obligation entered into within the framework of the WTO. This was explicitly recognised by the ECJ in *Nakajima* where it ruled that the applicant was not relying on the direct effect of the GATT Anti-dumping Code as the Council had argued.[48] A similar view has been defended by Eeckhout who explains that the *Nakajima* doctrine can justifiable be used to review the validity of EC law with reference to international obligations without producing conflict with the denial of direct effect of WTO law. The doctrine envisages that international obligations have been transposed into EC law. This obviates the need to rely on the international obligations directly. However, international obligations have to be fully and correctly transposed. The ECJ and CFI can therefore review whether this has been achieved.[49]

5.2 More than Consistent Interpretation

Some authors have argued that the *Nakajima* case law merely corresponds to the general obligation to interpret EC law consistently with international law and that 'the so-called Nakajima principle collapses into the principle of consistent interpretation'.[50] This is not entirely correct as the Nakajima line of case law 'offers more than mere consistent interpretation'.[51] In addition, it is different from consistent interpretation in that it may be relied upon in case of conflict between a provision of EC law and a provision of WTO law.[52]

---

[48] Case C–69/89 *Nakajima All Precision Co Ltd v Council* [1991] ECR I–2069, para 28. See also J Steenbergen 'Is there a Need for Constitutional Reform of Foreign Trade Law of the EEC?' in M Hilf and E-U Petersmann (eds) *National Constitutions and International Economic Law* (Deventer: Kluwer Law and Taxation Publishers, 1993) 564–5.

[49] P Eeckhout 'The Domestic Legal Status of the WTO Agreements: Interconnecting legal Systems' (1997) *CMLRev* 45–6. See also A Davies 'Bananas, Private Challenges, the Courts and the Legislature' in P Eeckhout and T Tridimas (eds) *Yearbook of European Law 2002* (Oxford: Oxford University Press, 2003) 318, fn 102.

[50] A Peters 'Recent Developments in the Application of International Law in Domestic and European Community Law' in *German Yearbook of International Law* (Berlin: Duncker & Humblot, 1997) 75. For a similar view, see A Ott *GATT und WTO im Gemeinschaftsrecht* (Köln: Carl Heymanns Verlag KG, 1997) 149.

[51] P Eeckhout 'The Domestic Legal Status of the WTO Agreements: Interconnecting legal Systems' (1997) *CMLRev* 42.

[52] A Davies 'Bananas, Private Challenges, the Courts and the Legislature' in P Eeckhout and T Tridimas (eds) *Yearbook of European Law 2002* (Oxford: Oxford University Press, 2003) 320 and P Eeckhout 'Judicial enforcement of WTO Law in the European Union – Some Further Reflections' (2002) *JIEL* 104–5.

5.3 Too Much Leeway for the EC legislator?

As far as the application of the *Nakajima* doctrine is concerned, it might not always be easy to know when the EC intends to implement a particular obligation undertaken in the framework of the WTO.[53] In *Nakajima*, the anti-dumping regulation clearly implemented the GATT Anti-dumping Code and references to this effect could be found in the recitals. A similar reasoning applies to the *Petrotub* case. The situation may not be so clear when an explicit reference is omitted. It is questionable, however, whether the absence of an explicit reference to the WTO Agreement(s) in an EC act would suffice to deprive applicants of the possibility to have the legality of the provisions of such an act assessed by the ECJ or CFI.[54] A rational reading of the *Nakajima* judgment reveals that the ECJ used a contextual and teleological approach.[55] It is therefore impossible for the EC to avoid review of the compatibility of a legal act with WTO law, simply by not referring to the relevant provisions of the WTO Agreement(s) which it intends to implement.[56] This would give too much leeway to the political institutions of the EC and would do injustice to private companies (and Member States) seeking to enforce WTO law within the boundaries of the *Nakajima* case law. One of the ECJ's main arguments for denying direct effect to WTO law is that it does not want to tie the hands of the legislator. If the same reasoning would be applied in the context of the *Nakajima* line of case law, private companies would be deprived of a legal avenue which enables them to invoke WTO law in order to test the legality of Community acts.

Bourgeois has – rightly – argued that by leaving it to the political institutions of the EC to decide on the effect of WTO law in the EC legal, the ECJ has introduced a sort of 'sovereignty shield' in the hands of these political bodies against the enforcement of WTO law.[57] It can

---

[53] As pointed out by F Castillo de la Torre 'The Status of GATT in EC Law, Revisited – The Consequences of the Judgement on the Banana Import Regime for the Enforcement of the Uruguay Round Agreements' (1995) *JWT* 53 at 59-60 and P Egli and J Kokott (2000) *AJIL* 744.
[54] F Castillo de la Torre 'The Status of GATT in EC Law, Revisited – The Consequences of the Judgement on the Banana Import Regime for the Enforcement of the Uruguay Round Agreements' (1995) *JWT* 53 at 60 and F Berrod 'La Cour de justice refuse l'invocabilité des accords OMC: essai de regulation de la mondialisation' (2000) *RTDE* 442.
[55] For a similar view, see GM Berrisch and HG Kamann 'WTO-Recht im Gemeinschaftsrecht – (k)eine Kehrwende des EuGH' (2000) *EWS* 95.
[56] *Contra*: S Griller 'Judicial Enforceability of WTO Law in the European Union. Annotation to Case C–149/96 *Portugal v Council*' (2000) *JIEL* 464.
[57] JHJ Bourgeois 'The European Court of Justice and the WTO: Problems and Challenges' in JHH Weiler (ed) *The EU, the WTO and the NAFTA Towards a Common Law of International Trade?* (Oxford: Oxford University Press, 2000) 107. Bourgeois refers to a report of the European Parliament of 24 September 1997 'on the relationship between international law,

continued ...

only be hoped that the EC legislator will not abuse this 'sovereignty shield' and that the European courts in Luxembourg will adopt a flexible interpretation of the *Nakajima* doctrine if the EC legislator would ever follow such an undemocratic approach. The explicit reference to a 'WTO compatible regime' in the proposed hormones directive is hopeful in this respect.[58]

6. Conclusion

Ehlermann has recently written that 'recognition of direct effect would harm, instead of help, the WTO'.[59] He argues that the granting of direct effect would further strengthen the quasi-judicial arm of the WTO, a situation which he considers to be dangerous in the context of the WTO 'as the (quasi-) judicial arm has proven already to be much stronger than the political arm of the WTO'. Ehlermann defends the view that a WTO member whose courts grant direct effect is likely to become an aggressive partner in the context of WTO dispute settlement if it wishes to uphold the balance of rights and duties between itself and its treaty partners. The imbalance to which he refers would be the result of an increase in legal actions brought by private companies against violations of WTO law before the domestic courts of the WTO member concerned, whereas there would be no comparable legal avenue in other countries. A WTO member exposed to such legal actions domestically will try to defend the interests of its exporters and investors before the WTO dispute settlement organs in order to restore the balance of rights and obligations.

However, the *Petrotub* case indicates that even the possibility of a limited reliance on WTO law might very well result in less litigation before the WTO dispute settlement organs, albeit not by the member granting this limited reliance. In the context of such a limited reliance on WTO law, Petrotub has been able to invalidate an EC regulation imposing anti-duties because the latter was incompatible with the WTO Anti-dumping Agreement. Petrotub has even obtained a reimbursement of the anti-duties paid following the annulment of the contested regulation by the ECJ.[60] If Romania would have decided to initiate WTO dispute settlement

---

Community law and the constitutional law of the Member States' (PE 220.225/fin) where this term is used. See p 14 of the report. It is ironic that this report has been written by Siegbert Alber, the Advocate General who took a 'revolutionary' approach with regard to the enforcement of WTO law in his Opinions in the *Biret* cases (n 2).

[58] REFERENCE Common position of ...

[59] C-D Ehlermann 'Six Years on the Bench of the "World Trade Court": Some Personal Experiences as Member of the Appellate Body of the World Trade Organization' (2002) *JWT* 637 and ibid, 'Tensions between the dispute settlement process and the diplomatic and treaty-making activities of the WTO' (2002) *World Trade Review* 307–8.

[60] See Notice concerning anti-dumping measures on imports of certain seamless pipes and tubes of iron or non-alloy steel originating in Romania [2003] OJ C30/14 of 8 February 2003.

proceedings against the EC, Petrotub could not have obtained a similar satisfactory result. The *Petrotub* judgment indicates that individual cases, where a WTO incompatible measure is being challenged, ought to be brought before the domestic courts of the WTO member concerned. It is indispensable therefore that private companies must be given the possibility to invoke WTO law to challenge WTO-incompatible legislation even without explicitly granting direct effect to WTO law.

CHAPTER XI

EC LIABILITY FOR NON-IMPLEMENTATION OF WTO DISPUTE SETTLEMENT DECISIONS – ARE THE DICE CAST?

The judgments of the ECJ in *Biret* seem to open the door for further discussions on the liability of the EC for non-implementation of WTO dispute settlement decisions. The ECJ refused to grant compensation to the applicants due the fact that the damages occurred before the adoption of the DSB decision and before the reasonable period of time accorded to the EC to implement this decision had lapsed. Since the ECJ did not explicitly pronounce itself on the question whether compensation could have been awarded if the damages had arisen after the reasonable period of time, it seems to have left the door half open. It is important that the ECJ does so without insisting – as it has done in its previous judgments concerning the effect of WTO law in the EC legal order – on reciprocity, that is without requiring whether any other of the EC's major trading partners would allow such damage claims. In addition, a recent judgment of the ECJ seems to indicate that the *Nakajima* line of case law, according to which the ECJ or the CFI may review the legality of an EC act in cases where the EC intends to implement a particular obligation entered into within the framework of the WTO, will play an essential role in the cases which are currently pending before the ECJ and CFI.

1. Introduction

The expectations amongst practising lawyers and legal scholars with regard to a further penetration of WTO law within the EC legal order[1] had almost risen to insurmountable heights when Advocate General Alber delivered his Opinions in the *Biret* cases on 15 May 2003.[2] The

---

[1] For recent contributions on this subject, see eg S Griller 'Enforcement and Implementation of WTO Law in the European Union' in F Breus, S Griller and E Vranes (eds) *The Banana Dispute. An Economic and Legal Analysis* (Vienna- New York: Springer, 2003) 247; C Kaddous 'Le statut du droit de l'OMC dans l'ordre juridique communautaire: développements récents' in *Mélanges en Hommage à Jean Victor-Louis*, (vol II, Brussels: ULB Presses Universitaires de Bruxelles, 2003) 107; D Luff, 'Considérations sur l'effet des règles de l'OMC dans les ordres juridiques Belge et Communautaire' in *Rapports belges au Congrès de l'Académie Internationale de Droit comparé à Brisbane* (Brussels: Bruylant, 2002) 671 and F Snyder 'The Gatekeepers: The European Courts and WTO Law' (2003) 40(2) *CMLRev* 313.
[2] Advocate General Alber, Opinions of 15 May 2003 in Case C–93/02 P *Biret International v Council* and in Case C–94/02 P *Établissements Biret and Cie SA v Council*, not yet published in the *ECR* but available at http://www.curia.eu.int (last visited 15 February 2004). For comments on the Opinions of the Advocate General, see eg S Hörmann and GJ Göttsche
continued ...

Advocate General had proposed a 'Copernican innovation' in the case law of the ECJ by opining that the WTO Agreements could have direct effect in the EC legal order, following an action for damages based on Article 288 EC Treaty, when the EC had neglected to adapt its WTO-incompatible legislation to a decision of the WTO Dispute Settlement Body (DSB) within the reasonable period of time accorded to it. It was obvious, in this context, that the judgments of the European Court of Justice (ECJ) would be impatiently awaited. In two judgments, rendered on 30 September 2003,[3] the ECJ declined to follow the Opinions of its Advocate General and seemed to have squashed the hopes of many. However, by not explicitly excluding the possibility that the EC could have been held liable if the factual circumstances of the cases had been different, the ECJ seems to have left the door half open. Since the ECJ and the Court of First Instance (CFI)[4] will have to pronounce themselves on similar cases in the not so far away future, the judgments of the ECJ in *Biret* can be quite significant.

2. Factual Background

The origins of the *Biret* cases can be traced back to the *Hormones* dispute between the EC and the United States (US). On 29 April 1996, the Council adopted Directive 96/22/EC concerning the prohibition on the use in stock farming of certain substances having a hormonal or thyrostatic action and of ß-agonists.[5] In January 1996, the US, considering that the EC legislation was restricting its exports to the EC of beef and veal treated with certain hormones, in breach of the obligations the EC

'Bleiben europäische Unternehmen rechtsutzlos bei Verstössen der EG gegen das Welthandelsrecht?' (2003) 14(15) *Europäische Zeitschrift für Wirtschaftsrecht*, 449; S Mann 'Beefing up the Direct Effect of WTO Agreements within the European Community' (2003) 9(5) *International Trade Law & Regulation* 133 and GA Zonnekeyn 'EC Liability for the Non-Implementation of WTO Dispute Settlement Decisions – Advocate General Alber proposes a "Copernican Innovation" in the Case Law of the ECJ' (2003) 6(3) *JIEL* 761.

[3] Case C–93/02 P *Biret International v Council* and Case C–94/02 P *Établissements Biret and Cie SA v Council*, not yet published in the *ECR* but available at http://www.curia.eu.int (last visited 15 February 2004). For a brief comment, see S Bartelt 'Die Haftung der Gemeinschaft bei Nichtumsetzung von Entscheidungen des WTO-Streitbeilegungsgremiums' (2003) 38(6) *EuR* 1077 and C Pitschas 'EuGH: kein Schadenersatz wegen Importvereibots für Hormonenfleisch'(2003) 14(24) *Europäische Zeitschrift für Wirtschaftsrecht* 758.

[4] See eg Case T–69/00 *Fiamm SpA and Fiamm Technologies Inc v Commission and Council* [2000] OJ C135/30; Case T–151/00 *Le Laboratoire du Bain v Council and Commission* [2000] OJ C247/30; Case T–297/00 *Claude-Anne de Solène v Council and Commission* [2000] OJ C355/30; Case T–301/00 *Groupe Frémaux SA and Palais Royal Inc v Council and Commission* [2000] OJ C355/32; Case T–320/00 *CD Cartondruck GmbH & Co KG v Commission and Council* [2000] OJ C355/39; Case T–383/00 *Beamglow Ltd v Council, European Parliament and Commission* [2001 OJ C 61/21; Case T–19/01 *Chiquita Brands International, Inc, Chiquita Banana Company BV and Chiquita Italia SpA v Commission* [2001] OJ C108/23; Case T–135/01 *Giorgio Fedon & Figli SpA v Commission* [2001] OJ C275/10 and Case T–109/03 *Arran Aromatics Limited, I. Russel and A Rennick v Commissie* [2003] OJ C135/33.

[5] [1996] OJ L125/3.

had entered into within the framework of the WTO, brought dispute settlement proceedings before the competent WTO organs.[6]

On 18 August 1997, the panel set up in respect of this procedure concluded that the EC was in breach of various provisions of the WTO Agreement on Sanitary and Phytosanitary Measures (SPS).[7] In response to an appeal lodged by the EC, the Appellate Body delivered a report on 16 January 1998 amending certain aspects of the report of the panel, but finding none the less that the EC was in breach of Article 3(3) and Article 5(1) of the SPS Agreement, essentially on the ground that there had not been a sufficiently specific scientific analysis of the cancer risks associated with the use of certain hormones as growth hormones.[8] The Appellate Body recommended that 'the Dispute Settlement Body request the European Communities to bring the SPS measures found ... to be inconsistent with the SPS Agreement into conformity with the obligations of the European Communities under that Agreement'. On 13 February 1998, the WTO Dispute Settlement Body (DSB) adopted the report of the Appellate Body and the reports of the panels, as amended by the Appellate Body.

As the EC had stated that it intended to comply with its WTO obligations but that it needed a reasonable time to do so,[9] under Article 21(3) of the Understanding on Rules and Procedures Governing the Settlement of Disputes (DSU), it was granted a period of 15 months for that purpose, which expired on 13 May 1999.[10]

On the basis of the results of further analysis of the risks associated with the use of the substances in question the European Commission adopted on 24 May 2000, and submitted to the Parliament and the Council on 3 July 2000, a proposal for a Directive of the European Parliament and the Council amending Directive 96/22 and seeking in particular to maintain the prohibition.[11] On 22 September 2003, Directive 2003/74/EC of the European Parliament and of the Council amending Council Directive 96/22/EC concerning the prohibition on the use in stock farming of

---

[6] Request for Consultations by the United States of 31 January 1996 *EC – Measures Concerning Meat and Meat Products ('Hormones')*, WT/DS26/1 and Request for the Establishment of a Panel by the United States of 25 April 1996 *EC – Measures Concerning Meat and Meat Products ('Hormones')*, WT/DS26/13.
[7] Panel Report *EC – Measures Concerning Meat and Meat Products ('Hormones')*, WT/DS26/R/USA, adopted on 13 February 1998.
[8] Appellate Body Report, WT/DS26/AB/R *EC – Measures Concerning Meat and Meat Products ('Hormones')*, adopted on 13 February 1998.
[9] Minutes of the Meeting of the DSB held in Geneva on 13 March 1998, WT/DS/M/43.
[10] Arbitration under Article 21.3(c) of the Understanding on Rules and Procedures Governing the Settlement of Disputes *EC – Measures Concerning Meat and Meat Products ('Hormones')*, WT/DS26/15, Award of the Arbitrator of 29 May 1998.
[11] OJ C337 E/163.

certain substances having a hormonal thyrostatic action and of beta-agonists was finally adopted,[12] thus more than four years after the reasonable period of time granted to the EC to comply with the adverse panel and Appellate Body rulings has lapsed. It is important to mention that the US has already expressed its doubts as to the WTO compatibility of the newly adopted 'hormones directive' during a meeting of the DSB in Geneva on 7 November 2003.[13]

In June 2000, *Biret* and its subsidiary brought an action against the Council before the CFI seeking compensation for damages suffered as a result of the ban on the import into the EC of hormone treated beef. The CFI dismissed the application for damages and referred to the now firmly established case law according to which: (i) the WTO Agreements do not in principle form part of the rules by which the ECJ and the CFI review the legality of acts adopted by the EC institutions under Article 230 EC Treaty; (ii) that individuals cannot rely on them before the courts; and (iii) that any infringement of them will not give rise to liability on the part of the EC.[14] In addition, the CFI emphasised that 'the purpose of the WTO Agreements is to govern relations between States or regional organisations for economic integration and not to protect individuals'.[15]

On 16 March 2002, *Biret* introduced an appeal against the judgment of the CFI, requesting, inter alia, that the ECJ should 'acknowledge that all or part of the WTO Agreements have direct effect'. The judgments of the ECJ in these cases will be further examined below.

3. The Judgments

The ECJ reiterated in both judgments the now firmly established case law on the non-recognition of direct effect of WTO law in the EC legal order, an analysis of which goes beyond the scope of this comment. The ECJ then argued that the CFI did not sufficiently motivate its judgments. In its judgments of 11 January 2002, the CFI had ruled that the decision of the DSB of 13 February 1998 was inescapably and directly linked to the plea alleging infringement of the SPS Agreement and could therefore only be taken into consideration if it had found that this Agreement had direct effect. This argument did not convince the ECJ. It ruled that the CFI should have replied to the argument whether the DSB decision of 13 February 1998 put into question the ECJ's finding that the WTO rules do

---

[12] OJ L262/17.
[13] Available at www.wto.org (last visited on 15 February 2004).
[14] CFI Case T-174/00 *Biret International SA v Council* [2002] ECR II-17, para 61 and CFI Case T-210/00 *Établissements Biret et Cie SA v Council* [2002] ECR II-47, para 71.
[15] CFI Case T-174/00 *Biret International SA v Council* [2002] ECR II-17, para 62 and Case T-210/00 *Établissements Biret et Cie SA v Council* [2002] ECR II-47, para 72.

not have direct effect and whether it could provide ground for a review of the legality of the contested directives.

Furthermore, the ECJ held that the *Atlanta* judgment,[16] to which the CFI had referred, was irrelevant in the case at hand. In *Atlanta*, the ECJ had found that a decision of the DSB, taken after the appeal had been brought and which established the incompatibility of an EC legal act with WTO law, was inescapably and directly linked to the plea of infringement of the provisions of GATT, which had been raised by the applicant before the CFI but had not been repeated by it in its pleas on appeal. Consequently, the ECJ rejected as inadmissible, on account of the late stage at which it had been invoked, the plea based on the decision of the DSB decision, raised before the ECJ for the first time in the reply, and the ECJ did not examine the substance of the plea. This implies that no real consequences could be drawn from the judgment, insofar as the effect of DSB decisions in the EC legal order was concerned, as the CFI had done.

The ECJ nevertheless concluded that the errors of law made by the CFI as regards the duty to state reasons and the scope of the *Atlanta* judgment, did not invalidate the contested judgment since the operative part thereof and in particular the rejection of the plea at first instance concerning the SPS Agreement, appeared founded on other legal grounds.

The ECJ determined that the decision of the DSB could not lead to the liability of the EC due to the specific factual circumstances of the case. Judicial liquidation proceedings in respect of *Biret* had already been initiated in 1995. Consequently, it could not be accepted that any damages to *Biret* arising from the maintenance in force, after 1 January 1995, of the contested directives could have been sustained during the period after 13 February 1998, the date on which the DSB decision relating to imports of meat containing hormones was adopted, and a fortiori after 13 May 1999, when the 15 month period granted to the EC for the purpose of complying with its obligations under the WTO rules expired. Moreover, for the period prior to 13 May 1999, the ECJ could not, in any event, carry out a review of the legality of the directives in question without rendering ineffective the grant of a reasonable period for compliance with the DSB decision.

The ECJ concluded that, in those circumstances, it was not necessary to consider what damage *Biret* might have suffered as a result of the EC's

---

[16] ECJ Case C–104/97 P *Atlanta AG Council and Commission* [1999] ECR I–6983. On this particular judgement, see GA Zonnekeyn 'The Status of Adopted Panel and Appellate Body Reports in the European Court of Justice and the European Court First Instance – The Banana Experience' (2000) 34(2) *JWT* 93.

failure to implement the DSB decision since, in the absence of any damage occurring after 13 May 1999, the EC could not have incurred any liability. The ECJ therefore concluded that the CFI was right in finding that the plea concerning infringement of the SPS Agreement was unfounded.

4. Comment – a Sparkle in the Dark or a Pandora's Box?

The rulings of the ECJ offer the possibility for a change in the case law with regard to the enforceability of WTO law since the ECJ has left open the question whether the EC can be held liable for measures that have been found to be WTO incompatible, if the damages arise subsequent to the period within the EC should have implemented the DSB decision. An *a contrario* reading of the ECJ's ruling could imply that if *Biret* had pursued its commercial activities also after 13 May 1999, the EC could have been liable if the conditions required for an action under Article 288 (2) EC Treaty were present. Important is that the ECJ does so without insisting – as it has done in its previous judgments concerning the effect of WTO law in the EC legal order – on reciprocity, that is without requiring whether any other of the EC's major trading partners would allow such damage claims.[17]

The essential question in these circumstances is whether a private party would be able to demonstrate that the conditions imposed by the ECJ for damages actions under Article 288 EC Treaty are present when the EC has acted in breach of its obligations under WTO law.[18] The ECJ has recently ruled that 'Community law confers a right to reparation where three conditions are met: the rule of law infringed must be intended to confer rights on individuals; the breach must be sufficiently serious; and there must be a direct causal link between the breach of the obligation resting on the author of the act and the damage sustained by the injured parties'.[19] In addition, the case law requires (i) that the rule of law infringed be intended to conger rights on individuals[20] and (ii) that

---

[17] On reciprocity, see J Klabbers 'Reciproci-what? The concept(s) of reciprocity and the EC Court' in P Helander, J Lavapuro and T Mylly (eds) *Yritys Eurooppalaisessa Oikeusyhteisössä* (Turku: Turun Yliopiston, 2002) 137 and A Ott 'Der EuGH und das WTO-Recht: Die Entdeckung der politischen Gegenseitigkeit – altes Phänomen oder neuer Ansatz?' (2003) 38(3) *EuR* 504.
[18] I have already defended the thesis that this ought to be possible. See GA Zonnekeyn 'EC Liability for Non-Implementation of Adopted WTO Panel and Appellate Body Reports. The example of the "innocent exporters" in the banana case' in V Kronenberger (ed) *The European Union and the International Legal Order: Discord or Harmony?* (The Hague: TMC Asser Press, 2001) 251. For a more recent contribution on this subject, see S Hörmann and GJ Göttsche 'Die Haftung der EG für WTO-Rechtverletzungen – Neue Tendenzen in der EuGH-Rechtsprechung?' (2003) 49(9) *Recht der Internationalen Wirtschaft* 689.
[19] ECJ Case C–312/00 P *Commission v Camar Srl and Tico Srl* [2002] ECR I–11355.
[20] The condition that the rule of law infringed be intended to conger rights on individuals does not entail that this rule of law should have 'direct effect'. This can be deducted from
continued ...

there is a sufficiently serious breach of law. An analysis as to whether these conditions could apply in cases where damages are claimed for a violation of WTO law goes beyond the scope of this comment.

It is my personal opinion that since the ECJ did not explicitly exclude the possibility for private parties to obtain damages for breaches of WTO law by the EC, there is still hope for these companies that are currently challenging the EC for breaches of WTO law before the CFI. Whether the *Biret* judgment should be seen as a 'sparkle in the dark' will thus very much depend on the outcome of these cases. The judgment does not imply, however, that the ECJ has opened a Pandora's box since the box can easily been closed when taking into consideration the prudent approach followed by the ECJ in *Biret*.

5. Conclusion – What about the Future?

In a recent judgment, the CFI declined to honour the requests for damages of two banana importers who claimed that they had suffered damages as a consequence of the EC's new banana regime as laid down in Regulations 1637/98 and 2362/98.[21] The CFI emphasised that the parties did not demonstrate that these regulations intended to implement any obligation entered into by the EC in the framework of the WTO and that the *Nakajima* line of case law did not apply.[22] In what could turn out to be a quite significant obiter dictum, the CFI said that the parties neither revealed that the aforementioned regulations referred to any specific provisions of the panel report of 12 April 1999 in the bananas case or to the decision adopting this report. This would imply that if such references had existed and the *Nakajima* case law would have applied, the WTO panel report could have served as a ground for judicial review.

It would seem that the application and interpretation of the *Nakajima* line of case law will be of major importance in the future judgments of the CFI. It is 'hopeful' for example that the new hormones directive

---

other case law of the CFI where it is said that the rule of law infringed must be aimed at protecting the individual. See eg CFI Case T–210/00 *Établissements Biret et Cie SA v Council* [2002] ECR II–47, para 52.

[21] CFI Joined Cases T–64/01 and T–65/01 *Afrikanische Frucht-Compagnie GmbH and Internationale Fruchtimportgesellschaft Weichert & Co v Council and Commission*, not yet published in the ECR but available at http://www.curia.eu.int (last visited 15 February 2004).

[22] Pursuant to this line of case law, WTO law can serve as a ground for review in cases where the EC intends to implement a particular obligation entered into within the framework of the WTO. ECJ Case C–69/89 *Nakajima All Precision Co Ltd v Council* ECR [1991] I–2069. For a recent overview of the application of the *Nakajima* line of case law, see GA Zonnekeyn 'The ECJ's *Petrotub* Judgement: towards a Revival of the *Nakajima* Doctrine?' (2003) 30(3) *LIEI* 249. In this particular contribution I argued that Regulations 1637/98 and 2362/98 did intend to transpose the results of WTO dispute settlement decisions in EC law. The same reasoning and criticism would obviously apply to these two recent cases.

explicitly refers to the 'results of a dispute settlement case brought before the World Trade Organisation'. In the event that a private party would challenge the WTO compatibility of this directive before the CFI or ECJ, it would seem that there would be no obstacles in applying the *Nakajima* line of case law. However, there is no doubt that the pending cases before the CFI will shed more light on the legal status of WTO dispute settlement decisions for challenging WTO-incompatible EC law before the European courts and their impact on the liability of the EC under Article 288 (2) EC Treaty. The dice have not been cast yet!

Chapter XII

Enforceability of WTO Law for Individuals:
Rien ne va Plus ?

1. Introduction

The European Court of Justice ("ECJ") and the Court of First Instance ("CFI") seemed to have firmly closed the door for virtually any form of enforceability of WTO law in the legal order of the European Community. After the judgment of the ECJ in *Biret*, there was still hope for a further penetration of WTO law, especially as far as the effect of WTO dispute settlement rulings was concerned.[1] These expectations came to an abrupt end by two judgments of the ECJ and the CFI, which both represented another sequel in the banana saga before the European courts in Luxembourg,[2] and were even further squeezed by the rulings of the CFI in the cases involving the so-called 'innocent exporters' claiming damages for the EC's non-compliance with WTO Panel and Appellate Body rulings.[3]

---

[1] Case C-93/02 P, *Biret International v Council* and Case C-94/02 P, *Établissements Biret and Cie SA v Council*, [2003] ECR I-10497 and I-10565. For a comment, see A. Alemanno, 'Judicial Enforcement of the WTO Hormones Ruling within the European Community: Toward EC Liability for the Non-Implementation of WTO Dispute Settlement Decisions', 45 (2) *Harvard International Law Journal* 547 (2004); S. Bartelt, 'Die Haftung der Gemeinschaft bei Nichtumsetzung von Entscheidungen des WTO-Streitbeilegungsgremiums', EuR 1077 (2003); Ch. Kaddous, 'The Biret Cases: an open door to EC liability for the non-implementation of WTO dispute settlement decisions?', *ELR* 54 (2004) and J. Wiers, 'One Day, You're Gonna Pay: The European Court of Justice in Biret', 31 (2) *LIEI* 143 (2004).

[2] Case T-19/01, *Chiquita Brands International, Inc., Chiquita Banana Co. BV and Chiquita Italia SpA v. Commission*, [2005] ECR II-315 and ECJ, Case C-93/02, *Léon Van Parys NV v. Belgisch Interventie- en Restitutiebureau (BIRB)*, [2005] ECR I-1465. For a comment, see W. Berg and J. Beck, 'Zur jüngsten Rechtsprechung der Gemeinschaftsgerichte zur unmittelbaren Anwendung von WTO-Recht im Gemeinschaftsrecht – Die Urteile Biret, Chiquita und Van Parys', 51 (6) RIW 401 (2005); J.M. Cortés Martin, 'Invocabilidad del las resoluciones del sistema de solución de controversias de la OMC ante las jurisdicciones comunitarias: 'Una excepción a la "Comunidad de Derecho?", in A. Remiro Brotóns and I. Blázquez Navarro (eds.), *El futuro de la acción exterior de la Unión Europea*, Tirant Lo Blanch, 2007, 389-428; F. Di Gianni and R. Antonini, 'DSB Decisions and Direct Effect of WTO Law: Should the EC Courts be more Flexible when the Flexibility of the WTO System has Come to an End?', 40 (4) *JWT* 777 (2006); G. Gattinara, 'On Dice and Doors: WTO Dispute Settlement Decisions in the System of Judicial Protection of the European Union', in A. Del Vecchio (ed.), *New International Tribunals and New International Proceedings*, giuffrè editore, Milan, 2006 and G.A. Zonnekeyn, 'De afdwingbaarheid van het WTO-recht voor particulieren: rien ne va plus?, 11 *Nederlands Tijdschrift voor Europees Recht* 197 (2005).

[3] Case T-69/00 *Fiamm SpA and Fiamm Technologies Inc. v. Commission and Council*; Case T-151/00 *Le Laboratoire du Bain v Council and Commission*; Case T-297/00 *Claude-Anne de Solène*

continued ...

The first two judgments were subject to criticism. Prof. Eeckhout, for example, argued that *"[I]f the EU courts are unwilling to give domestic legal effect to such [DSB] rulings, one can indeed ask questions about the EC's respect for international law."*[4] This view is corroborated by Lavranos who claims that the European courts are not adhering to one of the most fundamental principles of international law and that is the *pacta sunt servanda*-principle.[5] It must be said that not everybody shares these observations and that some have expressed strong arguments against judicial enforceability of WTO dispute settlement rulings.[6] One of the strongest opponents was Advocate General Léger who opined in *Ikea* that WTO dispute settlement rulings should be ignored by the ECJ since this would inevitably determine the ECJ's interpretation of the corresponding provisions of Community law. Such an outcome, according to the Advocate General, would jeopardise the autonomy of the Community legal order in the pursuit of its own objectives.[7]

In this chapter, some conclusions will be drawn from the most recent case law with regard to the future enforceability of WTO law in the EC legal order. As these judgments are to a large extent a mere confirmation of existing case law - apart from the views taken by some more audacious Advocates General from the ECJ - it does not come as a surprise that the future does not look too promising.

---

v Council and Commission; Case T-301/00 *Groupe Frémaux SA and Palais Royal, Inc. v Council and Commission*; Case T-320/00 *CD Cartondruck AG v Council and Commission*; Case T-383/00 *Beamglow Ltd v European Parliament, Council and Commission* and Case T-135/01 *Giorgio Fedon & Figli SpA and others v Council and Commission*, judgments of 14 December 2005, [2005] ECR II-5393. See S. Haack, 'Grundsäztliche Anerkennung der ausservertraglichen Haftung der EG für rechtmässiges Verhalten nach Art. 288 Abs. 2 EG', *Europarecht* 696 (2006); M. Schmauch, 'Non-compliance with WTO law by the European Community – neither unlawful conduct nor unusual damage', 4 (2) *ELR* 92 (2006) and A. Thies, 43 (4) *CMLRev* 1145 (2006). More in general, G. Gattinara, 'La responsabilità extracontrattuale della Comunità europea per violazione delle norme OMC', *Il Diritto dell'Unione Europea* 112 (2005); S. Görgens, *Die ausservetragliche Haftung der Europäischen Gemeinschaft für Verletzungen des WTO-Rechts durch ihre Organe*, Duncker & Hublot, Berlin, 2006, 227 p.; S. Held, *Die Haftung der EG für die Verletzung von WTO-Recht*, Mohr Siebeck, Tübingen, 2006, 343 p. And K. Höher, *Die Haftung der Europäischen Gemeinschaft für Verstösse gegen das WTO-Recht*, Nomos Verlag, Baden-Baden, 2006, 421 p.
[4] P. Eeckhout, *Does Europe's Constitution Stop at the Water's Edge? Law and Policy in the EU's External Relations*, Groningen, Europa Law Publishing 2005, at p. 17.
[5] N. Lavranos, 'The Chiquita and Van Parys Judgments: An Exception to the Rule of Law', 32 (4) *LIEI* 449 (2005), at p. 458.
[6] See for example A. Antoniadis, 'The Chiquita and Van Parys Judgments: Rules, Exceptions and the Law', 32 (4) *LIEI* 460 (2005), at p. 468-476 and P. J. Kuijper and M. Bronckers, 'WTO Law in the European Court of Justice', 42 (5) *CMLRev* 1313 (2005), at p. 1330-1342.
[7] Case C-351/04, *Ikea Wholesale Ltd v. Commissioners of Customs & Excise*, Opinion of 6 April 2006, at §78 to 98.

2. Prelude

It is well-known that – under the existing case law of both the CFI and the ECJ - WTO law cannot be used as a ground for judicial review of Community acts.[8] The more recent case law, however, concerns the question whether direct effect of WTO law needs to be assessed from a different perspective when there are specific WTO dispute settlement ruling against the EC. The crucial question seems to be whether decisions adopted by the Dispute Settlement Body [DSB] following a panel report, and possibly an Appellate Body report, which establish that the EC is in violation of WTO law of such a nature as to warrant an exception to the lack of direct effect?

In 2003, in *Biret*, the ECJ criticized the CFI for its failure to examine the argument of complainants that there is direct effect of DSB decisions, at least after the end of the reasonable period for implementation which WTO dispute settlement affords. The ECJ's criticism was *obiter dicta*, since the facts of the case predated the end of that period, and the issue did not therefore strictly arise. Therefore, the ECJ did not annul the CFI's judgment.[9]

The direct effect of DSB decisions was more fully considered in the *Chiquita* and *Van Parys* judgments, which did not pursue the route which *Biret* seemed to have opened.[10] The cases concerned imports of bananas and the EC's continuous failure to adopt a WTO compatible banana regime. Chiquita attempted to base a claim in damages on the failure to comply with the original DSB rulings. In *Van Parys*, a Belgian importer challenged refusals to grant import licenses, on the same grounds.

In both cases, the Luxembourg courts considered that the negotiating scope of the EC institutions, in the WTO, cannot be interfered with, even after the end of the reasonable period for compliance. They do not base

---

[8] Case C-149/96 *Portugal v Council* [1999] ECR I-8395. For a recent overview, see P.-J. Kuijper and M. Bronckers, 'WTO Law in the European Court of Justice', 42 (5) *CMLRev* 1313 (2005) and E.-U. Petersmann, 'On Reinforcing WTO Rules in Domestic Laws', in J. Barcelo and H. Corbet (eds.), *Rethinking the World Trading System*, Lexington Books, 2007.
[9] Case C-93/02 P, *Biret International v Council* and Case C-94/02 P, *Établissements Biret and Cie SA v Council*, [2003] ECR I-10497 and I-10565.
[10] Case T-19/01, *Chiquita Brands International, Inc., Chiquita Banana Co. BV and Chiquita Italia SpA v. Commission*, [2005] ECR II-315 and ECJ, Case C-93/02, *Léon Van Parys NV v. Belgisch Interventie- en Restitutiebureau (BIRB)*, [2005] ECR I-1465. See also Case T-69/00 *Fiamm SpA and Fiamm Technologies Inc. v. Commission and Council*; Case T-151/00 *Le Laboratoire du Bain v Council and Commission*; Case T-297/00 *Claude-Anne de Solène v Council and Commission*; Case T-301/00 *Groupe Frémaux SA and Palais Royal, Inc. v Council and Commission*; Case T-320/00 *CD Cartondruck AG v Council and Commission*; Case T-383/00 *Beamglow Ltd v European Parliament, Council and Commission* and Case T-135/01 *Giorgio Fedon & Figli SpA and others v Council and Commission*, judgments of 14 December 2005, [2005] ECR II-5393.

this on pure policy arguments. Both courts referred to legal provisions of the WTO Dispute Settlement Understanding [DSU] such as Articles 21.6 and 22.8 which provide, in essence, that the issue of compliance remains on the DSB's agenda as long as there is no agreement about compliance. The CFI even went so far as to say that the effectiveness of Art 21.6 would be undermined by judicial "intervention" in Luxemburg. It also stated that WTO dispute settlement is not a mechanism for judicial resolution by means of decisions with binding effects comparable with those of a court decision in domestic legal systems. The ECJ summarized the actions after the failed 1998 implementation attempt, up to the 2001 final resolution of the bananas dispute. It considered that this outcome could be compromised if there was something like direct effect of DSB rulings, and that the negotiation possibilities were not exhausted at the end of the reasonable period.

There are strong differences between the period before and after the end of the reasonable time for implementation. If one agrees with Jackson's analysis, to the effect that there is a clear international law obligation to comply with DSB rulings[11], the question whether the reasonable period has lapsed is irrelevant.[12] Practically WTO rulings are prospective, requiring a Member to bring its laws and regulations into compliance. There is a reasonable period of time for doing so. However, once it has expired there appears to be a legally perfect and complete obligation at that point in time even though the DSU provides that the issue of compliance will remain on the agenda of the DSB as long as there is no consensus on compliance and even though there are remedies, such as suspension of concessions, in the event of continued failure to comply. Arguing, however, that the effectiveness of these DSU provisions would be undermined by a municipal judicial decision which remedies the WTO violations does not convince. One could even say that such a decision would in fact contribute to realizing the DSU's objectives, and that is prompting compliance.

---

[11] J.H.J. Jackson, 'International Law Status of WTO Dispute Settlement Reports: Obligation to Comply or Option to Buy Out?', 98 *AJIL* 109 (2004).

[12] Di Gianni and Antonini argue that a DSB ruling cannot be used as a criterion for reviewing the legality of EC law. However, they do not exclude the possibility to rely on such a ruling in an action for damages based on Article 288 EC Treaty. See ; F. Di Gianni and R. Antonini, 'DSB Decisions and Direct Effect of WTO Law: Should the EC Courts be more Flexible when the Flexibility of the WTO System has Come to an End?', 40 (4) *JWT* 777 (2006), at p. 788. O'Connor - in a reaction to the article written by Di Gianni and Antonini - wrote that a DSB ruling can neither be used in a damages action. See B. O'Connor, 'Should Dispute Settlement Body Recommendations Give Rise to Rights in EC Damages Actions?', 2 (2) *Global Trade and Customs Journal* 293 (2007). Di Gianni and Antonini respectfully disagreed with O'Connor in a rebuttal published in 2 (2) *Global Trade and Customs Journal* 299 (2007).

3. Recent Case Law – Nil Novi Sub Sole ?

3.1 The Eggenberger Case – a voiceless Court ?

3.1.1 Factual Background

In *Eggenberger*, the Administrative Court of Frankfurt referred a question to the ECJ concerning the validity of Articles 25(1) and 35(2) of Regulation 2535/2001 laying down detailed rules for applying Regulation 1255/1999 as regards the import arrangements for milk and milk products and opening tariff quotas, in this case from New Zealand.[13] The reference was made in the context of legal proceedings between concerning the issue of an import licence for New Zealand butter at a reduced duty. The national court asked the ECJ whether the contested provisions of Regulation 2535/2001 are contrary to Article XVII(1)(a) of GATT and Article 1(3) of the WTO Agreement on Import Licensing Procedures. The referring court took the view that, in adopting Regulation 2535/2001, the intention of the EC legislator was to implement obligations assumed in the context of the WTO and could therefore, in application of the so-called *Nakajima* doctrine, review the legality of Community law in the light of the applicable WTO rules.

3.1.2 The Opinion of Advocate General Geelhoed

In an Opinion, dated 1 December 2005, Advocate General Geelhoed took a very proactive and reactive approach with respect to the arguments brought forward by the European Commission. The European Commission asked the ECJ to revisit the *Nakajima* case law and argued that that the rationale behind the ECJ's case law on the *Nakajima* exception could be better put into effect by a principle of consistent interpretation of Community legislation in conformity with international law.[14] The Commission observed that the unilateral nature of the *Nakajima* exception contradicts the balance of reciprocity inherent in the WTO legal framework, and warned that the practical consequences of the *Nakajima* exception are that the Community legislator would, in an attempt to avoid falling within the scope of the exception, avoid reference to WTO law in the preambles to Community legislation.[15]

---

[13] OJ L 349/29 of 22 December 2001
[14] That is, the principle that, when the wording of secondary Community legislation is open to more than one interpretation, the primacy of international agreements concluded by the Community over provisions of secondary Community legislation means that such provisions must, so far as is possible, be interpreted in a manner that is consistent with those agreements. See Case C-61/94 *Commission v Germany* [1996] ECR I-3989, paragraph 52.
[15] It is not surprising that Pieter-Jan Kuijper - former member of the EC legal service – has defended this line of reasoning in some of his legal writings. See e.g. P.-J. Kuijper and M. Bronckers, 'WTO Law in the European Court of Justice', 42 (5) *CMLRev* 1313 (2005) and
continued ...

Advocate Geelhoed strongly disagreed with this approach. He emphasized that the ECJ was fully aware of, and considered, the implications of the reciprocal nature of the WTO Agreements in its leading judgments setting out the circumstances in which WTO rules may form a ground of review of Community measures. For example, in *Portugal v. Council*, the ECJ recalled that the WTO Agreement is *"still founded, like GATT 1947, on the principle of negotiations with a view to "entering into reciprocal and mutually advantageous arrangements."* In all theses cases the ECJ none the less confirmed the *Fediol* and *Nakajima* exceptions to the general principle that Community measures may not be reviewed for compliance with WTO law. In addition, Advocate General Geelhoed opined that the existence of these exceptions does not conflict with what was a primary rationale for the general principle, namely, that according direct effect to WTO rules would *"deprive the legislative or executive organs of the Community of the scope for manoeuvre enjoyed by their counterparts in the Community's trading partners."* In a case where it is clear that a Community measure was specifically intended to implement a particular obligation of WTO law, the Community legislature has essentially chosen to limit its own scope of manoeuvre in negotiations by itself "incorporating" that obligation into Community law. Secondly, as regards the Commission's other argument in favour of removal of the Nakajima exception – namely, that in practice it could lead the Community legislator to avoid reference to WTO law in its legislation – this is, according to the Advocate General, both unattractive and irrelevant. Unattractive, because it suggests a deliberate attempt by the Community legislator to circumvent the judicial enforceability of binding WTO obligations in a situation where the conditions for direct effect are otherwise made out, which would amount to an attempt to bypass the principle of legality. Irrelevant, because evaluation of whether the Nakajima exception applies is not confined, in a purely formalistic manner, to checking the text of the measure for express reference to WTO law.

3.1.3 The judgment

The ECJ gave an answer to the first two questions by declaring that Regulation 2535/2001 was invalid inasmuch as it provided that applications for import licences for New Zealand butter at reduced duty may be lodged solely with the competent authorities of the UK and that Articles 25(1) and 35(2) of Regulation 2535/2001, read in conjunction with Annexes III, IV and XII to that Regulation, were invalid since they permitted discrimination in the issue of import licences for New Zealand butter at reduced duty.

P.-J. Kuijper, 'From Initiating Proceedings to Ensuring Implementation: The Links with the Community Legal Order', in G. Sacerdoti et al. (eds.), *The WTO at Ten*, Cambridge University Press, Cambridge, 2006.

It is surprising, however, that the ECJ remained tacit on the question whether Regulation 2535/2001 was contrary to WTO law. Two pertaining questions, i.e. the question whether the rationale behind the ECJ's case law on the *Nakajima* exception would be better put into effect by a principle of consistent interpretation of EC law in conformity with international law, and the question whether the "unilateral" nature of the *Nakajima* exception contradicted the balance of reciprocity inherent in the WTO legal framework, now remained unanswered as if the ECJ was afraid to open a Pandora's box full of unanswered legal questions.

3.2   Ikea – Much ado about nothing

3.2.1   Factual Background

In June 2002, Ikea Wholesale Ltd ["Ikea"] sought repayment from the Commissioners of Customs and Excise ["the Commissioners"] of anti-dumping duties paid in respect of imports of cotton-type bed linen from India and Pakistan in accordance with Regulation 2398/97.[16] The claim for repayment was made on the basis of Articles 236 and 239 of the Community Customs Code [Regulation 2913/92].[17] In support of its claim, Ikea pleaded the unlawfulness of Regulation 2398/97 and the subsequent Regulations 1644/2001[18], 160/2002[19] and 696/2002[20] and, in particular, of the methodology used in calculating the duty. Ikea relied in particular on the findings of a WTO Panel report of 30 October 2000[21] and a WTO Appellate Body report of 1 March 2001.[22] These reports concluded that the imposition by the EC of definitive anti-dumping duties on imports of cotton-type bed linen was inconsistent with the Agreement on Implementation of Article VI of the General Agreement on Tariffs and Trade 1994 [the "WTO Anti-Dumping Agreement"].

In November 2002, the UK authorities rejected the claim and confirmed the decision taken by the Commissioners to reject the claim for reimbursement of the anti-dumping duties. Ikea then brought an appeal against the Commissioners' review decision before the VAT and Duties Tribunal which, by decision of 8 September 2003, dismissed the appeal on the ground that, since Ikea had not brought an action for annulment pursuant to Article 230 EC Treaty, the regulations at issue had become definitive against it. In October 2003, Ikea appealed against the decision to the High Court of Justice of England and Wales, Chancery Division.

---
[16] OJ L 332/1 of 4 December 1997.
[17] OJ L 302/1 of 19 October 1992.
[18] OJ L 219/1 of 14 August 2001.
[19] OJ L 26/1 of 30 January 2002.
[20] OJ L 109/3 of 25 April 2002.
[21] WT/DS141/R of 30 October 2000.
[22] WT/DS141/AB/R of 1 March 2001.

It maintained, first, that the Regulations at issue were not of direct and individual concern to it for the purposes of Article 230 EC. Second, it submitted that those Regulations were unlawful. The High Court set aside the decision of the VAT and Duties Tribunal as it found that Ikea did not have standing to bring a direct action for annulment before the Courts in Luxembourg pursuant to Article 230 EC, since none of the contested Regulations were of direct and individual concern to it. The High Court held that Ikea was able to contest those Regulations in the proceedings before it and decided to refer a number of questions to the ECJ for a preliminary ruling on the validity of the contested Regulations.

In its first question, the national court was essentially asking the ECJ to determine whether Regulation 2398/97 was valid in the light of the WTO Anti-Dumping Agreement, as subsequently interpreted in the WTO Panel and Appellate Body reports, and also in the light of the EC anti-dumping Regulation.[23] As regards the final determination of the dumping margin, the national court wanted to ascertain whether the practice of 'zeroing' used in establishing the overall dumping margins, as it was applied in the anti-dumping investigation at issue in the main proceedings, was compatible with Article 2(11) of the EC anti-dumping Regulation.

3.2.2 The Opinion of Advocate General Léger

As mentioned above, Advocate General Léger opined that WTO dispute settlement rulings should be ignored by the ECJ since this would inevitably determine the ECJ's interpretation of the corresponding provisions of EC law. Such an outcome, according to the Advocate General, would jeopardise the autonomy of the EC legal order in the pursuit of its own objectives.[24] The Advocate General referred to the objectives pursued by the WTO, which is not to create either a legal order based on the rule of law or a single market similar to that developed within the EC.[25] According to Advocate General Léger, the WTO forms a common institutional framework within which the Contracting Parties negotiate "by entering into reciprocal and mutually advantageous arrangements" about their rights and obligations with a view, in particular, to reducing

---

[23] Council Regulation (EC) No. 384/96 of 22 December 1995 on protection against dumped imports from countries not members of the European Community, OJ L 56/1 of 6 March 1996 [as amended].

[24] Case C-351/04, *Ikea Wholesale Ltd v. Commissioners of Customs & Excise*, Opinion of 6 April 2006, at § 78 to 98. For a brief analysis, see M. Bronckers, 'The Relationship of the EC Courts with Other International Tribunals: Non-Committal, Respectful or Submissive?', 44 (3) CMLRev 601 (2007), at pp. 612 to 613.

[25] On this subject, see S. Weatherill, 'L'Applicazione Del Diritto Dell'Organizzazione Mondiale Del Commercio Nell'Ordinamento Giuridico Comunitario: "Doppio Standard" Della Corte Di Giusta?', in *Organizzaione mondiale del commercio e diritto della Communita' Europea nella prospettiva della risoluzione delle controversie*, F. Francesco et.al. (eds.), Giuffre, Milan, 2005, p. 133 to 153.

barriers to trade and eliminating discriminatory treatment in international trade relations. In the pursuit of those objectives, the provisions of the WTO Agreement(s) are interpreted in accordance with approaches and methods which are different from those which may be favored by the Community courts. In those circumstances, given the nature of the WTO and the Community and the objectives pursued by each of them, the Advocate General took the view that to acknowledge that the ECJ could be bound by the interpretation of the WTO dispute settlement rulings jeopardize the autonomy of the EC legal order and that to admit of the contrary view would also call in question the exclusive jurisdiction of the Community judicature under Article 220 EC in the interpretation of the rules of Community law.

3.2.3 The Judgment

The ECJ smoothly avoided ruling on the nature of the WTO legal system but did recall, as a preliminary point that, according to settled case-law, given their nature and structure, the WTO Agreements are not in principle among the rules in the light of which the ECJ is to review the legality of measures adopted by the Community institutions. It is only where the Community has intended to implement a particular obligation assumed in the context of the WTO, or where the Community measure refers expressly to the precise provisions of the WTO agreements, that it is for the Court to review the legality of the Community measure in question in the light of the WTO rules.

It then referred to Article 1 of Regulation 1515/2001 according to which the Council may, following a report adopted by the WTO Dispute Settlement Body, and depending on the circumstances, repeal or amend the disputed measure or adopt any other special measures which are deemed to be appropriate in the circumstances.[26] Regulation 1515/2001 applies, according to its Article 4, to reports adopted after 1 January 2001 by the DSB. In the present case, the DSB adopted the report of the Appellate Body on 12 March 2001 together with that of the Panel as amended by the Appellate Body's report. Pursuant to Article 3 of Regulation 1515/2001, any measures adopted pursuant to that Regulation are to take effect from the date of their entry into force and may not serve as basis for the reimbursement of the duties collected prior to that date, unless otherwise provided for. Recital 6 in the preamble to the Regulation provides in that

---

[26] OJ L 201/10 of 26 July 2001. For a comment, see D. Blanchard, 'Les Effets des Rapports de L'Organe de Règlement des Différends de l'OMC à la Lumière du Règlement (CE) 1515/2001 du Conseil de L'Union Européenne', *Revue du Marché commun et de l'Union européenne* [2003] 37; J. Branton, 'The EC Washes its Dirty Bed Linen – Is the Saga Over Yet?', *IntTLR* [2002] 64; D. Horovitz, 'A Regulated Scope for EU Compliance with WTO Rulings', *IntTLR* [2001] 153 and G.A. Zonnekeyn,.'The Bed Linen Case and its Aftermath. Some Comments on the EC's "WTO Enabling Regulation"', Part I, Chapter VI *supra*.

connection that the recommendations in reports adopted by the DSB only have prospective effect. Therefore, the ECJ emphasized, any measures taken under Regulation 1515/2001 will take effect from the date of their entry into force, unless otherwise specified, and do not provide any basis for the reimbursement of the duties collected prior to that date.

In this particular case, having regard to the provisions of Regulation 1515/2001 and to the DSB's recommendations, the Council first of all adopted Regulation 1644/2001 on 7 August 2001. Next, on 28 January 2002, it adopted Regulation No 160/2002, and finally, on 22 April 2002, Regulation No 696/2002 confirming the definitive anti-dumping duty imposed by Regulation 2398/97, as amended and suspended by Regulation 1644/2001. The ECJ concluded that it followed from all of the foregoing that, in circumstances such as those in the case at hand, the legality of Regulation 2398/97 could not be reviewed in the light of the WTO Anti-dumping Agreement, as subsequently interpreted by the DSB, since it was clear from the subsequent Regulations that the Community, by excluding repayment of rights paid under Regulation 2398/97, did not in any way intend to give effect to a specific obligation assumed in the context of the WTO.

What is crucial in the judgment is that the ECJ left it to the national authorities to draw the consequences, in their legal system, of a declaration of invalidity made in the context of an assessment of validity in a reference for a preliminary ruling, which has the consequence that anti-dumping duties, paid under Regulation 2398/97 are not legally owed within the meaning of Article 236(1) of Regulation 2913/92 and should, in principle, be repaid by the customs authorities in accordance with that provision, provided that the conditions to which such repayment is subject are satisfied, this being a matter for the national court to verify.

4. Merck Genéricos - A Different Approach for the TRIPS Agreement?

4.1 Factual Background

The facts from which this reference to the ECJ arose are of some antiquity. Merck & Co owned a Portuguese patent for which an application was filed on 4 December 1979 and which was granted on 8 April 1981. This patent was used for the production of a pharmaceutical product, known as Renitec, which was marketed from 1 January 1985 onwards. Merck Sharp & Dohme was granted the right to exploit that patent in Portugal. In 1996, Merck Genéricos started to market a pharmaceutical product under the trademark Enalapril Merck, which it sold at prices appreciably lower than those for Renitec and which, it claimed, was the same product as Renitec.

Merck & Co and Merck Sharp & Dohme decided to sue Merck Genéricos, seeking an order that the latter should refrain from importing, marketing in Portugal or exporting the product at issue under the trade mark Enalapril Merck or under any other commercial description without their express authorisation, and seeking compensation for the material and non-material damage caused by its unlawful conduct.

Merck Genéricos denied any liability. In its view, the period of patent protection had expired since the period of 15 years provided for by Article 7 of the 1940 Industrial Property Code [the law then applicable in Portugal] ended on 9 April 1996. Merck & Co and Merck Sharp & Dohme disagreed. They argued that, by application of Article 33 of the TRIPS Agreement according to which "*the term of protection available shall not end before the expiration of a period of twenty years counted from the filing date*", the patent ran until 4 December 1999. Merck & Co and Merck Sharp & Dohme lost at first instance. On appeal, however, the Court of Appeal ordered Merck Genéricos to pay damages on the ground that, under Article 33 of the TRIPS Agreement, which had direct effect under Portuguese law, that patent had expired not on 9 April 1996 but on 9 April 2001. Merck Genéricos appealed to the Supreme Court of Justice, claiming that Article 33 of the TRIPS Agreement was not directly applicable and decided to refer a number of questions to the ECJ under article 234 of the EC Treaty: (i) Does the Court of Justice have jurisdiction to interpret Article 33 of the TRIPs Agreement? (ii) If the first question is answered in the affirmative, must national courts apply that article, on their own initiative or at the request of one of the parties, in proceedings pending before them?

4.2 The Opinion of Advocate General Ruiz-Jarabo Colomer

4.2.1 Jurisdiction of the ECJ

The Advocate General rendered his opinion on 23 January 2007.[27] He started with an overview of the existing case law on mixed agreements, especially with regard to the TRIPS Agreement[28] and concluded that time had come to "*undertake a task of reorganisation in the interests of the Community, maintaining that the ECJ has unlimited jurisdiction to interpret the TRIPS Agreement*" for the reasons referred to hereinafter.[29]

First, more attention must be given to the inclusion of the WTO Agreements as part of international law, in which agreements are

---
[27] Opinion of Advocate General Ruiz-Jarabo Colomer of 23 January 2003 in Case C- 431/05, *Merck Genéricos – Produos Farmacêuticos Lda v Merck & Co. Inc. and Merck Sharp & Dohme Lda*, judgment of the ECJ of 11 September 2007, not yet reported in the ECR.
[28] See also G.A. Zonnekeyn, 'De Directe Werking van de TRIPS Overeenkomst – Een Stand van zaken', *IRDI* 132 (2002).
[29] Paragraph 54 of the opinion.

ratified with the intention of complying with them in good faith. It should be pointed out that GATT has undergone a change, in which its original 'contractual' nature has weakened and it has virtually become a 'constitutional' framework for world trade owing to its full alignment with the standards of the international treaties in accordance with the Vienna Convention on the Law of Treaties.[30]

Secondly, the agreements concluded by the Community and the Member States jointly reveal their common objective and bind them vis-à-vis the third countries which are party to those agreements. The principle of good faith laid down in Article 10 EC Treaty requires the Member States to cooperate not only in the process of negotiation and conclusion of those agreements, but also in their implementation. This must be read in conjunction with the duty to achieve the effectiveness of Community law not only in the legislative sphere but also in the executive and judicial spheres.[31]

Thirdly, the best way of guaranteeing observance of international agreements with third parties and of achieving the necessary harmony in the interpretation of mixed agreements is to ensure that they are interpreted uniformly, a view reinforced by the fact that the provisions of the Agreement may be interconnected. In this connection, the only body capable of carrying out that task is the ECJ, always with the invaluable help of the national courts by means of the preliminary ruling mechanism under Article 234 EC Treaty.[32]

Fourthly, that the ECJ may consider that it has the power to examine mixed agreements, in particular the TRIPS Agreement, does not imply transference to the Community of national legislative powers, nor of those which revert to the Member States because the Community institutions fail to exercise them. On the contrary, if there were uniform interpretation, binding on everybody, even in the fields in which there is as yet no Community legislation, the Member States could more easily comply with the provisions of Article 10 EC, making use of those powers.[33]

Fifthly and lastly, the situation caused by the current case law concerning mixed agreements is surprising, since to deny the ECJ jurisdiction to examine an agreement of that kind, ratified by the Community, until legislation has been adopted in respect of specific matters is as illogical as prohibiting a national court from

---
[30] Paragraph 55 of the opinion.
[31] Paragraph 56 of the opinion.
[32] Paragraph 57 of the opinion.
[33] Paragraph 58 of the opinion.

interpreting a framework law until the authorities to whom the legislative power has been delegated have exercised it.[34]

It is not surprising therefore that the Advocate General concluded that the ECJ had jurisdiction to interpret the TRIPS Agreement and more in particular Article 33 thereof.

4.2.2 Direct Effect of Article 33 TRIPS Agreement

The Advocate General – rightfully – expressed his dissatisfaction with the *Van Parys* judgment and wrote that *"the denial of direct effect to the WTO rules is absolute in tone, since the Court of Justice held that it was not possible to plead before a court of a Member State that Community legislation was incompatible with the WTO rules, even if the Dispute Settlement Body had stated that that legislation was incompatible with those rules."*[35] He clearly said that the ECJ "might" have infringed the principle pacta sunt servanda, contained in Article 26 of the Vienna Convention on the Law of Treaties, by disregarding the decisions of a body whose competence was accepted by the Community when it signed the WTO Agreements.[36]

The Advocate General further criticized the existing case law by stating that he could glimpse no chance of abandoning the dualistic system by which, on an uncertain legal basis, the ECJ transformed the implementation in the Community of the ius gentium, and of the WTO Agreements, into a means of evading its obligations.[37]

In addition, with regard to the direct effect of Article 33 of the TRIPS Agreement, the Advocate General said that if the real reason for which the ECJ refuses to acknowledge the direct effect of the WTO Agreements is that it does not wish to interfere with the powers of the Community political institutions to act within the margin for negotiation granted to them in the DSU that applies only to fields in which compromise is genuinely possible. Although the DSU includes the TRIPS Agreement, the nature of the legislation it seeks to harmonize - intellectual and industrial property rights - does not sit comfortably alongside the mechanism for settling disputes, since, by definition, those rights belong to individuals, not to the Member States.[38] The Advocate General doubted whether

---
[34] Paragraph 59 of the opinion.
[35] Paragraph 71 of the opinion.
[36] Paragraph 71 of the opinion.
[37] Paragraph 78 of the opinion.
[38] Paragraph 82 of the opinion. Zonnekeyn referred to TRIPS as a "lex specialis". See G.A. Zonnekeyn, 'De Directe Werking van de TRIPS Overeenkomst – Een Stand van zaken', *IRDI* 132 (2002), at p. 145-146. See also C.J. Hermes, *TRIPS im Gemeinschaftsrecht*, Duncker & Humblot, Berlin, 2002, p.297-302.

those different kinds of rules offer the same flexibility for achieving a compromise. In addition, the Advocate General opined that the importance which the approach of the ECJ accords the WTO system for settling disputes is disproportionate, because it puts the option of relinquishing the responsibilities assumed under the WTO Agreement before its binding value as a multilateral international treaty.[39]

The Advocate General concluded that Article 33 of the TRIPS Agreement had direct effect.

4.3 The judgment

Notwithstanding the elaborated opinion of the Advocate General, the ECJ decided to keep its analysis relatively simple and fully in line with the existing case law. The ECJ essentially ruled that it is not contrary to EC law for Article 33 of the TRIPS Agreement to be given direct effect in national law and to be applied directly by a national court. The ECJ also held that it had jurisdiction to interpret Article 33 of the TRIPS Agreement to ascertain whether it is contrary to EC law for that provision to be given direct effect.

5. Conclusion

The latest judgments of the ECJ seem to indicate that it is not willing to change its case law on the effect of WTO law and DSB rulings within the EC legal order and this notwithstanding the provocative opinions by some of its Advocate Generals. These opinions seem to reflect - more than before - a criticism towards the ECJ and CFI to alter its case law. As already indicated above, these voices have fallen on to deaf mans ears with the judges in Luxembourg.

---

[39] Paragraph 84 of the opinion.

PART II: THE EU TRADE BARRIERS REGULATION

CHAPTER I

THE EC 'TRADE BARRIERS REGULATION': MORE OPPORTUNITIES
FOR COMMUNITY INDUSTRIES?

This comment examines the EC's Trade Barrier Regulation adopted on 22 December 1994. The Regulation repealed the New Commercial Policy Instrument and introduced some major changes especially affecting the substantive issues of the Regulation. The comment focuses on those changes and assesses them from a Community industry perspective.

1. Introduction

In September 1984 the European Community ('EC') introduced Council Regulation 2641/84 'on the strengthening of the common commercial policy with regard in particular to protection against illicit commercial practices'.[1] This Regulation, known as the New Commercial Policy Instrument ('NCPI'), was primarily designed to give Community industries access to some form of relief under Community law when their trade opportunities were illicitly restricted by trade practices of third countries. It was also adopted in response to section 301 of the US Trade Act of 1974, as amended, which enables private parties to invoke the intervention of the US government against foreign trade practices which limit the commerce of the United States.[2]

Little use has been made of the NCPI. This was mainly due to some of the key concepts forming part of the NCPI which proved to be inappropriate to protect effectively the interests of Community industries in third country markets.

Council Regulation 3286/94 'laying down Community procedures in the field of the common commercial policy in order to ensure the exercise of the Community's rights under international trade rules, in particular

---

[1] OJ 1984 L252/1. See, for example, JHJ Bourgeois, EC Rules Against 'Illicit Trade Practices' - Policy Cosmetics or International Law Enforcement?', in 1988 Annual Proceedings of the Fordham Corporate Law Institute, BE Hawk (ed), M. Bender, New York, 1989, Chapter 6; F Schoneveld, The European Community Reaction to the 'Illicit' Commercial Trade Practices of other Countries', (1992) *Journal of World Trade* 17 and F. Castillo de la Torre, 'The EEC New Instrument of Trade Policy: Some Comments in the Light of the Latest Developments', (1993) *Common Market Law Review* 687.
[2] For a comparative analysis between the NCPI and section 301, see P Mavroidis, *Handelspolitische Abwehrmechanismen der EGW und ihre Vereinbarkeit mit den GATT-Regeln* (Stuttgart, Verlagsgesellschaft Internationales Recht, 1993).

those established under the auspices of the World Trade Organization',[3] best known in Community parlance as the 'Trade Barriers Regulation', repealed Regulation 2641/84 and introduced some major changes. The most important changes relate to the right of Community enterprises to submit complaints to the Commission when being confronted with trade obstacles on third country markets and the extension of the Regulation's scope to services. Other amendments have been included to strengthen the link between the Trade Barriers Regulation ('TBR') and the improved World Trade Organization ('WTO') dispute settlement mechanism.[4]

The present analysis gives a brief overview of the few cases which have been brought, or attempted, under the NCPI with a view to seeing whether those cases give an answer as to the usefulness and effectiveness of the NCPI. It will then describe - in a nutshell - the attempts made in the past at amending different aspects of this instrument. Finally, the main part of the analysis will focus on the substantive and procedural aspects of the TBR and assess it from a Community industry/enterprise perspective.

2. Experiences to Date

Regulation 2641/84 provided for actions to be brought under two 'tracks'. To date, there have been no cases brought under the so-called 'track B', that is referrals of a matter by a Member State, requesting the 'full exercise of the Community's rights' under international trade rules. The so-called 'track A' of the NCPI has been used at least a few times: there have been five cases in which the Commission formally opened an examination procedure, following a complaint by a Community industry that it was being injured by an illicit commercial practice of a third country, and two more complaints were lodged but rejected by the Commission.

3. The 'Full Exercise of the Rights of the Community': Complaints by Member States

Member States have not been particularly interested in the NCPI, including those who had advocated its adoption in the first place. This obviously begs the question of why they have not been interested. For some of them, the answer probably lies in the negative attitude that they

---

[3] OJ 1994 L349/71, as amended by Council Regulation 356/95, OJ 1995 L41/3.

[4] For an analysis of the new WTO dispute settlement system, see, for example, E-U Petersmann, 'The Dispute Settlement System of the World Trade Organization and the Evolution of the GATT Dispute Settlement System since 1948', (1994) *Common Market Law Review* 1157 and E. Vermulst and B Driesen, 'An Overview of the WTO Dispute Settlement System and its Relationship with the Uruguay Round Agreements', (1995) *Journal of World Trade* 131.

have had from the very beginning[5] and an unwillingness to 'legitimafe' its use. It is more difficult to see why those Member States who had been in favour of the Regulation never resorted to it. The most obvious reason is that Article 113 EC Treaty provided a sufficient legal basis for the Community to bring complaints before the GATT. Member States could raise issues in other *fora*, in particular the 113 Committee, in order to get the Community to act internationally, including in GATT.

4. 'Illicit Commercial Practices': Complaints by Community Industries

4.1 Akzo v United States

Regulation 2641/84 was first tested in December 1985, when Akzo brought a complaint challenging a US import ban on Akzo's aramid fibres in application of section 337 of the US Tariff Act of 1930, as amended.[6] After a thorough examination under the procedure set out in Regulation 2641/84, the Commission decided to initiate dispute settlement proceedings under GATT Article XXIII.[7] A panel was established to study the matter and some months later the panel report, which was issued in November 1988, found section 337 to be inconsistent with Article III:4 of GATT.[8] The United States accepted the panel report about a year after it had been issued. In the framework of its Uruguay Round implementing legislation, the US amended section 337 to bring it into conformity with the GATT panel finds. It is doubtful, however, whether this objective has effectively been reached.[9]

4.2 IFPI v Indonesia

In March 1987 IFPI (the International Federation of Phonogram Industries), representing the European sound recording industry, filed a complaint against the alleged failure by the Indonesian Government to grant adequate protection to European record producers against the unauthorised copying of their sound recordings in Indonesia.[10] The procedure was closed in May 1988 after the conclusion of an amicable settlement.[11]

---

[5] Especially Germany, Denmark and the Netherlands were rather reluctant to give private enterprises the right to bring a complaint directly before the Commission, see MCEJ Bronckers, 'Private Response to Foreign Unfair Trade Practices: US and EEC Complaint Procedures', in Selective Safeguard Measures in Multilateral Trade Relations: Issues of Protectionism in GATT, European Community and United States Law, Kluwer, Deventer, 1985, 157, at 225.
[6] OJ 1986 C25/20.
[7] OJ 1987 L117/18.
[8] BISD 36th Supp., 345.
[9] See the Commission's 1995 Report on US Barriers to Trade and Investment.
[10] OJ 1987 C136/3.
[11] OJ 1988 U23/51.

4.3 ECSA v Japan

In January 1989 ECSA (European Community Shipowners Association), acting on behalf of major European shipping companies, complained about port charges in Japan which did not correspond to any service actually performed, which were higher for international transport than for domestic transport.[12] The Commission argued that the Japanese practices were contrary to GATT and threatened to initiate dispute settlement proceedings under Article XXIII of GATT,[13] and that the Community might eventually initiate dispute settlement proceedings under Article XXIII of GATT. This resulted in the Japanese Government abolishing the fund and the case was terminated.[14]

4.4 IFPI v Thailand

Having first complained about piracy in Indonesia, IFPI now charged the Thai Government with failing to offer adequate protection to the Community sound recording industry against the unauthorised duplication of its sound recordings in Thailand.[15] Contrary to the first IFPI case, where Indonesia's copyright law was found to be contrary to its international obligations, Thailand's copyright law appeared to be in compliance with its international commitments. It was rather the non-enforcement of Thai copyright law which was alleged to be in breach of Thailand's international obligations. Bilateral consultations were held in the second half of 1992 which resulted in the Thai Government's commitment to reduce substantially the level of unauthorised duplication. The case is still open and subject to further monitoring by the Commission.

4.5 CIRFS v Turkey

In July 1993 CIRFS (International Rayon and Synthetic Fibres Committee) complained about increased customs duties and a special levy imposed on imports of certain fibres. Both were alleged to be in breach of the EC–Turkey Association Agreement and Articles II and III of GATT.[16] Bilateral consultations took place and resulted in a commitment of the Turkish Government gradually to eliminate both the customs duties and the import levy.

---

[12] OJ 1991 C40/18.
[13] The notice of initiation does not mention any GATT Articles but it is obvious that the following GATT provisions had been infringed: Article II:2.(c) in combination with Article VIII. I:(a) and Article III:2.
[14] OJ 1993 L166/45.
[15] OJ 1991 C189/26.
[16] OJ 1993 C235/4.

Besides these five cases, there have been two other complaints which were formally lodged by a Community industry. The first was lodged in 1986 by FEDIOL (European Seed Crushers and Oil Processors Federation) against Argentina's system of export taxation, pursuant to which higher taxes were levied on raw materials (soya beans) than on processed products (soya meal and soya oil), and quantitative restrictions on the exportation of soya beans. The Commission rejected the complaint because it did not contain sufficient evidence of the existence of illicit commercial practices on the part of Argentina.[17] The complainant appealed to the European Court of Justice under Article 173(2) EC Treaty[18] but the Court upheld the Commission's decision.

Another complaint was lodged in June 1988 when the Commission received a request from a pharmaceutical company, Smith Kline & French Laboratories Ltd, to take action against Jordan. Smith Kline argued that as a consequence of changes introduced in its patent legislation Jordan no longer afforded adequate protection for Smith Kline's products. The Commission rejected that complaint too, on the ground that Smith Kline had not provided sufficient evidence of the existence of an illicit commercial practice, and also because of insufficient factual data in the complaint.[19] This case is still pending.

The above cases show that in its ten years of existence, Community industries have resorted to the NCPI only occasionally. This may be due to some of the substantive defects of the Regulation, a lack of faith in the efficiency of the procedure and also to a lack of awareness of the procedures of the Regulation. In addition, the application of the NCPI has been hampered by the decision-making procedure provided for by the Regulation. This explains why the few attempts to amend the NCPI were aimed at 'streamlining' the decision-making mechanism.

5. Proposals to Amend the NCPI

5.1 The 1992 Proposal to Change the Decision-Making Procedures

In 1992 the Commission put forward a proposal to 'streamline' the decision-making procedures of certain instruments of commercial defence, including Regulation 2641/84.[20] As regards Regulation 2641/84 the proposal would have transferred to the Commission the power to take retaliatory measures if no other solution to a matter brought under

---
[17] See the Report for the Hearing in Case 70/87, FEDIOL v Commission [1989] ECR 1785.
[18] Now Article 173(4) EC Treaty.
[19] OJ 1989 L30/67.
[20] OJ 1992 C181/9.

the NCPI had been found, subject to the possibility for the Council to overturn the Commission decision by a qualified majority.

5.2 The 1994 Regulation on the Streamlining of Decision-Making Procedures

The main purpose of Regulation 522/94,[21] which was passed by the Council as one of the package of amendments to the EC's instruments of commercial defence, was to strengthen the link between the NCPI and the improved dispute settlement of the WTO. As Regulation 522/94 put it, the NCPI would be used in particular for initiating, pursuing and terminating international dispute settlement procedures in the field of the common commercial policy. It would be used as a privileged channel for Community industries to prompt the Community to international action against the infringement of its rights under international trade law.

The Regulation enabled the Council to proceed to dispute settlement (under the WTO) without a prior examination procedure. Such an initiative to follow formal consultation and dispute settlement was taken by a procedure which authorised the Commission to take a decision which would apply after ten days, unless the matter was referred to the Council by a Member State within that period. In the event of the matter being referred to the Council, the Commission's decision became effective after a period of 30 days if the Council had not given a ruling within that time. If the Community received authorisation to retaliate, the Council would act by qualified majority, in accordance with Article 113 EC Treaty, within 30 days after receiving the Commission's proposal.

6. The Trade Barriers Regulation: An Analysis

6.1 The Scope of the Trade Barriers Regulation

The TBR's scope has been extended to services, although its predecessor had already been applied to services in the Japan Harbour Management Fund case. Account should be taken of Opinion 1/94 given by the European Court of Justice ('ECJ') under Article 228(6) EC Treaty in response to the Commission's request concerning the competence of the Community to conclude international agreements concerning services and the protection of intellectual property.[22] The ECJ confirmed that the

---

[21] OJ 1994 L66/10.
[22] [1995] ECR 1-5267. For comments on the Opinion, see, for example, JHJ Bourgeois, 'The EC in the WTO and Advisory Opinion 1/94: An Echternach Procession', (1995) *Common Market Law Review* 763 and J Simor, The Competence of the Community Institutions to Conclude International Agreements Concerning Services and the Protection of IP', (1995) *International Trade Law & Regulation* 29.

EC has exclusive competence under Article 113 EC Treaty - the legal basis of the TBR – to conclude agreements relating to trade in goods. It also decided that Article 113 EC Treaty applies to measures concerning trade in services, provided no movement of persons is involved. On the other hand, it held that Article 113 EC Treaty does not cover the case where a service provider seeks to enter the EC market or to establish a branch there, in order to provide the service, nor where the recipient of the service crosses the border (for example as a tourist). It finally held that in these cases exclusive Community competence cannot be implied under the principle of implied powers. The result is that the Community has exclusive competence in relation to trade in services only where there is no movement of persons.

6.2   The Aims of the Trade Barriers Regulation

The TBR established procedures to enable the EC to exercise its rights under various international trade rules, in particular, those established under the auspices of the WTO, which are aimed at: (1) responding to obstacles to trade that have an effect on the Community market in order to remove the injury which results from such obstacles; and (2) responding to obstacles to trade that have an effect on third country markets in order to remove any resulting adverse trade effects.[23]

'Obstacles to trade' covers any trade practice adopted or maintained by a third country where international trade rules provide a right of action. Such a right of action will exist when these rules either prohibit a practice, or give another party affected by the practice a right to seek the elimination of the effect of the practice in question.[24] 'Adverse trade effects' are those which an obstacle to trade causes or threatens to cause, in respect of a product or a service, to Community enterprises on any third country market which have a material impact on the economy of the Community, a region of the Community or a sector of economic activity in the Community.[25] The requirement of material impact has been introduced to enable the Commission to weed out frivolous actions and concentrate on those actions which benefit the Community beyond the advantages they would bring to the complainant.[26]

---

[23] Article 1 of Regulation 3286/94.
[24] Article 2(1) of Regulation 3286/94.
[25] Article 2(4) of Regulation 3286/94.
[26] Explanatory Memorandum of the Commission's proposal for a Council Regulation 'on the strengthening of the common commercial policy, in particular with regard to protection against illicit commercial practices and adverse trade effects suffered by Community enterprises, and to the exercise of the Community's rights under international trade rules', COM(94) 414 final of 5 October 1994. The final Regulation as adopted by the Council underwent some major changes but the Explanatory Memorandum still provides some guidance on the concepts used by the TBR.

6.3 Who May Submit a Complaint to the Commission?

The TBR has expanded the scope of potential complainants who may submit a complaint to the Commission requesting that a procedure be initiated to examine alleged obstacles to trade. A complaint may now be lodged on behalf of the Community industry or on behalf of Community enterprises. Both terms are defined in the TBR and each is discussed in more detail below. Member States are, as was the case under the NCPI, also entitled to ask the Commission to initiate a procedure. Unlike the Community industry and the Community enterprises which are confined to lodging complaints based on, in the case of the Community industry, obstacles to trade which have an effect on the Community market which allegedly causes injury to the Community industry and, in the case of Community enterprises, obstacles to trade which have an effect on a third country market which allegedly causes adverse trade effects, Member States may ask the Commission to initiate a procedure based on both of these situations.

6.3.1 Complaints Submitted on behalf of the Community Industry

Any natural or legal person, or any association not having legal personality, acting on behalf of the Community industry can lodge a complaint with the Commission where it believes that it has suffered injury as a result of obstacles to trade that have an effect on the market of the Community.[27]

The term 'Community industry' covers all Community producers or providers, respectively, of products or services identical or similar to the product or service which is the subject of an obstacle to trade; or of products or services competing directly with that product or service; or who are consumers or processors of the product or consumers or users of the service which is the subject of an obstacle to trade; or all those producers or providers whose combined output constitutes a major proportion of total Community production of the products or services in question.[28]

Special considerations must, however, be taken into account in deciding whether or not the complainant constitutes the Community industry where there are related producers or providers and where there are producers or providers within a region of the EC.

---

[27] Article 4(1) of Regulation 3286/94.
[28] Article 2(5) of Regulation 3286/94.

6.3.2 Complaints Submitted on behalf of Community Enterprises

Any Community enterprise, or any association, having or not legal personality, acting on behalf of one or more Community enterprises may also lodge a complaint with the Commission where it believes that the Community enterprises concerned have suffered adverse trade effects as a result of obstacles to trade which affect a third country market. The complaint will, however, only be admissible if the alleged trade barrier is the subject of a right of action established under international trade rules laid down in a multilateral or plurilateral trade agreement.[29]

The concept of Community enterprise is defined in the TBR as a company or firm formed in accordance with the law of a Member State, having its registered office, central administration or principal place of business within the EC.[30] The enterprise must be directly concerned by the production of goods or the provision of services which are the subject of the obstacle to trade.

6.4 Injury and Adverse Trade Effects

Aside from identifying the alleged obstacles to trade complained of in each situation, the Commission must examine injury in the cases where the Community industry or a Member State has requested action on alleged obstacles to trade which affect the Community market, and adverse trade effects where the Community enterprises or a Member State have asked the Commission to examine obstacles which affect a third country market. The concepts of injury and adverse trade effects in these distinct types of proceedings under the TBR are examined further below.

6.4.1 Injury

The concept of injury under the TBR comprises three important elements. It requires that an obstacle to trade causes or threatens to cause, in respect of a product or service, material injury to a Community industry on the Community market.[31] As such, there must be a causal link between the material injury or the threat of material injury and the obstacle to trade in question. An examination of material injury must, where applicable, involve a number of factors which are set out in the TBR, such as the volume of Community imports or exports in question, the prices of the Community industry's competitors and, in particular,

---
[29] Article 3(1) of Regulation 3286/94.
[30] Article 2(6) of Regulation 3286/94.
[31] Article 2(3) of Regulation 3286/94.

price undercutting and the consequent impact on the Community industry taking into account trends in certain economic factors including production, utilisation of capacity, stocks, sales, market share, prices and profits.[32] Where a threat of injury is alleged, the Commission must assess whether it is clearly foreseeable that a particular situation is likely to develop into actual injury and may consider issues such as the rate of export increases and existing or proposed export capacity in the country of origin or export.[33]

6.4.2 Adverse Trade Effects

If a procedure relates to an allegation that obstacles to trade exist that have an effect on a third country market, no measures may be taken under the TBR unless adverse trade effects result from the alleged obstacles. The concept 'adverse trade effects' covers those which an obstacle to trade causes or threatens to cause in respect of a product or service to Community enterprises on a third country market.[34] Further, it must have a material impact on the Community's economy or the economy of a region of the Community or on a sector of economic activity. It is not sufficient to prove that the complainant suffers from adverse trade effects in isolation from the EC market. The examination of the impact of such adverse trade effects on the economy of the Community is essential to a determination of adverse trade effects.[35]

The Commission may consider a number of factors in reviewing this issue including those referred to above in the context of an examination of injury and a threat of material injury. The TBR provides examples of where adverse trade effects may arise such as where trade flows relating to a product or service are prevented and where obstacles to trade have materially affected the supply of parts and components of raw materials to Community enterprises.[36] The Commission must also consider the relevant international rules which relate to the trade barrier in question.

6.5 Relation with other Trade Policy Instruments

Just like its predecessor, the TBR provides that it will not apply in cases covered by other existing rules in the common commercial policy field such as the anti-dumping and anti-subsidy regulations.[37] However, nothing seems to exclude the use of the TBR as a complement to the anti-

---

[32] Article 10(1)(a), (b) and (c) of Regulation 3286/94.
[33] Article 10(2) of Regulation 3286/94.
[34] Article 2(4) of Regulation 3286/94.
[35] Ibid.
[36] Article 10(4) of Regulation 3286/94.
[37] Article 15(1) of Regulation 3286/94.

subsidy Regulation[38] for countering the effects of foreign subsidisation outside the EC market.[39]

7. Procedural Aspects

The TBR established procedures for the administration of complaints which closely resemble the procedural mechanism introduced by its predecessor.

7.1 Lodging a Complaint

As described above, complaints may be submitted on behalf of the Community industry or Community enterprises. The TBR does not contain any specific requirements regarding the form of the complaint. It only specifies that the complaint must be in writing.[40] Its content, however, must meet certain conditions. If a complaint is submitted on behalf of the Community industry, it must contain sufficient evidence of the existence of the alleged obstacles to trade and of the resulting injury.[41] where a complaint is lodged by a Community enterprise, again it must contain sufficient evidence of the obstacles to trade. It must, however, also contain sufficient evidence of the resulting adverse trade effects.[42] Evidence of injury and of adverse trade effects must be given on the basis of an illustrative list of factors required by the TBR. These have been dealt with above.

7.2 The Consultation Procedure

Copies of all complaints must be sent to the Member States. The Commission will then consult the Member State representatives sitting in advisory committee to determine whether there is sufficient evidence to justify the initiation of an examination procedure and whether it is in the Community interest to do so. If the Commission decides to reject the complaint, the complainant must be informed.

7.3 The Community Examination Procedure

If the Commission decides to open an examination procedure, it must publish a notice of initiation in the *Official Journal* setting out details

---

[38] Regulation 3284/94 of 22 December 1994, OJ 1994 L349/22 as amended by Regulation 1252/95 OH 1995 LI22/2.
[39] J H J Bourgeois (ed.), Kluwer, Deventer, 1991, 187, at 197 and C. Norall, ‚Impact of the New Rules on Subsidies and Countervailing Measures', in *The Uruguay Round Results. A European Lawyer's Perspective*, J H J Bourgeois, F. Berrod and E G Fournier (eds) (European Interuniversity Press, Brussels, 1995) 255, at 263.
[40] Articles 3(1) and 4(1) of Regulation 3286/94.
[41] Article 3(2) of Regulation 3286/94.
[42] Article 4(2) of Regulation 3286/94.

of the case such as the product or service concerned and a summary of the information received.[43] The Commission must also officially notify the representatives of the country or countries concerned with whom, as appropriate, consultation may be held and it must conduct an examination at a Community level, acting in co-operation with the Member States.[44] If appropriate, information may also be requested from the importers, traders, agents, producers and trade associations who are interested in the procedure. The Commission does not, however, have the power to compel these interested parties to co-operate and provide the necessary information.[45] Nevertheless, in the absence of voluntary submissions, it has the power to make its findings on the basis of the facts available.[46] On-the-spot investigations may take place if necessary.[47]

The parties primarily concerned (namely, complainants, the exporters and importers concerned as well as the representatives of the country or countries concerned) may inspect non-confidential information made available to the Commission, provided that the information concerned is relevant to the protection of their interests and it is used by the Commission for its investigation.[48] Interested parties also have the right to be heard. Parties who wish to be heard must, within the period indicated in the notice of initiation, apply in writing for a hearing showing that they are a party primarily concerned by the result of the procedure.[49] The TBR also gives these parties the opportunity to meet to discuss their views if necessary. Finally, interested parties may ask to be informed of the principal facts and considerations resulting from the examination procedure.

When the Commission has concluded its examination, it must submit an examination report to the Advisory Committee normally within five months of the announcement of initiation of the procedure, unless the complexity of the case is such that the Commission extends the period to seven months.[50]

7.4 The Outcome of the Procedure

There are basically four possibilities at the conclusion of an examination procedure. The procedure will be terminated where it is found that the interests of the Community do not require any action to be taken.[51] The

---
[43] Article 8(1)(a) of Regulation 3286/94.
[44] Article 8(1)(b) and (c) of Regulation 3286/94.
[45] Article 2(a) of Regulation 3286/94.
[46] Article 8(7) of Regulation 3286/94.
[47] Article 8(2)(b) of Regulation 3286/94.
[48] Article 8(4)(a) of Regulation 3286/94.
[49] Article 8(5) of Regulation 3286/94.
[50] Article 8(8) of Regulation 3286/94.
[51] Article 11(1) of Regulation 3286/94.

procedure may be suspended if the third country takes satisfactory measures to remove the obstacle to trade.[52] The examination procedure may also be suspended after the conclusion of an examination procedure (as well as any time before, during or after an international dispute settlement procedure) if it is appropriate to settle the matter by entering into an agreement with the third countries concerned.[53]

If the Commission decides that action is necessary in the interests of the Community to remove injury or adverse trade effects, the Community can adopt 'appropriate measures' such as the suspension or withdrawal of any concession resulting from commercial policy negotiations, the raising of existing customs duties or the introduction of any other charge on imports or the introduction of quantitative restrictions or any other measures modifying import or export conditions or otherwise affecting trade with the third country concerned.[54] It should be noted, however, that in some cases (that is, the WTO) the Community may be obliged, under internationally agreed rules, to participate in an international procedure for consultation or the settlement of disputes before taking any measures. If this is the case, then the Community may only decide to take measures in the light of the results of the procedure.[55] If the Community decides to retaliate, it may only do so in conformity with its international obligations and procedures.

7.5 Decision-Making Mechanism

The TBR contains detailed provisions governing the formalities which must be complied with in order to reach a decision on the measures to be imposed. The decisions adopted by the Council must be reasoned and published in the *Official Journal*.

8. Conclusion

The Commission, in its Explanatory Memorandum, emphasised that the objective of the TBR was not to relax the conditions for standing of Community industries and for the trade effects suffered, but to adapt the instrument as a tool for the opening of third country markets. It nevertheless appears that both aspects have been realised. By giving Community enterprises a right of standing, more complaints will be submitted in the future. The TBR allows European industry to adopt a more aggressive market-opening strategy.[56]

---

[52] Article 11(2)(a) of Regulation 3286/94.
[53] Article 11(3) of Regulation 3286/94.
[54] Articles 12(1) and 12(3) of Regulation 3286/94.
[55] Article 12(2) of Regulation 3286/94.
[56] In French, the TBR is referred to as 'Règlement pour l'ouverture des marchés', which clearly reflects the aim of the Regulation.

It appears that the Community has finally discovered the 'beauty' of this trade instrument and that it will use it as a vehicle to start international dispute settlement procedures under the new WTO dispute settlement mechanism. There is no danger that the TBR will develop into an equivalent of the US section 301 because it abides by the WTO dispute settlement procedures.

CHAPTER II

THE EC TRADE BARRIERS REGULATION
THE EC's MOVE TOWARDS A MORE AGGRESSIVE MARKET
ACCESS STRATEGY

1. Introduction

Following the conclusion of the Uruguay Round, there have been important changes to the EC's trade policy. The EC tends to move away from an approach which aims exclusively at protecting the EC market towards a more offensive strategy to open the markets of third countries.

Council Regulation 3286/94 laying down Community procedures in the field of the common commercial policy in order to ensure the exercise of the Community rights under international trade rules, in particular those established under the auspices of the World Trade Organization, best known in Community parlance as the Trade Barriers Regulation (the TBR),[1] was adopted on 22 December 1994 with the aim of helping European enterprises to eliminate trade barriers on third country markets which do not comply with international trade rules. The TBR gives access to a procedure by which the EC is requested to act, mainly through the European Commission (the Commission), internationally to obtain enforcement of international trade rules where third countries are adopting or maintaining barriers to trade. The principal means of taking action and exercising pressure to attain these objectives are international dispute settlement procedures and subsequent retaliatory measures if an actionable trade barrier is not removed. These procedures will primarily be those of the WTO, but also including other multilateral and bilateral agreements which provide for a dispute settlement mechanism.

---

[1] [1994] OJ L349/71 of 31 December 1994, as amended by Council Regulation 356/95 [1995] OJ L41/3 of 23 February 1995. See H Beekmann 'The 1994 Revised Commercial Policy Instrument of the European Union' (1995) *World Competition* 53; MCEJ Bronckers 'Private Participation in the Enforcement of WTO Law: the new EC Trade Barriers Regulation' (1996) *Common Market Law Review* 299; C Norall 'Some Thoughts on the New Community Trade Barriers Regulation' (1995) *International Trade Law & Regulation* 67; A Stewart 'Market Access: A European Community Instrument to Break Down Barriers to Trade' (1996) *International Trade Law & Regulation* 121 and G Zonnekeyn 'The EC "Trade Barriers Regulation": More Opportunities for Community Industries?' (1995) *International Trade Law & Regulation* 143. Comments also appear in I Van Bael and J-F Bellis *Anti-Dumping and Other Trade Protection Laws of the EC* (3rd edn, Oxfordshire: CCH, 1996).

The Commission has recently initiated seven procedures under the TBR. These procedures are the result of the Commission's efforts to promote this instrument of commercial policy[2] and demonstrates the EC's move towards a more aggressive market access strategy as it had been put forward in the Commission's communication entitled 'The Global Challenge of International Trade: A Market Access Strategy for the European Union'.[3]

This chapter provides an overview of the few cases which have been brought or attempted under the TBR's predecessor, the so-called New Commercial Policy Instrument (the NCPI). The main part of the chapter will focus on the substantive and procedural aspects of the TBR and the seven cases which have recently been initiated by the Commission.

2. Legislative Background

In September 1984, the EC introduced Council Regulation 2641/84 on the strengthening of the common commercial policy with regard in particular to protection against illicit commercial practices (the NCPI).[4] This regulation was primarily designed to give Community industries access to some form of relief under Community law when their trade opportunities were illicitly restricted by trade practices of third countries. It was also adopted in response to Section 301 of the US Trade Act of 1974, as amended, which enables private parties to invoke

---

[2] The European Commission has published an explanatory brochure entitled 'What is the Community's Trade Barriers Regulation? Opening New Trade Opportunities for European Businesses' and a brochure entitled 'A Market access Strategy for the European Union' which explains how to use the European Commission's new 'Market Access' database.
[3] COM (96) 53 final of 14 February 1996.
[4] [1984] OJ L252/1 of 20 September 1984. See eg JHJ Bourgeois and P Laurent 'Le "nouvel instrument de politique commerciale": un pas en vant vers l'élimination des obstacles aux échanges internationaux' (1985) *Revue Trimestrielle de Droit Européen* 41; JHJ Bourgeois 'EC Rules Against "Illicit Trade Practices" – Policy Cosmetics or International Law Enforcement?' in BE Hawk (ed) 1988 *Annual Proceedings of the Fordham Corporate Law Institute* (New-York: M Bender, 1989) ch 6; MCEJ Bronckers and MIB Arnold 'The EEC New Trade Policy Instrument: Some Comments On Its Application' (1988*) Journal of World Trade* 19; MCEJ Bronckers 'The Potentials and Limitations of the Community's New Trade Policy Instrument' in P Demaret, J Bourgeois and I Van Bael (eds) *Trade Laws of the European Community and the United States in a Comparative Perspective* (Brussels: Story-Scientia, 1992) 133–64; F Castillo de la Torre 'The EEC New Instrument of Trade Policy: Some Comments in the Light of the Latest Developments' (1993) *Common Market Law Review* 687; M Hilf and R Rolf 'Das Neue Instrument der EG. Eine rechtsstaatliche Stärkung der gemeinsamen Handelspolitik?' (1985) *Recht der Internationalen Wirtschaft* 297; F Schoneveld 'The European Community Reaction to the "Illicit" Commercial Trade Practices of Other Countries' (1992) *Journal of World Trade* 17 and J Steenbergen 'The New Commercial Policy Instrument' (1985) *Common Market Law Review* 421. Comments also appear in I Van Bael and J-F Bellis *Anti-Dumping and Other Trade Protection Laws of the EEC* (2nd edn, Bicester: CCH, 1990).

the intervention of the US Government against foreign trade practices which limit the commerce of the US.[5]

Little use has been made of the NCPI. This was mainly due to some of the key concepts forming part of the NCPI which proved to be inappropriate to effectively protect the interests of Community industries in third country markets. In addition, the application of the NCPI has been hampered by the decision-making procedure provided for by the regulation. This explains why the few attempts to amend the NCPI were aimed at 'streamlining' the decision-making mechanism.

In 1992, the Commission put forward a proposal to 'streamline' the decision-making procedures of certain instruments of commercial defence, including the NCPI.[6] As regards the NCPI the proposal would have transferred to the Commission the power to take retaliatory measures if no other solution to a matter brought under the NCPI had been found, subject to the possibility of the Council overturning the Commission decision by a qualified majority. The proposal has never been adopted.

In 1994, a package of amendments to the EC's instruments of commercial defence was adopted by the Council through Regulation 522/94.[7] Its main purpose was to strengthen the link between the NCPI and the improved dispute settlement system of the WTO. As Regulation 522/94 put it, the NCPI would be used in particular for initiating, pursuing and terminating international dispute settlement procedures in the field of the common commercial policy. It would be used as a privileged channel for Community industries to prompt the Community to international action against the infringement of its rights under international trade law.

Regulation 522/94 enabled the Council to proceed to dispute settlement (under the WTO) without a prior examination procedure. Such an initiative to follow formal consultation and dispute settlement was taken by a procedure which authorised the Commission to take a decision which would apply after 10 days, unless the matter was referred to the Council

---

[5] For a comparative analysis between the NCPI and Section 301, see WW Leirer 'Retaliating Action in United States and European Union Trade Law: A Comparison of Section 301 of the Trade Act of 1974 and Council Regulation 2641/84' (1994) *RCJ Int Law & Com Reg* 41, P Mavroidis *Handelspolitische Abwehrmechanismen der EWG und ihre Vereinbarkeit mit den GATT-Regeln* (Stuttgart: Verlagsgesellschaft Internationales Recht, 1993); D Petermann *Beschränkungen zur Abwehr von Beschränkungen, Sec 301 des US-amerikanischen Trade Act von 1974 und das neue handelspolitische Instrument der EG* (Heidelberg: Verlag Recht und Wirtschaft, 1989) and E Zoller 'Remedies for Unfair Trade: European and United States Views' (1985) *Cornell International Law Journal* 227.
[6] [1992] OJ C181/9 of 17 July 1992.
[7] [1994] OJ L66/10 of 10 March 1994.

by a Member State within that period. In the event of the matter being referred to the Council, the Commission's decision became effective after a period of 30 days if the Council had not given a ruling within that time. If the Community received authorisation to retaliate, the Council would act by qualified majority, in accordance with Article 113 EC Treaty, within 30 days after receiving the Commission's proposal.

3. Cases Brought under the NCPI

The NCPI provided for actions to be brought under two 'tracks'. There have been no cases brought under the so-called 'track B', that is referrals of a matter by a Member State, requesting the 'full exercise of the Community's rights' under international trade rules. The so-called 'track A' of the NCPI has been used at least a few times: there have been five cases in which the Commission formally opened an examination procedure, following a complaint by a Community industry that it was being injured by an illicit commercial practice of a third country, and two more complaints were lodged, but rejected by the Commission.

3.1 Akzo v United States

The NCPI was first tested in December 1985, when Akzo brought a complaint challenging a US import ban on Akzo's aramid fibres in application of Section 337 of the US Tariff Act of 1930, as amended.[8] After a thorough examination under the procedure set out in the NCPI, the Commission decided to initiate dispute settlement proceedings in GATT under Article XXIII.[9] A panel was established to study the matter and some months later the panel report, which was issued in November 1988, found Section 337 to be inconsistent with Article III.4 of GATT.[10] The US accepted the panel report about a year after it had been adopted and has adapted its legislation to the findings of the panel.

3.2 IFPI v Indonesia

In March 1987, IFPI (the International Federation of Phonogram Industries), representing the European sound recording industry, filed a complaint against the alleged failure by the Indonesian Government to grant adequate protection to the European record producers against the unauthorised copying of their sound recordings in Indonesia.[11] The procedure was closed in May 1988 after the conclusion of an amicable settlement.[12]

---

[8] See Notice of initiation [1986] OJ C25/2 of 5 February 1986.
[9] [1987] OJ L117/18 of 5 May 1987.
[10] BISD 36th Supp 345.
[11] See Notice of initiation [1987] OJ C136/3 of 21 May 1987.
[12] [1988] OJ L123/51 of 17 May 1988.

3.3 ECSA v Japan

In November 1989, ECSA (the European Community Shipowners' Association), acting on behalf of major European shipping companies, complained about port charges in Japan which did not correspond to any service actually performed, although they went into a 'Harbour Management Fund', and were higher for international transport than for domestic transport.[13] Bilateral consultations with Japan took place, in which the Commission took the view that the Japanese practice was in breach of GATT, and that the Community might eventually initiate dispute settlement proceedings under Article XXIII of GATT. This resulted in the Japanese Government abolishing the fund and the case was terminated.[14]

3.4 IFPI v Thailand

Having first complained about piracy in Indonesia, IFPI also charged the Thai Government for failing to offer adequate protection to the Community sound recording industry against the unauthorized duplication of their sound recordings in Thailand.[15] Contrary to the first *IFPI* case, where Indonesia's copyright law was found to be contrary to its international obligations, Thailand's copyright law appeared to be in compliance with its international commitments. It was rather the ineffective enforceability and non-enforcement of Thai copyright law which was alleged to be in breach of Thailand's international obligations. Bilateral consultations were held in the second half of 1992 which resulted in the Thai Government's commitment to reduce substantially the level of unauthorised duplication. The procedure was suspended in December 1995 since the entry into force of a new copyright act and the creation of a court specialised in IP infringements.[16] A tripartite working group was set up, including Commission officials, Thai officials both at government and police level and representatives of the European industry.

3.5 CIRFS v Turkey

In July 1993, CIRFS (the International Rayon and Synthetic Fibres Committee) complained about increased customs duties and a special levy imposed on imports of certain fibres for the benefit of the Turkish Mass Housing Fund. Both were alleged to be in breach of the EC-Turkey Association Agreement and Articles II and III of GATT.[17] Bilateral

---

[13] See Notice of initiation [1991] OJ C40/18 of 16 February 1991.
[14] OJ L166/45 of 8 July 1993.
[15] See Notice of initiation [1991] OJ C189/26 of 20 July 1991.
[16] [1996] OJ L11/7 of 16 January 1996.
[17] See Notice of initiation [1993] OJ C235/4 of 31 August 1993.

consultations took place and resulted in an elimination of both the customs duties and the import levy. The Commission therefore decided to terminate the procedure.[18]

3.6 Other Complaints

Besides these five cases, there have been two other complaints which were formally lodged by a Community industry. The first was lodged in 1986 by Fediol (the European Seed Crushers' and Oil Processors' Federation) against Argentina's system of different export taxation pursuant to which higher taxes were levied on the raw materials (soya beans) than on the processed products (soya meal and soya oil) and quantitative restrictions on the exportation of soya beans. The Commission rejected the complaint because it did not contain sufficient evidence of the existence of the illicit commercial practices on the part of Argentina.[19] The complainant appealed to the European Court of Justice but the court upheld the Commission decision.

Another complaint was lodged in June 1988, when the Commission received a request from a pharmaceutical company, Smith Kline & French Laboratories Ltd, to take action against Jordan. Smith Kline argued that as a consequence of changes introduced in its patent legislation Jordan no longer afforded adequate protection for its products. The Commission rejected the complaint too, on the ground that Smith Kline had not displayed sufficient evidence of the existence of an illicit commercial practice, as well as because of insufficient factual data in the complaint.[20]

4. The Trade Barriers Regulation

The TBR repealed the NCPI and introduced some major changes. The most important changes relate to the right of Community enterprises to submit complaints with the Commission when being confronted with trade obstacles on third country markets and the extension of the TBR's scope to services. Other amendments have been included to strengthen the link between the TBR and the improved WTO dispute settlement mechanism.[21]

---

[18] [1996] OJ L326/71 of 17 December 1996.
[19] See the report for the hearing in Case 70/87 *Fediol v Commission* [1989] ECR 1785.
[20] [1991] OJ L30/67 of 1 February 1991.
[21] For an analysis of the new WTO dispute settlement system, see eg N Komuro 'The WTO Dispute Settlement Mechanism. Coverage and Procedures of the WTO Understanding' (1995) *Journal of International Arbitration* 81; P-J Kuyper 'The New WTO Dispute Settlement System: the Impact on the Community' in *The Uruguay Round Results. A European Lawyer's Perspective* (Brussels: European Interuniversity Press, 1995) 87–114; E-U Petersmann 'The

continued ...

4.1 The Scope of the TBR

The TBR's scope has been extended to services although its predecessor had already been applied to services in the *Japan Harbour Management Fund* case. Account should be taken of Opinion 1/94 given by the European Court of Justice (the ECJ) under Article 228(6) EC Treaty in response to the Commission's request concerning the competence of the Community to conclude international agreements concerning services and the protection of intellectual property.[22] The ECJ confirmed that the EC has exclusive competence under Article 113 EC Treaty – the legal basis of the TBR – to conclude agreements relating to trade in goods. It also considered that Article 113 EC Treaty applies to measures concerning trade in services provided; no physical movement of persons is involved. On the other hand, it considered that Article 113 EC Treaty does not cover the case where a service provider seeks to enter the EC market or to establish a branch there, in order to provide the service, nor where the recipient of the service crosses the border (eg as a tourist). It finally held that in these cases exclusive Community competence cannot be implied under the principle of implied powers. The result is that the Community has exclusive competence in relation to trade in services only where there is no physical movement of persons.

As regards intellectual property rights, the ECJ considered that this was an area of shared competence between the EC and the Member States insofar as the Agreement on Trade Related Aspects of Intellectual Property Rights (TRIPs) involved modification of Community (and Member States') laws on intellectual property protection.

Dispute Settlement System of the World Trade Organisation and the Evolution of the GATT Dispute Settlement System since 1948' (1994) *Common Market Law Review* 1157; E-U Petersmann *The GATT/WTO Dispute Settlement System: International Law, International Organisations and Dispute Settlement*, (Deventer: Kluwer Law International, 1996); Y Renouf 'Le règlement des litiges' in *La Communauté Européenne et le GATT* (Rennes: Editions Apogée, 1995) 41–61; DP Steger 'The New Landscape for International Trade: WTO Dispute Settlement' paper presented at the 1997 International Trade Seminar at the University of Maastricht on 30 June 1997 and E Vermulst and B Driessen 'An Overview of the WTO Dispute Settlement System and its Relationship with the Uruguay Round Agreements' (1995) *Journal of World Trade* 131.
[22] [1995] ECR I–5267. For comments on the Opinion, see eg A Arnull 'The Scope of the Common Commercial Policy: A Coda on Opinion 1/94' in N Emiliou and D O'Keeffe (eds) *The European Union and World Trade Law After the GATT Uruguay Round* (Wiley: Chichester, 1994) 343; JHJ Bourgeois 'The EC in the WTO and Advisory Opinion 1/94: An Echternach Procession' (1995) *Common Market Law Review* 763, M Hilf 'The ECJ's Opinion 1/94 on the WTO – No Surprise, but Wise?' (1995) *European Journal of International Law* 245; A Maunu 'The implied external competence of the European Community after the ECJ Opinion 1/94 – Towards Coherence or diversity?' (1995) *Legal Issues of European Integration* 115 and P Van Nuffel 'Annotation on Opinion 1/94' (1995) *Columbia Journal of European Law* 338.

4.2 The Aims of the TBR

The TBR established procedures to enable the EC to exercise its rights under various international trade rules, in particular, those established under the auspices of the WTO, which are aimed at: (a) responding to obstacles to trade that have an effect on the Community market in order to remove the injury which results from such obstacles; and (b) responding to obstacles to trade that have an effect on third country markets in order to remove any resulting adverse trade effects.[23]

'Obstacles to trade' cover any trade practice adopted or maintained by a third country where international trade rules provide a right of action. Such a right of action will exist when these rules either prohibit a practice, or give another party, affected by the practice, a right to seek the elimination of the effect of the practice in question.[24] 'Adverse trade effects' are those which an obstacle to trade causes or threatens to cause, in respect of a product or a service, to Community enterprises on any third country market which have a material impact on the economy of the Community, a region of the Community or a sector of economic activity in the Community.[25] The requirement of material impact has been introduced to enable the Commission to weed out frivolous actions and concentrate on those actions which benefit the Community beyond the advantages they would bring to the complainant.[26]

4.3 Who May Submit a Complaint to the Commission?

The TBR has expanded the scope of potential complainants who may submit a complaint to the Commission requesting that a procedure be initiated to examine alleged obstacles to trade. A complaint may now be lodged on behalf of the Community industry or on behalf of Community enterprises. Both terms are defined in the TBR and each of these issues is described more in detail below. Member States are, as was the case under the NCPI, also entitled to ask the Commission to initiate a procedure. Unlike the Community industry and the Community enterprises which are confined to lodging complaints based on, in the case of the Community industry, obstacles to trade which have an effect on the Community

---

[23] Article 1 of Regulation 3286/94.
[24] Article 2(1) of Regulation 3286/94.
[25] Article 2(4) of Regulation 3286/94.
[26] Explanatory Memorandum of the Commission's proposal for a Council Regulation 'on the strengthening of the common commercial policy, in particular with regard to protection against illicit commercial practices and adverse trade effects suffered by Community enterprises, and to the exercise of the Community's rights under international trade rules' COM(94) 414 final of 26 September 1994. The final regulation as adopted by the Council underwent some major changes but the Explanatory Memorandum still provides some guidance on the concepts used by the TBR.

market which allegedly causes injury to the Community industry and, in the case of Community enterprises, obstacles to trade which have an effect on a third country market which allegedly causes adverse trade effects, Member States may ask the Commission to initiate a procedure based upon both of these situations.

4.3.1 Complaints Submitted on Behalf of the Community Industry

Any natural or legal person, or any association not having legal personality, acting on behalf of the Community industry can lodge a complaint with the Commission where it believes that it has suffered injury as a result of obstacles to trade that have an effect on the market of the Community.[27]

The term 'Community industry' covers all Community producers or providers, respectively of products or services identical or similar to the product or service which is the subject of an obstacle to trade; or of products or services competing directly with that product or service; or who are consumers or processors of the product or consumers or users of the service which is the subject of an obstacle to trade; or all those producers or providers whose combined output constitutes a major proportion of total Community production of the products or services in question.[28]

Special considerations must, however, be taken into account in deciding whether or not the complainant constitutes the Community industry where there are related producers or providers and where there are producers or providers within a region of the EC.

4.3.2 Complaints Submitted on Behalf of Community Enterprises

Any Community enterprise, or any association, having or not legal personality acting on behalf of one or more Community enterprises may also lodge a complaint with the Commission where it believes that the Community enterprises concerned have suffered adverse trade effects as a result of obstacles to trade which affect a third country market. The complaint will, however, only be admissible if the alleged trade barrier is the subject of a right of action established under international trade rules laid down in a multilateral or plurilateral trade agreement.[29]

---

[27] Article 3(1) of Regulation 3286/94.
[28] Article 2(5) of Regulation 3286/94.
[29] Article 4(1) of Regulation 3286/94.

The concept of Community enterprise is defined in the TBR as a company or firm formed in accordance with the law of a Member State, having its registered office, central administration or principal place of business within the EC.[30] The enterprise must be directly concerned by the production of goods or the provision of services which are the subject of the obstacle to trade.

4.4 Injury and Adverse Trade Effects

Aside from identifying the alleged obstacles to trade complained of in each situation, the Commission must examine injury in the cases where the Community industry or a Member State has requested action on alleged obstacles to trade which affect the Community market and adverse trade effects where the Community enterprises or a Member State have asked the Commission to examine obstacles which affect a third country market. The concepts of injury and adverse trade effects in these distinct types of proceedings under the TBR are examined further below.

4.4.1 Injury

The concept of injury under the TBR comprises three important elements. It requires that an obstacle to trade causes or threatens to cause, in respect of a product or service, material injury to a Community industry on the Community market.[31] As such, there must be a causal link between the material injury or the threat of material injury and the obstacle to trade in question. An examination of material injury must, where applicable, involve a number of factors which are set out in the TBR such as the volume Community imports or exports in question, the prices of the Community's industry's competitors and, in particular, price undercutting and the consequent impact on the Community industry taking into account trends in certain economic factors including production, utilisation of capacity, stocks, sales, market share, prices and profits.[32] Where a threat of injury is alleged, the Commission must assess whether it is clearly foreseeable that a particular situation is likely to develop into actual injury and may consider issues such as the rate of export increases and existing or proposed export capacity in the country of origin or export.[33]

4.4.2 Adverse trade effect

If a procedure relates to an allegation that obstacles to trade exist that have an effect on a third country market, no measures may be taken under

---

[30] Article 2(6) of Regulation 3286/94.
[31] Article 2(3) of Regulation 3286/94.
[32] Article 10(1) (a), (b) and (c) of Regulation 3286/94.
[33] Article 10(2) of Regulation 3286/94.

the TBR unless adverse trade effects result from the alleged obstacles. The concept 'adverse trade effects' covers those which an obstacle to trade causes or threatens to cause in respect of a product or service to Community enterprises on a third country market.[34] Further, it must have a material impact on the Community's economy or the economy of a region of the Community or on a sector of economic activity. It is not sufficient to prove that the complainant suffers from adverse trade effects in isolation from the EC market. The examination of the impact of such adverse trade effects on the economy of the Community is essential to a determination of adverse trade effects.[35]

The Commission may consider a number of factors in reviewing this issue including those referred to above in the context of an examination of injury and a threat of material injury. The TBR provides examples of where adverse trade effects may arise such as where trade flows relating to a product or service are prevented and where obstacles to trade have materially affected the supply of parts and components of raw materials to Community enterprises.[36] The Commission must also consider the relevant international rules which relate to the trade barrier in question.

4.5 Relation with Other Trade Policy Instruments

Just like its predecessor, the TBR provides that it will not apply in cases covered by other existing rules in the common commercial policy field such as the anti-dumping and anti-subsidy regulations.[37] However, nothing seems to exclude the use of the TBR as a complement to the anti-subsidy regulation[38] for countering the effects of foreign subsidisation outside the EC market.[39]

4.6 Procedural Aspects

The TBR established procedures for the administration of complaints which closely resembles the procedural mechanism introduced by its predecessor.

---

[34] Article 2(4) of Regulation 3286/94.
[35] ibid.
[36] Article 10(4) of Regulation 3286/94.
[37] Article 15(1) of Regulation 3286/94.
[38] Council Regulation 3284/94 of 22 December 1994 [1994] OJ L349/22 of 31 December 1994, as amended by Council Regulation 1252/95 of 29 May 1995 [1995] OJ L122/2 of 6 February 1995.
[39] MCEJ Bronckers 'Private Remedies Against Foreign Subsidization: A European View' in JHJ Bourgeois (ed) *Subsidies in International Trade. A European Lawyer's Perspective* (Deventer: Kluwer, 1991) 187 at 197 and C Norall 'Impact of the New Rules on Subsidies and Countervailing Measures' in JHJ Bourgeois, F Berrod and EG Fournier (eds) *The Uruguay Round Results. A European Laywer's Perspective* (Brussels: European Interuniversity Press, 1995) 255 at 263.

4.6.1 Lodging a Complaint

As described above, complaints may be submitted on behalf of the Community industry or Community enterprises. The TBR does not contain any specific requirements regarding the form of the complaint. It only specifies that the complaint must be in writing.[40] Its content, however, must meet certain conditions. If a complaint is submitted on behalf of the Community industry, it must contain sufficient prima facie evidence of the existence of the alleged obstacles to trade and of the resulting injury.[41] Where a complaint is lodged by a Community enterprise, again it must contain sufficient evidence of the obstacles to trade. It must, however, also contain sufficient evidence of the resulting adverse trade effects.[42] Evidence of injury and of adverse trade effects must be given on the basis of an illustrative list of factors required by the TBR.

4.6.2 The Consultation Procedure

Copies of all complaints must be sent to the Member States. The Commission will then consult the Member State representatives sitting in the Advisory Committee to determine whether there is sufficient evidence to justify the initiation of an examination procedure and whether it is in the Community interest to do so. If the Commission decides to reject the complaint, the complainant must be informed.

4.6.3 The Community Examination Procedure

If the Commission decides to open an examination procedure, it must publish a notice of initiation in the Official Journal setting out details of the case such as the product or service concerned and a summary of the information received.[43] The Commission must also officially notify the representatives of the country or countries concerned with whom, as appropriate, consultation may be held and it must conduct an examination at a Community level, acting in cooperation with the Member States.[44] If appropriate, information may also be requested from the importers, traders, agents, producers and trade associations who are interested in the procedure. It does not, however, have the power to compel these interested parties to cooperate and provide the necessary information.[45] Nevertheless, in the absence of voluntary submissions, the Commission has the power to make its findings on

---

[40] Articles 3(1) and 4(1) of Regulation 3286/94.
[41] Article 3(2) of Regulation 3286/94.
[42] Article 4(2) of Regulation 3286/94.
[43] Article 8(1) (a) of Regulation 3286/94.
[44] Article 8(1) (b) and (c) of Regulation 3286/94.
[45] Article 2 (a) of Regulation 3286/94.

the basis of the facts available.[46] On-the-spot investigations may take place if necessary.[47]

The parties primarily concerned (ie complainants, the exporters and importers concerned as well as the representatives of the country or countries concerned) may inspect non-confidential information made available to the Commission, provided that the information concerned is relevant to the protection of their interests and, it is used by the Commission for its investigation.[48] Interested parties also have the right to be heard. Parties who wish to be heard must, within the period indicated in the notice of initiation, apply in writing for a hearing showing that they are a party primarily concerned by the result of the procedure.[49] The TBR also gives these parties the opportunity to meet to discuss their views if necessary. Finally, interested parties may ask to be informed of the principal facts and considerations resulting from the examination procedure.

When the Commission has concluded its examination, it must submit an examination report to the Advisory Committee normally within five months of the announcement of initiation of the procedure, unless the complexity of the case is such that the Commission extends the period to seven months.[50]

4.6.4 The Outcome of the Procedure

There are basically four possibilities at the conclusion of an examination procedure. The procedure will be terminated where it is found that the interests of the Community do not require any action to be taken.[51] The procedure may be suspended if the third country or countries take satisfactory measures to remove the obstacle to trade.[52] The examination procedure may also be suspended after the conclusion of an examination procedure (as well as any time before, during or after an international dispute settlement procedure) if it is appropriate to settle the matter by entering into an agreement with the third countries concerned.[53]

If the Commission decides that action is necessary in the interests of the Community to remove injury or adverse trade effects, the Community can adopt 'appropriate measures' such as the suspension or withdrawal

---

[46] Article 8(7) of Regulation 3286/94.
[47] Article 8(2) (b) of Regulation 3286/94.
[48] Article 8(4) (a) of Regulation 3286/94.
[49] Article 8(5) of Regulation 3286/94.
[50] Article 8(8) of Regulation 3286/94.
[51] Article 11(1) of Regulation 3286/94.
[52] Article 11(2)(a) of Regulation 3286/94.
[53] Article 11(3) of Regulation 3286/94.

of any concession resulting from commercial policy negotiations, the raising of existing customs duties or the introduction of any other charge on imports or the introduction of quantitative restrictions or any other measures modifying import or export conditions or otherwise affecting trade with the third country concerned.[54] It should be noted, however, that in some cases (ie the WTO) the Community may be obliged, under internationally agreed rules, to participate in an international procedure for consultation or the settlement of disputes before taking measures. If this is that case, then the Community may only decide to take measures in the light of the results of the procedure.[55] If the Community decides to retaliate, it may only do so in conformity with its international obligations and procedures.

4.6.5 Decision-Making Mechanism

The TBR contains detailed provisions governing the formalities which must be complied with in order to reach a decision on the measures to be imposed. The decisions adopted by the Council must be reasoned and published in the Official Journal.

5. The EC's New Market Access Strategy

The Commission is determined to pursue a more active market opening strategy for the benefit of European enterprises. To this end, the Commission is committed to make full use of existing market opening instruments specifically adapted to this objective. In its Communication entitled 'The Global Challenge of International Trade: A Market Access Strategy for the European Union' the Commission stated that 'in addition to carrying out adequate policies to promote the international competitiveness of European industry, the Community must strive to achieve improved market access in third countries in parallel to the continued progressive opening of its own market, both by ensuring the full implementation by its partners of their Uruguay Round obligations and through other market access actions'.[56]

The Commission emphasised that one of the ways to achieve this objective is the application of the TBR, at the request of a Member State, Community industry or company. In order to help identifying the barriers which hamper European enterprises abroad, the Commission has set up a comprehensive database[57] identifying obstacles to market access with the active participation of the Member States and enterprises. The database

---

[54] Articles 12(1) and 12(3) of Regulation 3286/94.
[55] Article 12(2) of Regulation 3286/94.
[56] See COM(96) of 14 February 1996 at p 3.
[57] The database can be consulted at the following internet address: http://europa.eu.int

covers sectors and countries. The Commission emphasises that the 'new Market Access Strategy' can only work if everyone concerned pools the information available concerning export markets and provides continuous feedback on further developments. With this new Market Access Strategy the Commission is actively inviting the European enterprises to bring forward complaints about problems affecting Community exports.

6. Cases Brought under the TBR

As the result of the Commission's efforts to promote the TBR, seven complaints have been submitted to an examination procedure to date. Those seven cases will be reviewed here below.

6.1 Federtessile v United States

On 11 October 1996, Federtessile (the Federation of Italian Associations of Textile Industry), representing the Italian silk industry and the Italian luxury finishing textile industry, filed a complaint under the TBR against the US.[58]

Federtessile argues that the US' Uruguay Round implementing legislation has introduced new principles for determining the origin of textile and apparel products which are contrary to Article 4(2) of the WTO Agreement On Textiles and Clothing and Article 2(b) and (c) of the WTO Agreement on Rules of Origin.

Under Article 4(2) of the WTO Agreement on Textiles and Clothing, Members agreed that the introduction of changes in rules should not upset the balance of rights and obligations between the Members concerned under the Agreement, adversely affect the access available to a Member, impede the full utilisation of such access or disrupt trade under the Agreement.

Article 2(b) and (c) of the WTO Agreement on Rules of Origin provides that Members must ensure that rules of origin will not themselves create restrictive, distorting, or disruptive effects on international trade. Rules of origin may not impose unduly strict requirements or require the fulfilment of a certain condition not related to manufacturing or processing, as a prerequisite for the determination of the country of origin.

Federtessile contends that the changes in the United States rules of origin constitute obstacles to trade which threaten its members with suffering adverse trade effects. Those adverse trade effects are that imports to

---

[58] See Notice of initiation [1996] OJ C351/6 of 22 November 1996.

the United States of textile products from most of the countries which produce the grey fabric are subject to quantitative restrictions, the change of origin will require a change of labelling, with consequent loss of image and compliance with the changed and differentiated labelling requirements would cause stock management problems.

Moreover, as most of the Community silk industry is located in Italy, more in particular the Como area and most enterprises involved in textile finishing operations are located in Italian regions whose economy is highly dependent on the textile industry, there will be a material impact on the economy of these regions.

On 18 February 1997 the Commission decided to initiate international consultations and, where appropriate, dispute settlement procedures within the framework of the two WTO Agreements.[59]

This procedure was later suspended after the Commission had reached a negotiated settlement with the United States.[60] The United States agreed to modify its rules of origin either by adopting the solution resulting from the international harmonisation process or, if such negotiations failed to reach an agreement by the July 1998 deadline, by reverting to its previous rules of origin. The United States also agreed to a number of transitional measures aiming at ensuring that, in the meantime, the EC products' access to the United States market was not disturbed or diminished. The United States Congress did not amend its origin rules and the Commission therefore reactivated its request for WTO consultations.[61] The adopted legislation on silk marking, which was intended to implement the United States commitment of July 1997 but this was not considered satisfactory.[62]

Further bilateral negotiations resulted in a final settlement on 16 August 1999. The new compromise obligated the United States to amend its origin rules in Section 334 of the Uruguay Round Agreements Act in order to allow dyeing, printing, and two more finishing operations to confer origin on certain fabrics and goods. The United States amended its legislation accordingly and the EC therefore terminated the procedure in October 2000.[63]

---

[59] See decision on the initiation of international consultation and dispute settlement procedures [1997] OJ L62/43 of 4 March 1997.

[60] European Commission, Press Release, IP/97/744 of 7 August 1997. See also *United States – Measures Affecting Textiles and Apparel Products*, notification of mutually-agreed solution of 25 February 1998, WT/DS85/9.

[61] *United States – Measures Affecting Textiles and Apparel Products (II)*, request for consultations of 25 November 1998, WT/DS151/1.

[62] European Commission, *Report on United States Barriers to Trade and Investment*, Brussels, August 1999, at p. 16.

[63] See decision terminating the examination procedure concerning changes made by the United States of America in their rules of origin for textiles and apparel products, [2000] OJ

continued ...

6.2 Eurofer v United States

Further to a complaint lodged on 10 January 1997 by Eurofer (the European Confederation of Iron and Steel Industries), the Commission initiated an examination procedure on 25 February 1997.[64] The complaint alleges that the US Anti-Dumping Act of 1916 (the Act) is in breach with several obligations contained in the Agreement establishing the WTO, the WTO Anti-Dumping Agreement and GATT 1994.

According to Eurofer the Act prohibits the import and sale in the United States of products (primarily steel mill products) 'at prices substantially less than the actual market value in the principal markets of the country of their production'. The Act could potentially affect all EC exports to the US. Moreover, the Act provides for criminal penalties and the right to claim treble damages in case of import into, or resale in the US at dumped prices.

Eurofer contends that the Act threatens its members with suffering adverse trade effects. They are confronted with the risk of retroactive assessment of treble damages. In view of the same risk, US companies and users may decide to curtail purchases of steel produced in the EC and source steel products domestically. Finally, the mere opening of court proceedings of the type referred to above entails a considerable financial burden for defendant companies.

6.3 Cotance v Argentina

On 8 January 1997, the Confederation of National Associations of Tanners and Dressers of the European Community (Cotance) lodged a complaint with the Commission.[65] The Commission decided to initiate an examination procedure on 26 February 1997.

Cotance alleges that due to a tacit export ban, exports of raw hides and skins from Argentina are impossible, because of an export tax of 15 per cent and a control procedure before export. The complaint also relates to measures affecting the imports of finished leather, subject to an additional VAT of 9–10 per cent and an advance payment system of turnover tax, which apply only to imports of finished leather and not to the trade of locally produced goods, as well as a statistic duty of 3 per cent on imports.

L278/35 of 31 October 2000. See also *United States – Measures Affecting Textiles and Apparel Products (II)*, Notification of a Mutually Agreed Solution of 31 July 2000, WT/DS151/10.
[64] See Notice of initiation [1997] OJ C58/14 of 25 February 1997.
[65] See Notice of initiation [1997] OJ C59/6 of 26 February 1997.

Cotance contends that the abovementioned practices constitute obstacles to trade which are contrary to several provisions of the multilateral trade rules annexed to the WTO Agreement.

More in particular, the measures affecting the exports of raw hides and skins are alleged to be in breach of Article XI of GATT 1994 which provides for the elimination of quantitative restrictions on imports and exports. Furthermore, the complainant also alleges that the export tax as such is in breach of Article VII GATT 1994, which states, inter alia, that valuation of goods for customs purposes should be based on the actual value of the merchandise, whereas the tax base of the Argentinean export tax is calculated on the basis of the quotation of hides and skins on the Chicago commodities Market. Cotance finally argues that the participation of representatives of the Argentinean tanning industry in the administration of customs procedures constitutes a lack of impartiality in the sense of Article X.3(a) GATT 1994.

With regard to the measures affecting the imports of finished leather, Cotance alleges that the 9–10 per cent additional VAT and the advance turnover tax payment system do not apply on domestic products and are therefore in breach of the national treatment principle enclosed in Article III.2 GATT 1994. The complainant also states that the ad valorem character of the 3 per cent statistic duty maintained on imports of leather is in breach of Articles II.2(c) and VIII.1(a) GATT 1994.

Cotance claims that the Community producers are suffering or are threatened with suffering adverse trade effects as a result of the practices maintained by Argentina.

They result from the difficulties arising for Community enterprises' supply in raw materials, which affect the availability of hides and skins on the international market, and from the undercutting by Argentinean tanners of Community leather prices on the world market. As a result, EC operators have lost market share in their domestic and export markets.

The complainant contends that the Argentinean practices have accelerated the downward industry, where over 30.000 jobs have been lost 1981.

6.4 BNIC v Brazil

Further to a complaint by BNIC (the Bureau Interprofessionnel du Cognac), an examination procedure was opened by the Commission on 2 April 1997[66] concerning obstacles to export of Cognac to Brazil and

---
[66] See Notice of initiation [1997] OJ C103/3 of 2 April 1997.

other third country markets. BNIC alleges that lack of protection of the Cognac Appellation of Origin (AO) and the discrimination vis-à-vis other foreign and local geographical indications, the excessive administrative requirements for the marketing of Cognac, as well as discriminatory taxation adversely affect Cognac exports to Brazil.

According to BNIC, Brazilian legislation is in breach with the Cognac AO by allowing Brazilian brandy and other types of spirits be called 'conhague'. BNIC alleges that by providing legal coverage and protection to the use of the term conhague by Brazilian producers of spirits, Brazil is acting in breach with several provisions of the WTO Agreement on Trade-Related Aspects of Intellectual Property Rights (TRIPs), the Paris Convention for the Protection of Industrial Property, the Madrid Agreement for the Repression of False or Deceptive Indications of Source on Goods as well as the bilateral Agreements between the EC, Brazil and Mercusor.

BNIC alleges that the excessive administrative requirements for the marketing of Cognac are contrary to GATT 1994, notably Articles III and VIII, and to Articles 1 and 2 of the Agreement on the Application of Sanitary and Phytosanitary Measures. In addition, BNIC complained that the rate of tax is discriminatory since Cognac would be taxed from 150 to 600 per cent more than local conhague. The complaint cites Article III.1 and Article III.2 GATT 1994 to attack the Brazilian tax. BNIC claims that the Cognac sales in Brazil are currently de minimis in comparison to the conhague sales due to the practices maintained by Brazil.

BNIC estimates its loss in this market between Ffs <these don't exist any more?>50 and 100 million a year. As regards third country markets, BNIC emphasises the serious threat posed by exports of conhaque to such markets. BNIC further argues that the region of Cognac is highly dependent on exports of this product.

6.5 Cotance v Japan

On 24 February 1997, Cotance submitted its second complaint under the TBR.[67] The complaint now concerns trade barriers allegedly caused by Japanese practices and which adversely affect Community exports (of finished leather) to Japan.

The practices consist of quota management, subsidisation of the local industry and restrictive business practices which result in a de facto embargo on imports of finished leather originating in the EC.

---

[67] See Notice of initiation [1997] OJ C110/2 of 9 April 1997.

Cotance contends that the management of tariff quotas contravened Articles VIII and X of GATT 1994 and Article 3 of the WTO Agreement on Import Licensing Procedures. The subsidies granted to the local leather industry impede Community exports to Japan and are therefore actionable subsidies which fall under Part III of the WTO Agreement on Subsidies and Countervailing Measures. The restrictive business practices frustrate the benefits of the removal of quantitative restrictions which should have occurred after a GATT Panel Report in 1984.[68]

The adverse trade effects are demonstrated by the impossibility to enter the Japanese market in economically significant terms. The Japanese practices have been particularly damaging for the Community tanners who are specialized in quality and fashion markets.

6.6 IMRO v United States

Further to a complaint lodged by IMRO (the Irish Music Rights Organisation), the Commission initiated an examination procedure on 11 June 1997.[69]

The complaint concerns the obstacles to trade allegedly encountered in the US for the licensing of music works. The complaint contends that although the authorisation for the use of IMRO's repertoire in the US is covered by cross-border licensing agreements with US societies, such agreements are seriously [hindered] by the exemption contained in Section 110(5) of the USA 1976 Copyright Act.

The exemption contained in Section 110(5) covers the use of a home-type apparatus of radio or television in a shop, bar, restaurant, factory or any other place frequented by the public. The complainant alleges that a significant number of locations in the United States avail themselves of this exemption in order to avoid obtaining licenses for the performing of music works and thus paying appropriate remuneration to their authors.

IMRO contends that this practice is in breach of Article 9 of the TRIPS Agreement and the Berne Convention for the Protection of Literary and Artistic Works. As a result the music works of IMRO's members are claimed to be performed in the United States without their authorization and without remuneration in the situations in which Section 110(5) applies. The complainant estimates loses to IMRO's members caused by Section 110(5) at € 1,21 million a year and estimates Community loss at € 27 million a year.

---

[68] Panel on Japanese Measures on Imports of Leather, report of the Panel adopted on 15/16 May 1984, L/5623, BISD 32/94.
[69] See Notice of initiation [1997] OJ C177/5 of 11 June 1997.

The Commission concluded that there appears to be prima facie evidence of a material impact as the US practice is alleged to be of economic importance for Ireland and the EC, as well as of vital significance for a whole sector of the Irish and the Community's economy, i.e. music authors and composers.

The Commission further concluded that the Community interest in this matter was prima facie shown by the General Assembly of Gesac (the Groupement européen des societies d'auteurs et compositeurs).

The exemption contained in Section 110 (5) covers the use

6.7 Eurofer v Brazil

On 30 April 1997, Eurofer submitted its second complaint under the TBR.[70] The complaint relates to Brazil's practices in the area of import licensing as applied to stainless steel flat products.

Eurofer alleges that the importation of stainless steel flat products into Brazil is subject to a system of non-automatic import licensing. Import licences are being granted only if a payment term of maximum 30 days is foreseen for the goods to be imported whereas 180 days used to be internationally accepted practice. The complaints points out that no announcement of this change or explanation of the legal basis authorising the dismissal of licence applications was given by the competent authorities.

Eurofer contends that those practices constitute obstacles to trade contrary to Brazil's obligations under the WTO Agreement,, and in particular with articles XI, III.4 and X of GATT 1994 as well as Articles 1(4), 3(3), 5 and 1(9) of the WTO Agreement on Import Licensing Procedures.

The complainant alleges that its members and its members' affiliates are suffering adverse trade effects and are threatened with further adverse trade effects. According to the complainant, Community exports of flat steel products to Brazil have been adversely affected by supplementary housing costs, disrupting of contract performance and the loss of already secured business opportunities. More generally, the new requirement has entailed not only costly changes in production and market planning of Community exporters, but also the disruption of their established business relationships and thus of actual orders, as well of future orders. The complainant estimates that it may lose exports worth € 35 million per year.

---

[70] [1997] OJ C1972 of 27 June 1997.

7. Conclusion

Member States have not been particularly interested in the NCPI, including those who had advocated its adoption in the first place. This obviously begs the question of why they have not been interested. For some of them, the answer probably lies in the negative attitude that they have had from the very beginning[71] and of unwillingness to 'legitimate' its use. It is more difficult to see why those Member States who had been in favour of the Regulation never resorted to it. The most obvious reason is that Article 113 EC Treaty provided a sufficient legal basis for the Community to bring complaints before the GATT. Member States could raise issues in other fora, in particular the 113 Committee, in order to get the Community to act internationally, including in the GATT.

It appears that the EC's new market access strategy has so far been successful as it is demonstrated by the opening of seven procedures under the TBR. Although, the Commission, in its Explanatory Memorandum to the initial proposal for the TBR, emphasized that the objective of the TBR was not to relax the conditions for standing of Community industries and for the trade effects suffered, but to adapt the instrument as a tool for the opening of third country markets, it has certainly strengthened the position of European industry. The TBR allows European industry to make use of a more offensive market opening strategy.[72]

For the first time, enterprises may trigger a procedure which gives them at least an indirect right of access to the WTO dispute settlement procedures, notwithstanding the fact that the Commission will be responsible for carrying out the investigation and for the conduct of the dispute settlement procedure.

The content of the complaint is in hands of the industry or enterprise concerned. Should the Commission not fulfil its obligation to investigate and to proceed the case under the WTO dispute settlement mechanism, then the complainant has the right of judicial review.

It becomes visible that the Community has finally discovered the "beauty" of this trade instrument and that it will use it as a vehicle to start international dispute settlement procedures under the new WTO dispute

---

[71] Especially Germany, Denmark and the Netherlands were rather reluctant to give private enterprises the right to bring a complaint directly before the Commission; see MCEJ Bronckers 'Private Response to Foreign Unfair Trade Practices. US and EEC Complaint Procedures' in *Selective Safeguard Measures in Multilateral Trade Relations. Issues of Protectionism in GATT, European Community and United States Law* (Deventer: Kluwer, 1985) 157 at 225.

[72] In French, the TBR is referred to as "Règlement pour l'ouverture des marchés" what clearly reflects the aim of the Regulation.

settlement mechanism. The Commission has said that it is optimistic about the outcome of the ongoing TBR cases as the first investigation carried out under the TBR has proven to be an efficient instrument for dealing rapidly with the EC's industry market access problems.

CHAPTER III

THE PROTECTION OF INTELLECTUAL PROPERTY RIGHTS UNDER
THE EC TRADE BARRIERS REGULATION
AN ANALYSIS OF THE IMRO CASE

'US music copyright law gives EU the blues.'[1]

1.   Introduction

On 26 January 1999, the European Community and its Member States requested consultations with the United States under the dispute settlement mechanism of the World Trade Organization (WTO)regarding Section 110(5) of the 1976 US Copyright Act,[2] as recently amended by the 'Fairness in Music Licensing Act'.[3] The request is the outcome of a complaint submitted under EC Regulation 3286/94, the so-called Trade Barriers Regulation (TBR).[4] The TBR gives individual companies the possibility to lodge a complaint with the European Commission when their trade opportunities on third-country markets are restricted by foreign trade barriers. To date, eleven procedures have been initiated under the TBR, seven of which have led to the initiation of the WTO dispute settlement mechanism. The present article provides an in-depth analysis of the IMRO case and tries to assess how a WTO panel should rule if the case were to be submitted to the judgment of a panel.

---

[1] European Voice, 4-10 March 1999.
[2] Title 17 US Code.
[3] *United States–Section 110(5) of US Copyright Act*, Request for Consultations by the European Communities and their Member States, WT/DS160/1, 4 February 1999.
[4] Council Regulation (EC) No 3286/94 laying down Community procedures in the field of the common commercial policy in order to ensure the exercise of the Community's right under international trade rules, in particular those established under the auspices of the World Trade Organization, [1994] OJ L349171 of 31 December 1994 as amended by Council Regulation (EC) No 356/95, [1995] OJ L41/3 of 23 February 1995. A vast amount of literature has been devoted to the TBR during the first few years of its entry into force. Of a more recent date are MCEJ Bronckers, *Enforcing WTO Law through the EC Trade Barriers Regulation*, Int. TLR, 1997, 76; PC Mavroidis and W Zdouc, 'Legal Means to Protect Private Parties Interests in the WTO: The Case of the EC New Trade Barriers Regulation', *Journal of International Economic Law*, 1998, 407; N McNelis, 'The European Union Trade Barriers Regulation: A More Effective Instrument', *Journal of International Economic Law*, 1998, 149; M. Sanchez Rydelskt and G.A. Zonnekeyn, 'The EC Trade Barriers Regulation-The EC's Move Towards a More Aggressive Market Access Strategy', 31 *JWT* 5, October 1997, 147; and GA Zonnekeyn and J-C Van Eeckhaute, *De handelsbarrièreverordening en de vernieuwde markttoegangsstrategie van de EG*, SEW, 1998, 380.

2. Factual Background

On 21 April 1997, the Irish Music Rights Organization (IMRO),[5] unanimously supported by the Members of the *Groupement Européen des Sociétés d'Auteurs et Compositeurs* (GESAC),[6] lodged a complaint with the Commission under Article 4 of the TBR.[7] The complaint sought the elimination of US trade practices which were alleged to adversely affect cross-border licensing of music works.

The alleged obstacles result from the application of Section 110(5) of the 1976 US Copyright Act. The Act gives the owner of the copyright the exclusive right to authorise the performing of his music works but Section 110(5) allows that, subject to certain conditions, shops, bars, restaurants, and any other place frequented by the public are not required to obtain licences for the broadcast of music works by radio or television in their premises and, consequently, do not pay the right holder of the work any remuneration.[8]

IMRO alleges that this measure constitutes an obstacle to trade because it is contrary to the Agreement on Trade-Related Aspects of Intellectual Property Rights (the TRIPs Agreement). Moreover, IMRO claims that its members, as well as those from other EC collecting societies, are suffering adverse trade effects within the meaning of Article 2(4) of the TBR.[9] The complainant forwarded *prima facie* evidence that the losses caused to its members by the alleged obstacles were substantial. Furthermore, the US practices were alleged to have an effect on all EC right holders and not only on the complainant's members. The Commission therefore

---

[5] IMRO is a music licensing and collecting society which represents and acts on behalf of its members (more than one thousand five hundred authors, composers, arrangers of music, lyricists and music publishers), which are mainly based in Ireland.

[6] GESAC is an economic grouping of twenty-four of the largest licensing and collecting societies in Europe, representing nearly 480,000 authors and composers from all EC Member States.

[7] Notice of Initiation of an examination procedure concerning an obstacle to trade, within the meaning of Council Regulation (EC) No 3286/94, consisting of trade practices maintained by the United States of America in relation to cross-border music licensing, OJ 1997 C177/5 of 11 June 1997.

[8] For an analysis of Section 110(5) and the interpretation given to it by the United States courts, see eg DM Lilenfeld, *Why Congress should Eliminate the Multiple Performance Doctrine*, Ohio St LJ, 1997, 695; PH Luh, 'Pay or Don't Pay: Background Music and the Small Business Exemption of Copyright Law', *Loy, LA Ent L J*, 1996, 711; and J.B. MacDonald, *Defining the Limits of the Home-Type Receiver Exemption* in *17 U S C 110(5): Cam County Music Co v Muedini*, Vill. Sports & Ent L Forum, 1997, 147.

[9] Article 2(4) of the TBR defines 'adverse trade effects' as 'those which an obstacle to trade causes or threatens to cause, in respect of a product or service, to Community enterprises on the market of any third country, and which have a material impact on the economy of the Community or of a region of the Community, or on a sector of economic activity therein.'

concluded that it was in the EC's interests to start an examination procedure.

Following the initiation of the examination procedure, the Commission conducted an in-depth legal and factual investigation into Section 110(5) as well as into the amendments to the Act as discussed in the US Congress at the time of the investigation and enacted meanwhile. Since an amicable settlement could not be reached with the United States, the Commission decided to initiate WTO dispute settlement proceedings.[10]

3. The Activity Under Investigation: Cross-Border Licensing of Music Works

The complaint concerns the licensing by IMRO of its members' music works to users of these works in the United States. In its Notice of Initiation, the Commission defines the licensing of music works as a cross-border service within the meaning of Article 2(8) of the TBR which is questionable from a legal point of view.[11]

A musical composition entails two basic economic rights to the right holders to control the use of their creative materials, namely a performing right and a mechanical right. Whereas the latter refers to the incorporation of music in audio software, the first right consists of the right to authorise the communication of the work to the public (by means of live performance, radio and television broadcasting, performance of recorded music, etc.) in return for remuneration. The right holder's right to communicate the music to the public is an exclusive right. Third parties can only obtain such right when duly authorised ('licensed') to this effect by the right holder and under the conditions defined by the right holder. For reasons of (economic) efficiency, composers co-operate and license their music collectively through collecting societies. Such societies either license their music only (performing right organisations) or in combination with mechanical rights. The vast majority of these societies are organised on a national level. They grant licences to the users and collect and distribute royalties on behalf of their members or affiliates. The most common type of licence granted by these societies are 'blanket licences' covering the entire repertoire represented by such a society. In practice, such blanket licences cover practically the entire world repertoire, as all performing right organisations have entered into reciprocal agreements with each

---
[10] Commission Decision of 11 December 1998 under the provisions of Council Regulation (EC) No 3286/94 concerning Section 110(5) of the Copyright Act of the United States of America, OJ L346/60 of 22 December 1998.
[11] Article 2(8) of the TBR defines 'services' as 'those services in respect of which international agreements can be concluded by the Community on the basis of Article 113 of the Treaty.'

other to license their works in their respective markets. Cross-border licensing of musical works is thus usually provided through the collecting society operating on the market where the licence is granted, acting on the basis of a reciprocal agreement with the collecting society to which the right holder of the licensed musical works belongs. Of course, these societies only act as intermediaries for the right holder.

The complainant, IMRO, is a collecting society which administers, licenses and enforces the performing rights of its members. The authorisation for the use of IMRO's repertoire in the United States is covered by the cross-border licensing agreements which IMRO has concluded with US societies. However, the operation of those licensing agreements is seriously impeded by the exemption contained in Section 110(5) of the 1976 US Copyright Act.

4. The Obstacle to Trade

4.1 Section 110(5) of the 1976 US Copyright Act

Under the 1976 US Copyright Act, the right holder of a work has the exclusive right to reproduce the work, prepare derivative works and distribute copies of the work. Under Section 106(4) of the Act, the rightholder has also the exclusive right to 'perform the copyrighted [music] work publicly.'

However, Section 110 of the US Copyright Act exempts certain public performances from protection. Of the ten exemptions referred to in Section 110(5), IMRO's complaint refers to the exemption contained in Section 110(5) which provides that:

> Notwithstanding the provisions of Section 106, the following are not infringements of copyright: communication of a transmission embodying a performance or display of a work by the public reception of the transmission on a single receiving apparatus of a kind commonly used in private homes, unless (A) a direct change is made to see or hear the transmission; or (B) the transmission thus received is further transmitted to the public ...

The exemption thus covers the use of a 'home-style' radio or television in a shop, a bar, a restaurant or any other place frequented by the public. The exemption does not cover the playing of tapes, CD's or other mechanical instruments.

4.2 Legislative History of Section 110(5)

4.2.1 The Aiken Ruling

Section 110(5) was enacted as a reaction to the ruling of the US Supreme Court in *Twentieth Century Music Corp. v Aiken* in 1975.[12] Aiken was the owner of a small fast- food restaurant and operated a radio with an outlet to four speakers in the ceiling. This installation received the transmission of various radio stations including protected musical works. Since Aiken did not have a performing licence, he was sued for copyright infringement. At that time, it was inferred from the 1931 ruling from the US Supreme Court in *Jewell-La Salle* that a business establishment had to obtain a licence from the right holders of the musical works that were broadcast through the radio on its premises.[13] The Supreme Court exempted Aiken from liability under the 1909 Copyright Act since the actions of Aiken could not be considered as 'performing' within the meaning of the Act.

However, the ruling in *Aiken* contradicts the expansive definitions of the 1976 Copyright Act which considers turning on a radio in a public place as a public performance of the broadcasted music. A specific provision had therefore to be included in the Copyright Act to provide music-users with an exemption based on the *Aiken* case, hence the exemption is commonly referred to as the '*Aiken* exemption' or 'home-style exemption.'

In order to qualify for the exemption, the transmission must be received on a 'single receiving apparatus of a kind commonly used in private homes.' The benefit of the exemption is lost when a direct charge is made to the public. The exact breadth of the wording 'single receiving apparatus' is therefore crucial to benefit from the exemption. Technology is under constant evolution and has widened the scope of the home-style exemption.

4.2.2 The Congressional Intent

The scope of Section 110(5) has evolved over the years. At the time of the adoption of the 1976 Copyright Act, the US Congress favoured a narrow scope of the exemption which should only apply to small commercial establishments. The wording of the Congressional Intent makes this clear. The US Congress was of the opinion that:

---

[12] *Twentieth Century Music corp. v Aiken*, 422 US 151 (1975).
[13] *Busk v Jewell-La Salle Realty Co.*,283 US 191 (1931).

The basic rationale of this clause is that the secondary use of the transmission by turning on an ordinary receiver in public is so remote and minimal that no further liability should be imposed.

The Committee considers [the particular fact situation of *Aiken*] to represent the outer limit of the exemption, and believes that the line should be drawn at this point. Thus the clause would exempt small commercial establishments whose proprietors merely bring onto their premises standard radio or television equipment and turn it on for their customers' enjoyment, but it would impose liability where the proprietor has a commercial sound system installed or converts a standard home apparatus... into the equivalent of a commercial sound system.[14]

However, the Congressional Intent was rather ambiguous and also provided that:

... it applies to performances and displays of all types of works, and its purpose is to exempt from copyright liability anyone who merely turns on, in a public place, an ordinary radio or television.[15]

The US courts have also interpreted the exemption narrowly. If the receiving equipment and loudspeakers were too sophisticated and powerful, the exemption would not apply.[16]

4.2.3 The Evolution of the Case Law

The courts initially applied a teleological interpretation and focused on the intention of the legislator.[17] The factors that were taken into consideration were:

- the physical size of the establishment (in terms of square footage);
- the economic size of the establishment;
- the distance between the receiver and the speakers;
- the number of speakers;
- whether the speakers were free-standing or built into the ceiling;
- whether depending on its revenue the establishment was of a type that would normally subscribe to a background music service;
- the noise level of the areas within the establishment where the transmissions were made audible or visible;

---

[14] HR Rep No 1476, 94th Congress, 2nd Sess, 87 (1976).
[15] Ibid.
[16] Reply by the US Authorities to questions by Canada and the EC within the TRIPs Council of 30 October 1996, IP/Q/USA/1.
[17] B Ringer and H Sandison, *US Copyright Law*, in S M Stewart (ed.), *International Copyright and Neighboring Rights (London:* Butterworths, 1983) 596.

- the extent to which the receiving apparatus was to be considered as one commonly used in private homes; and
- the configuration of the installation.

Later, as a result of the ambiguous statutory language of Section 110(5), courts started to focus on the specific language of Section 110(5) to look for a broader interpretation of the exemption. Consequently, large chain store corporations were exempt from applying for a licence and paying a licence fee. An important number of large chain stores adapted their music installation in order to benefit from the exemption. Some of these chains even cancelled their subscription to background music. This is very well illustrated by the *Edison Brothers* case. This important chain of retail stores reached an understanding with Broadcast Music, Inc (BMI) on a 'radio policy' designed to exempt its more than one and a half thousand stores from copyright liability. Under the terms of the agreement, only two speakers could be attached to a radio receiver, the speakers had to be placed within fifteen feet of the receiver, and only portable speakers and radios could be used. In order to comply with this policy, Edison Brothers made considerable investments. However, in 1988, BMI changed its policy and took the view that the exemption of Section 110(5) could not apply to large chains of stores throughout the country, independent of the nature of the equipment used. The Edison Brothers stores successfully challenged this interpretation in court.[18]

The essential question in the *Edison Brothers* case, which also arose in the *Claire Boutiques* case,[19] was the potential application of the exemption to large chains of stores throughout the country and using the playing of music in stores as part of their commercial policy. In both cases, the Court's answer was affirmative. Both Courts argued that the only relevant factor in assessing the applicability of the exemption was the quantity and the quantity of the receiving apparatus used at a certain location.

IMRO alleges that Section 110(5) is in breach of the TRIPs Agreement. Under this Agreement, WTO Members are obliged to comply with the substantive provisions of the Berne Convention for the Protection of Literary and Artistic Works, as revised by the Pans Act of 1971 (the Berne Convention). Article 9(1) of the TRIPs Agreement imposes a mandatory obligation on WTO Members to comply with Articles 1 through 21 of the Berne Convention. Consequently, a WTO Member is in breach of its obligations under the TRIPs Agreement if it fails to comply with the Berne

---

[18] *Edison Brothers Stores, inc v Broadcast Music, Inc*, US District Court for the Eastern District of Missouri, No 90-328C(1), 3 April 1991. Confirmed on appeal in *Broadcast Music, Inc v Edison Brothers Stores, Inc*, US Court of Appeals for the Eighth Circuit, No 91-2115, 13 January 1992.

[19] *Broadcast Music, Inc, et al. v Claire's Boutiques, Inc*, US Court of Appeals for the Seventh Circuit, No 91-1232, 11 December 1991.

Convention. IMRO claims that Section 110(5) of the 1976 US Copyright Act does not comply with Article 11bis(1)(iii) of the Berne Convention. Due to the nature of the obligation contained in Article 9(1) of the TRIPs Agreement, the failure of the United States to comply with the Berne Convention would constitute a breach of the TRIPs Agreement. This legal argument will be further developed here below.

5. The Legality of Section 110(5)

5.1 The Berne Convention

5.1.1 Articles 11 and 11 bis of the Berne Convention

Article 11*bis*(1) of the Berne Convention gives the authors of literary and artistic works (including musical works) the exclusive right to authorise:

(i) the broadcasting and other wireless communication of their work;
(ii) the communication to the public by wire or by rebroadcasting of the broadcast of their work; and
(iii) the public communication of the broadcast of the works by loudspeaker or any other analogous instrument.

IMRO alleges that the exemption granted under Section 110(5) deprives right holders of the protection of their works to which they are entitled under Article 11*bis*(l)(iii) of the Berne Convention when broadcasts of their works are publicly communicated by loudspeakers or analogous instruments and under Article 11(l)(ii) of the Berne Convention when direct cable transmissions of their works are publicly communicated by such instruments.

The applicability of Article 11 *bis*(l)(iii) is subject to two conditions:

- the communication must be public; and
- the communication must be done by loudspeaker or any other analogous instrument transmitting by signs, sounds, or images of the broadcast of the work.

Radio and television sets (even when they are not operated with separate loudspeakers) must be considered as analogous instruments transmitting the broadcast of a work by signs, sounds or images. As far as the second condition is concerned, the circumstances in which a communication is public are not referred to in Article 11*bis*(1). It is the legislation of the country of protection that determines whether a communication is public. This discretion, however, is not unlimited because the Brussels Revision provides guidelines on what is to be understood as a public communication.[20]

In the United States, it is Section 101 of the Copyright Act which defines what is to be understood as the public performance or display of a work. It is defined as:

> (1) To perform or display at a place open to the public or at any place where a substantial number of persons outside of a normal circle of family and its social acquaintances is gathered; or

> (2) to transmit or otherwise communicate a performance or display of the work to a place specified by clause (1) or to the public, by means of any device or process, whether the members of the public capable of receiving the performance or display receive it in the same place or in separate places and at the same time or at different times.

Situations covered by Section 110(5) obviously come within the scope of this definition. This is expressly confirmed by the wording of Section 110(5) referring to a 'communication or transmission embodying a performance or display of a work by the public reception of'. It demonstrates that the objective of Section 110(5) is to exempt certain public 'performances' from protection and its very wording indicates that public communication by radio or television, be it in shops, pubs or restaurants, of the broadcast of a work is considered as a public performance within the meaning of the US Copyright Act. At international level, from the very beginning there was already a consensus that such kind of communication was 'public'.[21]

The playing of broadcast programmes in public requires the consent of the right holders whose work is included in the broadcasting programme, and there are no exceptions to this rule in Article 11*bis*(1) of the Berne Convention. Section 110(5) is therefore incompatible with the Berne Convention as it denies the right holders the protection granted to them by Article 11*bis*(1))iii) of the Berne Convention.

---

[20] S. Ricketson, *The Berne Convention for the Protection of Literary and Artistic Works: 1886-1986*, Kluwer, London, 1987, at p 453. The Brussels Revision refers to 'above all where people meet: in the cinema, in restaurants, in tea room, railway carriages' and also places where people work and conduct their business, such as factories, shops and offices.
[21] See eg Ricketson, ibid., at pp 452-453; and W Nordemann, K Vinck, PW Hertin and G Meyer, *International Copyright and Neighboring Rights Law: Commentary with special emphasis on the European Community* (Weinheim : VCH Verlagsgesellschaft, 1990) 125-126.

5.1.2 Exceptions to the Right Holder's Exclusive Right

(a) *Express Exceptions*

The Berne Convention contains a number of provisions which restrict the absolute protection of copyright. These provisions grant latitude to the signatories to limit the rights of the right holders in certain circumstances by providing for the possibility of using protected works in particular cases without having to obtain the authorisation of the right holder and mostly without having to pay any remuneration. These circumstances mainly cover situations in which, after careful balance of the interests of the right holders and the general public, it is considered that the public interest should prevail against the private interest of the right holders. Since the rights provided by the Berne Convention are exclusive rights, it goes without saying that any exception to these rights must be interpreted narrowly.

Under the Berne Convention, three distinct types of exceptions can be distinguished:[22]

- provisions denying protection in cases of particular categories of works, such as official texts of a legislative or administrative nature;
- provisions giving immunity from infringement proceedings to particular kinds of use. Typical examples are the use of copyright works for educational, informative or administrative purposes; and
- compulsory licensing systems. Here the right holder's rights are restricted, but only to a limited extent. The use of the work (in the circumstances covered by the exception) is no longer subject to the authorisation of the right holder, but the latter remains entitled to remuneration.

The only relevant exception to the principles contained in Article 11*bis*(1) of the Berne Convention can be found in Article 11*bis*(2). This provision provides that, while countries may impose conditions on the exercise of the exclusive rights set out in Article 11*bis*(1), such conditions may not be prejudicial to the author's right to obtain equitable remuneration. It provides as follows:

> It shall be a matter for the legislation in the countries of the Union to determine the conditions under which the rights mentioned in the preceding paragraph may be exercised, but these conditions shall

---
[22] Ricketson, ibid., at p 478.

apply only in the countries where they have been prescribed. They shall not in any circumstances be prejudicial to the moral rights of the author, nor to his right to obtain equitable remuneration which, in the absence of an agreement, shall be fixed by the competent authority.

This provision is generally understood as allowing the signatories of the Convention to substitute the right holder's exclusive rights specified in Article 11*bis*(1) with a system of compulsory licensing. A compulsory licence means that users do not need to request authorisation for the use of the work (the licence is 'automatic') but that payment is still required. In Article 11*bis*(2) the possibility of introducing a compulsory licensing system is bound to the express condition that such compulsory licence shall not be prejudicial to the right holder's right to obtain equitable remuneration.

Obviously, Section 110(5) of the US Copyright Act does not provide for a system of compulsory licensing. On the contrary, it not only abolished the right holders' rights to authorise the use of their music, it also deprives them of all remuneration in respect of the use of their works in situations covered by the home-style exemption. Section 110(5) therefore does not come within the scope of Article 11*bis*(2) of the Berne Convention.

(b) Implied or 'minor' Reservations

In its Notice of Initiation, the Commission also reviewed the so-called 'implied exceptions' or 'minor reservations'. These are not expressly contained in the text of the Berne Convention because the minor importance of the situations has never been found to justify the insertion of an express provision.

If 'minor exceptions' would apply to the exclusive rights set out in Article 11*bis*(l)(iii), the home-style exemption would obviously not qualify as a minor exception. Minor reservations are based on the *de minimis* principle of interpretation, namely that the law is not concerned with 'trifles'. Exceptions to the rights granted in the relevant Articles of the Convention must be concerned with minimal use, or use of no significance to the author.[23]

There is thus a *de minimis* threshold, under which exemptions are not considered in breach of the Berne Convention, as long as they are calibrated in such way to cause only minimal and insignificant, and thus negligible, economic impact on the copyright owner.

---

[23] Ibid., at pp 532-535.

The problem is now how to define the criteria to which an exemption should respond to be regarded as minor. In this regard, the criteria laid down in Article 9(2) of the Berne Convention may well provide an appropriate yardstick. Article 9(1) of the Berne Convention introduces an exclusive right of authorising the reproduction of works. The second paragraph of the Article gives the signatories to the Berne Convention the power to cut this down this exclusive right of reproduction:

> 2. It shall be a matter for legislation in the countries of the Union to permit the reproduction of such works in certain special cases, provided that such reproduction does not conflict with a normal exploitation of the work and does not unreasonably prejudice the legitimate interests of the author.

This power is thus subject to three conditions:

- limitations and exceptions must be confined to 'certain special cases';
- those special cases must not conflict with 'a normal exploitation of the work'; and
- those special cases must not unreasonably prejudice 'the legitimate interests of the right holder'.

Article 9(2) of the Berne Convention is flexible enough to make a domestic shading possible but it allows nothing more than that. The criteria referred to above could therefore provide an appropriate 'standard of reasonableness' to determine the *'de minimis'* nature of an exemption to exclusive copyrights.

        (i)   The Limitations and Exceptions Must be Limited to Certain Special Cases

This is a general criterion which embodies two distinct aspects.[24] Firstly, it implies that a broad exception cannot be justified and secondly, it means that it should serve a special purpose. There must be a reason of public policy or another exceptional circumstance that makes it virtually impossible or unreasonably cumbersome to enforce the right, or that enforcing the right would lead to costs exceeding its potential benefits.

The home-style exemption under Section 110(5) is not limited to 'special cases' due to the rather vague language used. There is only one important criterion for the application of the exemption (i.e. the use of a home-style apparatus) which certainly needs further clarification. One could argue that the use of 'single receiving apparatus of a kind commonly used in

---
[24] Ibid., at p 482.

private homes' refers to a specific situation, but the wording 'of a kind commonly used in private homes' is ambiguous and not precise enough to consider it as a 'special case' within the meaning of Article 9(2) of the Berne Convention. As a result of its vague statutory language, Section 110(5) potentially applies to a wide range of music-users. This is supported by the Congressional Intent which indicates that:

> ...it applies to performances and displays of all types of works, and its purpose is to exempt from copyright liability anyone who merely turns on, in a public place, an ordinary radio or television...

The use of the words all 'and 'anyone' in conjunction with the wording 'an ordinary radio or television' does not refer to a specific, limited situation.

Section 110(5) does not refer to a special purpose. The *ratio legis* for Section 110(5) can only be found in the Congressional Intent which refers to the exemption of small 'mom-and-pop' shops from copyright liability. Obviously, the application and interpretation of Section 110(5) goes far beyond the *ratio legis* referred to in the Congressional Intent as it also applies to large chain-store corporations. One could also question whether there is a public interest justifying the enactment of Section 110(5).

Virtually all the exceptions to the right holder's right to authorise the communication of a work to the public are justified by a reason of public interest. However, most of the exceptions contained in Section 110 do not serve a public interest but only the interests of particular interest groups. Lastly, it could also be argued that it would be too cumbersome to enforce the purchase of a performing licence upon every business throughout US territory. This runs counter to the very existence of Section 110(5) which does not aim at exempting every small business from copyright liability.

        (ii)   The Exemption Should Not Conflict with the Normal Exploitation of the Work

The communication to the public is part of the normal exploitation of a musical work. Article 11*bis*(l)(iii) of the Berne Convention regards the right to authorise the public communication of a broadcast work as an essential right for the right holder. Unlimited control by the right holder over the public communication of his work is thus part of the normal exploitation of a musical work. The only exception to that principle is the possibility to provide for compulsory licensing which nevertheless guarantees the right holder an acceptable level of remuneration for the use of his work.

All forms of commercial exploitation of a musical work (any transmission or retransmission to the public in a public venue) should be considered as part of 'the normal exploitation of a work', giving the right holder right to a remuneration.

> (iii) The Exemption Should Not Unreasonably Prejudice the Legitimate Interest of the Right Holder

The effect of Section 110(5) is that the right holder is deprived of his right to control the exploitation of his work and of his right to remuneration for such exploitation when the conditions of Section 110(5) are met. The right holder normally has a legitimate interest to expect to receive royalties for the use of his work. Any exception to the right holder's exclusive right therefore prejudices his commercial interests unless the loss of revenue is negligible. In view of the losses incurred by IMRO as a result of the application of Section 110(5), the *de minimis* test would not apply.[25]

In view of the above, the United States cannot justify the home-style exemption as a 'minor exception'.

5.2 The TRIPs Agreement

5.2.1 Article 9(1) of the TRIPs Agreement

The approach taken in the copyright provisions of the TRIPs Agreement is to adopt the regime of copyright protection provided for in the Berne Convention.[26] Article 9(1) of the TRIPs Agreement obliges WTO Members to comply with Articles 1 to 21 of the Berne Convention and the Appendix thereto. Consequently, a WTO Member will be in breach of its obligations under the TRIPs Agreement where it fails to comply with the said provisions of the Berne Convention. It was demonstrated above that Section 110(5) of the US Copyright Act contravenes Article 11*bis(1)* of the Berne Convention, and that it cannot be justified by any express or implied exemption under the Convention. This implies that Section 110(5) of the US Copyright Act is in breach of Article 9(1) of the TRIPs Agreement.

---

[25] According to the Notice of Initiation, IMRO's losses would amount to 1,21 million Euros per year.

[26] M Blakeney, *Trade-Related Aspects of Intellectual Property Rights: A Concise Guide to the TRIPs Agreement* (London, Sweet & Maxwell, 1996) p 45.

5.2.2 Article 13 of the TRIPs Agreement

Article 13 of the TRIPs Agreement requires Members to confine limitations or exceptions to exclusive rights to certain special cases which do not conflict with a normal exploitation of the work and do not unreasonably prejudice the legitimate interests of the right holder.

The United States could argue that the home-style exemption is compatible with the TRIPs Agreement if it could benefit from the exception referred to in Article 13. This Article applies to all rights covered by Part 11, Section I of the TRIPs Agreement (Copyright and Related Rights). Thus it covers the rights contained in Articles 1 to 21 of the Berne Convention (through Article 9 of the TRIPs Agreement) and those contained in Articles 10, 11, and 14 of the TRIPs Agreement (the so-called 'Berne-plus' rights).

It is questionable whether, under Article 13 of the TRIPs Agreement, the United States can impose conditions on the exercise of the right which eventually prevent the collection of the remuneration. Article 13 does not apply in the present case since Article 11*bis*(2) of the Berne Convention requires that the imposition of conditions cannot prejudice the right holder's right to obtain an equitable remuneration. Since the home-style exemption denies an equitable remuneration to the right holder, it cannot be invoked to justify the legality of Section 110(5).

6. Recent Amendments to Section 110(5) of the US Copyright Act

6.1 The Fairness in Music Licensing Act of 1998

While the Commission was investigating the home-style exemption, the US Congress was examining a bill amending Section 110(5) with a view to widening its scope. On 6 and 7 October 1998, the bill, entitled 'Fairness in Music Licensing Act', was adopted by, respectively, the US. House of Representatives and the US Senate. The bill adds a new sub-paragraph B to Section 110(5) which provides for a further exception to the right holders' exclusive rights to authorise public communication of their works, while the home-style exemption remains unchanged under sub-paragraph A. The new sub-paragraph B now applies to a much wider range of beneficiaries, namely eating, drinking and other commercial establishments, provided that they fulfil a certain number of conditions, mainly with regard to the surface area of the establishment and the number of loudspeakers used. It covers the use of any type of audiovisual device, and is thus not limited to the use of a 'home-style' apparatus only. The bill was signed by the President of the United States on 27 October 1998 and entered into force ninety days after its enactment.

The new sub-paragraph B of Section 110(5) also deprives right holders the protection they are entitled to under Articles 11bis(1)(iii) and 11(1)(ii) of the Berne Convention when broadcasts of their works or cable transmissions of their works are communicated to the public. Therefore, the analysis of the 1976 version of Section 110(5) (now under sub-paragraph A of the Section) fully applies to the new version of the law, which is thus equally in breach of the Berne Convention and the TRIPs Agreement.

6.2 Reaction to the Proposal in the United States

The proposal to amend Section 110(5) has been fiercely opposed by the US Copyright Office. In a statement before the House Subcommittee on Courts and Intellectual Property, at the occasion of a hearing on the proposed amendments to Section 110(5), the Registrar of Copyrights expressed her serious concerns on the 'substantial broadening of the existing exemptions...that would be accompanied by this bill.'[27] Referring to the ongoing Commission investigation as well as to Articles 11 and 11bis of the Berne Convention and Article 13 of the TRIPs Agreement, she also said that:

> As to the proposed expansion of the home-style exemption, we see significant problems. An exception this broad appears to be outside the scope of permissible 'small exceptions' to the Berne rights of public performance and communication. Allowing virtually every business to play music to its customers through loudspeakers or audiovisual devices would invite a difficult case against the United States for violating TRIPs obligations.
>
> ...
>
> A reasonable exemption of narrower scope could be crafted to clarify permissible conduct by small businesses that would clearly comply with the standards of Berne and TRIPs.

7. Conclusion

IMRO's allegations against Section 110(5) of the 1976 US Copyright Act seem fully justified in the light of the above. Section 110(5) constitutes a violation of Article 11bis(1) of the Berne Convention and consequently of Article 9(1) of the TRIPs Agreement.

It is difficult to see how this case will further develop. The EC and the United States are currently involved in other trade disputes (i.e. bananas, hormones and 'hush- kitted' aircraft) where the economic and political

---

[27] Statement of Marybeth Peters, Registrar of Copyrights, before the House Subcommittee on Courts and Intellectual Property, 105th Congress, 1st Session, 17 July 1997.

interests are more important. It could, therefore, very well be that the EC will not now pursue the case with the same vigour as it would normally have done. However, if the United States intends to keep the current legislation in force, the EC will have no choice but to request the establishment of a panel. As the United States appears to be of the opinion that Section 110(5) is fully in line with its international obligations,[28] the EC and the United States are heading for yet another trade dispute.

---

[28] Apparently, the United States refused to cooperate with the Commission during the investigation. Moreover, the recent enactment of the 'Fairness in Music Licensing Act' indicates that the United States does not intend to amend its legislation. This was already confirmed by the United States in 1996 when the EC questioned the United States on the legality of Section 110(5) in the WTO's TRIPs Council. Also, when the 1976 Copyright Act entered into force on 1 January 1978, the United States was not a party to the Berne Convention. It acceded to the Convention on 16 November 1988. When the Convention entered into force in November 1989, the United States revised the 1976 Copyright Act, leaving Section 110(5) as it was, and further declared that the Act, as amended, satisfied the obligations of the United States under the Berne Convention.

PART III: AMICUS BRIEFS AND THE WTO

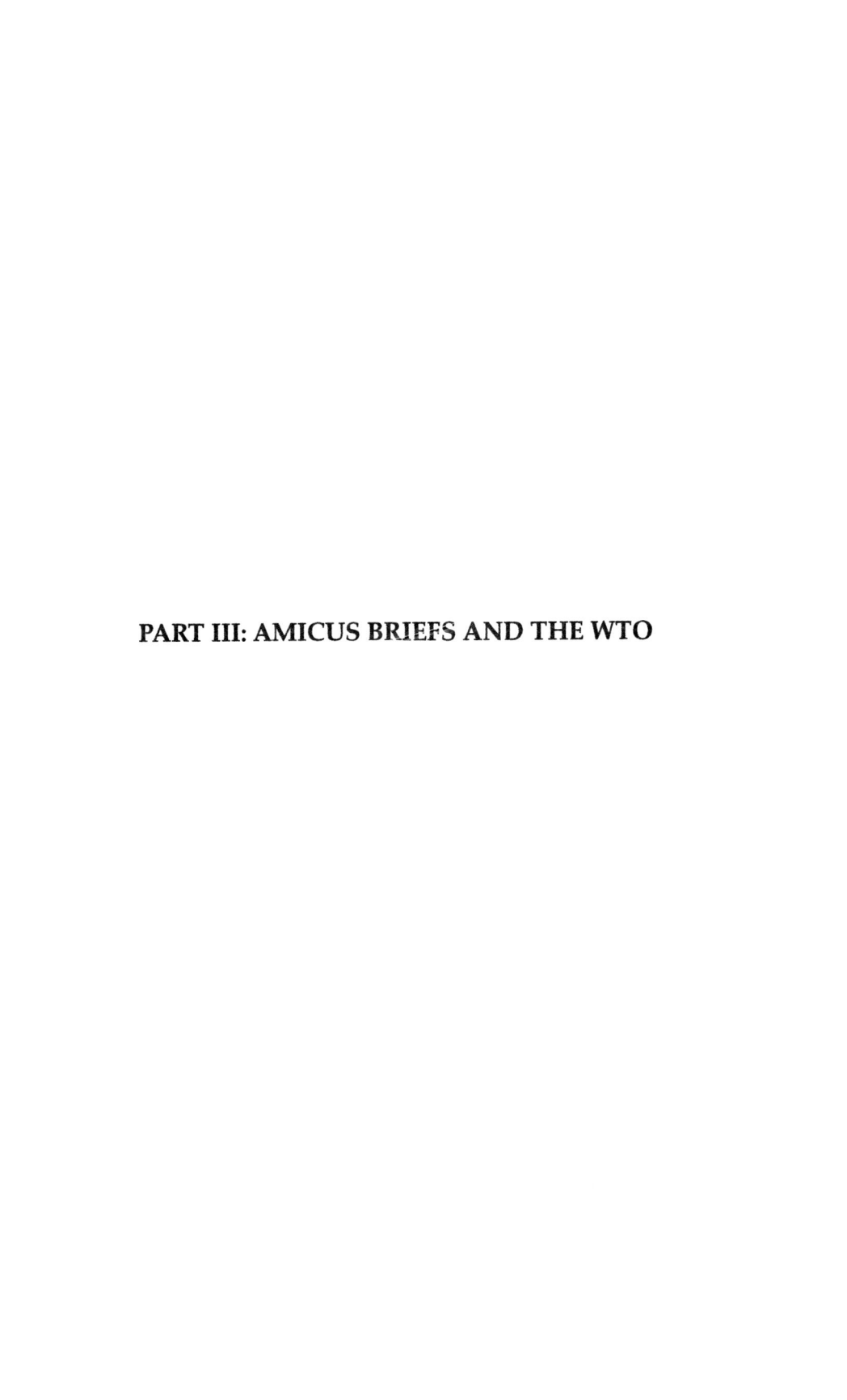

The Appellate Body's Communication on Amicus Curiae Briefs in the Asbestos Case - An Echternach Procession?

1. Introduction

The Luxembourg town of Echternach is known for its peculiar annual procession: for each three steps forward participants take two steps backward. This procession comes to mind when reflecting on how the Appellate Body applied the so-called 'Additional Procedure' which it established for the submission of amicus curiae briefs in Canada's appeal of a panel ruling in the *Asbestos* case.

WTO members have been at odds over non-governmental organisations' (NGOs) participation in trade disputes ever since the ruling of the Appellate Body in the *Shrimp/Turtle* case.[1] In that case, the Appellate Body held that unsolicited amicus curiae briefs are admissible in panel proceedings.[2] It must be emphasised that the question of admissibility of amicus curiae briefs in the *Shrimp/Turtle* case was dealt with in a preliminary decision of the Appellate Body, where it accepted such a brief for consideration. In its final decision, however, the Appellate Body confined itself to arguments raised by the parties and did not discuss its authority to accept unsolicited briefs. The controversy deepened with the Appellate Body's decision in the *British Steel* case, where it explicitly ruled that unsolicited amicus curiae briefs are admissible in Appellate Body proceedings.[3] It reached a climax after the Communication of the Appellate Body in the *Asbestos* case,[4] in which it established an Additional Procedure for the submission of amicus curiae briefs in Canada's appeal of a

---

[1] *United States – Import Prohibition of Certain Shrimp and Shrimp Products*, report of the Appellate Body of 12 October 1998, WT/DS58/AB/R. For a comment, see eg AE Appleton 'Shrimp/Turtle: Untangling the Nets' (1999) JIEL 477–96.

[2] See para 108 of the report (n 1).

[3] *United States – Imposition of Countervailing Duties on Certain Hot-Rolled Lead and Bismouth Carbon Steel Products Originating in the United Kingdom*, report of the Appellate Body of 10 May 2000, WT/DS138/AB/R. See in particular para 42 of the report where the Appellate Body held that '[W]e are of the opinion that we have the legal authority under the DSU to accept and consider amicus curiae briefs in an appeal in which we find it pertinent and useful to do so'.. For a comment, see AE Appleton 'Amicus Curiae Submissions in the Carbon Steel Case: Another Rabbit from the Appellate Body's Hat?' (2000) JIEL 691–9 and D Prévost 'WTO Subsidies Agreement and Privatised Companies. Appellate Body *Amicus Curiae* Briefs' (2000) LIEI 279–94.

[4] *European Communities – Measures Affecting Asbestos and Asbestos-Containing Products*, Communication of the Appellate Body of 8 November 2000, WT/DS135/9.

panel ruling that France's import ban on chrysotile asbestos was justified on public health grounds.[5]

It is not the objective of the present article to give an exhaustive analysis of the legal issues related to the submission of amicus curiae briefs in WTO dispute settlement proceedings.[6] The article will confine itself to an analysis and assessment of the controversial Communication.

2. The Communication – an Analysis

2.1 Genesis of the Communication

On 27 October 2000, the Appellate Body made its intention known to the parties and third parties to the dispute that it was mindful that, in the proceedings at the panel level, the panel had received five written submissions from NGOs, two of which it had taken into consideration. The Appellate Body recognized the possibility that it would also receive submissions from persons other than the parties and the third parties to the dispute and took the view that the fair and orderly conduct of the appeal could be facilitated by the adoption of appropriate procedures, for the purposes of the appeal only, pursuant to Rule 16(1) of the Working Procedures, to deal with any possible submissions received from such persons. To this end, it invited the parties and the third parties in the appeal to submit their comments on a number of questions, such as whether the Appellate Body should adopt a 'request for leave' procedure, what procedures would be needed to ensure that the parties and third parties would have a full and adequate opportunity to respond to submissions that might be received and whether it should take any other points into consideration if it decided to adopt a 'request for leave' procedure.

On 3 November 2000, all of the parties and third parties responded to the Appellate Body's proposal. Canada, the European Community (EC) and Brazil considered that issues pertaining to any such procedure should be

---

[5] See *European Communities – Measures Affecting Asbestos and Asbestos-Containing Products*, report of the panel of 18 September 2000, WT/DS135/R. Canada introduced an appeal on 23 October 2000. See *European Communities – Measures Affecting Asbestos and Asbestos-Containing Products*, Notification of an Appeal by Canada under paragraph 4 of Article 16 of the Understanding on Rules and Procedures Governing the Settlement of Disputes, notification of 23 October 2000, WT/DS135/8. The Appellate Body issued its report on 12 March 2001. See *European Communities – Measures Affecting Asbestos and Asbestos-Containing Products*, report of the Appellate Body of 12 March 2001, WT/DS135/AB/R.

[6] For a comprehensive analysis, see G Marceau and M Stilwell 'Practical Suggestions for *Amicus Curiae* Briefs before the WTO Adjudicating Bodies' (2001) *JIEL* 155 and J Peel 'Giving the Public a Voice in the Protection of the Global Environment: Avenues for Participation by NGOs in Dispute Resolution at the European Court of Justice and the World Trade Organization' (2001) *Colo J Int'l Envtl L & Pol'y* 47.

dealt with by the WTO members themselves. The United States welcomed adoption of a request for leave procedure, and Zimbabwe indicated that it had no specific reasons to oppose adoption of a request for leave procedure. Without prejudice to their positions, Canada, the EC and the United States each made a number of suggestions regarding any such procedure that might be adopted.

On 7 November 2000, and after consultations among all seven members of the Appellate Body, the Appellate Body adopted, pursuant to Rule 16(1) of the Working Procedures, an additional procedure, for the purposes of the appeal only, to deal with written submissions received from persons other than the parties and third parties to this dispute (the Additional Procedure). The Additional Procedure was communicated to the parties and third parties in this appeal on 7 November 2000. On 8 November 2000, the chairman of the Appellate Body informed the chairman of the Dispute Settlement Body (DSB), in writing, of the Additional Procedure adopted, and this letter was circulated, for information, as a dispute settlement document to the members of the WTO.[7]

2.2 Legal basis – stretching the limits?

The Appellate Body made it clear, at the outset of the Communication, that it did not have the intention to adopt a permanent new Working Procedure under Article 17.9 of the Understanding on Rules and Procedures Governing the Settlement of Disputes (DSU),[8] but a case-specific Additional Procedure pursuant to Rule 16(1) of the Working Procedures for Appellate Review.[9]

Some WTO members expressed their disapproval of this Additional Procedure.[10] They were particularly concerned that the rules would affect their rights and obligations and, moreover, would alter the relationship between the bodies within the WTO institutional framework. It was argued that although the Additional Procedure was presented as an explanatory

---

[7] *European Communities – Measures Affecting Asbestos and Asbestos-Containing Products,* Communication of the Appellate Body of 8 November 2000, WT/DS135/9.
[8] Article 17.9 DSU provides that '[W]orking procedures shall be drawn up by the Appellate Body in consultation with the Chairman of the DSB and the Director-General, and communicated to the Members for their information'.
[9] Rule 16(1) of the Working Procedures for Appellate Review states that '[I]n the interests of fairness and orderly procedure in the conduct of an appeal, where a procedural questions arises that is not covered by these Rules, a division may adopt an appropriate procedure for the purposes of that appeal only, provided that it is not inconsistent with the DSU, the other covered agreements and these Rules. Where such a procedure is adopted, the Division shall immediately notify the participants and third participants in the appeal as well as the other Members of the Appellate Body'.
[10] See Decision by the Appellate Body Concerning Amicus Curiae Briefs, Statement by Uruguay at the General Council on 22 November 2000, WT/GC/38.

note under Rule 16(1) of the Working Procedures for Appellate Review, its practical effect was that the Appellate Body adopted decisions on relations with NGOs, and that such decisions statutorily belong to the General Council under Article V:2 of the Agreement Establishing the World Trade Organization.[11] However, it is doubtful whether this provision would provide a proper argument for the rejection of amicus curiae briefs by panels and the Appellate Body. This article has clearly been written with the relations between a specific group of NGO's in mind, namely those 'concerned with matters related to those of the WTO', and the political organs of the WTO. Rejecting amicus curiae briefs is not exactly covered by 'consultations and cooperation with NGOs'.

It was also argued that the Additional Procedure affected the Working Procedures of the Appellate Body and should therefore have been subject to consultations with the Chairman of the DSB and the Director-General in accordance with Article 17.9 DSU. As far as the substance was concerned, the argument was brought forward that the Additional Procedure granted individuals and institutions outside the WTO a right that even WTO members themselves do not possess. It would allow them to influence the interpretation of the legal provisions applied in a particular case, whereas that right is solely reserved to the parties and third parties to a dispute. The concluding statement by the government of Uruguay at the General Council was remarkable. It was said that '[T]he Appellate Body must restrict itself to establishing whether a Panel has correctly applied or interpreted the rules in a specific case. However, insofar it knows that its decisions will set precedents, when it identifies difficulties that arise from the wider interpretation of the agreements it should inform the General Council so that the latter may take the decisions incumbent upon it. [Thus, we believe in the US – Shrimp case, referred to in the Secretariat's background document, when the Appellate Body decided to reject the Panel's interpretation of its powers under Article 13 of the DSU, it should have informed the General Council of this situation so as to obtain an interpretation that could be applied in other cases]'. This statement clearly indicates that some WTO members disagree with the interpretation given to Article 13 DSU by the Appellate Body in the *Shrimp/Turtle* case. In the following paragraphs, the question will be tackled whether the Appellate Body did act ultra vires, as maintained by some WTO members.

---

[11] Article V:2 of the Agreement Establishing the World Trade Organization provides that '[T]he General Council may make appropriate arrangements for consultation and operation with non-governmental organizations concerned with matters related to those of the WTO'.

2.2.1 Article 17.9 DSU and Rule 16(2) of the Working Procedures

In *British Steel*, the Appellate Body concluded that it follows from Article 17.9 DSU that it has a broad authority to adopt procedural rules and to accept and consider any information that it believes is pertinent and useful in an appeal.[12] This grant of authority is not unconditional since Article 17.9 DSU explicitly requires that these rules must be consistent with the provisions of the DSU and the covered agreements. In addition, Article 17.9 DSU provides a method for filling procedural gaps – the establishment of working procedures – and this involves a consultation and notification process, which might render the Appellate Body's authority less broad than it submits.[13] The requirements imposed by Article 17.9 DSU are quite burdensome. This could explain why, in the *Asbestos* case, the Appellate Body preferred to adopt a case-specific additional procedure in accordance with the less burdensome requirements of Rule 16(1) of the Working Procedures for Appellate Review. Rule 16(1) requires the Appellate Body: (1) to find that a procedural question not covered by the Working Procedures has arisen, (2) to find it was acting in the interest of fairness and orderly procedure, (3) to adopt an appropriate procedure for the purposes of that appeal only, (4) to adopt a procedure which is not inconsistent with the DSU and the other covered agreements and the Working Procedures, (5) to notify the procedure immediately to participants, third participants and the other members of the Appellate Body. It follows from the text of the Communication and the Appellate Body report that the Division of the Appellate Body hearing the appeal did respect these rules.

It can be argued that the Appellate Body had the legal authority to adopt and issue the Additional Procedure pursuant to Rule 16(1) of the Working Procedures for Appellate Review. The authority of the General Council to consult and cooperate with NGOs under Article V.2 of the Agreement Establishing the World Trade Organization is not an exclusive authority. Panels and the Appellate Body also have the authority to consider and solicit submissions and information from non-parties, including NGOs.[14] The adoption of a procedural avenue for receiving information from non-parties in a transparent and orderly manner by the Appellate Body does not upset the institutional balance between the WTO dispute settlement procedure and the authority of

---

[12] See para 39 of the report (n 3).
[13] AE Appleton (n 3) 696.
[14] *United States – Import Prohibition of Certain Shrimp and Shrimp Products*, report of the Appellate Body of 12 October 1998, WT/DS58/AB/R, paras 106–7 and *United States – Imposition of Countervailing Duties on Certain Hot-Rolled Lead and Bismouth Carbon Steel Products Originating in the United Kingdom*, report of the Appellate Body of 10 May 2000, WT/DS138/AB/R, para 39.

the General Council. In addition, the Additional Procedure does not prejudice WTO members' right to participate in disputes, nor does it extend the rights of non-members. All WTO members that have a substantial interest in a dispute are entitled to participate in dispute settlement procedures as third parties in accordance with Article 10 DSU. WTO members that have an interest in a dispute that arises after the adoption of a panel report, still have the possibility to make written submissions to the Appellate Body, which may be considered where it is 'pertinent and useful' to do so.[15] Moreover, WTO members also have the right to submit a request under the Additional Procedure.[16] Alternatively, such WTO members may choose to express their views on the Appellate Body report during the adoption procedure prescribed by Article 17.4 DSU.

2.2.2 Article 13 DSU

Article 13.1 DSU grants panels the right to seek information and technical advice from any individual or body. This was one of the Appellate Body's grounds for authorising the acceptance of unsolicited amicus submissions at the panel level in the *Shrimp/Turtle* case.[17] It is noteworthy that the DSU does not grant a similar right to the Appellate Body. In *British Steel*, however, the Appellate Body concluded that it has the legal authority under the DSU to accept and consider amicus curiae briefs in an appeal procedure. The Appellate Body concluded that '[In] considering this matter, we first note that nothing in the DSU or the Working Procedures specifically provides that the Appellate Body may accept and consider submissions or briefs from sources other than the participants and third participants in an appeal. On the other hand, neither the DSU nor the Working Procedures explicitly prohibit acceptance or consideration of such briefs. However, Article 17.9 of the DSU provides that 'Working procedures shall be drawn up by the Appellate Body in consultation with the Chairman of the DSB and the Director-General, and communicated to the members for their information.' This provision makes clear that the Appellate Body has broad authority to adopt procedural rules which do not conflict with any rules and procedures in the DSU or the covered agreements'. [followed by a footnote which provides that 'In addition, Rule 16(1) of the Working Procedures allows a division hearing an appeal to develop an appropriate procedure in certain specified circumstances where a procedural question arises that is not covered by the Working Procedures.] Therefore, we are of

---

[15] *United States – Imposition of Countervailing Duties on Certain Hot-Rolled Lead and Bismuth Carbon Steel Products Originating in the United Kingdom*, report of the Appellate Body of 10 May 2000, WT/DS138/AB/R, para 39.
[16] The Additional Procedure applied to 'any person, whether natural or legal, other than a party or a third party to this dispute'.
[17] Paragraphs 99–110 of the report (n 1).

the opinion that as long as we act consistently with the provisions of the DSU and the covered agreements, we have the legal authority to decide whether or not to accept and consider any information that we believe is pertinent and useful in an appeal'.

In the case at hand, it decided not to take the two amicus curiae briefs filed into account in rendering its decision. This ruling makes it clear, however, that the Appellate Body has the authority to accept amicus curiae briefs and may take these into consideration in its final ruling.[18] It would, in my view, also confirm that the Appellate Body did not act ultra vires when adopting the Additional Procedure.

2.3 Procedural Requirements

The Communication set out rigorous criteria for the application of a 'leave to file' with the Appellate Body for the purposes of the appeal in the *Asbestos* case. It provided that any person, whether natural or legal, other than a party or third party to the dispute, had until 16 November 2000 to submit an application or a leave to file. In addition, the application had to meet certain formal requirements. An application for leave to file an amicus curiae brief had: (a) to be made in writing, be dated and signed by the applicant, and include the address and other contact details of the applicant; (b) be in no case longer than three types pages; (c) contain a description of the applicant, including a statement of the membership and legal status of the applicant, the nature of the activities of the applicant, and the sources of financing of the applicant; (d) specify the nature of the interest the applicant had in the appeal; (e) identify the specific issues of law covered in the panel report and legal interpretations developed by the panel that are subject of the appeal, which the applicant intends to address in its written brief; (f) state why it would be desirable, in the interests of achieving a satisfactory settlement of the matter at issue, in accordance with the rights and obligations of WTO members under the DSU and the other covered agreements, for the Appellate Body to grant the applicant leave to file a written brief in this appeal and indicate, in particular, in what way the applicant will make a contribution to the resolution of the dispute that is not likely to be repetitive of what had already been submitted by a party or third party to this dispute; and (g) contain a statement disclosing whether the applicant has any relationship, direct or indirect, with any party or any third party to the dispute, as well as whether it has, or would, receive any assistance, financial or otherwise, from a party or a third party to this dispute in the preparation of its application for leave of its written brief.[19]

---

[18] See also R Howse 'The Most Dangerous Branch? WTO Appellate Body Jurisprudence on the Nature and Limits of the Judicial Power' paper prepared for the World Trade Forum, World Trade Institute, Berne, 21–22 August 2000 at pp 18–19 (I am grateful to the author for providing me with copy of his paper).

[19] Paragraph 3 of the Communication.

The Appellate Body had to review and consider each application for to file a written brief and take a decision whether to grant or deny such leave 'without delay'.[20] The grant of leave to file brief by the Appellate Body, did not imply that the Appellate Body was obliged to address the legal arguments brought forward in such a brief.[21]

These granted leave to file were to submit their briefs by 27 November 2000. The criteria included a maximum length of 20 pages and a substantive requirement to set out a precise statement, strictly limited to legal arguments, supporting the applicant's legal position on the issues of law or legal interpretations in the panel report with respect to which the applicant had been granted leave to file a written brief.[22] In addition, applicants granted leave had to provide a copy of their written brief to all the parties and third parties to the dispute. The latter would be given a full and adequate opportunity by the Appellate Body to comment and respond to any written brief by an applicant granted leave under the procedure.[23]

3. Administration of the Communication

The Appellate Body received thirteen written submissions from NGOs that were not submitted in accordance with the Additional Procedure.[24] Several of these were received while it was considering the possible adoption of an additional procedure. After the adoption of the Additional Procedure, each of these 13 submissions was returned to its sender, along with a letter informing the sender of the procedure adopted by the Appellate Body and a copy of the Additional Procedure. Only one of these associations, the Korea Asbestos Association, subsequently submitted a request for leave in accordance with the Additional Procedure.[25]

Pursuant to the Additional Procedure, the Appellate Body received seventeen applications requesting leave to file a written brief. Six of these 17 applications were received after the deadline specified in paragraph 2 of the Additional Procedure and, for this reason, leave to file a written brief

---

[20] Paragraph 4 of the Communication.
[21] Paragraph 5 of the Communication.
[22] Paragraphs 6 and 7 of the Communication.
[23] Paragraphs 8 and 9 of the Communication.
[24] Such submissions were received from: Asbestos Information Association (United States); HVL Asbestos (Swaziland) Limited (Bulembu Mine); South African Asbestos Producers Advisory Committee (South Africa); J & S Bridle Associates (United Kingdom); Associação das Indústrias de Produtos de Amianio Crisótilo (Portugal); Asbestos Cement Industries Limited (Sri Lanka); The Federation of Thai Industries, Roofing and Accessories Club (Thailand); Korea Asbestos Association (Korea); Senac (Senegal); Syndicat des Métallos (Canada); Duralita de Centroamerica SA de CV (El Salvador); Asociación Colombiana de Fibras (Colombia); and Japan Asbestos Association (Japan).
[25] See *European Communities – Measures Affecting Asbestos and Asbestos-Containing Products*, report of the Appellate Body of 12 March 2001, WT/DS135/AB/R, para 53.

was denied to these six applicants.[26] Each such applicant was sent a copy of the decision denying its application for leave because the application was not filed in a timely manner.

The Appellate Body received 11 applications for leave to file a written brief within the time limits specified in paragraph 2 of the Additional Procedure.[27] It reviewed and considered each of these applications in accordance with the Additional Procedure and, in each case, decided to deny leave to file a written brief. Each applicant was sent a copy of the decision denying its application for leave for failure to comply sufficiently with all the requirements set forth in paragraph 3 of the Additional Procedure.[28] However, the reasons given by the Appellate Body for rejecting the applications were – ironically – quite 'brief'. It merely referred to the failure to comply with all the requirements set forth in paragraph 3 of the Additional Procedure. A request to the Appellate Body made by some of the applicants to specify the reasons for rejecting the applications was ignored, the reason being that the applicants should await the publication of the Appellate Body report, where all the information would be provided.[29] Yet, the Appellate Body report does not contain this information.

---

[26] Applications from the following persons were received by the Division after the deadline specified in the Additional Procedure for receipt of such applications: Association of Personal Injury Lawyers (United Kingdom); All India AC Pressure Pipe Manufacturers' Association (India); International Confederation of Free Trade Unions/European Trade Union Confederation (Belgium); Maharashtra Asbestos Cement Pipe Manufacturers' Association (India); Roofit Industries Ltd (India); and Society for Occupational and Environmental Health (United States). See *European Communities – Measures Affecting Asbestos and Asbestos-Containing Products*, report of the Appellate Body of 12 March 2001, WT/DS135/AB/R, para 55.

[27] Applications from the following persons were received by the Division within the deadline specified in the Additional Procedure for receipt of such applications: Professor Robert Lloyd Howse (United States); Occupational & Environmental Diseases Association (United Kingdom); American Public Health Association (United States); Centro de Estudios Comunitarios de la Universidad Nacional de Rosario (Argentina); Only Nature Endures (India); Korea Asbestos Association (Korea); International Council on Metals and the Environment and American Chemistry Council (United States); European Chemical Industry Council (Belgium); Australian Centre for Environmental Law at the Australian National University (Australia); Associate Professor Jan McDonald and Mr. Don Anton (Australia); and a joint application from Foundation for Environmental Law and Development (United Kingdom), Center for International Environmental Law (Switzerland), International Ban Asbestos Secretariat (United Kingdom), Ban Asbestos International and Virtual Network (France), Greenpeace International (the Netherlands), World Wide Fund for Nature, International (Switzerland) and Lutheran World Federation (Switzerland).

[28] See *European Communities – Measures Affecting Asbestos and Asbestos-Containing Products*, report of the Appellate Body of 12 March 2001, WT/DS135/AB/R, para 56.

[29] Copies of such requests have been made available on the website of the International Ban Asbestos Secretariat (http://www.ibas.internet.co.uk).

4. Practice in other International Fora: the Example of the NAFTA *Methanex* Case

Pursuant to Chapter 11 of the North American Free Trade Agreement (NAFTA), the parties agreed to submit disputes with investors (including enterprises) of other parties to binding third-party arbitration (ie under the ICSID Convention or in accordance with UNCITRAL rules). Thus, private investors may have recourse against NAFTA governments under the third party arbitration provisions.[30] Article 1116 of NAFTA establishes standing for investors on their own behalf and Article 1117 of NAFTA establishes standing for investors on behalf of an enterprise that it owns directly or indirectly, but that is located in another party. Third-party intervention is permitted by Article 1128 of NAFTA but in favour of NAFTA parties only. Article 1133 of NAFTA allows a tribunal, under certain circumstances, to appoint 'one or more experts to report to it in writing on any factual issue concerning environmental, health, safety or other scientific matters raised by a disputing party'. Chapter 11 does not contain an explicit reference to amicus curiae briefs. However, in the *Methanex* case, an investor-state arbitral panel recently decided that it had discretion to consider amicus curiae briefs and exercised that discretion in favour of consideration in the case at hand.[31] The tribunal examined the due process issues surrounding amicus curiae practice in greater detail than the Appellate Body has done so far.

In *Methanex*, the arbitral tribunal had to rule on petitions from third parties to intervene as 'amici curiae'. The procedure was governed by the UNCITRAL Arbitration Rules of which Article 15(1) provides that '[S]ubject to these rules, the arbitral tribunal may conduct the arbitration in such manner as it considers appropriate, provided that the parties are treated with equality and that at any stage of the proceedings each party is given a full opportunity of presenting his case'. The tribunal emphasised that the central issue was whether this Article grants the tribunal any lesser procedural power in regard to non-party persons, such as the petitioners. It took –rightly – the view that the receipt of written submissions from a person other than the disputing parties was not equivalent to adding that person as a party to the arbitration since the rights of the parties to the dispute and the limited rights of non-disputing parties under Article 1128 of NAFTA are thereby not acquired by such third person. Their rights, both procedural and substantive, remain judicially exactly the same before and after receipt of such submissions and the third person acquires no rights at all.[32]

---

[30] See FM Abbott *Law and Policy of Regional Integration: The NAFTA and Western Hemispheric Integration in the World Trade Organization System* (Dordrecht: Martinus Nijhoff Publishers, 1995) 102.

[31] See *Methanex Corporation v United States of America* decision of the tribunal on petitions from third persons to intervene as 'amicus curiae', decision of 15 January 2001.

[32] Paragraph 30 of the decision (n 31).

The tribunal further argued that the decision to allow a third person to make an amicus curiae submission fell within its procedural powers under Article 15(1) of the UNCITRAL Arbitration Rules and that this approach was supported by the practice of the WTO.[33] The tribunal said that the distinction between parties to an arbitration and their right to make submissions and a third person having no such right had been adopted by the WTO Appellate Body in the *British Steel* case.[34] The tribunal further referred to the conclusions of the Appellate Body in *British Steel* that it has the authority to accept amicus submissions since Article 17(9) DSU gives the Appellate Body the capacity to draw up its own Working Procedures. It concluded that the procedural authority of the Appellate Body was significantly less broad than the authority accorded to the arbitral tribunal under Article 15(1) of the UNCITRAL Arbitration Rules to conduct the arbitration in such a manner as it considers appropriate. According to the tribunal, the WTO practice demonstrates that the scope of a procedural power can extend to the receipt of written submissions from non-party third persons, even in a judicial procedure affecting the rights and obligations of state parties and that the receipt of such submissions confers no rights, procedural or substantive, on such persons.[35] The tribunal therefore concluded that it had the power to accept amicus written submissions. The decision whether or not to receive such submissions would be made at a later stage of the arbitration proceedings.

5. Conclusion – Nil Novi Sub Sole?

'The Appellate Body, a court without friends?' This is how the Center for International Environmental Law expressed its dissatisfaction with the approach followed by the Appellate Body.[36] Also the Foundation for International Environmental Law and Development, Greenpeace International, the International Ban Asbestos Secretariat and WWF International conveyed their frustrations in a joint statement, saying that they were mystified as to why the Appellate Body invited and promptly rejected all requests to file non-party submissions.[37]

---

[33] Paragraphs 27 and 31 of the decision (n 31).
[34] See *United States – Imposition of Countervailing Duties on Certain Hot-Rolled Lead and Bismouth Carbon Steel Products Originating in the United Kingdom*, report of the Appellate Body of 10 May 2000, WT/DS138/AB/R. The tribunal quoted para 41 of the ruling where the Appellate Body held that '[I]ndividuals and organizations, which are not Members of the WTO, have no legal right to make submissions to or to be heard by the Appellate Body. The Appellate Body has no legal duty to accept or consider unsolicited amicus curiae briefs submitted by individuals or organizations, not Members of the WTO'. [footnote omitted].
[35] Paragraph 33 of the decision (n 31).
[36] See 'A court without friends. One year after Seattle, the WTO slams the door on NGOs' available at http://www.ciel.org.
[37] See 'NGOs welcome WTO Green Light to French Ban on Asbestos but remain Sceptical about the WTO Dispute Settlement Process' Joint Statement of 14 March 2001 (available at http://www.field.org.uk).

Indeed, the stance taken by the Appellate Body in the *Asbestos* case is not an example of good diplomacy. The Additional Procedure undoubtedly constitutes a good initiative taken within the boundaries of the law and case law. However, the strict application of the criteria set forth in the Additional Procedure rendered the 'effet utile' of the initiative meaningless. The outcome does not, in essence, differ much from the approach followed by the Appellate Body in the *British Steel* case. In this particular case, the Appellate Body emphasised its broad discretion in considering unsolicited briefs but found it unnecessary to take the two amicus curiae briefs into account that had been submitted. It had nevertheless recognised that these briefs were admissible. In the case at hand, third parties were not even given the opportunity to submit an amicus curiae brief. The most plausible reason for the U-turn made by the Appellate Body is the opposition of WTO members against what they saw as usurpation by the Appellate Body of their rights. This is evidenced by the criticism of the majority of WTO members at a special session of the General Council where the Communication and its implications were discussed.[38]

The conflict indicates that it is necessary to establish uniform rules or to apply a uniform practice for the consideration of amicus curiae briefs in WTO dispute settlement procedures. Amending the provisions of the DSU to establish a proper procedure for the treatment of amicus curiae briefs is not absolutely necessary. The case law of the Appellate Body shows that the legal framework, as interpreted by the Appellate Body, exists. It is just a matter of applying this legal framework in a consistent way so that non-state actors' organisations will at least be able to assess what their procedural rights are under the WTO dispute settlement system.

---

[38] See Decision by the Appellate Body Concerning Amicus Curiae Briefs, Statement by Uruguay at the General Council on 22 November 2000, WT/GC/38. See also ch 2.2 above.

About the Author

Geert A. Zonnekeyn, partner with Monard D'Hulst, has been practising WTO law and competition law for more than a decade and is included in the roaster of panellists of the WTO. He is also an academic consultant at the European Institute of the University of Ghent. He has published widely on various subjects and is a regular speaker at conferences.